Unity 4.x Game Development by Example Beginner's Guide

A seat-of-your-pants manual for building fun, groovy little games quickly with Unity 4.x

Ryan Henson Creighton

BIRMINGHAM - MUMBAI

Unity 4.x Game Development by Example Beginner's Guide

First published: September 2010

Second edition: September 2011

Third edition: December 2013

Production Reference: 1191213

Published by Packt Publishing Ltd.
Livery Place
35 Livery Street
Birmingham B3 2PB, UK.

ISBN 978-1-84969-526-8

www.packtpub.com

Cover Image by Dan John Cox (http://danjohncox.tumblr.com/)

Credits

Author

Ryan Henson Creighton

Reviewers

Trond Abusdal

Huzaifa Arab

John Hutchinson

Wei Wang

Acquisition Editors

Wilson D'souza

Mary Jasmine Nadar

Owen Roberts

Lead Technical Editors

Owen Roberts

Poonam Jain

Technical Editors

Tanvi Bhatt

Akashdeep Kundu

Edwin Moses

Nikhil Potdukhe

Tarunveer Shetty

Faisal Siddiqui

Sonali Vernekar

Project Coordinator

Venitha Cutinho

Proofreaders

Elinor Perry-Smith

Mario Cecere

Bridget Braund

Indexers

Mariammal Chettiyar

Mehreen Deshmukh

Rekha Nair

Tejal Soni

Graphics

Sheetal Aute

Production Coordinator

Nitesh Thakur

Cover Work

Nitesh Thakur

About the Author

Ryan Henson Creighton is a veteran game developer, and the founder of Untold Entertainment Inc. (`http://www.untoldentertainment.com`) where he creatively consults on games and applications. Untold Entertainment creates fantastically fun interactive experiences for players of all ages. Prior to founding Untold, Ryan worked as the Senior Game Developer at Canadian media conglomerate Corus Entertainment, where he created over fifty advergames and original properties for the YTV, Treehouse TV, and W networks. Ryan is the co-creator of Sissy's Magical Ponycorn Adventure, the game he authored with his then five-year-old daughter Cassandra. Ryan is the Vice President of the IGDA Toronto Chapter. He is also the author of the book that you are currently reading.

When Ryan is not developing games, he's goofing off with his two little girls and his fun-loving wife in downtown Toronto.

Big thanks to Cheryl, Cassandra, and Isabel for their love, their support, and their cinnamon rolls. Thanks to Jean-Guy Niquet for introducing me to Unity; to Jim "McMajorSupporter" McGinley for help with the book outline and ongoing mentorship; to the technical reviewers and Packt Publishing staff for letting me leave a few jokes in the book; and to David Barnes, for having such a great sense of humor in the first place. Special thanks to Michael Garforth and friends from the #unity3d IRC channel on Freenode. I also want to thank Mom, God, and all the usual suspects.

About the Reviewers

Trond Abusdal, though having been interested in computers since his parents bought him and his brother a C64 in the early 90s, he first got into programming years later when writing a modification for Quake2 with a childhood friend.

This interest lead to a bachelor's degree in Computer Science in 2006, after which he started working for TerraVision, a company using game technologies as a tool for education and visualization. In 2008, he first got introduced to Unity, which is still his main game development tool, although knowledge of other technologies and tools often come in handy.

Since 2010, he is a programmer and more recently a partner at Rock Pocket Games, which makes games for a variety of different platforms, both client projects and internal projects.

Huzaifa Arab is a Game Designer by choice and a Game Programmer by need. He has been playing games since young age, which progressed to Modding/Map-making/Scripting, when he realized that some games could be a whole lot more fun if he could put his own twist in them. And so, his hobby became a professional career choice after formally graduating from DSK Supinfogame, India (where his team won the prestigious Square Enix Game Dev Competition). After a year of freelance Game Development, he currently works at Tiny Mogul Games, India, as a Principal Game Designer.

He loves to connect with people interested in Human Computer Interface, Game Engines/VR Tech, Game Design in Education, and Instrumental music. You can drop him a line at arabhuzaifa@gmail.com.

I would like to thank Packt Publishing for giving me an opportunity to review a book on Unity 3D, a technology I am so passionate about. I would like to thank my best friend Angad for recommending me to Packt Publishing and I would like to thank my family and co-workers/friends for their support as I took time out to review such a wonderful book.

John Hutchinson is the founder of Rubber Ducky Games, an independent game development studio based in California.

In addition to being an exceptional programmer in multiple languages and frameworks, he is an experienced graphic designer, talented game system architect and gets excited about experience-focused design (and rubber duckies).

He is especially interested in games which push the boundaries of twitch-reflex response, explore human emotion, or leverage the interactive medium for more powerful learning experiences.

He is currently working with Making Friends Inc. as Lead Engineer and as part of the core design team, to deliver a game intent on teaching kids on the Autism-Asperger's spectrum valuable social skills.

When his face isn't glued to a computer screen he likes to play with his kids, explore board game design, and read technical books like this one.

> Thanks to my brothers, for providing feedback (and teaching me some things about games). To my sister, for making me feel like a hero (not a robot). To my parents, for teaching me to be caring and to work my butt off. And to my kids, for just being you. I love you all more than words can express.

Wei Wang made his first iOS casual game with Unity 3D in his college time, which got big success with more than 5 million downloads world-wide. Since then, he has discovered it's a great thing to make great games. After earning his master's degree from Tsinghua University (one of the best universities in China), he joined a game company in Japan and now he is trying to create interesting games with Unity 3D.

Right now, he is a skilled engineer and always eager to learn more. He now lives in Kawasaki with his wife. You can know more about him from his project's page `http://project.onevcat.com` or find him on his blog `http://onevcat.com` (Chinese). You can also follow him on twitter @onevcat.

www.PacktPub.com

Support files, eBooks, discount offers and more

You might want to visit www.PacktPub.com for support files and downloads related to your book.

Did you know that Packt offers eBook versions of every book published, with PDF and ePub files available? You can upgrade to the eBook version at www.PacktPub.com and as a print book customer, you are entitled to a discount on the eBook copy. Get in touch with us at service@packtpub.com for more details.

At www.PacktPub.com, you can also read a collection of free technical articles, sign up for a range of free newsletters and receive exclusive discounts and offers on Packt books and eBooks.

http://PacktLib.PacktPub.com

Do you need instant solutions to your IT questions? PacktLib is Packt's online digital book library. Here, you can access, read and search across Packt's entire library of books.

Why Subscribe?

- Fully searchable across every book published by Packt
- Copy and paste, print and bookmark content
- On demand and accessible via web browser

Free Access for Packt account holders

If you have an account with Packt at www.PacktPub.com, you can use this to access PacktLib today and view nine entirely free books. Simply use your login credentials for immediate access.

Table of Contents

Preface

A word about the third edition

As I sit here in my luxurious velvet smoking jacket, taking a long draw on a pipe, and admiring the various stuffed hunting trophies around the room in an attitude of quiet contemplation, it dawns on me that I don't smoke or advocate sport-hunting, and that I have no idea what I'm doing in this room. The jacket, however, is quite nice. I think I'll keep it.

It's wonderful to see that this book, one of the very first instructional guides about Unity 3D on the market, has withstood both the test of time, and Unity Technologies' relentless release schedule. Owing to the rapid pace of technology, many things have changed in a few short years. C# has largely overtaken UnityScript as a preferred language; to that end, all of the code in the book has been supplemented with a C# translation, including notes on how to perform that translation yourself for past and future projects.

In the time since the first edition, computers have increasingly become our evil, dominating overlords. With that in mind, the third edition includes two bonus chapters that teach you how to build a two-player game, and then how to program the computer to act as the merciless second player who never loses. That chapter also contains information on how to *make* the computer player lose, which I present as secret codified data to be used by the resistance movement during the inevitable machine uprising. Stay ever vigilant!

Your future as a game developer

"Game Developer" has rapidly replaced "firetruck" as the number one thing that kids want to be when they grow up. Gone are the days when aspiring developers needed a university education, a stack of punch cards, and a room-sized computer to program a simple game. With digital distribution and the availability of inexpensive (or free) game development tools like Unity 3D, the democratization of game development is well underway.

But just as becoming a firetruck is fraught with peril, so too is game development. Too often, aspiring developers underestimate the sheer enormity of the multidisciplinary task ahead of them. They bite off far more than they can chew, and eventually drift away from their game development dreams to become lawyers or dental hygienists. It's tragic. This book bridges the gap between "I wanna make games!" and "I just made a bunch of games!" by focusing on small, simple projects that you can complete before you reach the bottom of a bag of corn chips.

What this book covers

Chapter 1, That's One Fancy Hammer!, introduces you to Unity 3D—an amazing game engine and game authoring tool that enables you to create games and deploy them to a number of different devices. You'll play a number of browser-based Unity 3D games to get a sense of what the engine can handle, from a massively-multiplayer online game all the way down to a simple kart racer. You'll download and install your own copy of Unity 3D, and mess around with one of the demos that ships with the product.

Chapter 2, Let's Start with the Sky, explores the difference between a game's skin and its mechanic. Using examples from video game history, including Worms, Mario Tennis, and Scorched Earth, we'll uncover the small, singular piece of joy upon which more complicated and impressive games are based. By concentrating on the building blocks of video games, we'll learn how to distil an unwieldy behemoth of a game concept down to a manageable starter project.

Chapter 3, Game #1 – Ticker Taker, puts you in the pilot seat of your first Unity 3D game project. We'll explore the Unity environment and learn how to create and place primitives, add Components like Physic Materials and rigidbodies, and make a ball bounce on a paddle using Unity's built-in physics engine without ever breaking a sweat.

Chapter 4, Code Comfort, continues the keep-up game project by gently introducing scripting. Just by writing a few simple, thoroughly-explained lines of code, you can make the paddle follow the mouse around the screen to add some interactivity to the game. This chapter includes a crash course in game scripting that will renew your excitement for programming where high school computer classes may have failed you.

Chapter 5, Game #2 – Robot Repair, introduces an often-overlooked aspect of game development—"front-of-house" User Interface design—the buttons, logos, screens, dials, bars, and sliders that sit in front of your game—is a complete discipline unto itself. Unity 3D includes a very meaty Graphical User Interface system that allows you to create controls and fiddly bits to usher your players through your game. We'll explore this system, and start building a complete two-dimensional game with it! By the end of this chapter, you'll be halfway to completing Robot Repair, a colorful matching game with a twist.

Chapter 6, Game #2 – Robot Repair Part 2, picks up where the last chapter left off. We'll add interactivity to our GUI-based game, and add important tools to our game development tool belt, including drawing random numbers and limiting player control. When you're finished with this chapter, you'll have a completely playable game using only the Unity GUI system, and you'll have enough initial knowledge to explore the system yourself to create new control schemes for your games.

Chapter 7, Don't Be a Clock Blocker, is a standalone chapter that shows you how to build three different game clocks—a number-based clock, a depleting bar clock, and a cool pie wedge clock, all of which use the same underlying code. You can then add one of these clocks to any of the game projects in this book, or reuse the code in a game of your own.

Chapter 8, Hearty Har Har, revisits the keep-up game from earlier chapters and replaces the simple primitives with 3D models. You'll learn how to create materials and apply them to models that you import from external art packages. You'll also learn how to detect collisions between game objects, and how to print score results to the screen. By the end of this chapter, you'll be well on your way to building Ticker Taker—a game where you bounce a still-beating human heart on a hospital dinner tray in a mad dash for the transplant ward!

Chapter 9, Game #3 – The Break-Up, is a wild ride through Unity's built-in particle system that enables you to create effects like smoke, fire, water, explosions, and magic. We'll learn how to add sparks and explosions to a 3D bomb model, and how to use scripting to play and stop animations on a 3D character. You'll need to know this stuff to complete The Break-Up—a catch game that has your character grabbing falling beer steins and dodging explosives tossed out the window by his jilted girlfriend.

Chapter 10, Game #3 – The Break-Up Part 2, completes The Break-Up game from the previous chapter. You'll learn how to reuse scripts on multiple different game objects, and how to build Prefabs, which enable you to modify a whole army of objects with a single click. You'll also learn to add sound effects to your games for a much more engaging experience.

Chapter 11, Game #4 – Shoot the Moon, fulfills the promise of *Chapter 2, Let's Start with the Sky,* by taking you through a re-skin exercise on The Break-Up. By swapping out a few models, changing the background, and adding a shooting mechanic, you'll turn a game about catching beer steins on terra firma into an action-packed space shooter! In this chapter, you'll learn how to set up a two-camera composite shot, how to use code to animate game objects, and how to re-jig your code to save time and effort.

Chapter 12, Game #5 – Kisses 'n' Hugs, teaches you to build a two-player 3D Tic Tac Toe game entirely within the Unity 3D game authoring tool. You'll learn about writing return values for your custom functions, and using 3D objects to build an essentially 2D game. This simple strategy game forms the basis for the following chapter.

Chapter 13, AI Programming and World Domination, steps you through the process of developing an artificial intelligence program, enabling your computer to win at Tic Tac Toe. From there, you'll modify the terrifyingly perfect AI algorithm so that it randomly makes "mistakes", and gives humankind a slim chance at Tic Tac Toe survival.

Chapter 14, Action!, takes you triumphantly back to Ticker Taker for the coup de grace—a bouncing camera rig built with Unity's built-in animation system that flies through a model of a hospital interior. By using the two-camera composite from The Break-Up, you'll create the illusion that the player is actually running through the hospital bouncing a heart on a tin tray. The chapter ends with a refresher on bundling your project and deploying it to the Web so that your millions of adoring fans (including your grandma) can finally experience your masterpiece.

Appendix is an essentially vestigial component of the colon, which can be surgically removed if it gives you any trouble.

What you need for this book

You'll need to be in possession of a sturdy hat, a desk chair equipped with a seatbelt, and an array of delicious snack foods that won't get these pages all cheesy (if you're reading the e-book version, you're all set). Early chapters walk you through downloading and installing Unity 3D (`http://unity3d.com/unity/download/`). A list of resources and links to additional software can be found in the *Appendix*.

Who this book is for

If you've ever wanted to develop games, but have never felt "smart" enough to deal with complex programming, this book is for you. It's also a great kick start for developers coming from other tools like Flash, Unreal Engine, and Game Maker Pro.

Conventions

In this book, you will find a number of styles of text that distinguish between different kinds of information. Here are some examples of these styles, and an explanation of their meaning.

Code words in text are shown as follows: "The `audio.PlayOneShot` command is perfect for collision sound effects."

A block of code is set as follows:

```
for(var i:int=0; i<totalRobots; i++)
{
    var aRobotParts:List.<String> = new List.<String>();

    aRobotParts.Add("Head");
    aRobotParts.Add("Arm");
    aRobotParts.Add("Leg");
}
```

When we wish to draw indicate that a line of code needs to be added or edited, the relevant lines or items are set in bold:

```
function Awake()
{
    startTime = Time.time + 5.0;
}
```

New terms and **important words** are shown in bold. Words that you see on the screen, in menus or dialog boxes for example, appear in the text like this: "When you click on the **Apply** button, Unity creates its set of raster images based on the font that you're importing".

[Warnings or important notes appear in a box like this.]

[Tips and tricks appear like this.]

Reader feedback

Feedback from our readers is always welcome. Let us know what you think about this book—what you liked or may have disliked. Reader feedback is important for us to develop titles that you really get the most out of.

To send us general feedback, simply send an e-mail to `feedback@packtpub.com`, and mention the book title through the subject of your message.

If there is a topic that you have expertise in and you are interested in either writing or contributing to a book, see our author guide on `www.packtpub.com/authors`.

Customer support

Now that you are the proud owner of a Packt book, we have a number of things to help you to get the most from your purchase.

Downloading the color images of this book

We also provide you a PDF file that has color images of the screenshots/diagrams used in this book. The color images will help you better understand the changes in the output. You can download this file from `https://www.packtpub.com/sites/default/files/downloads/5268OT_ColoredImages.pdf`

Downloading the example code

You can download the example code files for all Packt books you have purchased from your account at `http://www.packtpub.com`. If you purchased this book elsewhere, you can visit `http://www.packtpub.com/support` and register to have the files e-mailed directly to you. Each project in the book is intended to be built from the "ground up", beginning with an new project file. The downloadable `.unitypackage` files for this book contain the assets (sounds, images, and models) you need to build the projects. You may also download completed, working versions of each project for your reference, though these are not intended to be your "first stop" – they're more like the answer sheet at the back of a text book.

Errata

Although we have taken every care to ensure the accuracy of our content, mistakes do happen. If you find a mistake in one of our books—maybe a mistake in the text or the code—we would be grateful if you would report this to us. By doing so, you can save other readers from frustration and help us improve subsequent versions of this book. If you find any errata, please report them by visiting http://www.packtpub.com/support, selecting your book, clicking on the **errata submission form** link, and entering the details of your errata. Once your errata are verified, your submission will be accepted and the errata will be uploaded to our website, or added to any list of existing errata, under the Errata section of that title.

Piracy

Piracy of copyright material on the Internet is an ongoing problem across all media. At Packt, we take the protection of our copyright and licenses very seriously. If you come across any illegal copies of our works, in any form, on the Internet, please provide us with the location address or website name immediately so that we can pursue a remedy.

Please contact us at copyright@packtpub.com with a link to the suspected pirated material.

We appreciate your help in protecting our authors, and our ability to bring you valuable content.

Questions

You can contact us at questions@packtpub.com if you are having a problem with any aspect of the book, and we will do our best to address it.

1

That's One Fancy Hammer!

Technology is a tool. It helps us accomplish amazing things, hopefully more quickly, more easily, and more amazingly than if we hadn't used the tool. Before we had newfangled steam-powered hammering machines, we had hammers. And before we had hammers, we had the painful process of smacking a nail into a board with our bare hands. Technology is all about making our lives better and easier. And less painful.

Introducing Unity 3D

Unity 3D is a piece of technology that strives to make life better and easier for game developers. Unity is a **game engine**, and a **game authoring tool**, which enables creative folks like you to build video games.

By using Unity, you can build video games more quickly and easily than ever before. In the past, building games required an enormous stack of punch cards, a computer that filled a whole room, and a burnt sacrificial offering to an ancient god named Fortran. Today, instead of spanking nails into boards with your palm, you have Unity. Consider it your hammer—a new piece of technology for your creative tool belt.

The engine, the tool, and the all-weather tires

You may have heard people call Unity and other tools "game engines". That's almost correct. The confusion here comes from the fact that we have three distinct things, and we call them all "Unity".

When you download Unity, as you'll do in a moment, you're downloading the Unity 3D game authoring tool. To use a car analogy, the authoring tool works like your auto body shop. You use it to design and build the car's chassis, its handling, and its sweet, sweet leather interior and boss rims.

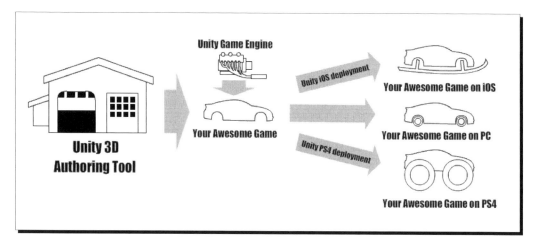

Under the hood, the authoring tool uses the Unity game engine, which is like the driving force behind your game. Unless you work out a pricy licensing deal with **Unity Technologies**, you are not allowed to mess around with the engine itself, but the engine is the piece that makes your car run.

When you're finished designing your game with the Unity authoring tool, your content gets bundled with the Unity game engine, and the two of them are packaged together with an extra piece that enables the game to run in a certain situation. The analogy gets weaker here, but consider tires: you can add snow tires to your car so that it can drive in the tundra, or dune buggy tires so that it can drive in the desert. In this way, you package your game content with a certain target platform in mind: PC, Mac, iOS, Android, or one of the various home video game consoles.

Unity takes over the world

Throughout this book, we'll be distilling our game development dreams down to small, bite-sized nuggets instead of launching into any sweepingly epic open-world game. The idea here is to focus on something you can actually finish instead of getting bogged down in an impossibly ambitious opus. This book will teach you how to build five games, each of which focuses on a small, simple gameplay mechanic. You'll learn how to build discrete pieces of functionality that you can apply to each project, filling the games out to make them complete experiences. When you're finished, you can publish these games on the web, Mac, PC, and Linux systems. If you spring for an additional software license for one of Unity's many add-ons, you may be able to publish your games for other platforms, including home video game consoles.

The team behind Unity 3D is constantly working on packages and export options ("snow tires") for other platforms. At the time of this writing, Unity could additionally create games that can be played on iOS, Android devices, Xbox One, PS4, and Wii U. Each of these tools is an add-on functionality to the core Unity package, and comes with an additional cost, while console development usually requires a developer relationship with the platform owner. These licenses are constantly in flux, however, and the mobile development add-ons that used to cost an additional fee are now free. By the time you read this book, who knows? To be safe, we'll stick to the core Unity 3D program for the remainder of this book.

With the initial skills that you learn in this book, you'll be able to expand on your knowledge to start building more and more complex projects. The key is to start with something you can finish, and then for each new project that you build, to add small pieces of functionality that challenge you and expand your knowledge. Any successful plan for world domination begins by drawing a territorial border in your backyard; consider this book as your backyard.

Why choose Unity?

There are a great many game authoring tools, engines, and frameworks that you may have explored or read about before investigating Unity 3D. What makes Unity an attractive option? Here are a few selling points:

♦ **Large community**: You want to avoid going with a tool that only you and some middle-schooler in Siberia know how to operate. Unity has a very large user base, which makes it much quicker and easier to find answers to your questions, and to find online videos, tutorials and books like this one that explain new concepts. A large community also implies that development on the software will continue. Nothing's worse than training on a tool that is later abandoned.

- **Social proof**: The fact that large companies have bought into or partnered with Unity Technologies bodes very well. **Electronic Arts** has purchased a site-wide license, and (at the time of this writing) two out of three major console manufacturers have struck licensing deals with Unity to spur development on their systems.

- **Bang for the buck**: If you ever "go pro", you'll want to invest some pennies against a full version of Unity. While it's not chicken scratch, the amount of power and the number of options you get from Unity vastly outweigh the cost outlay.

- **Market success**: On any given day, a survey of the chart-topping iOS games turns up a proportionately large number of Unity-developed titles. Unity is being used by a great many developers to create games that survive in the market, and thrive once they're there.

- **Customizability**: The entire Unity authoring tool can, itself, be authored. Developers can create their own windows, buttons, and panels to add to the Unity authoring tool, which has led to a very active secondary market called the **Unity Asset Store**, where you can download toolmakers' creations to make your development experience even better.

- **Multiplatform**: It mystifies me why people pour so much energy into tools like XCode, which can target exactly one platform (or maybe two? I honestly don't care enough to check). When faced with such a diverse marketplace, it's a savvy developer who chooses a technology that targets multiple platforms.

Why burn this book and run away screaming?

Of course, no game development tool is perfect, and in certain areas, other tools have the advantage over Unity. Here are a few places where Unity doesn't stack up against its rivals:

- **Learning Curve**: Even with the abundance of training available, Unity largely requires developers to learn how to program and to deal with complex concepts such as **shaders** and the **third dimension**. If you've come to Unity after hearing "it makes game development simple! Anyone can do it!", you've been fed a hot bowl full of filthy lies.

- **Cost**: Bang for buck notwithstanding, when you get into a situation where you're buying pro versions of Unity for an entire development team, and the Unity Asset Server on top of that, as well as copies of the deployment add-ons, the cost begins to add up. I may have knocked XCode in the previous section, but it does have the advantage of being free.

- **Purity**: If you're coming from a "pure" programming background, some of the ways in which you solve different problems in Unity may seem outright sacrilegious to you. If the thought of working within a GUI and dragging things on top of other things to create reflexive relationships gives you the willies, you may not dig the way Unity gets things done.

Browser-based 3D – welcome to the future

One of Unity's most astonishing capabilities is that it can deliver a full 3D game experience right inside your web browser. It does this with the **Unity Web Player**—a free browser plugin that embeds and runs Unity content on the web.

Time for action – install the Unity Web Player

Before you dive into the world of Unity games, download the Unity Web Player. Much the same way the Flash player runs Flash-created content, the Unity Web Player is a plugin that runs Unity-created content in your web browser.

1. Go to `http://unity3d.com/webplayer` (click either the **Windows** or **Mac OS X** button on the page to select your platform).

2. Click on **Download**.

3. Follow all of the onscreen prompts until the Web Player has finished installing.

4. The install process is only slightly more involved on a Mac. You have to download and run a `.dmg` file, and then enter your administrator password to install the plugin, but it's relatively quick and painless.

Welcome to Unity 3D!

Now that you've installed the Web Player, you can view the content created with the Unity 3D authoring tool in your browser.

What can I build with Unity?

In order to fully appreciate how fancy this new hammer is, let's take a look at some projects that other people have created with Unity. While these games may be completely out of our reach at the moment, let's find out how game developers have pushed this amazing tool to its very limits.

FusionFall

The first stop on our whirlwind Unity tour is **FusionFall**—a **Massively Multiplayer Online Role-Playing Game (MMORPG)**. You can find it at `fusionfall.com`.

FusionFall was commissioned by the **Cartoon Network** teevee franchise, and takes place in a re-imagined, anime-style world where popular Cartoon Network characters are all grown up. Darker, more sophisticated versions of *The Powerpuff Girls*, *Dexter's Laboratory*, *Foster's Home for Imaginary Friends*, and the kids from *Codename: Kids Next Door* run around battling a slimy green alien menace.

Completely hammered

While it's not the newest game on our tour, FusionFall remains one of the largest, most expensive and technically complex Unity games around. FusionFall is historically important to Unity Technologies, as it helped draw a lot of attention to the then-unknown Unity game engine when the game was released. As a tech demo, it's one of the very best showcases of what your new technological hammer can really do! FusionFall has real-time multiplayer networking, chat, quests, combat, inventory, NPCs (non-player characters), basic AI (artificial intelligence), name generation, avatar creation and costumes. And that's just a highlight of the game's feature set. This game packs a *lot* of depth.

Should we try to build FusionFall?

At this point, you might be thinking to yourself, "Heck YES! FusionFall is exactly the kind of game I want to create with Unity, and this book is going to show me how!"

Unfortunately, a step-by-step guide to creating a game the size and scope of FusionFall would likely require its own flatbed truck to transport, and you'd need a few friends to help you turn each enormous page. It would take you the rest of your life to read, and on your deathbed, you'd finally realize the grave error that you had made in ordering it online in the first place, despite having qualified for free shipping.

Here's why: the FusionFall credits

```
http://fusionfall.cartoonnetwork.com/game/credits.php
```

This page lists all of the people involved in bringing the game to life. Cartoon Network enlisted the help of an experienced Korean MMO developer called **Grigon Entertainment**. There are over 80 names on that credits list! Clearly, only two courses of action are available to you:

1. Build a cloning machine and make 79 copies of yourself. Send each of those copies to school to study various disciplines, including marketing, server programming, and 3D animation. Then spend a year building the game with your clones. Keep track of who's who by using a sophisticated armband system.

2. Give up now because you'll never make the game of your dreams.

Another option

Before you do something rash and abandon game development for farming, let's take another look at this. FusionFall is very impressive, and it might look a lot like the game that you've always dreamed of making. This book is not about crushing your dreams. It's about dialing down your expectations, putting those dreams in an airtight jar, and taking baby steps. *Confucius* said:

> *"A journey of a thousand miles begins with a single step."*

I don't know much about the man's hobbies, but if he was into video games, he might have said something similar about them—creating a game with a thousand awesome features begins by creating a single, less feature-rich game.

So, let's put the FusionFall dream in an airtight jar and come back to it when we're ready. We'll take a look at some smaller Unity 3D game examples and talk about what it took to build them.

Off-Road Velociraptor Safari

No tour of Unity 3D games would be complete without a trip to `Blurst.com`—the game portal owned and operated by independent game developer **Flashbang Studios**. In addition to hosting games by other independent game developers, Flashbang has packed **Blurst** with its own slate of kooky content, including **Off-Road Velociraptor Safari**:

In Off-Road Velociraptor Safari, you play with a dinosaur in a pith helmet and a monocle driving a jeep equipped with a deadly spiked ball on a chain (just like in the archaeology textbooks). Your goal is to spin around in your jeep doing tricks and murdering your fellow dinosaurs (obviously).

For many independent game developers and reviewers, Off-Road Velociraptor Safari was their first introduction to Unity. Some reviewers said that they were stunned that a fully 3D game could play in the browser. Other reviewers were a little bummed that the game was sluggish on slower computers. We'll talk about optimization a little later, but it's not too early to keep performance in mind as you start out.

Fewer features, more promises

If you play Off-Road Velociraptor Safari and some of the other games on the Blurst site, you'll get a better sense of what you can do with Unity without a team of experienced Korean MMO developers. The game has 3D models, physics (code that controls how things move around somewhat realistically), collisions (code that detects when things hit each other), music, and sound effects. Just like FusionFall, the game can be played in the browser with the Unity Web Player plugin. Flashbang Studios also sells downloadable versions of its games, demonstrating that Unity can produce standalone executable game files too.

Maybe we should build Off-Road Velociraptor Safari?

Right then! We can't create FusionFall just yet, but we can surely create a tiny game like Off-Road Velociraptor Safari, right? Well... no. Again, this book isn't about crushing your game development dreams. But the fact remains that Off-Road Velociraptor Safari took five supremely talented and experienced guys eight weeks to build on full-time hours, and they've been tweaking and improving it ever since. Even a game like this, which may seem quite small in comparison to full-blown MMO like FusionFall, is a daunting challenge for a solo developer. Put it in a jar up on the shelf, and let's take a look at something you'll have more success with.

I bent my Wooglie

`Wooglie.com` is a Unity game portal hosted by M2H Game Studio in the Netherlands. One glance at the front page will tell you that it's a far different portal than `Blurst.com`. Many of the Wooglie games are rough around the edges, and lack the sophistication and slick professional sheen of the games on Blurst. But here is where we'll make our start with Unity. This is exactly where you need to begin as a new game developer, or as someone approaching a new piece of technology like Unity.

Play through a selection of games on Wooglie. I'll highlight a few of them for your interest:

Big Fun Racing

Big Fun Racing is a simple but effective game where you zip around collecting coins in a toy truck. It features a number of different levels and unlockable vehicles. The game designer sunk a few months into the game in his off-hours, with a little help from outsource artists to create the vehicle models.

Diceworks

Diceworks is a very simple, well-polished game designed in Unity 3D for iPhones. We won't be covering any iPhone development, but it's good to know that your Unity content can be deployed to a number of other devices and platforms.

Diceworks was created by one artist and one programmer working together as a team. It's rare to find a single person who possesses both programming and artistic talent simultaneously; scientists say that these disciplines are split between two different lobes in our brains, and we tend to favor one or the other. The artist-programmer pairing that produced Diceworks is a common setup in game development. What's your own brain telling you? Are you more comfy with visuals or logic? Art or programming? Once you discover the answer, it's not a bad plan to find someone to make up the other half of your brain so that your game handles both areas competently.

At any event, with Diceworks we're definitely getting closer to the scope and scale that you can manage on your own as you start out with Unity.

It's also interesting to note that Diceworks is a 2D game created in a 3D engine. The third "D" is largely missing, and all of the game elements appear to exist on a flat plane. Nixing that extra dimension when you're just starting out isn't a half-bad idea. Adding depth to your game brings a whole new dimension of difficulty to your designs, and it will be easier to get up and running with Unity by focusing on the **X** and **Y** axes, and leaving the **Z**-axis in one of those dream jars. With a few sturdy working game examples under your belt, it won't be long before you can take that Z-jar down off the shelf and pop it open. The games that we'll be building in this book will stick to a two-dimensional plane, using three-dimensional models. Even so, certain games have taken this concept and ran with it: New Super Mario Bros. Wii locked its 3D characters to a 2D plane and wound up an extremely complex and satisfying platformer.

Lovers in a Dangerous Spacetime

With their game **Lovers in a Dangerous Spacetime**, the talented three-person team at the **Asteroid Base** adds half a "D" to that formula. This is a *two-and-a-half-D* game, which combines the advantages of a 2D game with all the eye-popping pizzazz of all 3Ds.

Showcase Showdown

Unity portals—game sites that feature Unity-made games—are popping up all over the place. Here are a few more sites to hit in your survey of what Unity can do:

Unity Technologies – "Made with Unity" page

`http://unity3d.com/gallery/made-with-unity/game-list`

Unity's own showcase of games features titles that aren't all playable, but they're sure to blow your mind.

Kongregate

`http://www.kongregate.com/unity-games`

Once the king of Flash game portals, Kongregate also features Unity-made games. Any developer can submit a game to Kongregate, and once the game is live, the Kongregate community can play, rate, and comment on it. If you're a first-time developer, that may sound a little scary. And if you're a veteran developer, you know *exactly* how scary it is! But an excellent goal for you to set, after reading this book, is to develop something of your own in Unity, and submit it to the scrutiny of complete strangers on a portal like Kongregate. Let's be honest... Mom is going to like everything you do. This may be your best shot at getting honest feedback, and it will help you grow as a developer.

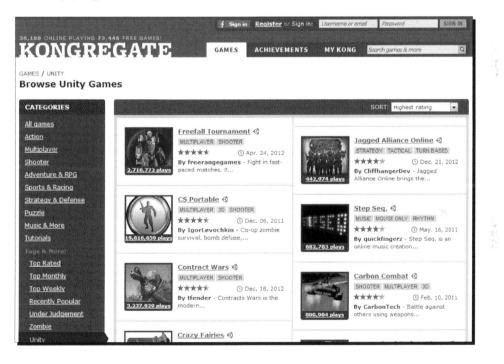

The iOS App Store

Unity developers have taken to Apple's App Store in a big way. On any given day, a good number of the games on the "Top 100" list are Unity-made titles. For a particularly good time, try **The Room**, which is a short-and-sweet **MYST**-like game that will have you safe-cracking increasingly complex puzzle boxes nested inside one another. Again, a significant amount of time, talent, and effort went into creating The Room, but this tour is about getting a feel for what Unity can do—and what you can do with it (given enough time, talent, and effort!).

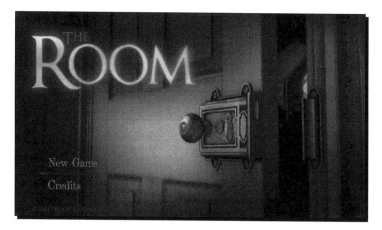

Walk before you can run (or double jump)

A common mistake that new game developers make is biting off more than they can chew. Even experienced game developers make this mistake when they get really excited about a project, or when they approach a new technology and expect to be immediately proficient at using it. The real danger here is that you'll sit down and try to create your dream—let's say it's a sword and sorcery RPG epic that combines all the best parts of **League of Legends**, **ChuChu Rocket!**, and Microsoft Excel. When you've sunk days and weeks and months into it and it still looks nothing like the game you envisioned, you give up. You figure that since you failed at creating your dream game, you were never really cut out to be a game developer to begin with.

You owe it to yourself to start small! Rome wasn't built in a day, and neither was your dream cart-racing game starring famous figures from Roman history. By taking smaller steps, you can experience success with a number of smaller games. Then you can take what you learn and add to it, slowly building your expertise until you're in a position to take that dream game jar off the shelf.

For now, let's keep our dream shelf fully stocked, and turn our attention to something small and achievable. By the end of this book, you'll have a collection of working games that started out simply, and grew more and more complex as you got smarter. My hope is that once you finish this book, you'll be well-equipped to dream up new incremental features for your games, and to hunt down the resources you will need to fill the gaps in your new-found knowledge.

In *Chapter 2, Let's Start with the Sky*, we'll go into detail about where you should start when you're deciding what kind of game to create. We'll also see some real-world examples of games that began as simple, effective ideas and later grew into enormously complex and feature-rich titles. From small acorns, mighty multiplayer oak tree games grow.

There's no such thing as "finished"

We'll be learning a lot about iteration throughout this book. Some game developers who produce content for fixed media like game disks and cartridges are used to producing a "gold master"—the final build of the game—and calling it a day. One of the joys of deploying games to the web or mobile is that they're never truly finished. You can continue tweaking your web games and modifying them until you end up with a far more fun and polished game than you started with.

If you follow Flashbang Studios on Twitter or if you read the studio's blog, you'll see that it's constantly modifying and improving its games, even years after they were "finished". The Flashbang team continued to tweak and modify Off-Road Velociraptor Safari even three years after the game was finished.

Likewise, we'll be creating some games that are raw and unfinished at first. But as we learn more about how to program the crucial bits and pieces common to many games, we'll keep revisiting our rough, early games to add those pieces and improve them.

Stop! Hammer time

Now that you've seen some of what Unity can do, it's time to download the program and kick the tires! The free version of Unity is available for a low price of... well, free (at the time of this writing) from the Unity 3D website.

1. Go to `http://unity3D.com`.

2. Click on the **Download** button.

3. Download the latest version of the Unity 3D authoring tool for your platform—Mac or PC. If you are given the option, make sure to download the sample project along with the program.

4. Follow all the onscreen prompts until the Unity authoring tool has finished installing.

5. Launch Unity!

Fight Some Angry Bots

After a quick registration process, Unity is ready to go. With any luck, the **AngryBots Demo** will automatically open. If it doesn't, and you're faced with a dialogue asking you to open a project, you can find the AngryBots Demo in the following location by default:

◆ Max OS: `/Users/Shared/Unity/4-0_AngryBots`

◆ Windows XP: `C:\Documents and Settings\All Users\Documents\Unity Projects\4-0_AngryBots`

  or

◆ `C:\Documents and Settings\All Users\Shared Documents\Unity Projects\4-0_AngryBots`

◆ Windows 7/ 8/ Vista: `C:\Users\Public\Public Documents\Unity Projects\4-0_AngryBots`

If you thought you'd be a rebel and you unchecked the sample projects box when you downloaded Unity, you may find yourself re-downloading Unity to get the AngryBots Demo. You can pull down other sample learning projects, such as the AngryBots Demo from the Unity website:

`http://unity3d.com/support/resources/example-projects/`

 These paths may change depending on which version of Unity you've downloaded. As the Unity Technologies team improves the software, they launch new and more impressive demos to show off what Unity can do. If you're reading this book, and your copy of Unity 3D launches a different demo project, or if the Angry Bots Demo is no longer available by the time you begin reading this book, don't freak out! Everything we're about to discuss can be generally applied to most demos.

When the Angry Bots Demo first opens, you may see a splash screen referring you to different tutorial resources and language guides. How helpful! Now close it (don't worry, it'll be there next time, unless you uncheck the **Show at Startup** box). If you checked the box but you'd really like to see that welcome screen again, look in the menus under **Help | Welcome Screen**. In the menus, click on **Window | Layouts | 2 by 3** to see the different panels that we're about to tour.

After the panels have repositioned themselves, look for the **Project** panel. It should be one of the three vertically oriented panels on the right half of your screen. At the top right of the **Project** panel is a very small button that looks like a downward-facing triangle next to three horizontal lines. Click there, and choose **One Column Layout** from the resulting context menu. This will get an annoying split view out of your way:

If you don't see all the fancy highfalutin' 3D jazz going on in the **Scene** and **Game** windows, you may just need to load the main game scene. To do this, find the Scene called **AngryBots** at the top of the **Project** panel (it has a black-and-white Unity icon next to it), and double-click it.

To try out the demo, click on the **Play** button at the top center of the screen:

You can walk around the Angry Bots Demo using the *WASD* keys on your keyboard. Hold down the left-mouse button to fire your boomstick at the aggravated automatons. When you're finished **exploring**, press the *Esc* key to pause the game and regain mouse control. Then click on the Play button again to end the demo:

The wonders of technology!

Much of what you see in the AngryBots Demo can't be built directly in Unity. Most of the assets were created with other software; Unity is the program you use to put everything together and to make it interactive. The Demo contains special models, such as the airlocks, which were imported from 3D software packages like **3D Studio Max**, **Maya**, or **Blender**. Certain elements, like robot enemies, have scripts attached to them. **Scripts** are lists of instructions that tell the items in the game world how to behave.

Throughout the book, we'll learn how to import 3D models and write scripts to control them. Let's take a quick look around the Unity interface and note a few points of interest.

The Scene window

The **Scene** window is where you can position your **GameObjects** and move them around. This window has various controls to change its level of detail. Use these controls to toggle lighting on and off (in the editor only—not in your actual game), and to display the window contents with textures, wireframes, or a combination of both. You can use the colorful **Gizmos** at the top-right corner to constrain the view to the **X**, **Y**, and **Z** axes to view the top and sides of your scene. Click on the white box in the middle to return to Perspective view. This window also features a search field.

Try clicking on the gizmo's green **Y** cone to view the AngryBots Demo from above, and then type rock into the search field. Every object with rock in its name lights up, while the rest of the scene fades to grayscale. Click the tiny **x** button to clear the search field:

The Game window

The **Game** window shows you what your players will see. When you click on the Play button to test your game (as you just did with the Angry Bots Demo), the results of your efforts play out in this window. Toggle the **Maximize on Play** button to test your game in full-screen mode:

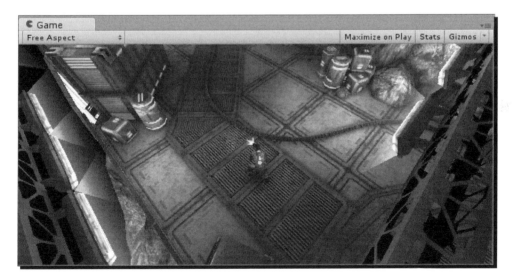

The Hierarchy panel

The **Hierarchy** panel lists all of the **GameObjects** in your **Scene**. **GameObjects**—cameras, lights, models, and prefabs—are the things that make up your game. They can be "tangible" things like the generators or the giant robot arm in the Angry Bots Demo. They can also include intangible things, which only you as the game developer get to see and play with, such as the cameras, the lights, the scripts, and *colliders*, which are special invisible shapes that tell the game engine when two game objects are touching.

The AngryBots Demo **Hierarchy** panel contains **GameObjects** for the cannisters, the tables, the airlocks and the computer terminals, to name a few. It also lists the **Player**, a very complicated GameObject that controls how the hero moves and collides with his environment. The player character has a camera following him. That camera is our eye into the game world. The Demo lists a collection called **Environment(sounds)**—a series of **GameObject** that determine what the player hears when he walks through different parts of the level (for example, torrential rain outside, and the droning equipment hum when he moves indoors). So, **GameObject** can include touchy-feely "physical" objects such as cannisters and airlocks, as well as behind-the-scenes intangible things such as lights, cameras, and actions (scripts).

Click on a **GameObject** in the **Hierarchy** panel, and then hover your mouse over the **Scene** window. Press the *F* key on your keyboard, and the **Scene** window will automatically pan and zoom directly to that object. Alternatively, you can navigate to **Edit | Frame Selected**, which can be more reliable than using the keyboard shortcut. (I like to think of the *F* key standing for "Focus" to help me remember what this shortcut does). You can also double-click on the **GameObjects** in the **Hierarchy** panel.

The Project panel

The **Project** panel lists all of the elements that you'll use to create **GameObjects** in your project. For example, look for the `mech_bot` in the **Objects | Enemies** folder. The AngryBots Demo `EnemyMech` **GameObjects** is made up of a series of meshes that represent the mech's shape, a material to depict its "skin" or coloring, and an animation to describe its movement. All of these types of goodies are listed in the **Project** panel.

The **Project** panel displays the contents of a special folder called `Assets` on your computer's operating system. Unity automatically creates the `Assets` folder for you when you create a new project. If you drag a compatible file, like a 3D model, a sound effect, or an image into the **Project** panel, Unity copies it to the `Assets` folder behind the scenes, and displays it in the **Project** panel.

The Inspector panel

The **Inspector** is a context-sensitive panel, which means that it changes depending on what you select elsewhere in Unity. This is where you can adjust the position, rotation, and scale of **GameObjects** listed in the **Hierarchy** panel. The **Inspector** can also display controls to configure components that add functionality to the **GameObjects**. Between the three main panels in Unity (Hierarchy, Project, and Inspector), the **Inspector** is where you'll likely spend most of your time because that's where you'll be tweaking and fiddling with every aspect of the elements that comprise your game projects.

This screenshot of the **Inspector** panel shows the components attached to the **Player GameObject** in the Angry Bots Demo. This includes:

- A number of scripts (including **Free Movement Motor** and **Player Move Controller**)
- A **Rigidbody** component
- A **Capsule Collider**

To see the same content on your computer, click to open the **Player** GameObject in the **Hierarchy** panel. In later chapters, we'll dive deeper to learn what these various components are all about.

Heads Up?

Let's use the **Inspector** panel to make a quick change to the orientation of the character. We'll begin the demo with the hero standing on his head (which is a sure-fire way to make those bots even angrier, by the way).

We can use the **Inspector** panel to change the rotation of the player. Follow these steps:

1. In the **Hierarchy** panel, click to select the **Player** game object.
2. Click on the **Rotate** button near the top left of the screen, which looks like two arrows sniffing each others' behinds:

A globe appears around the bottom of the **Player** GameObject in the **Scene** view. (If you don't see the player, hover over the **Scene** view and press the *F* key on your keyboard.) The blue **Z**-axis rotator handle encircles the player's body. Clicking and dragging it rotates the player model as if he were standing in a very dodgy canoe. The red **X**-axis rotator handle rotates the player as if he was a foosball player, stuck on a metal rod. If we click and drag that handle, the player rotates to either fall flat on his face, or flat on his back, like he's got space sickness. And the green **Y**-axis rotator handle runs around the player like a hula hoop. Dragging this handle around makes the player spin to face different directions. The Player **GameObject** can get pretty hairy; in order to isolate the rotation controls, type `player` into the **Scene** window's search field to exclude all other **GameObject**.

3. You can click-and-drag the red **X**-axis rotator handle to turn the player upside down, but a better method is to change the X-axis rotation in the **Inspector** panel. Expand the gray arrow next to **Transform** in the **Inspector** panel if it's not already open, and change the **X** value under **Rotation** to `180`. The player flips upside down.

4. Now, when you click on the **Play** button to test the game, the player will break-dance his way around the Angry Bots Demo, electric boogaloo-style. The robots are freaking out, thinking "ERROR! DOES NOT COMPUTE!" Way to keep them on their mechanical toes.

The **Transform** is the component that governs a GameObject's **Position**, **Rotation**, and **Scale**. Every object in the scene has a Transform component that determines where it is (Position), how big or small it is (Scale), and how it's oriented (Rotation). Objects can be stretched and deformed by scaling them along one axis, as we'll see in later chapters.

Layers and layout dropdowns

Above the **Inspector** panel, you'll see the **Layer** and **Tag** drop-down menus. Game objects can be grouped into layers, somewhat like in Photoshop or Flash. Unity stores a few commonly used layouts in the **Layout** drop-down menu (mine is set to the **2 by 3** configuration). You can also save and load your own custom layouts.

Playback controls

As we've seen, these three buttons help you test your game and control playback. The Play button starts and stops your game. The Pause button works as expected—it pauses your game so that you can make changes to it on the fly. The third button is a **step-through** control; use it to advance frame-by-frame through your game so that you can more tightly control what's going on.

Scene controls

At the top-left of your screen, you'll see four controls that help you move around your **Scene**, and position GameObjects within it. These controls are mapped to the *Q*, *W*, *E*, and *R* keys on your keyboard. From left to right, they are.

◆ **The Hand tool** (*Q*): Use it to click-and-drag around your scene. Hold down the *Alt* key on your keyboard to rotate the view. Use your mouse wheel to zoom the scene in and out. Hold down the *Shift* key to pan, zoom, and rotate in larger increments to speed things up. This is a way for *you* to navigate around the game world. It doesn't actually impact the way the player sees the game. To modify the **Game** view, you need to use the **Move** or **Rotate** tools to modify the **Camera** position. Hold *Shift* to make the camera move farther. Hold the right or alternate mouse button to pivot the scene as if you're viewing it through a 3D camera.

◆ **The Move tool** (*W*): This tool lets you move the **GameObjects** around your scene. You can either drag the object(s) around by the X, Y, or Z-axis handles, or by the square in the center for freeform movement. Holding down the *Ctrl* key or the *command* key (Apple) will snap movement to set grid increments.

◆ **The Rotate tool** (*E*): Use it to spin your objects around using a neat spherical gizmo. The red, green, and blue lines map to the X, Y, and Z axes.

◆ **The Scale tool** (*R*): This tool works much the same as the Move and Rotate tools. Use it to make your game objects larger or smaller. Dragging an X, Y, or Z handle will non-uniformly scale (squash and stretch) the object, while dragging the gray cube in the center will uniformly scale it.

Don't stop there – live a little!

We've glanced briefly at the key elements of the Unity interface, but there's no need to stop poking around. Far beyond the scope of this book, there is a wealth of menu options, buttons, and controls that we haven't covered. Why not explore those menus or start randomly clicking on things that you don't yet understand? Now is the time to safely break stuff. *You* didn't work hard to create the Angry Bots Demo, so why not mess around with it a little bit?

Some of the changes you make to the Demo will "stick", even if you don't explicitly choose to save your changes. Duplicate the entire Angry Bots Demo folder before you go crazy.

Here are some things to try:

◆ Select some of the GameObjects in the **Hierarchy** panel and move them around in the **Scene** window using the **Scene** controls. What happens when you put an airlock in the middle of the sky? Can the player still pass through? What if you put the canisters or the computers over the player's head before the game starts? Do they fall, or do they hover? Can you remove objects to help the player career off the edge of the balcony? What happens when he does?

- Randomly right-click / alternate-click in the three different panels and read through the context menu options to see what you're getting yourself into.

- Poke around in the **GameObject | Create Other** menu. There's a whole list of interesting things that you can add to this scene without even touching a 3D modeling program.

- What happens when you delete the lights from the scene? Or the camera? Can you add another camera? More lights? How does that affect the **Scene**?

- Can you move the player to another part of the Demo to change your starting position? Can you replace the audio files to make the gun "moo" whenever you fire it?

- Download a picture of kittens from the Internet and see if you can wrap it around a boulder model. Kittens rock! You can pull the kitties into your project using the **Assets | Import New Asset** option in the menu.

Summary

This chapter was all about getting a feel for what Unity can do and for what the program interface had to offer. Here's what we found out:

- Massive 80-person teams, all the way down to tiny one- or two-person teams are using Unity to create fun games.

- By thinking small, we'll have more success in learning Unity and producing fully functional games instead of huge but half-baked abandoned projects.

- Different flavors of Unity help us deploy our games to different platforms. By using the free version, we can deploy to the web, and to Mac, PC, Linux, and certain mobile platforms.

- The Unity interface has controls and panels that let us visually compose our game assets, and test games on the fly right inside the program!

I hope you've taken some time to thoroughly vandalize the Angry Bots Demo. If you save the file by clicking on **File | Save Project**, you'll have a perma-upside-down space marine in your Demo. If you want to return to a pristine AngryBots Demo later to wreak more havoc, don't bother saving the hilarious (but meaningless) changes we've made in this chapter.

Big ambition, tiny games

Now that we've trashed the joint, let's take a quick trip through some game design theory. In the next chapter, we'll figure out the scope and scale of a game that a solo, beginner developer should actually tackle. Crack your knuckles and put on your favorite hat because you're about to dip yourself in awesome sauce.

2
Let's Start with the Sky

*So, you've downloaded and cracked the seal on a fresh copy of Unity. You've seen some examples of what other people have done with the game engine, and you've taken a whirlwind tour of the interface. You can clear out the Angry Bots Demo project by clicking on **File | New Project** in the menu. After choosing an empty folder for the new project (you can call it Intro), Unity will close down completely and start up again. Once it does, you're left staring at a 3D plane.*

Click on the little landscape icon at the top middle of the Scene view to see this plane, as shown in the following screenshot. It stretches on forever in all directions—seemingly infinitely to either side of you, ahead of you, behind you, straight down to the deepest depths, and straight up to the sky.

It's time to build a game, right? But how do you start? Where do you start?

That little lightbulb

The idea's the thing. Every game starts with an idea—that little lightbulb above your head that flicks on all of a sudden and makes you say, "Aha!" If you've gone as far as picking up a book on Unity, you probably have at least one game idea floating around in your noggin. If you're like me, you really have *10,000* game ideas floating around in your head, all clamoring for your attention. "Build me! Build me!" Which of these ideas should you go ahead with?

The quality that defines a successful game developer is not the number of ideas he has. The guy with 10 game ideas is equally as valuable as the girl with 500 game ideas. They're both essentially worthless! *A game developer develops games*. The one thing that separates you from success is not the number of ideas you've had or the number of projects you've started and abandoned. It's the games you've finished that count. To put it another way: *he who executes, wins*. Don't worry about getting it right just yet; worry about getting it *done*.

And what's with all this pressure to make your first game good—anyway? Before he directed *Titanic* and *Avatar*, James Cameron worked on the sequel to *Piranha*—a zero-budget, B-movie schlockfest about murderous fish. Don't worry—you'll be the game world's answer to Cameron some day. But for now, let's finish the fish.

The siren song of 3D

The biggest barrier between you and your success as a Unity game developer is finishing a project. The idea stage that you enter when you sit staring at that endless 3D plane is crucial to you overcoming that barrier. If you choose the right idea, you will have a much better shot at finishing. Choose the wrong idea, and you might crash and burn. Then you'll probably go back to school and study to be an accountant. Starting in game development and ending in accounting is your worst-case scenario. Let's avoid that at all costs.

Before you even begin, the odds are stacked against you. That endless 3D plane is calling you, begging you to start a project that's way over your head. You may begin thinking of the other 3D games you've played: gritty, wide-open "sandbox" games like **Saints Row** or **Grand Theft Auto**; tightly-controlled platformer games with lots of exploration and interesting challenges like **Super Mario 64**; sweeping, epic role-playing games like **Skyrim** or **Fallout 3**. All of these games have a few things in common: an animated character or first-person camera moving around in a physics-based environment; a rich and detailed 3D world with maps, quests, non-player characters, and pick-ups; and teams of hundreds of people burning through multimillion dollar budgets.

Odds are that you're not reading this book with 99 of your closest, wealthiest friends who all want to help you build your game. You need to ignore the dizzying and endless scope that eternal 3D plane implies—and foster the creativity and resourcefulness that will get you from point A to point B; that is, from an idea to a finished game.

Features versus content

Another trap fledgling game developers fall into is reducing the scope of their ideas in ways that still prove the project impossible. For example, they'll say, "I don't want to set my sights too high, so I'm going to make a game such as **Gran Turismo**, except with fewer cars," or "I want to make **Diablo III** with smaller levels," or "I'm going to build **World of Warcraft** with fewer classes and about half the items".

To understand why this approach is so dangerous we'll have to understand a little more about how games are put together. The two issues here are **features** and **content**. All things being equal, a game with 50 levels has more **content** than a game with 5 levels. The 50-level game has ten times more content, but both games have the same feature: levels. A role-playing game with twelve character classes has more content than a game with three character classes, but they both have the same feature: character classes.

So, while you may recognize that it's more work to build additional **content** for a game, try to peer behind the curtain and recognize the number of **features** that go into a game. Every feature that your game supports takes more work, and sometimes it's easier to build 20 different enemies for a game than to actually build the enemies **feature**.

A game with no features

We see how it can be dangerous and self-defeating to choose a game with many features and reduce the amount of content in that game. And, because some features are so time-consuming to develop, it's also dangerous to choose a fully featured game and start stripping features to reduce the scope of our project.

A much better approach, and one that you'll have much more success with, is to start with a game that has *zero* features, and then add them slowly, one by one. Using this approach, you can decide when your game is good enough to unleash on your players, and any additional features you had planned can go into the sequel. This is a winning approach that will see you through many small victories, and many finished games!

Mechanic versus skin

One skill that may help you finish a game is recognizing the difference between **mechanic** and **skin**. Your game's mechanic is how it physically functions. The very best games contain a simple mechanic that's easy to learn, hard to master, and compelling enough to keep a player interested. The mechanic in **Tetris** is to move and rotate falling blocks into place to create and eliminate one or more solid lines. The mechanic in many golf games is to simulate swinging a golf club by moving the controller's thumbstick around or tapping a button when the "Power" and "Accuracy" meters are at the right level. The mechanic in **Breakout** is to move a paddle back and forth to bounce a ball into a wall of fragile bricks.

A game's **skin** is how it looks and sounds. It's the animated cutscenes that establish a story. It's the theme that you choose for your game. Imagine a game where you've programmed an object to follow the mouse cursor. There are "bad" objects on the screen that you must avoid, and "good" objects on the screen that you must collect. That's the game mechanic. The game skin could be practically anything. The player object could be a mouse collecting "good" cheese objects and avoiding "bad" rat objects. Or it could be a spaceship collecting space gold and avoiding black holes. Or it could be a fountain pen collecting verbs and avoiding conjunctive pronouns. As they say, "the sky's the limit!"

Trapped in your own skin

The advantage that you gain by separating a mechanic from a skin is that you can shuck off video game conventions and free yourself to develop anything you want. If you think, "I'd like to create a space-themed strategy game," and you think back to all of the space-themed strategy games that you've played, you might think of 4X games like **Alpha Centauri** or **Master of Orion**—they both pit you in a massive quest to conquer the universe. They are *huge* games that you likely won't finish alone. So, you start trimming them down for sanity's sake—"I'll just build Master of Orion with fewer planets," or "I'll just build Alpha Centauri with fewer features". Now you've unwittingly fallen into that self-defeating trap. Your project is still too huge. You eventually abandon all hope. A few years later, you're an accountant wondering what might have been.

That singular piece of joy

Instead of going down that doomed copycat road, start asking yourself questions about the outer space theme and the strategy mechanic. What's fun about each of them? Which moments in a game like Master of Orion really turn your crank? Do you like mining a planet for resources and buying new stuff? Do you like the thrill of discovering a new planet? Or does building an armada of spaceships and conquering enemies really get you excited?

Distill your game down to that one thing—that *singular piece of joy*. Create that one joyful experience for your player, and nail it. That's your game. Everything else is just feature creep.

One percent inspiration

The Internet is packed with small, simple, and free-to-play games that offer the cheap thrill of a singular piece of joy. Let's analyze some of these games to see what we can learn. For each example, we'll identify:

- The core game mechanic—that singular piece of joy
- The skin
- The feature set
- Possible additional features
- Alternate skin ideas

These games require the Flash Player plugin, which you probably already have. If, for some weird reason, your computer's been living under a digital rock and you need to install it, browse to `http://get.adobe.com/flashplayer/` and follow the instructions there.

Motherload

Motherload by **XGen Studios** (`http://www.xgenstudios.com/play/motherload`) distills a complicated 4X game, like Master of Orion, down to two joy-inducing tasks: mining for resources and shopping for stuff. Here's a screenshot from the game:

The core mechanic: Pilot your vehicle by using the arrow keys—dig, fly, and avoid long falls—with a finite fuel source. There's only one real "level" in the game, and it stretches down your screen for a long time. Your drill-enabled vehicle can only dig down so deep and dig up so many pieces of ore before having to return to the surface to sell off the goods and clear some cargo space. The trick is to dig up and sell enough ore to upgrade your ship so that it can dig deeper, carry more loot, and survive longer falls. The initial goal is to rack up ludicrous cash, but a story eventually develops that adds meaning to your loot-lust. This mechanic is similar to the much simpler game **Lunar Lander**, where the player must gently land a spacecraft on a single non-scrolling screen with limited fuel. You can look at Motherload as either a dramatically toned-down Master of Orion or a trumped-up **Lunar Lander**!

The skin: A quasi-cartoony space mine with a layer of grit and grime over it. The player character is a futuristic mining vehicle. The only non-player character is a human being (... or is he??).

The feature set:

- Vehicle control
- Vehicle upgrades (which include both vehicle and terrain strengths and attributes)
- Shops
- Diggable terrain
- Scrollable story or dialog windows
- The save game option
- Front-of-house features

Front-of-house

We'll be looking at front-of-house game wrappers later on. They include things such as the title screen, instructions screen, pause screen, and win or lose screens, and are an essential part of your finished game. The best part is that if you build them well, you can reuse a lot of your work for every new game that you create!

Possible additional features:

Sequel features for Motherload include:

- Switching between vehicle types

- Mining on different planets

- Managing multiple vehicles at the same time

- A character mode where you get out and run around as a little guy, as in **Blaster Master**

Alternatively, the sequel could just add new content: more ship upgrades, more ore types, a larger play area, more story sequences, more sound effects and music tracks, and so on. This is what game reviewers can derisively call a **MOTS (more-of-the-same)** sequel. These days, you can get away with it by calling it an "expansion pack".

For a look at what a completely different team has done with a nearly identical mechanic, check out **I Dig It** and **I Dig It Expeditions** from **InMotion Software**, which counts underwater exploration among its innovations:

Stretch your skills

We're looking way down the road here, but if you create a sequel for your game, be sure to add at least one new feature. And, because you'll still be learning Unity, make sure that developing the new feature requires a skill that you don't already have. In this way, each game that you create will stretch your capabilities farther and wider, until you're an unstoppable Unity pro.

Heads up!

Pay close attention to a game's **Head-up display** (**HUD**). Video game HUDs contain graphical elements that usually don't make sense within the context of the game world, but they provide vital information to the player. A great example is the heart health meter in any **Zelda** game, or the energy bar in any fighting game. The Motherload HUD includes draining Fuel and Hull bars. It displays dynamic money and depth tallies. Three clickable elements lead the player to the **Inventory**, **Options**, and **Instructions** screens. Finally, a piece of text lets the player know that there are more shops to be found past the borders of the viewable game area.

Unity has great features for building game HUDs. Every HUD item type that you see in Motherload—the graphical bar, the dynamic (changeable) text, the clickable icons, and the flashing helper text—can all be built in the Unity game engine. Skip ahead to *Chapter 4, Code Comfort* if you're dying to try it!

Artillery Live!

Artillery Live! (http://www.gamebrew.com/game/artillery-live/play) is one of the many, many iterations of the classic **Artillery** game mechanic, which is nearly as old as video games themselves. It was also built in Flash, but there's no reason it couldn't be built in Unity using 3D tank models and some awesome exploding particle effects.

The core mechanic: Artillery games share a familiar mechanic where the player sets the trajectory and power of his shot to demolish the enemy tanks. This version also has a wind speed feature that affects the way the tank shells travel through the air. Over time and in other incarnations, the game mechanic evolved into a pull-back-and-release experience, mimicking a slingshot. Other versions have the gun turret automatically angling towards the mouse, and the player holds down the mouse button to power up his shot.

The skin: The **Gamebrew** version is a classic tanks-and-mountains affair, holding true to the very first Artillery games developed by game development pioneers in the 1970s. These games transformed from text-only titles to primitively illustrated games with pixelated tanks. An obvious alternate skin is to replace the tank with a man holding a bow and arrow (refer to the **Bowman** series of online games):

Among the more interesting Artillery skins in recent memory is the **Worms** series, which replaces tanks with teams of anthropomorphic annelids bent on heavily armed destruction, and **GunBound**, an online multiplayer game where players pilot giant vehicles and mounts into battle. In addition to tanks, GunBound throws animals and mythical creatures into the mix. It could even be argued that the pull-back-and-release slingshot mechanic of **Angry Birds** is an evolution of the Artillery mechanic.

The feature set: In addition to the core mechanic, the front-of-house features, and computer-controlled players, the Gamebrew version of Artillery offers turn-based multiplayer gameplay. Multiplayer games are a huge topic and deserve a book of their own. Unity does have features to enable multiplayer play. Unity interfaces nicely with out-of-the-box socket server solutions, or any server you decide to write on your own. Multiplayer play is largely outside the scope of this book, but *Chapter 12, Game #5 – Kisses 'n' Hugs*, has you creating a two-player game with a computer-controlled opponent. If you've never programmed a multiplayer game before, you should know that they come with a universe of headaches all their own! As a general rule, you're better off tackling single-player games if you're just starting out.

The skinny on multiplayer

More and more, gaming is moving from the lonely, isolated hobby of teenage boys in their moms' basements to a pastime that people enjoy in groups, either in person or virtually. Any time you move beyond a single-player experience, you're spending more time, money, and brain power to build the game. Here's a list of multiplayer features in order from the *most expensive* or difficult to the *least*:

- **Multiplayer, different computers, real-time**: Think of an action game such as **Quake**, where everyone's running around and shooting all at once. Real time is the most expensive to develop because you need to make sure all the computers "see" the same thing at once. What if the computer drops a connection or is slower than the rest?

- **Multiplayer, different computers, turn-based, synchronous**: **Boggle**, **Battleship**, and various card and parlor games fit into this category. You don't have to worry about the computers constantly sending and receiving the right messages multiple times per second, so it's a little more forgiving.

- **Multiplayer, different computers, turn-based, asynchronous**: Instead of people playing at the same time, their latest turn is sent via a Facebook message or an e-mail. Enabling players to grow old and die between moves really takes the messaging pressure off. The **Scrabble**-like **Words With Friends** is a great example.

- **Multiplayer, human versus computer**: This is a costly option because you have to write code to make the computer player intelligent enough to defeat a human player. The difficulty in doing this changes depending on the type of game. It's easier to program artificial intelligence for a game such as **Connect Four** than **Chess**.

- **Multiplayer, same computer, human versus human**: This is the easiest to do. There's no complicated messaging going back and forth between computers, and you don't have to write artificial intelligence for a computer player. Regardless, it's still more effort to build than a strictly single-player game.

Possible additional features: The **Worms** series did a great job of iterating on the Artillery concept by adding a slew of additional features:

- Weapons inventories (including the standard-issue bazooka, and the not-so-standard-issue Super Sheep and Holy Hand Grenade)

- Limited or collectible ammo

- Team-based play with turn time limits

- Environmental extras such as land mines, oil barrels, and cargo drops

- Moving and jumping

- Physics-based platforming with the ninja rope

- Cutscenes

- Nameable characters

- Single-player levels

- Unlockable extras

The Worms series is an excellent example of how you can take a simple, fun mechanic, skin it creatively, and go nuts with a bevy of brilliant features. But, the most important thing is to start by building Artillery, not Worms.

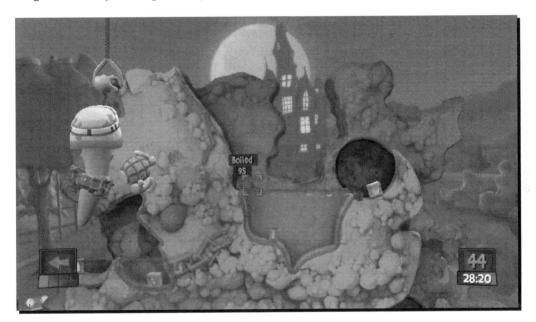

Bang for your buck

By far, the Holy Grail of feature development is finding features that are fast and cheap to build, but that give players the most pleasure. Being able to name your team of worms provided untold entertainment. I remember spending a lot of time with one version of the game creating my own custom sound effects for the worms to say whenever they'd blow stuff up. It wasn't too tough a feature for the developers to build, and I almost spent more time customizing my team than I did playing the game!

Build a game, buy a house?

If you think that players only notice the big ideas and the big games with hundreds of people working on them, Artillery offers you a re-education! iPhone developer *Ethan Nicholas* released a version of Artillery on the iPhone and reported to Wired magazine that he had earned $600, 000 on his game. It's definitely possible to be small and successful.

Pong

Seriously, **Pong**? Yes, Pong. The British Academy of Film and Television Arts hosts an online version of the classic game (`http://www.bafta.org/games/awards/play-pong-online,678,BA.html`). The original Pong is credited with kick-starting the commercial video game industry that we know today:

The mechanic: Pong takes its name from "ping pong"—a real-world activity where two players use paddles to bounce a ball at each other across a table with a tiny net. Ping pong was adapted from tennis, after people finally realized that all that running around was too much effort.

Some real-world activities lend themselves very well to video game mechanics. Not quite 50-years old, the video game industry is still very much in its infancy. There is an enormous wealth of fun stuff in the physical world (such as playing ping pong or blowing up tanks) that's waiting to be adapted to a terrific video game mechanic. Are you clever enough to find one of those undiscovered mechanics and build the next Pong?

The skin

Like many early games, Pong obviously leaves a lot to be desired. Video game skins of tennis and ping pong have come a very long way, and can be radically diverse. Compare the ultra-realistic treatment of ping pong in **Rockstar Games presents Table Tennis** with the all-out insanity of Nintendo's **Mario Tennis** games, which add spinning stars and carnivorous plants to the playing field.

In both cases, be aware of the HUD elements. All three games—**Pong**, **Table Tennis**, and **Mario Power Tennis**—display a dynamic (changeable) piece of text on the screen to show the score data. Table Tennis also has player names, an exertion meter, and little circles that display how many games each player has won. Look at the positioning of those elements. In all cases, and in our Motherload example, these HUD elements are displayed at the top of the screen.

The feature set: As Pong evolved, the feature set became far richer. Satisfied that the simple mechanic of hitting a virtual ball back and forth was enough to hang a game on, both Rockstar Games and Nintendo were able to blow out Pong with feature sets so juicy that the games' Pong origins are barely recognizable. By implementing tennis-style scoring, they made these games much more like tennis with very little effort. Both games add tournaments, rankings, and different player characters with varying skill sets. Mario Power Tennis adds about 30 new features involving mushrooms. Pong is a true testament to the level of complexity a simple, strong game mechanic can aspire to. But, again, if you want to make a fully featured game like Table Tennis or Mario Power Tennis, the key is to start with is a simple game like Pong.

The mechanic that launched a thousand games

The Pong game mechanic is so simple and so effective that its impact can be felt far and wide throughout the annals of video game history.

From Pong, we get Breakout. The innovation here is to turn Pong into a single-player game like real-world handball or squash, with the addition of a breakable brick wall. Breakout introduces stages or levels to the Pong concept, each with a different configuration of bricks:

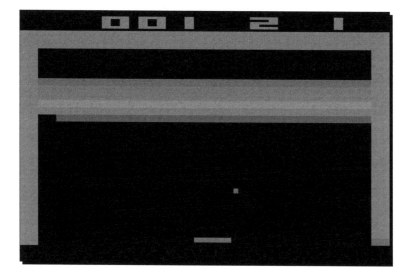

Arkanoid iterates on Breakout by changing the skin to a sci-fi theme. The paddle becomes a spaceship. Arkanoid adds a few new features, most importantly power-ups that come in the form of capsules that are released when the ball smashes into the bricks. When the player catches the capsules with the spaceship, the game rules get bent. The spaceship can become longer. It can become sticky so that the player can catch the ball and plan the next shot. My favorite Arkanoid power-up is the red capsule marked **L**; it enables the spaceship to fire laser beams to destroy the bricks!

The Pong legacy brings us all the way to the present day, with **Peggle** by **PopCap Games**. Peggle combines a few different game mechanics: the brick-smashing and ball-bouncing of Breakout, the angular aiming of **Bust-A-Move** or **Puzzle Bobble**, and the random insanity of real-world pachinko games. To jazz up the skin, PopCap adds cartoon unicorns and gophers, and in one of the most-talked-about payoffs in video game history, Peggle rewards players with an absolutely over-the-top slow-motion winning shot while blaring the climax of Beethoven's ninth symphony!

Peggle teaches us some important lessons:

- A few small twists on a timeless mechanic will still sell. Peggle has been downloaded over 50 million times!

- Small games and large games can play nicely together. The famed MMORPG **World of Warcraft (WoW)** is embedded with a special version of Peggle, along with another blockbuster PopCap Games hit, **Bejewelled**. WoW players can use Peggle to decide how to distribute loot among the party members, which is probably more fun than flipping a coin.

- You stand to reach a broad audience if you package your game with friendly, well-illustrated unicorns and gophers instead of dark and brooding axe-wielding superwarriors named "Kane" or "Glorg".

- Music and sound play a crucial role in your design. They can make the game.

Have a go hero – redesign your favorite games

What if *you* were in charge of creating sequels to some very well-known games? Sequels to Pac-Man added 3D mazes, jumping, and a red bow to the main character's head. Is that what you would have done? Take a look at this list of popular games and think about which gameplay features you might add if you were in charge of the sequel:

- Pac-Man
- Tetris
- Wolfenstein 3D
- Wii Sports – Boxing
- Chess
- Space Invaders

Toy or story

The approach that we're taking to your initial idea phase is not an approach that comes naturally. Usually, new game developers want to start with setting the story and characters, as if writing a book. That's how we've always been taught to begin a creative project. As there's often so much overlap between narrative forms such as books, movies, and teevee shows, it's tempting to start there. "My game is about a dark, brooding superwarrior named Kane Glorg who doesn't know who his parents are, so he travels the wasted landscape with his two-handed axe and his vicious battle sloth, slicing through hordes of evil slime demons in his ultimate quest to punch Satan in the face."

The take-away from this chapter is that all that stuff is window dressing. When you're just starting out (and unless you're building an explicitly narrative game like a graphic or text-based adventure), story, setting, and character are the end point, not the start point. Too many would-be game developers get caught up in the epic implications of their story design instead of worrying about what's most important: does my game have a fun, simple mechanic that players will enjoy?

When you're designing a game, you're not creating a narrative. You're creating a toy, which can be wrapped like a sausage roll in flaky layers of delicious storytelling, character arcs, and twist endings, but you need to start with the toy. You need to start with that small, singular piece of joy that puts a smile on your player's face. As Shigeru Miyamoto, the man who created **Mario**, **Donkey Kong**, and **Zelda**, said in his 2007 keynote at the Game Developers Conference,

> *"Start by imagining your player having fun with your game, and work backwards from there."*

Shopping for ideas

One great place to find inspiration for games is your local toy store. Ignore the toy skins, like the high-seas adventure of Lego Pirates sets, and focus on the mechanic: building. Ignore the giant fire-breathing scorpion head skin on that Hot Wheels track set, and think about the mechanic: the fun, the physical way the little cars fly over the ramps. And be sure to investigate the small, simple toys in the end aisles, in the nickel bins, and inside those chocolate eggs and bags of caramel popcorn. You're bound to find game mechanic ideas there.

Pop Quiz – finding that singular piece of joy

What follows is a list of video games that are all based on a real-world physical game mechanic. In some cases, they're based on a physical game, and in other cases, they're based on goofing around. Can you identify the singular piece of joy from which these games take their cue? The answers are written on a folded piece of paper that I've hidden underneath your chair.

- **Super Monkey Ball**: Tilt the level to guide a sphere along ramps, spirals, and treacherously thin platforms suspended above a bottomless void.
- **Metal Gear Solid**: Hide behind crates and other pieces of cover while heavily armed guards seek you.
- **Boom Blox**: Throw a ball at a stack of blocks that have different physical properties to knock them all down or to make them explode.

◆ **Katamari Damacy**: Roll a ball around in random detritus scattered around the level and watch it grow ever larger. Roll up a writhing junk wad of sufficient size to reach the goal.

◆ **Dance Dance Revolution**: Light up a series of scrolling arrows by stepping on their corresponding buttons on a flat input pad. The button presses are timed to the beat of a backing soundtrack.

Redefining the sky

The sky's the limit, and Unity starts us off with an endless sky. But through this chapter, we've seen that that endless sky can actually trap us into an ambitious concept that we'll have no chance of completing. So, let's redefine the sky. Instead of wondering how big and complex your game can be, think about the endless array of simple interactions and moments of joy our world contains. Throwing and catching a ball, knocking a pile of stuff over, feeding an animal, growing a plant—the world is packed with simple, effective interactions that ignite our most primitive, most basic "Joy Cortices", which is a neurological term that I've entirely invented just now.

If you want to discover one of these joy-producing real-world moments, study a child. Because games are all about playing, the simple things that amuse and delight children and babies are the stuff of award-winning games. What is **Metal Gear Solid** if not a complex game of hide and seek? **Rock Band** and **Guitar Hero** are digital versions of all those times you played air guitar and pretended to be a rock star in front of the mirror with your bedroom door closed. Have you ever rolled snow into giant balls to build a snowman? **Katamari Damacy** is the video game expression of that joy-producing activity.

Creative limitation is not something to rebel against—it's something to be embraced! It's when we're under restriction that we come up with the most creative and interesting solutions to problems. Conversely, when we have absolutely no limitations, we're at risk of producing junk. This is a common criticism leveled at George Lucas for creating his vastly inferior *Star Wars* prequels; so the theory goes, no one dared to tell George "no", and the horrifying result was Jar Jar Binks.

It's even possible that in the midst of your limitations, you'll stumble upon a game bug or a strange behavior that's so fun and interesting, it becomes your core gameplay mechanic! In the world of video games, anything is possible.

Summary

In case you ever need to answer a multiple-choice quiz on this chapter, here's a quick rundown of what we've learned:

- ♦ Big game ideas are the enemy! Consider thinking small and building slowly to achieve big success.
- ♦ By cutting **features** from your game ideas, you can whittle your design down to a more manageable size than by cutting **content**.
- ♦ A game's **mechanic** is distinct from its **skin**. A single, strong game mechanic can support myriad different skins through a whole host of great games.
- ♦ Start taking notice of the front-of-house aspects and HUDs in the games that you play. You'll be building your own a few chapters from now!

Let's begin

For the rest of this book, we're going to ignore the epic implications of that endless Big Sky Country 3D plane in the Unity Scene view. We're going to focus on small, simple, and fun game mechanics. Once you close the back cover of this book, you can take those simple concepts and iterate on them, even blowing them out to ambitious fully featured crazy-fests such as Master of Orion or Mario Power Tennis. But stick to the strategy that will make you successful throughout—start at zero, discover that singular piece of joy, and iterate until your game is finished.

3
Game #1 – Ticker Taker

So far, we've taken a look at what other developers, large and small, are doing with Unity. We talked about what it's going to take for you to become a small developer and succeed—to finish a fully functional game. Now it's time to roll up your sleeves, tie up your inner procrastinator and lock it in the trunk of your car, and start learning to build a game with Unity.

Here's what we're going to do:

1. Come up with a game idea.
2. Distil it down to that small, singular piece of joy.
3. Start building the game in Unity using placeholder objects.
4. Add lighting to the **Scene**.
5. Tie into Unity's built-in physics engine.
6. Modify a game object using components to bend it to your steely will.

Let's get cracking!

Kick up a new Unity project

Let's get to that crucial decision-making stage where we're staring at a wide-open 3D frontier in an empty project file:

1. Open Unity 3D. The last project you had open should appear. (This might be the AngryBots Demo from *Chapter 1, That's One Fancy Hammer!*).

2. In the menu, click on **File | New Project...**.

3. Under **Project Location**, type in or browse to the folder where you want your project created. It's a good idea to create a new folder somewhere on your computer where you'll be able to find it again, and name it something that makes sense. I created a folder on my desktop called `UnityProjects`, and created my new project in an empty folder called `Chapter3Game`.

4. Unity gives us the option to import a bunch of useful ready-made goodies into our new project. We don't need any of these yet, so make sure all the boxes are unchecked:

5. Next, click on the **Create** button. Unity will briefly close and restart. After importing the assets we selected, the program will open.

6. Close the **Welcome to Unity** start screen if it's open. You'll find yourself staring face-to-face with that wide-open 3D plane.

Where did everything go?

If you're staring at nothing but a 3D plane in the **Scene** view, Unity has pulled a switcheroo on you. To get back to a layout, like the one you saw in the AngryBots Demo, choose **2 by 3** from the **Layout** drop-down menu at the top right of the screen. Note that there are other choices here, and that Unity enables you to save and restore your own custom layouts:

Layers ▼   2 by 3 ▼

2 by 3
4 Split
Default
Tall
Wide

Save Layout...
Delete Layout...
Revert Factory Settings...

'Tis volley

What kind of game are we going to make? Well, let's pretend that you are totally pumped up about volleyball (work with me here). All you can think about night and day is volleyball. You dream about it at bedtime. You play it at every chance you get. So, when it comes to making your first game in Unity, there's no question: you *have* to make a volleyball game.

Let's back away from that idea a little and, using what we learned in *Chapter 2, Let's Start with the Sky*, evaluate the difficulty level of a volleyball game. Volleyball features two teams of six players on either side of a net. A "server" hits a ball with his/her hands over the net, and the teams compete to keep the ball in the air, hitting it back and forth over the net. The rally ends when:

- One team lets the ball hit the floor
- The ball goes out of bounds
- An angry puma bursts onto the court and starts chewing on the star players

The first team to score 25 points wins the set. A match is best-of-five. Then there are a number of rules that govern how often and in what way a player may hit the ball (hint: no grabsies).

Hopefully, it's clear that volleyball is a BIG game with lots of rules and a heap of helping of complexity. Multiple teams means that you have four options:

♦ **Two-player, same computer**: Both players share the keyboard and mouse to compete against each other

♦ **One-player, same computer**: So, you'd have to program AI (Artificial Intelligence) to enable the computer to play against a human

♦ **Two-player, different computers**:

♦ **Multiple players, multiple computers**: Where every human player controls a team of volleyball team members

We saw in the last chapter that these multiplayer options can add significant layers of complexity to a simple game. Right out of the gate, the challenge is daunting. In addition to providing for two teams, having multiple players on each team means that you have to program a way for the player to switch between different characters. And who knows *how* you're ever going to animate that puma?

Keep the dream alive

All this results in the simple mathematic equation: *you + volleyball game = badIdea^{10}*. That's a bad idea to the *power of ten*, which (mathematically) makes it an *exponentially* bad idea.

But volleyball is your passion. Does that mean you can never follow your dreams and make the kinds of games you'd always hoped to build? Of course not! Let's see if we can distil the game of volleyball down to its barest essentials—to that small, singular piece of joy.

Slash and burn!

If you want to finish a game, you need to cut the complexity and the features. Bring out your red pen and/or machete, and follow along:

1. Scrap the sets and the best-of-five match structure

2. Kibosh the teams

3. Jettison the multiple players

4. Ditch the net

5. Nix the referee and the spectators

   What do we have? Just a person with a ball, looking kind of lonely. Hmm! That person might be a little tricky to model, texture, rig, and animate. Let's keep slashing.

6. Next, trash the player

Now where are we? We have a ball, floating in midair; a ball that can't hit the floor. So, we need something simple to hit the ball with. A human character is too complicated, so let's just say it's a surface. We'll have some kind of thing that we can bounce the ball on.

The many faces of keep-up

You know what? This game is starting to sound a lot like **keep-up**. You might have played that as a kid with a balloon that couldn't hit the ground. Or you might have played it in a circle of hippies and called it "Hacky Sack" or footbag. You might have played it in a soccer drill by bouncing the ball on different parts of your body. You may even have played it by taking something scalding hot out of the oven, calling it "Ow! Ow! Ow! It burns! Get me an oven mitt already! OW!"

Keep-up looks a whole lot like Pong or Breakout from *Chapter 2, Let's Start with the Sky*. You have an object to keep up and an object to keep it up with. The innovation is a little bit of physics—in this case, gravity—which is the force that constantly pulls the object towards the ground. It's simple, it's effective, and your players will instantly get it. It distills volleyball down to that singular piece of joy. It's what volleyball was meant to be, before *Johnny McBuzzkill* came along and added all of those formalized rules and unflattering shorts. And, because little kids play and enjoy keep-up, you know that you're tapping into some primal, intuitive game mechanic that will stand the test of time.

Keep-up sounds like a *great* first project for learning Unity. Let's do it! Let's build a keep-up game!

Creating the ball and the hitter

For now, we'll use Unity's built-in 3D primitives to create our game objects. Besides the terrain editor, Unity doesn't have any great modeling tool built in. You'll need a piece of 3D software for that. Let's see what we can manage with what Unity gives us.

Time for action – create the Ball

Let's add a built-in `GameObject` to the **Scene** view:

1. In the menu, click on **GameObject**.
2. Point to **Create Other**.
3. Click on **Sphere**.

What just happened – that's all there is to it?

Well, yeah, actually! Unity has a number of prebuilt simple 3D models, also known as **primitives**, which we can use to get started. You've just created a built-in game object with four components on it. A component is a piece of functionality that modifies or augments a **GameObject**. Look at the **Inspector** panel to see what the Sphere's components are:

◆ **Transform**: This determines how a game object is positioned, rotated, and scaled (made big or small) in your **Scene** view.

◆ **Mesh Filter**: This component takes a mesh, and runs it through the **Mesh Renderer**. A **Mesh** defines the connected vertices that comprise a 3D structure.

◆ **Sphere Collider**: This is a sphere-shaped boundary on our game object that helps Unity figure out when instances of game object colliders touch, overlap, or stop touching.

◆ **Mesh Renderer**: This component enables the player to see our meshes. Without it, meshes don't get drawn or rendered to the screen.

We'll get a better understanding of what exactly a **Mesh** is when we add the **Paddle** to the **Scene** a few steps from now.

A ball by any other name

Let's make a few changes to our ball. We should rename it and move it up into the "air" so that it has some place to fall from.

Time for action – rename the Ball

1. In the **Hierarchy** panel, find the **GameObject** called **Sphere**, beneath **Main Camera**.

2. To rename the sphere, you can either right-click/alternate-click it and choose **Rename**, or press *F2* on the keyboard if you're on a PC. Mac users can press the *Return* or *Enter* key to rename the **Sphere**. You can also rename a **GameObject** by selecting it and typing a new name into the field at the top of the **Inspector** panel.

3. Rename the game object to `Ball`:

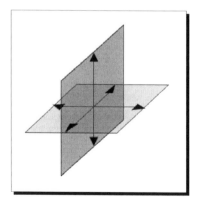

Your project can fill up fast with generically named game objects and other assorted things, so let's stay on top of our project by naming game objects as we create them.

Origin story

The center of your game world is called the **origin**. The origin is the magical place in 3D space where everything begins. 3D space is divided into three axes: **X**, **Y**, and **Z**. If you remember your Cartesian grid from grade school, or if you've ever seen a bar or line graph, the X-axis runs one way (usually horizontally), and the Y-axis runs perpendicular to it (usually vertically). 3D is like taking a second piece of paper and sticking it at a right angle to your graph so that this axis is perpendicular to both X and Y-axis and you have a third axis firing straight up at your face from your desk, and down into the floor in the opposite direction.

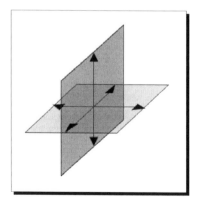

The orientation (the way the X, Y, and Z axes are positioned) varies from program to program. Unity has a Y-up orientation. The X and Z axes run perpendicular to each other on the "floor". If you hold your arms out like a scarecrow, your arms are the X axis, and the Z axis runs through your belly button. The Y axis runs straight up into the sky, and straight down to the center of the Earth where there are probably goblins or some such creatures.

Let's get a better look at that ball. To orbit around the **Scene** view, hold down the *Alt* key or *option* key on your keyboard (depending on whether you're using a PC or a Mac) and press and hold the primary (usually left) mouse button. If the ball is centered near the origin, you should notice that the "ground" plane slices right through it. That's because the ball's transform ("registration" or "pivot point" in other software) is at its center. Half the ball is above ground, half the ball is below. If the ball's X, Y, and Z position values are all zero, the center of the ball is at the origin, where the three 3D planes converge. It's entirely likely that your ball is floating around somewhere else in the scene. Let's fix that right now.

Disoriented?

If you ever get lost orbiting, panning, and zooming around the **Scene** view, remember that you can reorient yourself by clicking on the gizmo at the top-right of the **Scene** view. Click on the green **Y** cone to view the scene from the Top-down. Click the red **X** cone to view the scene from the Right. Clicking on the blue **Z** cone focuses us at the Front of the **Scene**. Click the gray box in the middle of the gizmo to return to a perspective view. If you want to completely reverse your view, you can click on the white cone sitting opposite to your orientation—doing this will flip the view around so that you're looking at things from the opposite angle. The label beneath the cone tells you which view you're currently using.

Remember, you can always use the *F* key to frame (or focus) the selected game object.

XYZ/RGB

If you've ever listened to your science or art teacher drone on about color spectrum of light, you might have noticed that X, Y, and Z map onto Red, Green, and Blue. Red, Green, and Blue are the primary colors of light, and are always listed in that order. If you're visually-oriented, it might help you to know that X is Red, Y is Green, and Z is Blue, when you're looking at any depiction of axes in Unity. Most often, your selected axis turns yellow when you hover over or select it.

Time for action – move the Ball Into the "Sky"

We want the ball to start somewhere in the "sky" (the area above the ground plane) so that it will have somewhere to fall from:

1. Make sure that the **Ball** game object is selected. Click on it in the **Hierarchy** panel.

2. See the control gizmo poking out from the center of the ball? You can either click-and-drag the green Y-axis to move the ball up, or type a new Y position for it in the **Inspector** panel. As we want to stay on the same page together, let's type it. Look in the **Inspector** panel and find the **Y** field—it's next to **Position** in the **Transform** component of the **Ball**:

3. Change the **Y** position from 0 to 2.

4. Press the *Enter* key to commit this change.

5. Your ball may not have begun life at the origin. Make sure that the values for its **X** and **Z** position are at **0**.

6. The **Ball** game object should now be hovering two units above the ground plane, which is a marvelous height from where any self-respecting ball can endeavor to fall:

Time for action – shrink the Ball

The units in our 3D world are arbitrary. When you're working on your game, it may help to ascribe real-world measurements to these units. Perhaps one unit equals one foot or one meter? If you're building a real-time strategy game where the scale is much larger, maybe one unit equals one mile or one kilometer? The ball that we've just created is a little large for our purposes, so let's shrink it down:

1. With the **Ball** still selected, type 0.4 for the **X**, **Y**, and **Z** scale values in the **Transform** component of the **Ball**.

2. Press *Tab* to move the cursor to each new field, and press *Enter* after typing in each field to commit the change:

The **Ball** should shrink down to 0.4, or 40 percent of its original size. Note that if you enter 0.4 only into one or two of the three **Scale** fields, you'll accidentally create a weird-looking egg or an ovoid-shaped ball. If you dig gizmos, you can also use Unity's **Scale** gizmo which, as we've seen, is mapped to the *R* key. Click and drag the grey box in the middle of the gizmo to scale the ball uniformly.

Size matters

When it comes to including **GameObjects** in Unity's physics simulation, as we'll do by the end of this chapter, scale does actually matter. The Unity manual recommends that you treat 1 unit as 1 real-world meter (that's 3.2 feet, for you imperial users).

Time for action – save your scene

A computer teacher of mine once gave me sage advice: "Save often, cry seldom." Throughout the book, I won't pester you to save your project in every other paragraph—that's up to you and how comfy you feel with your dodgy power cable and the fact that you're reading this book during a lightning storm. At the very least, let's learn how to save the **Scene** that we're working on. Save frequency is up to you from this point on!

1. Click on **File | Save** (or **Save Scene As**) in the menu. You're asking Unity to save the current named **Scene**, but there really is no named **Scene** for it to save yet. Let's fix that.

2. In the resulting dialog, type a name for your **Scene**. I chose to call mine Game.

3. Click on the **Save** button. Unity actually creates a **Scene** asset in the **Project** panel called **Game**. You know that it's a **Scene** because it has a Unity 3D icon next to it:

4. Now that you've named your **Scene**, you can quickly save changes at any point by pressing *Ctrl* or *Command + S*, or by clicking on **File | Save Scene** in the menu. Clicking on **File | Save Project** will do a blanket save across your entire project.

Time for action – add the Paddle

We'll borrow a term from Pong by naming our hittable surface paddle. The paddle will be the thing the player uses to bounce the ball and keep it up in the air. We can build the paddle using Unity's built-in **Cube** primitive, like we did with the **Sphere**.

1. In the menu, navigate to **GameObject | Create Other | Cube**, as shown in the following screenshot:

Now, according to **Hierarchy**, we have three instances of **GameObject** in our **Scene**: the **Ball**, a **Cube**, and the **Main Camera**. Let's rename our **Cube** to remind us what it will do in the game:

2. If the **Cube** is not selected, click on its name in the **Hierarchy** panel and rename it `Paddle`:

Now, we should make the **Paddle** more paddle-like by changing the **Scale** properties of the **Transform** component.

3. Make sure that the **Paddle** is still selected in the **Hierarchy** panel.

4. In the **Inspector** panel, change the **X Scale** value of the **Paddle** to `1.1`.

5. Change the **Y Scale** value of the **Paddle** to `0.04`.

6. Make sure the Position values are zeroed out to move the **Paddle** to the origin.

Ah, that's better! The **Paddle** looks like a thin, flat, smackable surface—perfect for whacking around our **Ball**.

What's a Mesh?

Although technology is constantly changing, most often a piece of 3D artwork comprises three types of pieces: vertices, edges, and faces. A vertex is a point in 3D space. The **Paddle** that we just added has eight vertices (points)—one on each corner. In these illustrations, we'll depict a cube mesh to make this easier to grasp:

Edges connect the dots—building lines between the vertices. Our **Paddle** has 12 visible edges: four along the top, four along the bottom, and four edges at each corner connecting the top and bottom.

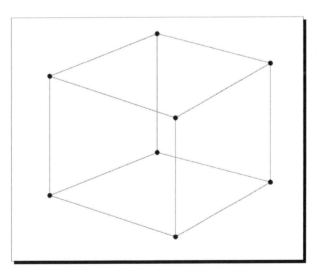

Faces are surfaces that are drawn between (usually) three vertices. Our **Paddle** has six faces, like a die. Edges help define where one face ends and another begins:

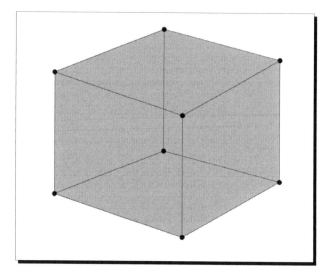

Each face in our **Paddle** actually has a hidden edge splitting it up into two triangles. So, the **Paddle** is made up of *6 x 2 = 12* triangles:

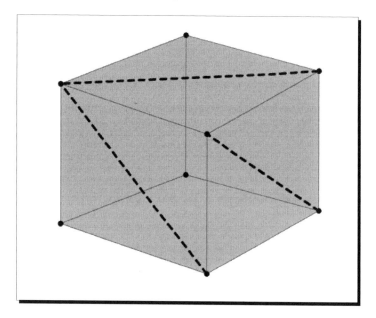

3D models, then, are made up of three-sided (or sometimes four- or more-sided) surfaces. A multisided shape is called a **polygon**. When you hear someone say "polygon count", he's talking about the number of triangles that make up a 3D model. The fewer the polygons, the less work the computer needs to do to render, or draw, the model. That's why you may have heard that game artists need to produce low-polygon (or "low-poly") count models, while film and teevee artists are free to produce high-poly count models. In film or teevee, a shot only has to be rendered once before it's committed to a frame of the movie forever. But video game engines such as Unity have to constantly draw and redraw models on the fly. The fewer the polygons, the faster the game will potentially run.

A low-polygon model looks more crude and roughly hewn than a high-polygon model. As video games are built for better and faster systems, the models start featuring higher polygon counts. Compare the character models in a game such as **Half-Life** with the higher-polygon count models in the game's sequel, which requires a faster computer to run it. The difference is clear!

Poly wants to crack your game performance?

The number of polygons that Unity can handle in a single **Scene** really depends on the hardware that's running your game. Unity games are hardware-accelerated—the faster the machine that runs your game, the more polygons you can push. The best thing to do is to build your models with as few polygons as you can get away with, without making your game a giant cube-fest (unless you're making **Minecraft**, in which case, more power to you). Decide on a minimum system specification, then test early and often on that minimally-powered system to ensure that your game actually runs!

Of course, it entirely depends on your game, but you might try staying between 1,500 and 4,000 triangles per mesh to keep things humming.

Keep in mind that a number of factors beyond polygon count determine how quickly or slowly your game runs. Learning how to put together a lean, mean, and optimized game is something you'll learn over time as you gain experience as a game developer.

When you bring a 3D model into Unity from another program (as you'll be doing later in this book), Unity converts the model's "whatever-gons" into triangles. When you read about model architecture in Unity, "triangles" is the term that crops up most often.

Keeping yourself in the dark

If you've kept an eye on the **Game** view, which is what the player sees, you've noticed that the Mesh game objects in our **Scene** are a dark, dreary gray color. Would you believe me if I told you they're actually closer to white?

Just like on a real movie or teevee set, 3D scenes require lights to illuminate objects. The lights aren't actually "real" objects (such as our **Ball** and **Paddle** meshes), they're virtual objects in 3D space that determine whether the faces on a mesh will appear bright or dark. The computer figures this out for us based on the kind of light we use, the way we position and rotate it, and the settings we give it.

So, while you can move a light around your scene just like the **Ball** or the **Paddle**, there's no actual geometry or triangles comprising the light. Lights aren't made of triangles, they're made of data. In Unity, as in many 3D programs, lights are represented in the **Scene** view by icons (or as Unity calls them—"gizmos"), with lines indicating their direction or their area of influence.

Time for action – add a light

Let's add one of these virtual lights to our **Scene** so that we can see our objects a bit better:

1. If you're still in **Wireframe** mode (where your game objects look like they're made from chicken wire), you'll need to switch to textured mode. In the **Scene** view frame, click on the **Wireframe** button and choose **Textured** rendering. Then click on the little light icon (it looks like a sun) a few buttons over to see the effects of our (as-yet-non-existent) lighting. Your ball and paddle should look as dreary and dark gray as they do in the **Game** view.

2. In the menu, navigate to **GameObject | Create Other**. The three types of lights that Unity supports are listed there: point light, spotlight, and directional light.

3. Choose **Directional Light**.

A new directional light is added to the **Scene**. The icon also looks like an iconic white sun. When the light is selected (as it is now), a tube of yellow rays shoots out from it. That tube shows us which way the light is pointing.

Notice that one portion of your ball is now lit, and the objects in the **Game** view have brightened up.

Time for action – move and rotate the light

This new light is kind of in the way, and a big chunk of our ball isn't properly lit. Let's fix that.

1. Ensure that the **Directional Light** is still selected. If you deselected it, click on the **Directional Light** label in the **Hierarchy** panel.

2. In the **Inspector** panel, change the light's position to move it up and out of the way. Enter 0 for the **X** position, 4 for the **Y** position, and -4 for the **Z** position. moving a directional light like this does not alter its intensity, but we're just making sure it's within reach in the **Scene** view.

3. Rotate the light so that it shines down on the objects. Enter a value of 44 for the light's **X Rotation** in the **Inspector** panel. The other two rotation values should be zero.

4. Now, the light is casting its sunny rays a bit more pleasantly on our **Scene**:

Have a go hero

If you're feeling adventurous, now's a great time to get a better feel for these virtual lights. Switch to the Rotate mode by using the controls at the top-left corner of the screen, or press the *E* key on your keyboard. You can freely rotate the light around to see how it affects your objects:

Switch to Move mode by clicking on the Move icon or by pressing *W* on the keyboard. Click on the **Transform** gizmo to move the light around the scene. How does moving the light affect the way your objects appear?

Kill the light by pressing *Delete* on the keyboard (*command + Delete* if you're on a Mac). Add one of the other two types of lights—a spotlight or a point light—by navigate to **GameObject | Create Other** and choosing another light. You can also change an existing light's type in the **Type** drop-down menu in the **Inspector** panel. What's the difference between the light you chose and the directional light? Move the new light all around to get a sense of how each light type treats your objects slightly differently.

Here are the differences between the lights in a nutshell:

- **Directional light**: This light can travel an infinite distance and illuminate everything in the **Scene**. This kind of light works like the sun. As we've seen, it doesn't matter how large or small a directional light is, or where you place it in the **Scene**—only by rotating it can we determine which surfaces it illuminates.

- **Point light**: These lights start at a point in 3D space and shine all around like a light bulb. Unlike directional lights, point lights have a range—anything outside of that range doesn't get lit.

- **Spotlight**: Spotlights are cone-shaped. They have a range *and* a direction. Objects outside a spotlight's cone don't get lit by that light.

- **Ambient**: This is the default type of lighting that you see in your **Scene**, without adding any light game objects. Ambient lighting is the most efficient, but it's also the most boring. You can crank the level of ambient lighting in your **Scene** up and down by fiddling with the render settings (**Edit | Render Settings**). Try clicking on the **Ambient Light** swatch to cast a creepy, bright green glow over your entire **Scene**, as shown in the following screenshot:

Extra credit

If this lighting stuff really revs you up, check out all of the settings and things to fiddle with within the **Inspector** panel when you select a light. You can get more information on what these and any other **Component** settings do by clicking on the blue book icon with the question mark on it in each **Component** section in the **Inspector** panel.

Are you a luminary?

Unity takes care of the science behind lighting our scenes, but arranging the lights is an art. On many 3D animated movies and teevee shows, as well as on large game development teams, there's often at least one person dedicated to lighting the scene, just as there are lighting specialists on real-world film sets. Virtual lights are built to mimic the properties of real-world lights. Lighting, like modeling, can be an entirely unique discipline in the world of 3D game development.

When you're finished exploring lights, follow the steps mentioned previously in the *Time for action – move and rotate the light* section to restore your directional light, or just press *Ctrl + Z* or *command + Z* on the keyboard to undo everything back to when you started messing around.

Who turned out the lights?

When you light a scene with multiple lights, it can be tricky to see which light is affecting which area. To turn a light off, select the light in the **Hierarchy** panel. Then, uncheck the checkbox at the top of the **Inspector** panel. Poof! The light is gone; but not forgotten. Check the checkbox again to make it reappear.

In fact, you can turn any **GameObject** on and off by using this checkbox. It's a handy way to isolate things in your **Scene** without deleting your hard work.

Darkness reigns

If you're working on a particularly grim game and you want to be able to see what's going on in your **Scene**, toggle the internal lighting by pressing the sunny little button at the top of your **Scene** view. When it's lit, your light game objects take over. When it's unlit, internal lighting hits your meshes so that you can see what's what:

Cameramania

If you had a good time playing with all the light settings, you're going to lose your mind when you check out the camera! Cameras in 3D programs are simulations of how the light rays bend around from a single perspective point. 3D cameras can simulate many different lenses, focal lengths, and effects. For now, we're just going to ensure that our camera is adjusted properly so that we're all on the same page, but don't be afraid to goof around with the camera controls if you're dying to get into some trouble.

1. In the **Hierarchy** panel, click to select the **Main Camera** game object. You'll notice you get a cool little **Camera Preview** picture-in-picture to show you what the camera "sees":

2. In the **Inspector** panel, adjust the camera's position to **X**: 0, **Y**: 1, and **Z**: -2.5. The paddle and ball should now be nicely framed in the **Game** view:

Time for action – test your game

We have a well-lit and nicely framed **Scene** containing a **Ball** and a **Paddle**. The **Ball** is poised in midair, ready to fall. Everything looks good. Let's test our game to see what happens next:

1. Click on the Play button to test your game.

Ack! That was anti-climactic. The **Ball** is just sort of sitting there, waiting to fall, and the **Paddle** is not moving. Somewhere in the distance, a slow, sad strain of violin music plays.

But not to worry! We're one step away from making something amazing happen. Press the Play button again to stop testing the game.

The pitfalls of Play

Remember that when you're testing your game with the Play button activated, you can still make changes to your **Scene**, but these changes don't get saved! When you stop testing, everything will go back to the way it once was, like Cinderella after the royal ball. To make it very clear that you're in this potentially confusing game-testing mode, click on the **Maximize on Play** button at the top of the **Game** window. Now, whenever you test your game, the window will fill the screen to prevent you from absentmindedly messing with stuff.

Let's get physical

I wanted you to test your game at this point, even though nothing happened, to pinpoint that magic moment when Unity becomes awesome. If you're already having a good time, you ain't seen nothing yet!

Add physics to your game

Let's tap into Unity's built-in physics engine by adding a **Rigidbody** component to the **Ball**:

1. Select the **Ball** from the **Hierarchy** panel.

2. In the menu, navigate to **Component | Physics | Rigidbody**.

3. A **Rigidbody** component is added to the **Ball**. You can see it in the list of the components of the **Ball** game object in the **Inspector** panel:

4. Make sure that the **Rigidbody** component's **Use Gravity** checkbox is checked in the **Inspector** panel.

5. Press Play to test your game.

6. Press Play again when you've recovered from how awesome that was.

No way! When you tested your game, you should have seen your **Ball** plummet straight down and land on the **Paddle**. How cool was that? If you answered, "Especially cool", give yourself ten points.

Understanding the gravity of the situation

Unity's built-in physics engine is ready for you to hook into it, but it will ignore your game objects unless you opt to add a component like **Rigidbody** to your game object. The **Rigidbody** component is so-named to differentiate it from **soft body dynamics**, which are calculations that actually distort and deform your meshes.

Unity's Gone Soft

Soft bodies like cloth are partially supported in Unity 4.*x*, after numerous developers requested the feature. You can view and vote on upcoming Unity features here:

`http://feedback.unity3d.com/`

Rigidbody dynamics treat all of our objects as if they're made of wood, steel, or very stale cake. **Collider** components tell Unity when game objects crash into each other. As both our **Ball** and our **Paddle** already have sphere- and cube-shaped colliders surrounding their meshes, the missing link is the **Rigidbody** component. By adding a **Rigidbody** component to the **Ball**, we include the **Ball** in Unity's physics calculations. The result is hot ball-on-paddle action.

More bounce to the ounce

The **Ball** hits the **Paddle** and comes to a dead stop. Pretty cool for such a small effort, but it won't do for a keep-up game. We need to get that **Ball** bouncing!

Select the **Ball** and take a close look at its **Sphere Collider** component in the **Inspector** panel. One of the parameters, or options, is called **Material**. Next to that, we see the label **None (Physic Material)** (this text may be slightly cut off depending on your screen resolution—to see the whole label, click-and-drag the left edge of the **Inspector** panel to increase its width). There's a small circle with a dot in the middle next to the label that means we can pop open a selection window. What hidden wonders await us in that window?

Time for action – make the Ball bouncy

1. Let's import a new package with certain goodies we'll need to make the **Ball** bounce. In the menu, navigate to **Assets | Import Package | Physic Materials**, then click on the **Import** button. A bunch of Physic Materials (whatever *they* are) get added to our **Project** panel:

2. Make sure that the **Ball** is selected.

3. In the **Inspector** panel, find the **Sphere Collider** component of the **Ball**. If it is closed, click on the gray triangular arrow to expand it so that you can get at its goodies.

4. Find the **Material** parameter of the **Sphere Collider**.

5. Click the small black circle next to the label that reads **None (Physic Material)**.

6. Double-click **Bouncy** from the list.

7. Test your game by clicking on the Play button.

8. When you finally snap out of it, press Play again to escape the mesmerizing results.

The Physic Materials package that we just imported includes a number of useful prebuilt physic materials. These special materials change what happens when a collider hits another collider. We chose the one called **Bouncy**, and lo and behold, when the **Ball** game object's **Sphere Collider** hits the **Cube Collider** of the **Paddle**, it reacts like a bouncy ball should. At our current phase of human technological progress, this is as close to a **Make Game** button as you're going to get!

Have a go hero

Unity's **Standard Assets** package provided us with a **Bouncy** physic material to use, but we could just as easily have created our own. If you want to create your own physic material from scratch, right-click/alternate-click on a blank area of the **Project** panel, and choose **Create | Physic Material**. Alternatively, you can click-and-hold the mouse button on the **Create** button at the top of the **Project** panel and choose **Physic Material**:

A new **Physic Material** called (appropriately enough) **New Physic Material** appears in the **Project** panel. You can rename it the same way you renamed the **Ball** and **Paddle** game objects. Call it **BouncyBall**.

Click to select the **Physic Material** in the **Project** panel. Its parameters are listed in the **Inspector**. If you're desperate to know what everything does, click on the blue book icon with the question mark on it, and prepare to be bored to tears by talk of anisotropic friction. Yawn! What you really want to do is change the **Bounciness** to 1, and set the **Bounce Combine** to **Maximum**. Or choose your own settings if you just want to see what they do:

Inspector	
BouncyBall	Open
Dynamic Friction	0.4
Static Friction	0.4
Bounciness	1
Friction Combine	Average
Bounce Combine	Maximum
▶ Friction Direction 2	
Dynamic Friction 2	0
Static Friction 2	0

Select the **Ball** again. Find where the **Sphere Collider** component's **Material** parameter is set to that built-in **Bouncy Physic Material**. Drag-and-drop your **BouncyBall** physic material into the slot where the built-in **Bouncy** one is. Alternatively, you can choose your **BouncyBall** physic material from the menu. The **Bouncy** physic material is swapped out for your own custom-created **BouncyBall** physic material.

What a drag!

We'll be pulling that same drag-and-drop maneuver again and again as we use Unity. If you weren't feeling up to trying those last steps, don't worry; you'll get plenty of chances to drag stuff around the interface as we build more games.

Test the game by clicking the Play button. The paddle is flat, the ball is bouncy, and everything seems right with the world! We haven't programmed any interactivity yet, but try moving and rotating the paddle around while the game is running using the Unity tools to get a sense of how the ball might react when we rig up mouse control in the next chapter. (You'll have to deselect **Maximize on Play** to gain access to your tools to try this out in the **Scene** view.) While any changes you make to **GameObjects** in the **Hierarchy** don't "stick" while the game is playing, changes you make to elements in the **Project** panel do get saved. This feature allows you to adjust things such as the **BouncyBall** material's bounciness live while you play.

Summary

In this chapter, we started to put the Unity 3D engine through its paces. We learned how to:

- Add built-in **GameObjects** to our **Scene**
- Position, rotate, and scale those game objects
- Add lighting to the **Scene** to brighten things up
- Add **Rigidbody** components to our **GameObjects** to tie into Unity's physics calculations
- Create **Physic Materials**
- Customize **Collider** components to make **GameObjects** become bouncy

We took an impossibly complex game idea and hacked it down to its fun, naked essentials. We explored the origin point—the center of our game's universe. We learned about the building blocks of 3D construction: vertices, edges, and faces. We talked about how polygon counts can affect game performance. We laughed, we cried. It was profound.

Following the script

What we have so far is not a game, but a very dull movie about the best keep-up player in the world who never, ever drops the ball. One key thing that distinguishes movies from games is popcorn. Also, games are interactive. We need to introduce interactivity to our game so that the player can move that paddle around.

We do this by writing a **Script**. Just like in the movies where everyone follows a list of stage cues, lines, and notes to put the finished product together, **GameObjects** in Unity can follow scripts to determine what to do. Scripts are essentially lists of instructions for people, or **GameObjects**, to follow. In the next chapter, we'll learn how to add scripts to our **GameObjects** to add interactivity to our game.

4
Code Comfort

*We've reached the precipice: we're staring at a game that doesn't do much and **won't** do much more unless we write some code. If you're brand new to this stuff, code is scary—or, rather, the **idea** of code is scary. Will you have to type a bunch of ones and zeroes or cryptic punctuation along thousands of monotonous line numbers? If you've ever tried developing a game or if you've ever been taught to program using some ancient language in a high school computer course, code might have been the thing to undo you. But, here you are giving it one more crack at the bat. The world needs a three-dimensional keep-up game, by gum! It's time to show the world what you're made of.*

What is code?

Code is just a series of instructions that you give to Unity to make it do stuff. We write lines (sentences) of code describing what we want to accomplish; these lines are called **statements**. Unity reads these statements and carries out our instructions. In Unity, you usually take a set of instructions and "stick" it to a **GameObject**. From now on, we'll use Unity's terminology **Script** to describe a collection of code statements.

Time for action – write your first Unity Script

Let's open our keep-up game project from the previous chapter, if it's not already open. We'll write a really simple Script and stick it to our **Ball** GameObject.

1. In the **Project** panel, right-click/alternate-click on an empty chunk of space and navigate to **Create | JavaScript** as shown in the following screenshot:

2. Alternatively, you can navigate to **Assets | Create | JavaScript** in the menu at the top of the screen, or use the **Create** button at the top of the **Project** panel. A new Script is added to the **Project** panel, inviting you to type a name for it. Call the script DisappearMe. It's also a good idea to use the same **Create** menu to make a folder and name it Scripts, then drag your new DisappearMe script into it to keep your **Project** panel organized.

3. When you double-click to edit your new `DisappearMe` Script, a brand new window opens up. This is Unity's default Script editor (or **Integrated Development Environment (IDE)**), called MonoDevelop. Its main panel looks a lot like a basic text editor, because that's all that Scripts really are—plain old boring text.

Rolling your own

If you have your own favorite Script editor/IDE, you can configure Unity to launch it instead. But, for the remainder of the book, we'll use the default MonoDevelop editor.

A leap of faith

The first piece of code (the first line of our Script) looks like this:

```
#pragma strict
```

What on Earth does that mean? We've been hit with confusing nerd talk right out of the gate. The simple explanation for this line is that it makes writing your code more fussy, but your code runs faster. We'll learn what that's all about later; for now, turn your attention further down to the Start function:

```
function Start () {
}
```

Click to place your cursor after the first curly brace, and press the *Enter* key to make some space between the top and bottom curly braces. Press the *Tab* key to indent, to make your code look pretty, if the editor doesn't automatically do it for you. Then, type a single line of code so that your Script looks like this:

```
function Start () {
    renderer.enabled = false;
}
```

You'll notice that as you type each word in this line of code, entire drop-down lists pop open with a dizzying list of strange-looking options. This is called **Code Hinting**, and while it may seem annoying when you first encounter it, you'll be erecting a shrine to it by the time you finish this book. Code Hinting brings a programming language's entire dictionary to your fingertips, saving you the hassle of looking things up or misspelling special keywords.

You may also notice that the word `false` lights up after you type it in. MonoDevelop highlights special reserved code words (*keywords*) to signify that they have special meaning to Unity.

A little asterisk ("star") appears next to your Script's name in the menu bar of MonoDevelop whenever you have unsaved changes, as shown in the following figure. Save your Script by pressing *Ctrl + S* or *command + S* on the keyboard, or by navigating to **File | Save** from the menu. For the remainder of this book, we'll assume that you've saved any modifications that you've made to your Scripts before trying them out.

The Sound of One Hand Clapping

Careless coders often wind up banging their heads against their desks when they test their code and nothing new happens—usually because they've forgotten to save their code files! Even though you've typed a bunch of code, nothing new will happen when you run your program unless your files are saved, so don't forget!

Lick it and stick it

Return to Unity. You should still see your `DisappearMe` Script in the **Project** panel. To attach it to the ball, drag-and-drop the file over the **Ball** GameObject in the **Hierarchy** panel.

If drag-and-drop isn't your thing, you can also select the **Ball** GameObject, and navigate to **Component | Scripts | Disappear Me** from the menu. You could also click on **Add Component** in **Inspector**, click on **Scripts**, and then choose the **DisappearMe** script from the resulting list. Once you do this, it may not look as if anything happened. To confirm that you did it correctly, click on the **Ball** in the **Hierarchy**. At the bottom of the **Inspector** panel where components of the **Ball** are listed, you should see your `DisappearMe` Script .

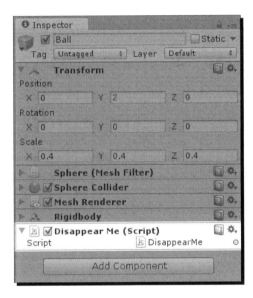

Disappear me!

Uncheck the **Maximize on Play** button in the **Game** view to experience the full effect of your script. (Cue circus music) And now, ladies and gentlemen, thrill to the astounding spectacle that you have created with a single line of code! Press the **Play** button to test your game, and watch with amazement as your **Ball** disappears!

What just happened?

A good magician never reveals his tricks, but let's break down that piece of code we wrote to see what's going on behind the scenes.

It's all Greek to me

First, we created a JavaScript Script. Unity Scripts are written in three languages that are somewhat like English: JavaScript, C#, and Boo. Of these, JavaScript and C# are the two most commonly used languages in Unity. You may have already dabbled in JavaScript if you've tried your hand at web development. Unity's version of JavaScript (called "UnityScript") is a bit different because it talks about Unity-related things and runs much faster than your father's JavaScript.

In this book, we'll use JavaScript because it's the simplest of the three languages to learn. For this reason, many of the online Unity scripting tutorials you'll find are also written in JavaScript.

Look Sharp

One major difference between JavaScript and C# is that C# is more formal, more rigidly structured, and more "strictly" typed. It's a bit like the difference between grabbing a milkshake at a greasy spoon with your best friend, and having high tea with the Queen of England; expect C# to constantly correct you on your table manners.

Among the advantages of a strictly-typed and structured language like C# is that it may be better suited to much larger projects, and with C# you tend to see fewer *run-time errors*—that is, problems that crop up while your game is running.

JavaScript is an excellent choice for beginner programmers, but many readers of previous editions have asked if this book could also include C# examples. From this point on, wherever you use JavaScript code, you'll find the completed and commented C# translation at the end of the chapter.

The first thing that we did was to write a line of code between two curly braces. I like to think of curly braces as delicious sandwich buns that group code together. The single lines of code are like the thin layers of salami or tomato in the sandwich. Above the curly braces is the description, or declaration, of the sandwich. It's like saying: *We are now going to make a hoagie*—top sandwich bun, yummy ingredients, bottom sandwich bun.

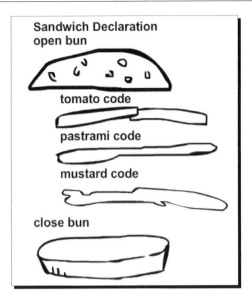

In more technical, less sandwich terms, the area grouped by the buns is called a **statement block**. The layers between the buns are called **statements**. And the type of sandwich we're making, the *Update* sandwich, is known as a **function**.

You'll never go hungry again

A **function** is a piece of the Script that can be executed, or called, over and over again. It's like having a sandwich that you can eat as many times as you want. We use functions to organize our code, and to house lines of code that we may need more than once.

The function we used is called Update. Just as there's an ongoing physics process in the background of our game that we can tap into to make our ball move and bounce, there's an ongoing Update loop as well. Update is eaten (or called) again and again and again while our game runs. Any Script lines, or statements, that we put inside the Update function tap into that loop.

Notice the way the `Update` function is declared. On a restaurant menu, we might declare that our Street-Fightin' Hoagie is a scrumptious offering of mile-high pastrami with lettuce, tomatoes, bacon, and cucumbers, topped with a fried egg, and slathered with mustard. We can declare a function much more simply. It starts with the word `function`, and adds the function name and a pair of round brackets. If our hoagie was a JavaScript function, it might look like this:

```
function Hoagie() {
}
```

Certain functions, like `Start()` and `Update()`, are special functions that are inherent to Unity. At the time of writing, Unity 3D does not have a built-in `Hoagie()` function, which means it's a *custom* function.

With great sandwich comes great responsibility

There are a few rules and *best practices* to follow when declaring functions. They are as follows:

- ◆ Your function name should start with a capital letter.

- ◆ You must never start a function with a number or some weirdo character like the Rod of Asclepius or you will get an error. An error is a written notice that Unity sends you when something you typed doesn't work or doesn't make sense.

- ◆ You can press the *Enter* key to drop the top sandwich bun down a line. Some programmers (like me) prefer writing code this way so that they can see the open or closed sandwich buns lined up, but other programmers prefer code that doesn't spread out too much.

```
DisappearMe.js
DisappearMe  ▸  Start
  1   #pragma strict
  2
  3   function Start ()
  4   {
  5       renderer.enabled = false;
  6   }
  7
  8   function Update (){
  9
 10   }
```

In this book, we'll use both approaches just to keep you on your toes.

Examining the code

Let's look closely at the line of code that we wrote:

```
renderer.enabled = false;
```

The semicolon at the end of the line is like the period at the end of a sentence. Nearly all single-line statements must end in a semicolon or the code might break. When code breaks, Unity uses a special pop-up window called the **console** to tell us about it. When you have code that throws an error, we say there is a *bug* in your code.

> **Semi-confusing**
>
> So why doesn't the function declaration have a semicolon? Why don't the curly braces each have one? It's because they're a different beast. They're not a single line of code—they're more like a house where code lives. If you start seeing the declaration and statement block as one complete thing instead of three different things, you'll be well on your way to getting past the confusing bracket hurdle that many new programmers face.

In order to understand the rest of that line, you need to realize that there is a *lot* of code going on behind the scenes that you can't see. It looks like a bunch of pretty pictures to you and me, but the Unity team had to write code to make it look that way. Behind each instance of your **GameObject**, and behind the Unity program itself, there are thousands of lines of code telling your computer what to show you.

Renderer is one such piece of code. When you set the `enabled` property of your Ball's renderer to `false`, you're saying that you don't want Unity to draw the triangles in the mesh that makes up your ball.

Time for action – find the Mesh Renderer component

Does "renderer" sound familiar to you? We already saw a component called **Mesh Renderer** when we created our **Paddle** and **Ball** GameObjects. If you don't remember, have a look:

1. Select the **Ball**, if you haven't already.

2. Look in the list of the components of the **Ball** in the **Inspector** panel. There should be one component there called **Mesh Renderer**.

3. If you see only the name of the component, click on the gray arrow next to the component name to expand the component.

Aha! What do we have here? Something called **Mesh Renderer**—it has a checkmark next to it. What happens if you click on it to uncheck that checkbox?

Go on—try it!

The ball disappeared. No surprises there. We saw something similar happen when we clicked on the checkmark beside an entire **GameObject** in the previous chapter.

But, I wonder, does this **Mesh Renderer** component have anything to do with the "renderer" we talked about in our `DisappearMe` Script? Checking that checkbox certainly seemed to have the same effect as running a Script that said `renderer.enabled = false;`.

Let's be bold here. We need to figure this out. We'll leave the checkbox unchecked and modify our Script to get a solid answer.

Time for action – make the ball re-appear

1. Double-click on the `DisappearMe` Script. MonoDevelop will open up and display the Script.

2. Change the word `false` to `true`.

3. Save the Script.

4. Click on the **Play** button to test your game.

Your Script should look like this:

```
function Update () {
    renderer.enabled = true;
}
```

Bingo! The **Ball** started out invisible and then magically appeared. That means that the **Mesh Renderer** component and the renderer that we referred to in our Script are the same thing. And the checkbox in the **Inspector** panel is actually the `enabled` property in checkbox form—instead of `true` and `false`, it shows us checked and unchecked states! In fact, you can even keep an eye on the checkbox when you click on **Play** and see it change states. That tingling sensation means it's working.

Ding!

Hopefully, a little lightbulb has appeared above your head at this point. You may be wondering what *else* you see in that **Inspector** panel that you can get your grubby mitts on through code. Let's take a quick glance at what else is in that **Mesh Renderer** component:

◆ A checkbox labeled **Cast Shadows** (this is a Unity Pro feature)

◆ Another checkbox labeled **Receive Shadows**

◆ Something a little more complicated involving **Materials**

Unless you're some kind of whiz kid, it's unlikely that you'll figure out how to fiddle with this stuff on your own. Let's take a trip to the Unity Script Reference to see what it tells us about the **Renderer** class.

Time for action – journey to the Unity Script Reference

The **Unity Script Reference** is like a dictionary that contains every single word of Unity JavaScript we'll ever need. It's organized extremely well, is searchable, and has hyperlinks to related sections. Look *that* up in your Funk and Wagnalls.

1. Make sure that the **Ball** is still selected.

2. Find the **Mesh Renderer** component of the **Ball** in the **Inspector** panel.

3. Click on the blue book icon with the question mark on it to open the manual.

Your default browser should open, and the **Mesh Renderer** page of the Unity manual will load. Note that you're not viewing this information online. These are HTML files stored locally on your computer that Unity displays in your browser. You can find this same Unity manual online at the following URL: `http://unity3d.com/support/documentation/Manual/index.html`

The manual tells you how to work with the things that you see in the Unity interface. The page you're looking at now tells you everything you always wanted to know about the **Mesh Renderer** component. Click on one of the **Scripting** links at the top-left or top-right of the page; the Unity Script Reference should appear.

| Manual | Reference | Scripting |

Scripting Reference

As we want to explore the Renderer class, type the word Renderer into the search field at the top-left of the page. Click on the link to the Renderer class at the top of the resulting list.

Scripting Overview

This is a short overview of how scripting inside Unity works.

Scripting inside Unity consists of attaching custom script objects being the following:

Update:
This function is called before rendering a frame.

Q▼ Renderer   ✕

Menu
Overview
Runtime Classes
    Attributes
    Enumerations
Editor Classes
    Attributes
    Enumerations

The Renderer class

The Renderer class lists a bunch of stuff that might look like so much gibberish to you. It has these lists:

- Variables
- Messages sent
- Inherited variables
- Inherited functions
- Inherited class functions

From that list, the only familiar word might be "functions", which we just learned are reusable bundles of code (or endlessly eatable sandwiches, if you prefer). As we write more code in this chapter, we'll come to understand what variables are. For now, focus on the things listed under the **Variables** section.

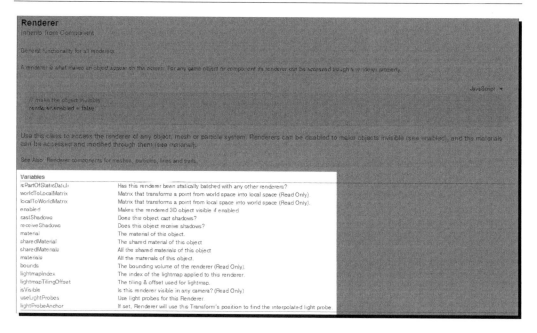

One of the variables is called `enabled`. Do you remember when you wrote `renderer.enabled = false;`? You've already used a variable, perhaps without knowing it. And, check it out—some of the other things that we noticed in the **Mesh Renderer** component are listed here. There are variables called `castShadows` and `receiveShadows`, which we saw as checkboxes in the **Inspector** panel. There are also some material-related variables. At the bottom of the list, there's a variable called `isVisible`, which appears to do something different compared to the `enabled` variable.

Downloading the example code

You can download the example code files for all Packt books you have purchased from your account at `http://www.packtpub.com`. If you purchased this book elsewhere, you can visit `http://www.packtpub.com/support` and register to have the files e-mailed directly to you. Each project in the book is intended to be built from the "ground up", beginning with an new project file. The downloadable .unitypackage files for this book contain the assets (sounds, images, and models) you need to build the projects. You may also download completed, working versions of each project for your reference, though these are not intended to be your "first stop" – they're more like the answer sheet at the back of a text book.

Have a go hero – pulling the wings off of flies

If you were the type of kid who disassembled your parents' clock radio, or got up close and personal with the insects in your backyard to see what made them tick, this is your time to shine. The Script Reference is your gateway to every special reserved word ("keyword") in the Unity language. Try clicking on the `enabled` variable in that list. The resulting page not only repeats the explanation of the variable, but it also provides an example of how you might use that variable in code. You can even use the drop-down lists on the right to see the C# and Boo translations. (Go ahead—check them out! Fortune favors the bold).

Renderer.enabled

var **enabled** : boolean

Description
Makes the rendered 3D object visible if enabled.

JavaScript ▼

```
// make the object invisible
renderer.enabled = false;
```

Another example:

JavaScript ▼

```
// Toggle the Object's visibility each second.
// make the object visible
renderer.enabled = true;
function Update () {
    // Find out whether current second is odd or even
    var seconds : int = Time.time;
    var oddeven = (seconds % 2) == 0;
    // Enable renderer accordingly
    renderer.enabled = oddeven;
}
```

If you're wired a certain way, you've already thrown this book down and are eagerly scouring the Script Reference looking for code you can mess around with. That's okay. We'll be here when you get back. If you are still a little wary of this foreign language and would like a little more guidance using it, read on.

What's another word for "huh"?

Perhaps the most challenging thing about using a language reference as a beginner is that you don't know what you don't know. The language is searchable to the tiniest detail, but if you don't know Unity's particular word for something, you'll still be lost. It's like not knowing how to spell a certain word. You can look it up in a dictionary, but if you don't know how to spell it, you might have trouble looking it up!

If you can't find what you're looking for, your best plan of attack is to bust out the synonyms. Try typing in any word you can think of that's related to what you want to do. If you want to hide or show something, try searching words like visible, visibility, visual, see, show, appearance, draw, render, hide, disappear, and vanish! Even if it's a long shot, try "POOF!" You never know.

| Dictionary | Thesaurus | Encyclopedia | Translator | Web |

Thesaurus.com
An Ask.com Service

visible   Search

Related Searches

When will mars be vis...

Which planets are vis...

Which planets will be...

Visible light

Planets visible now

Visible blue veins

Visible light spectru...

Visible light wavelen...

Visible light waves

When are the northern...

Why do veins pop out

Are bed bugs visible ...

Main Entry:	visible
Part of Speech:	*adjective*
Definition:	apparent, seeable
Synonyms:	arresting, big as life, <u>bold</u>, <u>clear</u>, <u>conspicuous</u>, detectable, <u>discernible</u>, discoverable, distinguishable, <u>evident</u>, in sight, in view, <u>inescapable</u>, macroscopic, <u>manifest</u>, <u>marked</u>, not hidden, <u>noticeable</u>, observable, <u>obtrusive</u>, <u>obvious</u>, ocular, <u>open</u>, out in the open, <u>outstanding</u>, <u>palpable</u>, <u>patent</u>, perceivable, <u>perceptible</u>, <u>plain</u>, <u>pointed</u>, <u>pronounced</u>, revealed, <u>salient</u>, seen, <u>signal</u>, <u>striking</u>, to be seen, unconcealed, under one's nose, unhidden, unmistakable, viewable, <u>visual</u>
Antonyms:	<u>concealed</u>, <u>hidden</u>, <u>invisible</u>, obscured, unseeable

If you've exhausted your vocabulary and you still come up short, you can randomly click on words in the documentation and read about what they do. Another approach is to start scouring the Internet for Unity tutorials. Many developers like to share their code to help beginners like you learn new things. You might not understand what all this code does, but in grazing through it, you could find a line of code that looks like it might do what you're trying to do. Copy it, paste it into your own Script, and start playing around. If it breaks your game, then good! You might think that you're not learning anything, but you are: you're learning how to **not** break your game. One final resource is chat channels, which you can find by using an Internet Relay Chat client, but as a Unity n00b (new user), you have to be careful and respectful of the way you speak to real people who know far more than you do. In most chat channels, there's very little love for new users who don't exhaust existing online resources before asking a question.

Be sure to also check the *Appendix* at the back of this book for a great list of Unity resources.

It's been fun

Our first attempt at scripting has been a laugh and a half, but we're no closer to making that paddle work in our keep-up game than when we started. Let's undo some of the work we did and get started on a Script that's crucial to our game.

Time for action – unstick the Script

Let's remove the Script from the **Ball** and recheck the **Mesh Renderer** component to make sure everything's back to normal:

1. Make sure that the **Ball** is still selected.

2. Find the **Mesh Renderer** component of the **Ball** in the **Inspector** panel, and make sure that the component is checked. The **Ball** should reappear in your **Scene** view.

3. Find the `DisappearMe` Script at the bottom of the **Inspector** panel.

4. Right-click/alternate-click on the name of the component, and click on **Remove Component**. On a Mac, you can *command* + click, or click the little black gear icon and choose **Remove Component** from the drop-down menu. Now, the Script is no longer associated with your **GameObject**.

Gone, but not forgotten

It's just as important to learn how to remove a Script from a **GameObject** as it is to learn about adding one. Note that we could also have unchecked the checkbox in the DisappearMe Script component to temporarily disable it. The DisappearMe Script is no longer acting on **Ball**, but we haven't deleted it. You should still be able to see it in the **Project** panel. To delete it, click on the Script and press the *Delete* key on your keyboard, or *command* + *delete* if you're on a Mac. If you want to keep the Script around to remember what you did in this chapter, leave it be.

A Script for all seasons

You may already have guessed that the DisappearMe Script is not exclusive to the **Ball** GameObject. You can drag-and-drop the Script on top of the **Ball**, the **Paddle**, or any other **GameObject** in your **Scene**. As long as that **GameObject** has a renderer component, the Script will work.

Why code?

We'll write our next Script armed with some juicy knowledge. We know that **GameObjects** are backed by code. Some of that code is invisible to us, and we can tap into it only through scripting. Other code is exposed to us in the **Inspector** panel in the form of components with a GUI (like checkboxes and drop-down menus) on top.

You may already wonder why, when Unity gives us such a friendly and easy-to-use checkbox to click, we would ever want to bother writing code to do something? It's because the controls you fiddle with while you build your game are no good to you while your game is actually *running*.

Imagine you want a **GameObject** to suddenly appear in response to something your player does while playing your game. What if your player can grab a power-up that displays a second paddle on the screen? In that case, that checkbox is useless to you. Your player isn't going to enjoy your game inside the Unity 3D authoring tool, and it's silly to suggest that you'll be there sitting on his lap to click that checkbox whenever he collects the Double Paddle power-up. You need to write code to tell Unity what to do when you're not there anymore. It's like equipping a baby bird with all the skills it needs to survive in the world, and then booting it out of the nest. No one's going to be around to click that checkbox for you, baby bird.

Equip your baby bird

Let's teach Unity what to do when we're not around, and the player wants to move the paddle to bounce the ball. Make sure that the **Mesh Renderer** component of your **Ball** is enabled (checked). We're going to create a brand new Script and attach it to the paddle.

Time for action – create a new MouseFollow Script

1. In the **Project** panel, right-click/alternate-click on an empty chunk of space and navigate to **Create | JavaScript**. Alternatively, you can navigate to **Assets | Create | JavaScript** in the menu at the top of the screen, or use the **Create** button at the top of the **Project** panel.

2. A new Script is added to the **Project** panel. Name it `MouseFollow`.

3. Drag-and-drop your new `MouseFollow` Script onto your **Paddle** GameObject.

4. Double-click to open the Script in MonoDevelop. Just as before, we're going to add a single, simple line of code inside the curly braces (sandwich buns) of the `Update` function (sandwich):

```
function Update () {
    transform.position.x = 2;
}
```

5. Add a **Rigidbody** component to **Paddle** by navigating to **Component | Physics | Rigidbody**.

6. In the **Inspector** panel, find the **Rigidbody** component and check box next to **Is Kinematic**. The Unity manual warns against moving colliders around through code without adding a **Rigidbody** component because it could add a lot of overhead (unnecessary calculation processing), so we've added **Rigidbody**. The **Is Kinematic** option excludes the **Paddle** GameObject from Unity's physics simulation.

7. Save the Script and press **Play** to test your game. Like pulling the chair out from beneath someone when he tries to sit down, your **Paddle** should act like a total jerk, and pop out of the way to let your **Ball** plummet to its doom. Not cool, Paddle. Not cool.

What just happened?

Just as we saw with the **Mesh Renderer** component, **Transform** is also a component of your **GameObject**. It's the first attached component on the list in the **Inspector** panel when you select your **Paddle**. As we learned in *Chapter 3, Game #1 – Ticker Taker*, the **Transform** component decides how the **GameObject** is positioned, rotated, and scaled (made larger or smaller).

In the Unity environment, the **Transform** component of our **Paddle** was set to position **0** in the X-axis. But, we changed this with our line of code, setting the x property of the paddle's transform to 2. The result is that the first time the Update function is called, the paddle appears to jump out of the way to two units along the X-axis.

The thought may have already struck you: if you can control the x position of the **Paddle**, you can probably also control its y and z positions just as easily. And if `position` is available to you, `rotation` and `scale` can't be far behind! But, which keywords should you use to change these properties? `rotation` and `scale` are two good guesses, but we'd rather be sure.

To satisfy your curiosity, let's hit the Unity Script Reference again; this time, we'll take a shortcut. Highlight the word `transform` in your Script and press *Ctrl + '* on your keyboard, or *command + '* on a Mac (that's the apostrophe character). You'll zip directly to the Script Reference with a list of hits as if you'd searched for `transform` in the search field. What wonders await you within?

Transform
Inherits from Component, IEnumerable

Position, rotation and scale of an object.

Every object in a scene has a Transform. It's used to store and manipulate the position, rotation and scale of the object. Every Transform can have a parent, which allows you to apply position, rotation and scale hierarchically. This is the hierarchy seen in the Hierarchy pane. They also support enumerators so you can loop through children using:

JavaScript ▼

```
// Moves all transform children 10 units upwards!
for (var child : Transform in transform) {
    child.position += Vector3.up * 10.0;
}
```

See Also: The component reference, Physics class.

A capital idea

The **Transform** component is listed as **Transform** with an uppercase *T*. When we refer to it in code, we use a lowercase *t*. In the Script Reference, it has an uppercase *T* again. But, if you've already made the mistake of using an uppercase *T* in your code, Unity threw you an error in the console window. What gives?

Unity's language is **case sensitive**, which means that a word with a capital letter is treated as a completely different thing than the same word with a small letter. So, `transform` and `Transform` are as different from each other as the words *night* and *day*.

Transform is a class. A **class** is like a blueprint that you use to make other things. You might implement power-ups in your keep-up game. Your capital-P Powerup class describes what a power-up should look like and how it should behave. You might create a new power-up using your Powerup class, and label it powerup with a small *p*. The capital-P Powerup class contains the instructions for building something, and lowercase-p powerup is the name you gave to the thing you've built with that blueprint.

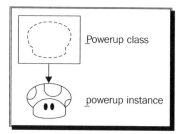

So, in this case, capital-*T* Transform is the class, or blueprint, that describes how a transform works. Small-*t* transform is the name our **GameObject** gives to its own transform instance, which was built using the Transform blueprint. This upper-case class/lower-case instance is a coding *convention*, and so is not shouting at the dinner table; let's follow the convention to keep things civil.

Here are a few more examples to help you understand:

◆ Car is the class (blueprint). We use it to make a new car instance, which we call car (small *c*).

◆ House is the class (blueprint). We use it to build a new house instance, which we call house (small *h*).

We can use these classes to create multiple copies, or instances, of a thing. The Car class could stamp out many things, which we could call car1, car2, and car3. We could also call those things sedan, convertible, and suv. In Unity-land, the developers decided to call the thing that was created with the Transform class transform. It could just as easily have been called pinkElephant, but transform makes more sense.

Animating with code

We talked about how the Update function is called again and again by Unity. We're about to see what that really means by making a slight adjustment to our code.

Time for action – animate the Paddle

1. Jump back into your `MouseFollow` Script if you're not there already by double-clicking on it in the **Project** panel.

2. Change the line of code in the `Update` function ever so slightly so that it reads as follows:

    ```
    function Update () {
        transform.position.x += 0.2;
    }
    ```

The changes are very subtle. We added a plus sign (+) before the equals to sign (=), and we made the number smaller by adding a zero and a decimal place in front of it, changing it from 2 to 0.2.

Save the Script and test your game. The **Paddle** should scoot out the way, and fly straight off the right-edge of the screen!

What just happened – what witchcraft is this?

We made the 2 smaller, because the **Paddle** would have just rocketed off the screen in a twinkling and we may not have seen it. But, there's a tiny bit of code magic going on in that += bit.

By changing the `transform.position.x` property with += instead of =, we're saying that we want to *add* 0.2 to the x property on every update. The special built-in `Update` function automatically gets called again and again by Unity as your game plays. While this happens, the x position constantly increases. Let's follow the following logic:

◆ The first time `Update` is called, x is 0. We add 0.2, and the **Paddle** moves to 0.2.

◆ The second time `Update` is called, x is 0.2. We add 0.2, and the **Paddle** moves to 0.4.

◆ Every time `Update` is called, the **Paddle's** x position increases. We get a real sense of how often the `Update` function is called by how quickly the **Paddle** moves across the screen in tiny 0.2 increments.

Any excuse to work less

+= is a bit of programmer shorthand. It's the same as typing:

```
transform.position.x = transform.position.x + 0.2;
```

But that's *way* more typing, and the less you have to type the better. Excessive typing kills 80 percent of computer programmers before their 40th birthdays. I just made that stat up, so it's probably off by a few percentage points.

Why didn't the Paddle animate before?

When we wrote the line `transform.x = 2`, the **Paddle** just jumped into position; it didn't go anywhere, like it does now. Why is that?

The `Update` function is still getting called multiple times. But each time, it's putting the **Paddle** at two units on the X-axis. The value of `x` changes on every `Update`, but it changes to the *same thing*. So, once **Paddle** is in position, it doesn't appear to move.

With our new modified line of code, the `x` position of the **Paddle** is changing by `0.2` every time the `Update` function is called, so **Paddle** moves across the screen.

An important part of being a beginner programmer is keeping a positive attitude. You should start with the assumption that what you want to do **can** be done—anything is possible. We now know how to set the position of the paddle. With your positive, can-do attitude, you might imagine that to get the paddle moving around with the mouse, you could find the position of the mouse, and set the `transform.position.x` property to match.

But, what *words* do you need to use to get the position of the mouse? For the answer, let's dive back into the Unity Script Reference.

Pick a word – (almost) any word

We're going to put the Script Reference through some serious stress testing here. We're going to arm ourselves with every synonym of *mouse* we can think of. Here's a list that I painstakingly brainstormed: mouse, screen position, cursor, pointer, input device, small rodent, two-button, aim, and point. One of those *has* to do the trick. And, if we come up empty-handed, we're going to hit those online tutorials *hard* until we find our answer.

Go ahead, fire up the Unity Script Reference and type `mouse` into the **Search** field. Scour the resulting list. We will *not* back down. We will *not* take "no" for an... oh, hello, what's this?

Midway down the list, there's this entry, as highlighted in the following screenshot:

Input.mousePosition

The current mouse position in pixel coordinates.

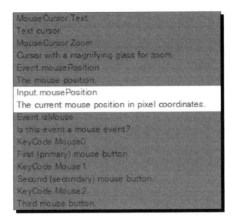

Well, uh... ahem. That was easy. I guess we won't be needing this synonyms list then.

Screen coordinates versus World coordinates

Click on the `Input.mousePosition` entry and check out the resulting page. The Script Reference tells us that we have a new origin to deal with. Unity treats our screen like a flat, 2D plane, with (0, 0)—the origin—in the bottom-left corner of the screen like a bar graph from fourth grade.

Input.mousePosition

static var **mousePosition** : Vector3

Description
The current mouse position in pixel coordinates. (Read Only)

The bottom-left of the screen or window is at (0, 0). The top-right of the screen or window is at (Screen.width, Screen.height).

JavaScript ▼

```
var particle : GameObject;
function Update () {
    if (Input.GetButtonDown ("Fire1")) {
        // Construct a ray from the current mouse coordinates
        var ray : Ray = Camera.main.ScreenPointToRay (Input.mousePosition);
        if (Physics.Raycast (ray)) {
            // Create a particle if hit
            Instantiate (particle, transform.position, transform.rotation);
        }
    }
}
```

We have a code example here, but it looks a little hairy. What's a `Physics.Raycast`? I have no idea. And how do we get the x, y, and z values for `Input.mousePosition`?

The answer is a tiny bit sneaky. Look at the top of the screen where it tells us that `Input.mousePosition` is a `Vector3`. What's a `Vector3`? I dunno. Click on it. Ah, the resulting page tells us that a `Vector3` has x, y, and z properties along with a slew of other useful stuff. That shall do nicely.

Vector3
Struct

Representation of 3D vectors and points.

This structure is used throughout Unity to pass 3D positions and directions around. It also contains functions for doing common vector operations.

Besides the functions listed below, other classes can be used to manipulate vectors and points as well. For example the Quaternion and the Matrix4x4 classes are useful for rotating or transforming vectors and points.

Variables

x	X component of the vector.
y	Y component of the vector.
z	Z component of the vector.
this [int index]	Access the x, y, z components using [0], [1], [2] respectively.
normalized	Returns this vector with a magnitude of 1 (Read Only).
magnitude	Returns the length of this vector (Read Only).
sqrMagnitude	Returns the squared length of this vector (Read Only).

Move the Paddle

We are ready to rock. If we just set the x position of **Paddle** to the mouse's screen position by using `Input.mousePosition`, we should be able to use the mouse to move the paddle. Change your line of code so that it looks like this:

```
transform.position.x = Input.mousePosition.x;
```

Save your Script and try it out.

Worst. Game. Ever.

It may look like nothing actually happened. Your paddle is gone. Super. Obviously, controlling the paddle with the mouse isn't so simple.

But don't despair. Try placing your mouse at the left edge of the screen, and then move it very, very slowly. You should see your paddle pass rapidly across the screen. You'll notice that even the tiniest horizontal movement of your mouse sends the paddle rocketing off into Never Neverland. This will not do.

See the matrix

We need to figure out what kind of numbers our mouse is throwing out. We can do this by using the Debug.Log() function. Whatever information we ask Debug.Log() to display will show up at the bottom of the screen while we test our game.

Time for action – listen to the paddle

1. Add this line of code beneath the existing line of code:

    ```
    Debug.Log(Input.mousePosition.x);
    ```

2. Your entire Script should look like this:

    ```
    function Update () {
            transform.position.x = Input.mousePosition.x;
            Debug.Log(Input.mousePosition.x);
    }
    ```

3. Save and test your game.

Look at the very bottom of the screen for the results of your Debug.Log() statement. If nothing shows up, follow these steps to enable **Console** statements:

1. Navigate to **Window | Console** in the menu.

2. This is an important window! Dock it to your layout by clicking and dragging it beneath your **Game** view.

3. Ensure that Console messages are enabled by clicking on the little button with the comic book speech bubble.

As you move the mouse cursor left and right, you'll see this number changing. It goes from **0** when your mouse is at the left edge, and rapidly increases. The upper limit depends on your monitor resolution; on my screen, `Input.mousePosition.x` maxes out at 1279! Earlier, a value of 2 put the paddle nearly all the way off the screen. With `Debug.Log()` reporting these crazy big numbers, we can see why our code behaves the way it does.

A tiny bit o' math

This code's not going to work. Our paddle moves only to the right, along the positive X-axis, because we're working only with positive numbers. We need some negative numbers in there so that the paddle will move to the left at some point. But, at what point?

Hmm... what if we take half of the screen's width and *subtract* it from `Input.mousePosition.x`? What does that do for us?

A quick trip to Unity Script Reference tells us how to find the width of the screen in pixels. Let's divide that number by 2 and subtract it from the mouse position.

Change the `Debug.Log()` function call to look like this:

```
Debug.Log(Input.mousePosition.x - Screen.width/2);
```

Save and test. Watch the bottom of the screen for the result.

Tracking the numbers

When the mouse cursor is near the left edge of the screen, you get negative numbers. When it's closer to the right edge, you get positive numbers. And, if you try to position your cursor at exactly the halfway point, you get zero. This makes sense. We know that when the mouse is at the left edge, `Input.mousePosition.x` is zero. If we subtract half of the screen width from zero (on my monitor, that's 640 pixels), we get **-640** at the left edge instead.

My screen is 1280 pixels wide, so I'm using 640 to represent half of its width. Your mileage may vary! Common screen widths are 800, 1024, 1152, 1280, 1600, or 1920.

When the mouse is in the middle of the screen, `Input.mousePosition.x` is 640. It's at the halfway point. If we subtract half the screen width (640 in my case), we get zero.

When the mouse position is at the right edge of the screen, `Input.mousePosition.x` is almost at 1280 on my 1280-pixel-wide display (again, your mileage may vary). Subtract half the `Screen.width` and we get 640. **-640** at the left edge, **0** in the middle, and **640** at the right edge.

Futzing with the numbers

This is promising, but we already know that these numbers are still too big. If we move the paddle to `640` units along the X-axis, it's going to wind up in Timbuktu. We've got a good positive or negative number scale going—we just need to shrink that number down somehow. Let's try dividing our number by half of the screen's width.

Time for action – Log the New Number

1. Change your `Debug.Log()` call so that it looks like this:

```
Debug.Log( (Input.mousePosition.x -Screen.width/2) /
    (Screen.width/2) );
```

Ack! So many brackets! We use those brackets because we want the division and subtraction stuff to happen in the right sequence. You may remember order of operations rules from algebra class. **BEDMAS**: evaluate the Brackets first, then the Exponents, then Division, Multiplication, Addition, and finally Subtraction.

To wrap your brain around it, here's what we're doing, in pseudocode:

(first thing)/(second thing)

We're dividing something by something else. The first thing is the -640 to 640 number range that we cooked up. The second thing is `Screen.width/2` (the screen's midpoint). We wrap all of that in a tasty `Debug.Log()` shell:

Debug.Log((first thing)/(second thing));

> **Pseudocode** is fake code that will not work if you type it into a Script. We're just using it to better understand the real code that we're writing. Some programmers use pseudocode to type their thoughts out with English words to help them puzzle through a problem. Then, they go back over the pseudocode and translate it into a language that the computer will understand—JavaScript, C#, and so on.

Now, we really have something. If you save and test and move the mouse cursor around, you'll see that as you get closer to the left edge of the screen, you get closer to -1. And, as you get closer to the right edge, you approach 1. In the middle, it's zero.

Copy or rewrite the chunk of code from the `Debug.Log()` statement to the line above it so that it now reads:

```
transform.position.x = (Input.mousePosition.x -Screen.width/2) /
    (Screen.width/2);
```

Save and test your file.

She's a-work!

That's what we're after. The paddle moves at a reasonable rate along with the mouse, and now we can actually bounce the ball around a little. Success! To get more than just a straight vertical bounce, try clipping the ball with the edge of the paddle. The ball should bounce off the screen at an erratic angle. Game over!

Press the **Play** button again to stop testing your game.

Somebody get me a bucket

A common programmer mantra is "duplication is evil". The idea is that any time you type the same thing twice, you could be wasting time and effort. Remember that the less typing we do, the less likely we are to drop dead from the programmer illness I totally fabricated. The less duplication we do, the less "maintenance" we have to do if something goes wrong later—correcting one chunk of code is easier than correcting multiple duplicated chunks. But the rule for beginners is this: make it work first—*then* make it elegant.

Notice that we have some duplication in this line:

```
transform.position.x = Input.mousePosition.x - Screen.width/2)/
    (Screen.width/2);
```

We've typed `Screen.width/2` twice. That won't do! For starters, typing makes my hands tired. What's more, we're forcing the computer to do that complicated math calculation twice. Why not do the calculation once and ask the computer to remember the result? Then, any time we want to talk about the screen's midpoint, we can ask the computer to retrieve the result.

We do this by creating a *variable*. A *variable* is a reserved storage locker in memory. I like to think of it as a **bucket that can hold one thing**. Just as we saw with functions, variables are created by declaring them.

(To be totally honest, an extra division operation isn't going to bring your game to its knees. But, there are more "costly" operations we could ask Unity to perform, and learning to put things in variable buckets now is good practice to prepare us for the heavy lifting that we'll do later).

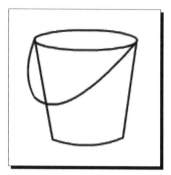

Time for action – declare a variable to store the Screen midpoint

1. Modify your Script so that it looks like this (you can get rid of the `Debug.Log()` function call):

```
function Update () {
  var halfW : float = Screen.width/2;
  transform.position.x = (Input.mousePosition.x -halfW)/halfW;
}
```

That code looks a lot cleaner. Not only is it easier to read, but we've knocked out some of those confusing brackets in the second line.

What just happened – we've gone too var

We've used the special `var` keyword to declare our variable (bucket). I chose the name `halfW`, which is short for "half width"—half the width of the screen. You can choose any name you like for a variable as long as it isn't a reserved Unity keyword, and it doesn't break any of the naming rules that we discussed when we looked at naming functions. For example, `1myvar funfun` will **not** work, because it begins with a number and has a space in the middle. Also, it sounds ridiculous and doesn't make any sense. Try your best to keep your variable names logical.

F is for function

The biggest difference between naming a function and naming a variable in Unity is that a function name should start with a capital letter, while a variable name should not. This is not a hard and fast rule, but it's called a "best practice", which means that everyone else does it, so you should too. Jump off a bridge with us!

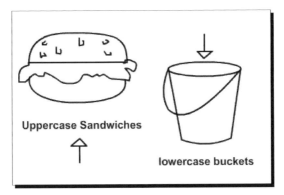

Uppercase Sandwiches

lowercase buckets

We stuck a colon and the word `float` at the end of our variable name. Why? By using a colon, we're telling Unity what *type* of variable we're using. This lets the program know how big of a bucket in memory to create. Giving a variable a type speeds up our game because Unity doesn't have to keep guessing what type of bucket `halfW` is.

`float` is short for a *single-precision floating point*. To you and me, that's a number with a decimal point in it. Here are a few more data types that Unity uses:

◆ `String`: An alphanumeric bunch of characters such as "Hello, my name is Herb" or "123 Fake St"

◆ `Boolean`: Like a light switch, a `Boolean` can be only one of two states—`true` or `false`

◆ `int`: An integer, such as 28 or -7

Our `halfW` variable is typed as `float` because we need that decimal place. But we're not splitting the atom or anything, so we don't need to make it a `double`, which is a more accurate numerical data type that can store a number with many more digits in it.

Save the Script and test your game to make sure everything is working correctly.

Using all three dees

Now that we know how to track the mouse left and right with the paddle, it's not a huge leap of logic to make our paddle track the y position of the mouse, and translate it into z coordinates. Remember that we're working with two different planes here:

◆ The flat, two-dimensional plane of the computer screen

  ❏ Horizontal X-axis

  ❏ Vertical Y-axis

  ❏ Origin point (0, 0) at the bottom-left of the screen

◆ The deep, three-dimensional intersecting planes of our game world

  ❏ Horizontal X-axis

  ❏ Vertical Y-axis

  ❏ Deep Z-axis

  ❏ Origin point (0, 0, 0) in the middle of the world where the three planes meet

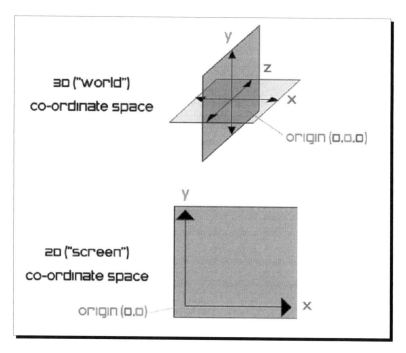

We're going to track the y movement of the mouse, and map it onto the z movement of the paddle to make it move toward and away from the player. If instead we map the y position of the mouse to the y position of the **Paddle**, the **Paddle** will move up and down from the ground to the sky, which is not quite what we're after.

Time for action – follow the y position of the mouse

1. Modify your code to add a few familiar-looking lines:

```
function Update ()
{
 var halfW:float = Screen.width/2;
 transform.position.x = (Input.mousePosition.x - halfW)/halfW;
 var halfH:float = Screen.height/2;
 transform.position.z = (Input.mousePosition.y - halfH)/halfH;
}
```

The two new lines of code are almost identical to the first two lines. We've created a new variable and called it `halfH` (half height) instead of `halfW`. We're changing the z property of `Input.mousePosition` instead of x. When you save the Script and test your game, you'll have a fully movable paddle to bounce your ball on.

Math effect

I actually put a little cheat into my code. I wanted the paddle to travel deeper and farther along the Z-axis with less mouse movement, so I changed my `halfH` variable declaration to this:

```
var halfH:float = Screen.height/3;
```

That's a third of the screen, not a half. Really, I should change the name of my variable to something like `thirdH`. You can rip through all of your code easily and make this change by navigating to **Search | Replace**, typing `halfH` in the top field, `thirdH` in the bottom field, and clicking the **All** button to replace all instances in the code.

A keep-up game for robots

After all this effort for getting our paddle to move, the game still doesn't have much oomph to it. It's very easy to keep the ball bouncing because there's nothing to send it spinning off in any crazy directions. At least in **Breakout** or **Arkanoid**, you had interesting angles to work with. Our game doesn't have any walls to angle off, but we do have that paddle.

What if we angled the paddle as the player moved it around? An angled paddle would make the ball bounce in different directions and keep the player on her toes.

Once more into the breach

How do we make the paddle angle? Let's consult the Script Reference, armed with words that describe what we want to do: angle, rotation, rotate, spin, turn, bank, tilt, yaw, or roll. Our second idea, rotation, holds the secret.

Time for action – re-visit the Unity Language Reference

1. Type `rotation` into your Script. It lights up. It's one of the magic keywords!

2. Double-click to select the `rotation` keyword.

3. Press *Ctrl + '* or *command + '* to warp to the Unity Script Reference. You could also type `rotation` into the **Search** field of the reference if you already have it open.

A quick look at the resulting list turns up `Transform.rotation`. We've already been using `Transform.position` to move our paddle around—it's not such a stretch to figure out that this is what we need. Click on the link!

Transform.rotation

var **rotation** : Quaternion

Description
The rotation of the transform in world space stored as a Quaternion.

Unity stores rotations as Quaternions internally. To rotate an object, use Transform.Rotate. Use Transform.eulerAngles for setting the rotation as euler angles.

JavaScript ▾

```
// Reset the world rotation
transform.rotation = Quaternion.identity;
```

Another example:

JavaScript ▾

```
// Smoothly tilts a transform towards a target rotation.
var smooth = 2.0;
var tiltAngle = 30.0;
function Update () {
    var tiltAroundZ = Input.GetAxis("Horizontal") * tiltAngle;
    var tiltAroundX = Input.GetAxis("Vertical") * tiltAngle;
    var target = Quaternion.Euler (tiltAroundX, 0, tiltAroundZ);
    // Dampen towards the target rotation
    transform.rotation = Quaternion.Slerp(transform.rotation, target,
                        Time.deltaTime * smooth);;
}
```

Our work here is done

Well, would you look at that—while we were sleeping, some kind programmer elves cobbled together some shoes for us! The `Transform.rotation` page of the Script Reference has a chunk of code that "smoothly tilts a transform towards a target rotation". That sounds a lot like what we're trying to do.

Hey, I have an idea: I'll keep an eye on the door. You copy and paste this code into your game. If anyone asks, tell them "the book made me do it".

Time for action – add the sample code to your Script

1. Add the new code to your existing game code. You'll need to shuffle a few lines around. Here is the code with the new stuff highlighted:

```
var smooth : float = 2.0;
var tiltAngle : float = 30.0;
function Update ()
{
    var halfW:float = Screen.width/2;
    transform.position.x = (Input.mousePosition.x - halfW)/halfW;

    var halfH:float = Screen.height/3;
    transform.position.z = (Input.mousePosition.y - halfH)/halfH;

    // Smoothly tilts a transform towards a target rotation.
    var tiltAroundZ : float = Input.GetAxis("Horizontal") *
        tiltAngle;
    var tiltAroundX : float = Input.GetAxis("Vertical") *
        tiltAngle;
    var target : Quaternion = Quaternion.Euler (tiltAroundX, 0,
        tiltAroundZ);
    // Dampen towards the target rotation
    transform.rotation = Quaternion.Slerp(transform.rotation,
        target,Time.deltaTime * smooth);
}
```

Nobody's perfect

In my version of the Script Reference, there's a typo. The last line ends with two semicolons instead of one. If your version has the same typo, just delete the extra semicolon.

Note that two variables, `smooth` and `tiltAngle`, are outside the `Update` function at the top of the Script. We'll discover why in a moment.

If you save the Script and run the game now, the new rotation code won't work. We have to make a few adjustments. I've highlighted what you need to change in the following code:

```
var smooth : float = 5.0;
var tiltAngle : float = 60.0;

function Update ()
{
  var halfW:float = Screen.width/2;
  transform.position.x = (Input.mousePosition.x - halfW)/halfW;

  var halfH:float = Screen.height/3;
  transform.position.z = (Input.mousePosition.y - halfH)/halfH;

  // Smoothly tilts a transform towards a target rotation.
  var tiltAroundZ : float = Input.GetAxis("Mouse X") * tiltAngle;
  var tiltAroundX : float = Input.GetAxis("Mouse Y") * tiltAngle;
  var target : Quaternion = Quaternion.Euler (tiltAroundX, 0,
    tiltAroundZ);
  // Dampen towards the target rotation
  transform.rotation = Quaternion.Slerp(transform.rotation, target,
    Time.deltaTime * smooth);
}
```

Here's what's new:

◆ We bumped up the smooth variable from `2.0` to `5.0` to make the motion more… well, quick.

◆ We asked Unity for `Mouse X` and `Mouse Y` instead of `Horizontal` and `Vertical`. `Horizontal` and `Vertical` are, by default, mapped to the arrow keys and the *WASD* keys on your keyboard. `Mouse X` and `Mouse Y` will report mouse movement.

Available for comment

Notice the line in the code that says "Smoothly tilts a transform towards a target rotation," and the one a bit farther down that says "Dampen towards the target rotation." That sounds like plain English—not code at all. The double-slashes before these two lines make them comments. Comments are ignored by Unity when we run our game. Comments enable you to type whatever you want in your code as long as you've got those two slashes in front. Many programmers use comments to explain to other programmers (or to themselves, in the future) what a piece of code is supposed to do. While you learn Unity, you can use comments to take notes on the new code concepts that you're learning.

Save the Script and test your game. The paddle should tilt as you move your mouse around.

It sort of works, but the way it tilts around the Z-axis makes the paddle fire the ball into crazy town. Stop testing your game. We're close—very close.

One final tweak

One small adjustment stands between you and a fun keep-up game mechanic. We want the paddle to angle in the opposite direction to keep the ball bouncing inside the play area. We can multiply by `-1` to flip the effect:

```
var tiltAroundX : float = Input.GetAxis("Mouse Y") * tiltAngle * -1;
```

Save and test. Hooray! The paddle tilts around the play area inclusively, keeping the ball more or less within our reach—unless we get twitchy, and then we drop the ball. But that's the fun of keep-up—moving the paddle just so as to keep the ball in play.

What's a quaternion?

Well, that was lots of fun! We've got a working keep-up game mechanic. Now let's go and do something else.

Wait, what's a quaternion?

Oh, that? Don't worry about it. We have bigger fish to fry! In the next chapter, we'll...

WHAT THE HECK IS A QUATERNION??

Gosh, you're persistent. Can't you just leave it well enough alone?

I'm not going to sugarcoat it: 3D math is complex. A **quaternion** (like the one we used in our rotation code just now) is a beast of a mathematical concept. According to my Mathematics Dictionary (which I often pull out for light reads in the bathroom), "a quaternion forms a four-dimensional normed division algebra over the real numbers". There. *Now* do you understand?

Quaternions are clearly outside the scope of a beginner book. But, we can't just go swiping code from the Script Reference without even partially understanding it, so let's give it the old college try.

Educated guesses

These are the two lines from our code we'd like to understand better:

```
var target : Quaternion = Quaternion.Euler (tiltAroundX, 0,
    tiltAroundZ);
// Dampen towards the target rotation
transform.rotation = Quaternion.Slerp(transform.rotation,
    target,Time.deltaTime * smooth);
```

Let's actually start from the bottom up.

In the final line of code, we're setting `transform.rotation` to something, which will turn the paddle somehow. That much, we get. We can probably also guess that `Quaternion` is one of those built-in classes that we looked at, like `Input`—both `Quaternion` and `Input` start with a capital letter, and light up when we type them.

`Slerp` sounds weird, but it starts with a capital letter and has round brackets next to it. We've seen that same structure when we called functions earlier in our code, like `Input.GetAxis()` and `Debug.Log()`. And, just like those two functions, `Slerp()` needs some extra information to do what it does. These are called **arguments**, and we've used them a few times already. We stuck something inside the brackets of `Debug.Log()` to make it appear at the bottom of the Unity window. Giving data to a function to make it do what it does is called **passing arguments**.

So, what do we have? A class (or blueprint) called `Quaternion`, with a function called `Slerp()` that asks for three pieces of information—three **arguments**. For a better idea of which arguments `Slerp()` needs, type `Quaternion.Slerp(` into the Script, and read the code hinting that pops up). `Slerp()` needs these three arguments to do what it does:

♦ `From`, which needs to be of type `UnityEngine.Quaternion`

♦ `to`, which needs to be of type `UnityEngine.Quaternion`

♦ `t`, which needs to be of type `float`

We can already see that we're passing in the `transform.rotation` value of the **Paddle** as the `from` argument, which means that `transform.rotation` must be of type `Quaternion`.

For the `to` argument, we're passing `target`, which is a variable of type `Quaternion`. We defined it one line earlier.

Finally, for the `t` argument, we're passing `Time.deltaTime` and multiplying it by the value of our `smooth` variable, which we defined way up at the top of our Script as `5.0`.

Time.deltaTime

You'll see `Time.deltaTime` very often in your Unity travels. `deltaTime` is a property of the `Time` class; it represents the amount of time that elapsed between this frame and the last. You usually use it to make your game move according to time rather than according to the frame rate. Frame rates can change depending on how powerful a player's computer is, but time remains consistent.

Think back to when we were moving the paddle 2 units on each `Update` call. If you were running a fast computer that ran your game at 100 frames per second, then in one second the paddle will travel 200 units. If you were running your game on a slower computer that ran at only 50 fps, the Paddle would only travel 100 units in 1 second.

`Time.deltaTime`, conversely, is the great equalizer. Using `Time. deltaTime`, the amount that you want to move your **GameObject** is calculated and spread out across 1 second. By switching from a frame-based model to a time-based model, your game will run more consistently on both the slow computer and the fast computer, because 1 second is 1 second, no matter how zippy the computer may be.

More on Slerp

We've used our brains to try to figure out what this code is doing, so now it's time to fill in our knowledge gaps a little more.

Slerp is a frankenword meaning **Spherical linear interpretation**. You might already have guessed that it lets us move from one `Quaternion` rotation to another. The interpolation (or spread-outedness of the motion) happens across `t`, or time.

If we were to pseudocode this statement:

```
transform.rotation = Quaternion.Slerp(transform.rotation,
    target,Time.deltaTime * smooth);
```

It might go something like this:

On every frame, rotate the paddle, starting at the paddle's current rotation. Rotate towards our target rotation. Use the amount of time that's elapsed between frames to stretch out (interpolate) the motion. Reduce the jerkiness of the motion by constantly supplying the paddle's updated rotation value.

Right on target

Last but not least, let's look at how we get that `target` Quaternion. We know *why* we need it: because we have to feed a `to` Quaternion to the `Slerp()` function. To better understand the penultimate line, let's break it down like we did before.

```
var target : Quaternion = Quaternion.Euler (tiltAroundX, 0,
    tiltAroundZ);
```

We're creating a variable called `target`, which is a bucket. Then, we're putting something in that bucket that we know is going to be of type `Quaternion`. We're calling the `Euler` function of the `Quaternion` class and passing to it, three arguments.

Try typing `Quaternion.Euler(` into your Script, and reading the tooltip that pops up. The `Euler` function needs three arguments of type `float`. Notice also that there's a little page 1/2 indicator in the tooltip. If you press the down arrow on your keyboard, you'll see that this method will also take one argument of type `Vector3`. We've seen the `Vector3` class before (earlier in this chapter). A quick trip to the Script Reference reminds us that `Vector3` is made up of three different parts: x, y, and z, which are all of `float` type. Hmm!

Quaternion.Euler is what's called an *overloaded method*. That means it has more than one function signature, so that it can accept two different sets of arguments. You want to pass it `Vector3`? You pass it `Vector3`. You wanna pass it three floats? You pass it three floats. You wanna pass it seven ints and a boolean? TOUGH NUTS! That's not one of the overloaded options.

The rest is history. We're using our `TiltAroundX` and `TiltAroundZ` variables in the x and z slots, and because there's no change in the y rotation, we're passing zero. The `Euler` function gives us a **return value**, which is like putting money into a vending machine and getting change. We feed it values for x, y, and z (or a single `Vector3`), and it spits out a crazy-complex `Quaternion` for us that we probably couldn't have constructed on our own. With any luck, we'll get a candy bar too!

We take the resulting `Quaternion`, store it in a variable (bucket) called `target`, and use that as the `to` argument in the `Slerp()` function of the last line.

Have a go hero – time to break stuff

But don't take my word for it. If you're still confused about what does what or you want to put this sample code through its paces, go for it. Here are a few things to try:

◆ Change the values for the `smooth` and/or `tiltAngle` variables, and test your game (make sure that whatever value you try still has a decimal point). What effect do the new numbers have on the movement of the paddle?

- Reverse any number in the code by putting a minus sign (-) in front of it.

- Divide instead of multiplying.

- Subtract instead of adding.

- Try creating separate variables called `tiltAngleX` and `tiltAngleZ` to control the `x` and `z` tilt amounts independently.

- Try creating a new variable of type `Vector3` using the `tiltAroundX`, 0, and `tiltAroundZ` values. Then, pass the resulting `Vector3` as a single argument to the `Quaternion.Euler` function. Does your code still work?

Keep it up

That was some heavy-duty book-learnin'! Feel free to leave the room for a moment if you need to empty your brain. In this chapter, we:

- Wrote our first Unity JavaScript

- Applied the Script to a **GameObject**

- Learned how to modify components through code

- Removed a Script from a **GameObject**

- Moved a **GameObject** with code

- Hooked the position and rotation of a **GameObject** up to the mouse's position and movement

- Dove into the Unity Script Reference and Component Reference to understand and to "borrow" some code

- Took a crash course in programming to learn about:

    - functions and statement blocks

    - classes

    - data types

    - arguments

    - comments

    - logging

If you're still not grasping every little detail about programming, don't fret. Certain people are wired to just immediately get it, and some of us have to keep trying, failing, and trying again until that little light turns on. I tried and failed at programming my whole life, from the time I was about ten years old, until I gradually understood it. For me, it was less of a sudden light turning on, and more of a slow, steady burn, as the light bulb filament steadily heated up as if on a dimmer switch. If you want to learn programming in Unity, you're not bound by your intelligence—only by your determination and drive.

Beyond the game mechanic

We've added code to our keep-up game to control the paddle, and the game mechanic is amusing, but it's not a game! There's *so* much more to game development than just the core mechanic. Our game needs a proper starting point. It needs an ending. It needs a cue telling the player that he's failed when the ball falls on the ground... it needs a ground! Currently, you have to shut down and restart the game every time you drop the ball. We need some kind of **Play Again** button. And wouldn't it be nice to have a score counter on the screen telling the player how many bounces he got before dropping the ball? What about sound effects and music? And the box art! We *have* to have nice box art!

We may not get as far as shipping our game out to the shopping mall, but there's still a lot more we can do to make our game more *gamey*. We're going to come back to this game mechanic in a bit because there's definitely something promising here. But, first, we should learn how to put some of those crucial buttons and score counters on the screen. While we figure that out, we're going to use our new-found programming skillz to build a whole other game. Are you ready? Then journey with me to the laboratory of Professor Wrecker...

C# Addendum

The C# version of the `DisappearMe` script is nearly identical to the JavaScript version. There are just a few differences between the way in which JavaScript and C# scripts are set up.

```csharp
using UnityEngine;
using System.Collections;

public class DisappearMeCSharp : MonoBehaviour {

  // Use this for initialization
  void Start () {

  }

  // Update is called once per frame
  void Update () {
    renderer.enabled = false;
  }
}
```

Notice that the C# script has two `using` statements at the top. This is because there are thousands of collections of code and keywords that you can tap into with C#, and if we assume that every project needs to have access to every nook and cranny of the C# language, we'll wind up with a massive final file! The `using` keyword tells Unity which specific sections of the C# language this script needs to access.

Another difference is the "class" declaration beneath the `using` statements. Every C# script is its own class (like the `Renderer` class we discussed earlier).

The word `class` is prefaced with the word **public**. Public is an **access modifier** that determines which bits of this script other scripts can "see" and futz around with. The four different access modifiers in C# are **public**, **private**, **protected**, and **internal**. We'll deal exclusively with the **public** and **private** access modifiers throughout this book.

There are some more salient changes in the C# version of the `MouseFollow` script:

```
using UnityEngine;
using System.Collections;

public class MouseFollowCSharp : MonoBehaviour {


  private float smooth = 5.0f;
  private float tiltAngle = 30.0f;


  // Use this for initialization
  void Start () {

  }



  // Update is called once per frame
  void Update () {
    float halfW = Screen.width / 2;
    float halfH = Screen.height/2;
    transform.position = new Vector3 ((Input.mousePosition.x
      -halfW) / halfW, transform.position.y, (Input.mousePosition.y
      - halfH)/ halfH);

    // Smoothly tilts a transform towards a target rotation.
    float tiltAroundZ = Input.GetAxis("Mouse X") * tiltAngle * 2;
    float tiltAroundX = Input.GetAxis("Mouse Y") * tiltAngle * -2;
    Quaternion target = Quaternion.Euler (tiltAroundX, 0,
      tiltAroundZ);

    // Dampen towards the target rotation
    transform.rotation = Quaternion.Slerp(transform.rotation,
      target,Time.deltaTime * smooth);
  }
}
```

Note, first of all, that the **member variables**—the ones we declared up top, outside of any functions, have **private** access modifiers next to them. Technically speaking, these access modifiers aren't required, and indeed, we could have added them to our member variables in our JavaScript code. Including them here is good form. (Remember—the Queen is watching).

Another change is the way we type variables in C#. In JavaScript, the format is **variableName : datatype**. In C#, the format is **datatype variableName** (note: no colon required). C# also does away with the `var` keyword when declaring variables. Finally, when a float definition has a decimal place in it, you need to append the lowercase letter *f*.

Here are the differences, side by side:

```
var someNumber : float = 3.5; // JavaScript member variable
   declaration
private float  someNumber = 3.5f; // C# member variable declaration
```

A little further down in the C# code, there's another change. Whereas with JavaScript, we were able to set the `transform.position.x` and `transform.position.z` values of the paddle individually, C# is a little less kind and friendly. C# wants us to change the entire `transform.position` all at once, which means passing it a newly-minted `Vector3` with all three of the float values it requires.

So while in the JavaScript code, we were allowed to set the `x` and `z` parameters like so:

```
transform.position.x = whateverX;
transform.position.z = whateverZ;
```

In a C# script, we have to knock it all out in one shot, like this:

```
transform.position = new Vector3(whateverX, whateverY, whateverZ);
```

The `new` keyword is how we stamp out an instance using the industrial Class mold, as we discussed earlier in the chapter. `Vector3` is the template, and the `new` keyword is how we use it to crank out an instance of that template. To put it another way, the `Vector3` class is our cookie cutter, and the `new` keyword is how we cut new gingerbread men out of the dough.

It's interesting, because in the case of this script, we know what the `whateverX` and `whateverZ` values are, but there should be no change to the paddle's `transform. position.y` value. So what do we put in there that means "no change"? Your first instinct might be to leave it blank, but Unity will surely throw an error if we try to feed the `Vector3` class an non-existent value. Your second instinct might be to pass a value of zero, but that's not quite what we're after either. What if the paddle's initial `y` value isn't zero?

The way to pass a value that means "no change" is to simply pass the current transform value of **GameObject** for a given axis. This line of code, for example, will not change the position of **GameObject** at all:

```
transform.position = new Vector3(transform.position.x,
    transform.position.y, transform.position.z);
```

To change the paddle's x and z transform.position values, then, without changing its y transform.position value, the code (as above) looks like this:

```
transform.position = new Vector3 ((Input.mousePosition.x -halfW) /
    halfW, transform.position.y, (Input.mousePosition.y -
    halfH)/ halfH);
```

You may have already sniffed out the fact that C# requires you to write more code than JavaScript does. Nobody said high tea with the Queen was going to be easy.

5
Game #2 – Robot Repair

*One of the secret aspects of game development is that getting a mechanic
working is often less challenging than getting an entire GAME working.
Our keep-up game has a working mechanic, but it's clearly nothing like
a finished game.*

*In this chapter, we'll take a break from our keep-up game to add an important
tool to our Unity game development tool belt: Graphical User Interface
programming. Graphical User Interfaces, or GUIs for short, include all of
the buttons, sliders, dropdowns, arrows, and on-screen text that help players
understand and move through your game. Unity has a whole separate GUI
(pronounced "gooey") system that we'll start digging around in to flesh out
our games a bit better. To get a good grasp on what the GUI system can do,
we're going to program an entire working 2D flip n' match memory game
in that system!*

A language by any other name

There's nothing particularly Unity-centric about what we're going to learn
in this chapter. The techniques you learn here can generally be applied
to other scripting languages to build the same game. Programming a
memory game in Unity GUI is not much different from building one in
VB6, Flash, XNA, or OBJ-C for iOS.

In this chapter, we'll:

♦ Start building a working memory game called **Robot Repair** using only the Unity GUI controls

♦ Learn how to add buttons and images to the screen

♦ Connect multiple scenes with buttons

♦ Practice our programming, including one-dimensional and two-dimensional Collections

All set? Then let's get GUI!

You'll totally flip

Let's make sure we're on the same page when I say "flip n' match memory game". That's the kind of game where you take a deck of playing cards and lay them out in a grid on the table. Then, two or more players take turns flipping over a set of two cards. If the pair of cards matches (that is, two 10s, two queens, and so on), then that player clears the matching pair from the table and gets to flip again. Otherwise, the cards are turned back facedown and the next player gets a turn. The game ends when the grid is cleared. The winning player is the one who collects the most matching cards.

To start, we're going to build the basic solitaire (one-player) flip n' match game in the Unity GUI, using robots on the cards. Here's how it will look when you're finished:

There are lots of things that make flip n' match memory an ideal learning game for new developers. It's extremely versatile! The pictures on the cards can be anything you like—you can skin the game in endless ways. You can build it for any number of players; a solitaire version just needs a few extra goodies, like a timer, to make it more compelling. You can quite easily crank the difficulty up and down by tweaking the number of cards on the table, the timer length, and the types of allowable matches.

I can't wait to start! Let's go!

A blank slate

Start a new Unity project by navigating to **File | New Project...**. Create a new folder called `robotRepair` on your computer's operating system. Follow the same steps as before to choose a folder for the new project, call the project `robotRepair`, and click **Create**. You don't need to import any extra unityPackage files if you don't want to—we won't be using anything from them in this project.

When Unity has finished building your project, you should see that big, wide-open, empty 3D world. We're going to completely ignore the 3D world for this project and focus instead on the invisible 2D plane sitting in front of it. Imagine that your 3D world sits behind a sheet of glass. That sheet of glass is where the Unity GUI controls exist. We'll tack up buttons and images to that sheet of glass as if they're stickers that the player can interact with.

You're making a scene

Until now, we've only been working with one **Scene**. Unity lets you create multiple scenes, and then daisy-chain them together. You can think of a scene as a level or area in your game. In our case, we're going to create a scene for the title screen of our game and another scene for the game itself.

Time for action – set up two scenes

The new project you just created automatically starts with a single scene. Let's rename it `title`.

1. Navigate to **File | Save Scene As** and choose `title` for the name of the scene. You'll notice that the title bar in Unity now says **title.unity – robotRepair**. There's also a new scene in the **Project** panel called **title**. You can tell that it's a Scene because it has a little black-and-white Unity logo next to it.

2. Create a second scene by navigating to **File | New Scene**.
3. Navigate to **File | Save Scene As...** and call this new scene `game`.

4. To keep things more organized, create a folder to hold your two scenes. Click on the **Create** button in the **Project** panel and choose **Folder**. A new folder called **New Folder** appears in the **Project** panel.
5. Rename the folder `Scenes`.

6. Click-and-drag your **game** and **title** scenes into the **Scenes** folder in the **Project** panel. All tidy!

7. Click on the little gray arrow to expand the **Scenes** folder. Double-click on the **title** scene to make it the active scene. You'll know that you've done it correctly if the Unity title bar says **Unity – title.unity – robotRepair**.

Now, we have a scene to hold our title screen, and a scene to hold all of our game logic. Let's get to work building that title screen!

No right answer

The more you explore Unity, the more you'll discover that there are many possible ways to do one thing. Often, there's no right way to do something, it all depends on what you're building and how you want it to look. There can, however, be better ways to do things: as we saw earlier, programmers call these preferred methods "best practices".

You can build a title screen for your game in a number of different ways. If you have a 3D world, maybe you want the camera to fly around the world as a piece of 2D title work fades up over it? Maybe the title work should be in 3D, and you start the game by moving a controllable character through a doorway? For this introduction to Unity GUI controls, we'll take a flat 2D graphic of our game title work and add a **Play** button on top of it. This is how it will look when we're finished:

Time for action – prepare the GUI

In Unity, GUIs are coded in `Scripts`, which are attached to **GameObject**. Let's create an empty **GameObject** and then attach a new script to it:

1. Navigate to **GameObject | Create Empty**. A **GameObject** called "GameObject" appears in the **Hierarchy** panel:

2. Click on the **GameObject** in the **Hierarchy** panel and press *F2*. Rename it `TitleScreen`:

3. In the **Inspector** panel, position the **TitleScreen** GameObject at x:0 y:1 z:0.

4. Right-click /alternate-click on a blank space in the **Project** panel and navigate to **Create | JavaScript**.

5. Rename the new script `TitleGUI`.

6. Click-and-drag the **TitleGUI** script from the **Project** panel to the **TitleScreen** GameObject you just created in the **Hierarchy** panel. The **TitleScreen** GameObject should light up blue before you release the mouse button.

7. To make sure the **TitleGUI** script is linked to the **TitleScreen**, click on the **TitleScreen** in the **Hierarchy** panel. In the **Inspector** panel, you should see the **TitleGUI** script listed beneath **Transform** as one of the components of the **TitleScreen**:

Our script won't get executed unless it's hooked up to a **GameObject**. We've created an empty **GameObject** called **TitleScreen** and connected our new **TitleGUI** script to it. We're almost ready to start scripting!

GUICam

Some developers prefer to hook their GUI scripts up to the main camera in the scene. If this makes more sense to you than hooking the script up to an empty GameObject, don't let me hold you back. Go for it!

The beat of your own drum

We're going to take a few extra steps to ensure that our GUI looks different from the standard built-in Unity GUI. If you visit the Unity game portals in *Chapter 1, That's One Fancy Hammer!*, you may notice that the buttons and UI controls in many of the games look the same or similar: dark, semi-transparent buttons with gently-rounded corners. This is because those game developers haven't bothered to give their UI controls any unique flair.

Time for action – create and link a custom GUI skin

Custom styling your UI controls is definitely more work than sticking to the Unity default, but the results are worth it! If you've ever worked with **Cascading Style Sheets** (**CSS**), you'll have a better idea of what's going on here. CSS enables you to define the way a website looks; how the images are displayed, the font and size of the text, and the spacing of elements. All of the website's pages use that stylesheet to display their elements the same way. So you've got the thing, and then you've got the way the thing looks. It's like putting a costume on a kid at a birthday party. You can make the kid look like a pirate, a princess, a superhero, or a giant walking cupcake, but the foundation of the kid doesn't change. It's still little Billy under that foam cupcake suit. Two different websites can have the exact same content, but their stylesheets could make them appear radically different.

When you custom style your UI, you create a new "costume" for it. You can apply different costumes to the GUI, but the bones stay the same. You still have the same number of buttons at the same size and in the same position on the screen. Those buttons and controls all behave the same way as they did before—they're just wearing a different costume.

Let's take the first few steps towards setting up our game to use a custom UI—a different costume (or "skin") for our controls:

1. Double-click on the **TitleGUI** script in the **Project** Panel to open the default script editor, **MonoDevelop**.

2. At the top of the script, create a member variable to hold your custom GUI skin:

```
var customSkin:GUISkin;
function Start() {
}

function Update() {
}
```

3. Save and close the **TitleGUI** script.

4. Right-click or alternate-click any empty space in the **Project** panel, then navigate to **Create | GUI Skin**. You can also click on the **Create** button at the top of the **Project** panel.

5. Rename the newly created GUI skin `MyGUI`.

6. Click on the **TitleScreen** GameObject in the **Hierarchy** panel.

7. Look for the **TitleGUI** script component in the **Inspector** panel. Notice that the `customSkin` variable that we just created in code is now listed in the **TitleGUI** script component! Strangely, Unity has decided to capitalize our variable name and add a space between the words, but rest assured it's the same variable.

8. Click-and-drag the **MyGUI** GUI skin that you just created and drop it into the `customSkin` variable in the **Inspector** panel. You can also choose **MyGUI** from the drop-down list in that same variable field.

What just happened?

We've created a skin for our GUI, which works like a costume on a kid at a birthday party. Now, we're all set up to fiddle with the fonts, colors, and other parameters of our custom **MyGUI** skin. We have the costume, now we just need to describe the kid underneath it. Let's build ourselves a button, and then we'll see the difference that a custom GUI skin can make.

▼ Js ☑ **Title GUI (Script)**		🖪 ⚙,
Script	Js TitleGUI	⊗
Custom Skin	▫ MyGUI (GUISkin)	⊗

Time for action – create a button UI control

We're going to add a button to the title screen through code, using Unity's built-in OnGUI function:

1. Double-click on the **TitleGUI** script, or switch over to the script editor if it's already open.

2. We won't need the Update function any longer. Instead, we'll be using the built-in OnGUI function. Change the word Update to OnGUI:

    ```
    var customSkin:GUISkin;
    function OnGUI() {
    }
    ```

3. Add a chunk of code that creates a button inside the OnGUI function:

    ```
    var customSkin:GUISkin;
    function OnGUI() {
      if(GUI.Button(Rect(0,0,100,50),"Play Game"))
      {
        print("You clicked me!");
      }
    }
    ```

4. Save the script and press the Unity **Play** button to test your game.

A button labeled **Play Game** appears at the top-left of the screen. When you click on it, the message **You clicked me!** appears in the status bar at the bottom of the Unity interface. It will also appear in the **Console** window if you have it open.

Great! With a very tiny bit of code, we have a working, labeled button up on the screen! It lights up when you roll over it. It goes back to normal when you roll off. Its appearance changes when you press and hold the mouse button on it. The text label is automatically centered inside the button. Somebody spent a bunch of time behind the scenes programming this GUI stuff to save us time. Thanks, Unity Team!

Where it all begins

This **Play Game** button is a crucial element of our flip n' match memory game, and every game you'll ever build with Unity, or any other game-building tool for that matter! It's a part of the understood language of the video game medium that games start in a paused state on a title screen and the player takes an action to start the game. In a coin-operated arcade setup, that action is inserting a quarter. In modern console gaming, that action is pressing a button on the controller. In a web game like ours, that action is clicking on a button that says **Start**, **Play**, or **Play Game**.

What just happened?

If you've never programmed user interfaces before, this should all seem peachy. But, if you have done some coding, you might be looking at the lines we just wrote with a completely confused look on your face. This may not be like any interface programming that you've ever seen before.

Unity uses what's called an *immediate mode GUI*. The term is borrowed from graphics programming, and it requires you to program a little differently than you may be used to. Let's break it down line by line.

```
if(GUI.Button(Rect(0,0,100,50),"Play Game"))
```

Like the `Update` function, the `OnGUI` function is called repeatedly as your game runs. This line is called twice per frame: once to create the button, and once to see if the button has been clicked. This code is stateless. On every frame, your entire interface is recreated from scratch based on the code in your `OnGUI` function.

So, if you imagine this code as a split second in time, your `if` statement asks whether the button that you're creating in this instant is being clicked on. It's kind of a strange thing to get used to, but it makes sense the more you use it. The `if` statement in this case is like saying, "if the button was clicked". Without that `if`, the button won't respond to input.

The rest of the line is a bit easier to understand. The `GUI.Button` method needs two arguments: a rectangle defining the top-left corner and size of the button, and a label for the button.

```
if(GUI.Button(Rect(0,0,100,50),"Play Game"))
```

`Rect` takes four inputs: x position, y position, width, and height. The origin of the two-dimensional screen is at the top-left, so a value of 0,0 places the button at the top-left of the screen. (Note that this is in opposition to the bottom-left origin we just learned about when tracking mouse movement. This is the THIRD co-ordinate system we've encountered so far!) The width and height values of `100` and `50` make the button 100 pixels wide and 50 pixels tall.

```
print("You clicked me!");
```

This line is straightforward. When the button is clicked, the message we typed is printed to the status bar and the Console window's log. Remember that the status bar is the skinny 20 pixel high gray bar at the bottom of the Unity interface. Let's check it out one more time with a big fat arrow to help us out:

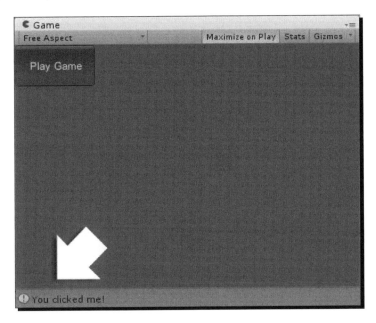

`print` is another way to throw messages to the console window or the status bar. I prefer it to `Debug.Log()` because it's faster and easier to type, but be aware that it won't work in all situations. If you ever find yourself tearing your hair out because your `print()` statements aren't working, try switching back to `Debug.Log()`.

Have a go hero – no sense sitting around on your button

Why stop there? To fully appreciate what this code is doing, try this:

- Change the button label, the button position, and the button width and height.
- Change the message that gets printed when you click on the button.
- Try taking the button creation code out of the `if` statement. What happens?

Fiddling with this code is a sure-fire way to better understand it.

Want font?

As promised, we're going to try overriding the default look of the UI button control using our custom GUI skin (or child's cupcake costume). At the top of the OnGUI function, between the curly brackets, add this line:

```
GUI.skin = customSkin;
```

Save the script. Now, the custom GUI skin called **MyGUI** that we linked to this script will knock out the default skin like putting on a different costume. Let's make a quick change to **MyGUI** so that we can see the results.

Click on **MyGUI** in the **Project** panel. Now, check out the **Inspector** panel. There's a loooong list of goodies and controls that we can customize. This is why many of the Unity projects that you see use the default GUI—customizing all this stuff takes a long time!

Click on the arrow next to **Button** to expand it, and then click on the arrow next to **Normal**. There's a color swatch here labeled **Text Color** (it has an eye dropper icon next to it). Click on the swatch and choose a new color—I chose light blue. Press the **Play** button to test your game.

Voila! The text color on your button is blue! When you roll over the button, though, the text reverts to white. There are separate colors and graphics for the hover, normal, and pressed states of the button. Yikes! Fully customizing a GUI skin takes a while.

To change the font on your buttons, navigate to a directory on your computer where you keep your fonts, and click-and-drag the font file into the **Project** panel. Now, you can choose that font from the drop-down list labeled **Font** in the **Inspector** panel of your MyGUI skin.

Where my fonts is?

If you're running Windows, your fonts are likely to be in the `C:\Windows\Fonts` directory. If you're a Mac user, you should look in the `/Library/Fonts/` folder.

You could spend hours messing around with your custom GUI skin. Don't let me hold you back! If you want to go nuts customizing **MyGUI**, be my guest. When you're ready to come back, we'll build out the rest of the title screen.

Cover your assets

Download the `Assets` package for this chapter from the Packt Publishing website:

> `http://www.packtpub.com`

To import the package, navigate to **Assets | Import Package | Custom Package....** Navigate to wherever you saved the package and double-click to open it, an **Importing Package** dialog will open. All assets should be checked by default, so click on the **Import** button to pull them into your `Assets` folder.

Open the **Resources** folder in the **Project** panel. All of the graphics that we need to build the game are now in there, including the title screen graphic (it's the one called **title**). Click on it, and you should see a preview of the **Robot Repair** title screen in the **Inspector** panel.

With the title screen graphic selected, navigate to **GameObject | Create Other | GUI Texture**. Unity analyzes the width and height of our graphic and sets it up as the background to our GUI. Press the **Play** button to test your game, you should now see the **Play Game** GUI button superimposed over the **Robot Repair** title screen graphic (or floating off from the top-left corner of the image, depending on your screen resolution).

Don't forget to select the image

Unity does a few extra steps for us when we create a GUI texture with an image selected. If you try to create a GUI texture and the image is not selected, you'll have to manually hook up the image and set a few parameters for it. Why bother? Make sure that the **Robot Repair** image is selected first and you'll save a bit of time.

Beautify the background

Depending on your screen resolution, you may see the default blue background color around the edges of the title screen GUI texture. To change this color, click on the **Main Camera** in the **Hierarchy** panel. Click on the color swatch labeled **Background** in the **Inspector** panel. Change the color to white—it looks the best.

Time for action – nix the mip-mapping

There's an unwanted sparkly effect that can occur when a 3D camera gets closer and farther away from a 2D image. A technique called **mip-mapping** reduces this effect. Unity creates a series of images from your texture that are each half the size of the previous image, which allows the computer to figure out the best pixel colors to show to the player, reducing the sparkle effect.

Because our title screen is presented as-is with no 3D camera movement, we're not really concerned about sparkle. And, as you can imagine, with all those extra images, mip-mapping requires a decent amount of extra memory for storage. As we don't need mip-mapping—adding that extra bulk—let's disable it:

1. With the "title" texture image selected, find the **Generate Mip Maps** checkbox in the **Inspector** panel.

2. Uncheck the box.

3. Click on **Apply** to save these changes.

4. The rest of the images that you imported should not be mip-mapped, but there's no harm in checking them for peace of mind.

Front and center

Our title screen is almost complete, but a glaring problem is that the **Play Game** button is in a really goofy place, at the top-left of the screen. Let's change the code so that the button is centered on the screen and sits just beneath the title work.

Time for action – center the button

In order to center the button on the screen, you need to adjust the **TitleGUI** script:

1. Double-click on the **TitleGUI** script in the **Project** panel, or switch over to the script editor if it's already open.

2. Write a few new variables at the top of the script, and define them in the `Start` function:

```
// button width:
var buttonW:int = 100;
// button height:
var buttonH:int = 50;

// half of the Screen width:
var halfScreenW:float;
// half of the button width:
var halfButtonW:float;

function Start()
{
  halfScreenW = Screen.width/2;
  halfButtonW = buttonW/2;
}
```

3. Modify the button creation line in the `OnGUI` function to incorporate these new variables:

```
if(GUI.Button(Rect(halfScreenW-halfButtonW, 460, buttonW,
  buttonH),"Play Game"))
```

What just happened – investigating the code

The code is just a touch hairier now, but those variable declarations help to clarify it. First, we're storing the width and height of the button that we're going to create:

```
// button width
var  buttonW:int = 100;
// button height
var  buttonH:int = 50;
```

Next, we're creating a variable that will hold the value of half the screen width, which we get by dividing the `Screen.width` property by 2 later on in the `Start` function. **Screen** refers to what Unity calls **Screen Space**, which is the resolution of the published player—the box or window through which the player experiences your game. By referring to Screen Space, we can center things on the screen regardless of the resolution our gamer's computer is running.

```
// half of the Screen width
var halfScreenW:float;
```

(and then later, in the `Start` function)

```
halfScreenW = Screen.width/2;
```

Below that, we're storing half of the button width by dividing our earlier stored value, button, by 2:

```
// Half of the button width
var halfButtonW:float;
```

(and then later, in the `Start` function)

```
halfButtonW = buttonW/2;
```

The waiting game

The reason why we're declaring these variables at the top of the script, and defining them (giving them their values) further down in the `Start` function, is partly stylistic, and partly practical. There's a potential problem here: because Unity is superfast at calculating the `Screen.width` property, it might do so before the game screen has finished resizing and initializing, returning an incorrect value. By moving the variable definition to the `Start` function, we're giving Unity a few CPU cycles to make itself decent before we go barging in demanding screen properties.

Defining `halfButtonW` at the top of the class won't break anything, but some programmers would prefer to see the definition separated from the declaration.

The easiest button to button

We're storing all of these values so that we can clarify the button creation line, which looks like this:

```
if(GUI.Button(Rect(halfScreenW-halfButtonW,460, buttonW, buttonH),
    "Play Game"))
```

Note that if we didn't store these values ahead of time, the button creation line could have been written as:

```
if (GUI.Button(Rect((Screen.width/2)-(100/2),460,100,50),"Play Game"))
```

There are too many brackets and mysterious numbers in there for my liking! The line where we use variable names instead is a lot easier to read and understand.

> **Math will divide us**
>
> Computers are faster at multiplication than they are at division. If you are a stickler for speed, you can amp up this code by multiplying the values by 0.5 instead of dividing them by 2.
>
> By declaring and defining these variables at the top of the script, any of our script's functions can refer to them. They'll also show up in the **Inspector** panel, where we can fiddle with their values without having to open a script editor.

So, what we're doing here is putting the button halfway across the screen. Because the button builds out from its top-left corner, we're bumping it back by half its own width to make sure it's perfectly centered. The only other thing we're doing here is placing the button at 460 pixels down the screen along the y axis. This puts the button just beneath the title work.

Here's what your complete code should look like:

```
var customSkin:GUISkin;

// button width:
var buttonW:int = 100;
// button height:
var buttonH:int = 50;

// half of the Screen width:
var halfScreenW:float;
// half of the button width:
var halfButtonW:float;

function Start()
{
  halfScreenW = Screen.width/2;
  halfButtonW = buttonW/2;
}
```

```
function OnGUI () {
  GUI.skin = customSkin;
  print("screenW = " + Screen.width);
  print("halfScreenW = " + halfScreenW);
  if(GUI.Button(Rect(halfScreenW-halfButtonW, 460, buttonW, buttonH),
    "Play Game"))
  {
    print("You clicked me!");
  }
}
```

Save your code. From the drop-down list of screen dimensions in the **Game** view, choose **Standalone (1024x768)** instead of **Free Aspect**. Try out your game with **Maximize on Play** selected. It's starting to look pretty good!

To the game!

The title screen is built and the button's in place. The only thing left to do is to link the **Play Game** button up to take us to the **game** scene.

Modify the line inside the button call where you're printing **You clicked me!**. Wipe out the whole line (or comment it out using double-slashes if you want to save it for later) and type this line:

```
Application.LoadLevel("game");
```

The `Application.LoadLevel` call moves us from this scene to whichever scene we pass as an argument. We're passing the name of our game scene, so that's where we'll end up when we click on the button.

Time for action – add both scenes to Build List

There's just one last thing we need to do. Unity keeps a laundry list of scenes to bundle together when we run the game called the **Build List**. If we call a scene that is not on the **Build List**, Unity will throw an error and the game won't work. And we don't want that.

1. Navigate to **File** | **Build Settings...**; the **Build Settings** panel appears.

2. Click on the **Add Current** button to add the title scene to the **Build Settings** page.

3. Close the **Build Settings** panel.

4. Navigate to **File | Save Scene**, to save the title scene.

5. In the **Project** panel, double-click on the **game** scene to switch to it.

6. Follow the same process to add the **game** scene to the **Build Settings**, and then close the **Build Settings** window. Alternately, you can click-and-drag the game scene from the **Project** panel into the **Build Settings** panel.

7. Press the **Play** button to test the game.

> **Order! Order!**
>
> The order in which you add scenes to the **Build List** matters. Scenes appear from the top to down. If you put your title scene at the bottom of the list, it won't appear first when you build or export your game. If you added the scenes in the wrong order, you can easily reorder them by clicking-and-dragging the scenes around in the **Build Settings** list.

Now that both of our scenes are on the **Build List**, the `Application.LoadLevel` call will take us to the **game** scene when you click on the **Play Game** button. Save the **game** scene, and switch back to the title scene. Run your game. When you click on the **Play** button, you should see a blank screen. That's because we haven't actually built anything in the game scene, but the button totally works! Huzzah!

> **Get Off My Case**
>
> Case sensitivity is in effect here, too! You need to make sure that the scene name you pass into `Application.LoadLevel` is consistent with the actual name of the scene, including its capitalization, or else this command won't work.

Set the stage for robots

The excitement is palpable! We have a shiny-looking title screen promising something about robots. There's a glistening **Play Game** button that, when clicked, takes us to a new scene where our flip n' match memory game will live. It's time now to build that game.

Make sure your game's not still running—the **Play** button at the top of the screen should not be lit up. Double-click on the **game** scene in the **Project** panel. Unity may ask you to save the **title** scene if you haven't already—if that's the case, click on **Save** when you're prompted.

Just as we did with the **title** scene, we should change the camera background color to white. Select the **Main Camera** from the **Hierarchy** panel, and change its view color by clicking on the color swatch in the **Inspector** panel.

Time for action – prepare the game scene

We need to repeat a few steps that we followed in the **title** scene to set up our **game** scene.

1. Navigate to **GameObject | Create Empty**, and rename the new GameObject `GameScreen`.

2. Create a new JavaScript file from the **Project** panel and name it `GameScript`.

3. If you'd like to stay tidy, create a folder in the **Project** panel and rename it `Scripts`. Drag your **TitleGUI** and **GameScript** scripts into the new **Scripts** folder to keep them organized.

4. Drag-and-drop the **GameScript** script from the **Project** panel onto the **GameScreen** GameObject in the **Hierarchy** panel to link the script to a GameObject.

5. If you feel so inclined, you can set up a `customSkin` variable in the script, and link up your `MyGUI` custom GUI skin to the script. This step is not necessary to complete the rest of this chapter.

These steps are repetition of what we've already done on our title scene. For more detailed instructions, just jump back a few pages!

The game plan

One of the best ways to learn game development is to build a learning project. Choose a very basic game and recreate it on your own. Many programmers use Tetris as their learning project. For a very basic introduction to a language or tool, I like to use Memory.

"But, wait!" you say: "Memory games are stupid and boring, and they're for babies, and I'll positively die if I have to build one!" Of course, you're right. You're not going to be lauded by critics and raved about by gamers for building a simple memory game. But, it's a fun challenge to set for yourself: how can you take a game that everyone has played before a million times, and put a simple twist on it to make it more interesting? How can you work within those constraints to make it your own, and to showcase your creativity?

In **Robot Repair**, we'll lay out a 4 x 4 grid of 16 cards. There are four different robot types: a yellow robot, a red robot, a blue robot, and a green robot. To make things interesting, we're going to break these robots; rip off an arm here, tear off a leg there. The player has to match each broken robot with its missing body part!

Once the player wins, we'll give him the option to play again. The **Play Again** button will link him back to the title screen.

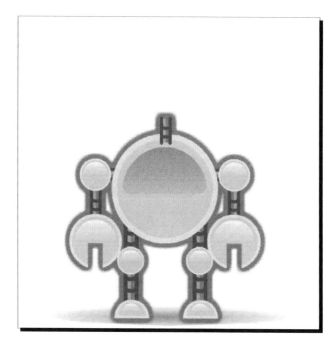

Starting your game development career by building simple starter games like Memory is like eating a big slice of humble pie. But this is all in the spirit of crawling before you walk. While you're crawling, how can you make things interesting for yourself? And, if you can't flex a little creative muscle in the confines of a simple game, how will you survive when you're building your dream project?

Have some class!

To start building **Robot Repair**, we need to write a custom class in our **GameScript** script. We've already seen some built-in Unity classes in the previous chapter: the `Renderer` class, the `Input` class, and so on. We're going to create our own class called `Card`. You guessed it, the `Card` class is going to represent the cards in the game.

1. Double-click to open the **GameScript** script.

2. Add the following code to the script, beneath (and outside) the `Update` function:

    ```
    class Card extends System.Object
    {
    ```

```
    var isFaceUp:boolean = false;
    var isMatched:boolean = false;
    var img:String;

    function Card()
    {
        img = "robot";
    }
}
```

Just like the keyword `var` declares a variable, we use the keyword `class` to declare a class. Next comes the name of our class, `Card`. Finally, our `Card` class extends `System.Object`, which means that it inherits all of its stuff from the built-in `System.Object` class much the same way I inherited my fabulous good looks and my withered left knee that smells like almond bark.

System.Object

What does it mean to inherit from `System.Object`? That class is like Adam/Alpha/the Big Bang—it's the class from which (generally speaking) everything in Unity is derived. It's about as nondescript as anything can get. You can think of `System.Object` as being synonymous with "thing" or "stuff". Every single other *thing* we build in Unity, including our Memory game's `Card` class, derives from this primordial ur-thing called `System.Object`.

In the next few lines, we will declare some variables that all `Card` instances must have. `isFaceUp` determines whether or not the card has been flipped. `isMatched` is a true or false (**boolean**) flag that we'll set to true when the card has been matched with its partner. The `img` variable stores the name of the picture associated with this card.

The function called `Card` inside the class called `Card` is a special piece of code called the **constructor function**. The constructor is the very first function that gets called, automatically, when we create a new `Card` instance. Unity knows which function is the constructor function because it has the same name as the class. The only thing that we're doing in the constructor function is setting the `img` variable to **robot**.

Great! That's all we need in our `Card` class for now. Let's create some important game variables off the top of the script.

Time for action – store the essentials

There are a few crucial values we need to remember throughout our game. Let's declare some variables at the very top of the **GameScript** (remember that typing the comments is optional, but the comments may help you understand the code).

```
import System.Collections.Generic;

var cols:int = 4; // the number of columns in the card grid
var rows:int = 4; // the number of rows in the card grid
var totalCards:int = 16;
var matchesNeededToWin:int = totalCards * 0.5; // If there are 16
    cards, the player needs to find 8 matches to clear the board
var matchesMade:int = 0; // At the outset, the player has not made
    any matches
var cardW:int = 100; // Each card's width and height is 100 pixels
var aCards:List.<Card>; // We'll store all the cards we create in
    this List
var aGrid:Card[,]; // This 2d array will keep track of the shuffled,
    dealt cards
var aCardsFlipped:List.<Card>; // This generic array list will store
    the two cards that the player flips over
var playerCanClick:boolean; // We'll use this flag to prevent the
    player from clicking buttons when we don't want him to
var playerHasWon:boolean = false; // Store whether or not the player
    has won. This should probably start out false :)
```

> **Speed kills**
>
> Remember that this line:
>
> ```
> var matchesNeededToWin:int = totalCards * 0.5;
> ```
>
> is exactly the same as this:
>
> ```
> var matchesNeededToWin:int = totalCards / 2;
> ```
>
> But, because the computer can multiply faster than it can divide, getting into the habit of multiplying could speed up your more complicated games in the future.

A matter of great import

That's a big list of variables! It all starts with an `import` statement. If you read through the code addendum at the end of *Chapter 4, Code Comfort*, you'll remember that C# code requires **using** declarations that tell Unity we'd like to certain chunks of the code base. The JavaScript keyword `import` is identical to the C# keyword `using`. We use it to tell Unity that we're accessing `System.Collections.Generic` chunk of code, which isn't normally available to us by default. Try typing `List<>` into your code without the `using` declaration. Then, add the `using` declaration and type `List<>` again. When we declare that we're using `System.Colletions.Generic`, we get access to a whole new bunch of stuff.

Why do we need access anyway? Because the generic `List` object we declare a little farther down requires it. But what the heck is a List? It's one in a family of datatypes called Collections, which includes its (perhaps) more well-known cousin, array.

If a variable is a bucket that can hold one thing, then an array is a bucket that can hold many things. Unity JavaScript has a class called `Array` that allows us to create these handy buckets-of-stuff.

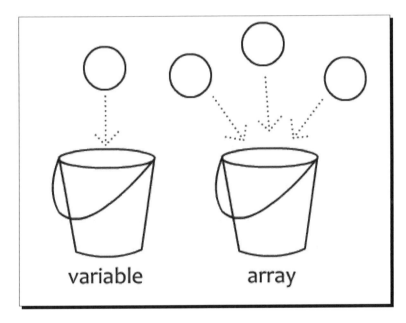

In fact, the Collections family has many members, including Built-in Array, Generic List, ArrayList, Hashtable, Generic Dictionary, and 2D Array. Knowing which family member to call on for a given task is a matter of taste and experience. In this chapter, we'll be using two types of Collections: the Generic List, and the 2D Array. Let's start by looking at that Generic List:

```
var aCards:List.<Card>; // We'll store all the cards we create
    in this List
```

Just like the variables we've used previously, Generic Lists are typed. We can put any type we want inside those pointy brackets. The `aCards` Generic List is typed `Card`, so we can only ever put `Card` instances inside.

Generally speaking

If a Generic List takes a specific type, why do we call it a *Generic* List? "Generic" refers to the parameter we pass to the Collection. It can be (generically) anything we want it to be ... but once we declare it, it can only ever contain that type of thing.

Building a better bucket

By *typing* a Collection, we're telling Unity which *type* of thing we'll put in there. That speeds up Unity's calculations, because the software doesn't have to worry about sorting through different types of things in the Collection.

Imagine if you brought home a bucket of mystery fried chicken, but were warned that it also contained a tennis shoe, a wrench, 175 ball bearings, and a well-worn copy of Big Al's Bathroom Reader. It would take you longer to sort out what was chicken and what was scrap metal than if it was 100% chicken, and consequently, you wouldn't be able to eat your way through the bucket quite as quickly. (Of course, if you made any dire mistakes, that Bathroom Reader would probably come in handy.)

Typing the array (giving it a *type*) also speeds you up as a programmer, because when you pull things out of a mystery bucket of fried chicken, you constantly have to tell Unity, "this is a shoe. This is fried chicken. This is a ball bearing," using a technique called **casting** via the `as` keyword:

```
var friedChicken:FriedChicken = aMysteryBucket[0] as FriedChicken;
// This is definitely not a shoe, Unity.
// Using the 'as' keyword, I'm explicitly telling you that what I've
// just pulled out of the bucket is absolutely a piece of fried
    chicken.
```

How big is your locker?

Some Collections, like Built-in Arrays, have a set size. You need to tell Unity how many things you're putting inside, and that number can never change. Other Collections, like Generic Lists, can take whatever we throw at them—their length is elastic, and they don't have to have a set size. Which approach is better? As you'll see, there are advantages and disadvantages to each.

You'll remember that when we define a variable (a bucket that can hold one thing), we're actually carving out a storage locker in the computer's memory. By *typing* the variable (giving it a *type*), we're telling the computer how big that storage locker needs to be. An `int` variable needs a different amount of room in memory than a `string` variable or a `boolean` variable, and so on.

It's the same idea with a Collection. If we tell Unity how many elements an array needs to hold, Unity can reserve the right amount of space in memory and call it a day. Imagine if you were moving house, and you had to rent a storage locker, but the amount of stuff you needed to store was constantly changing. You'd need to rent more lockers, or bigger lockers, and then get rid of them and consolidate your things, and then rent another few lockers again. What a hassle! We reap the benefit of a fast Collection when we use a built-in Array, and tell Unity exactly how many things it needs to hold.

This is what it might look like if we used one line of code to declare and define a 20-piece bucket of fried chicken with absolutely no tennis shoes in it:

```
var aDefinitelyFriedChicken:FriedChicken[] = new FriedChicken[20];
```

So if you had the choice of using a sleek, speedy Built-In Array with its fixed size, why would we ever want to use the slower `Generic List` class, with its flexible size? Well, one advantage of the `Generic List` class is that it has a few methods that the stripped-down, no-nonsense Built-in Array doesn't have. We're going to use one of those methods unique to the `Generic List` class a little later in the code. And who the heck knows how much stuff they're going to want to cram into their storage locker ahead of time? Flexible Collection size is a real advantage in some situations. For now, let's keep on trucking. We have a game to build!

> **"A" is for Anal Retentive**
>
> Programmers develop their own naming conventions for things. My own best practice when declaring Collections like Arrays and Lists is to begin them with a lowercase letter "a". It's just a code organization technique that helps me keep everything straight in my head.

Start me up

Remember that we're building this game with Unity GUI controls. Just as we created a clickable **Play Game** button on the title screen, we're going to build all of our clickable game cards using the same button control. Our grid of cards will be a grid of GUI buttons aligned on the screen.

Let's add some code to the default `Start` function to get the ball rolling. `Start` is another one of those built-in Unity functions that gets called before `Update` or `OnGUI`, so it's a good place to initialize some stuff. Type the following code near the top of your script, beneath the list of variables we just declared:

```
function Start () {
  playerCanClick = true; // We should let the player play, don't you
    think?

  // Initialize some empty Collections:
  aCards = new List.<Card>(); // this Generic List is our deck of
    cards. It can only ever hold instances of the Card class.
  aGrid = new Card[rows,cols]; // The rows and cols variables help us
    define the dimensions of this 2D array
  aCardsFlipped = new List.<Card>(); // This List will store the two
    cards the player flips over.
  // Loop through the total number of rows in our aGrid List:
  for(var i:int = 0; i<rows; i++)
  {

      // For each individual grid row, loop through the total number
        of columns in the grid:
      for(var j:int = 0; j<cols; j++)
      {
        aGrid[i,j] = new Card(); // stuff a new card instance into
          the 2D array
      }
    }
}
```

In these first few lines, we're flagging `playerCanClick` to `true` so that the player can start playing the game right away. Then, we're using the `new` keyword to create a new, empty Generic List to hold our deck of cards (`aCards`). The `new` keyword is used again in the next line to create an empty 2D Array to hold the grid of cards that gets dealt to the table (`aGrid`), and we declare another Generic List that will store the two cards that the player flips over (`aCardsFlipped`).

Going loopy

The piece of code that follows is a touch trickier. We want to create 16 new cards and put them into our deck, the `aGrid` array. To do that, we're using an "iterative loop" to populate our two-dimensional array.

An iterative loop is a piece of code that repeats itself, with special instructions telling it when to start and when to end. If a loop never ends, our game crashes, and we're flooded with angry tech support calls.

This line begins an iterative loop:

```
for(var i:int=0; i<rows; i++)
```

The variable `i` is called the iterator. That's what we use to figure out how many times to loop, and when to stop. You don't have to use the letter `i`, but you'll see it a lot in other people's code. It's a best practice. And, as we'll see shortly, when you start putting loops inside other loops, you'll actually have to start using other letters, or else your code will break.

The anatomy of a loop

An iterative loop always starts with the `for` keyword. It has three important sections:

- Where to start
- Where to end
- What to do after every loop finishes

In this case, we start by declaring an iterator variable called `i` of type `int` (integer), and set that iterator `i` to zero.

```
var i:int = 0
```

Next, we say that we're going to loop as long as the value of `i` is less than (`<`) the value of **rows**. Because we've already set **rows** to 4, this code will loop four times.

```
i<rows
```

In the third section, we increase the value of `i` by one. Here's how the interpreter chews through our loop:

1. Set an integer variable called `i` to 0.
2. Check to see if `i` is less than `rows` (4). 0 is less than 4, so let's go!
3. Run the code inside the loop.
4. When we're finished, increase `i` by one. (`i++`). `i` is now 1.
5. Check again to see if `i` is less than `rows` (4). 1 is less than 4, so let's keep going.

6. Run the code inside the loop.
7. Repeat until we increase i to 4 on the fourth loop.
8. Because i is no longer less than rows (**4**), stop repeating the loop.

To nest is best

The structure that we've set up is called a "nested loop" because we have one iterative loop running inside another.

Inside the second loop, we're using j as the iterator because i is already in use. We're using the new keyword to create a new instance of the Card class, and we're adding it to the array at index aGrid[i,j].

Talk it through and it's not too tricky to understand:

◆   The first time through the outside loop, we're at index 0 of our 2D Array.
◆   Then in the inner loop, we loop four times. Each time, we stuff a new card into the 2D Array called aGrid.
◆   Next, we do the main loop again. The outer index value i increases to 1.
◆   On to the inner loop, we cram four new cards into the empty. Now, aGrid contains 8 cards.
◆   We keep going until this whole thing plays out. At the end of the nested loop, aGrid is an array containing four arrays, and each of those arrays has four cards in it, for a total of 16 cards.

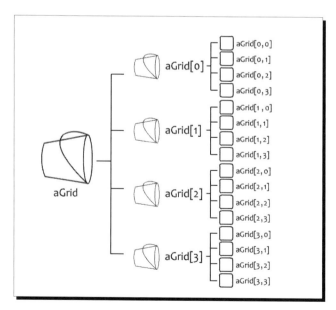

The reason why 2D Arrays are so handy is that we can easily access stuff inside them using grid coordinates, just like in that old board game Battleship. If we want to talk about the card three slots over and one slot down, we call it using `aGrid[1,2]`. In fact, if we were building a digital version of Battleship, we might use nested loops to build 2D arrays to build that game as well.

Note that arrays are zero based. The card at `aGrid[0,0]` is the card at the top-left of the grid. Next to that is the card in `aGrid[0,1]`. Next to that is the card in `aGrid[0,2]`. To get the card one row down, we increase the first index: `aGrid[1,2]`. Here's what you should try picturing in your head:

aGrid[0,0]	aGrid[0,1]	aGrid[0,2]	aGrid[0,3]
aGrid[1,0]	aGrid[1,1]	aGrid[1,2]	aGrid[1,3]
aGrid[2,0]	aGrid[2,1]	aGrid[2,2]	aGrid[2,3]
aGrid[3,0]	aGrid[3,1]	aGrid[3,2]	aGrid[3,3]

Hopefully, you're already seeing how a grid like this relates to a grid of cards laid out on the table for a Memory game. If not, take it on faith and keep reading! It should become clearer as we go.

Seeing is believing

So far, everything we've done has been theoretical. Our cards exist in some imaginary code space, but we've done nothing to actually draw the cards to the screen. Let's build our `OnGUI` function and put something on the screen to see where all this is leading.

On the title screen, we used a Fixed Layout to position our **Play Game** button. We decided exactly where on the screen to put the button, and how big it should be. We're going to build our grid of cards using an Automatic Layout to illustrate the difference.

With an Automatic Layout, you define an area and place your GUI controls inside it. You create your controls using the built-in GUILayout class, instead of the GUI class. The controls that you create with GUILayout stretch to fill the layout area.

Time for action – create an area to store the grid

Let's create one of these Automatic Layout areas in our **GameScript**.

   1. We don't need the Update function in this script. As we did earlier, change Update to OnGUI to create an OnGUI function:

```
function OnGUI () {
```

   2. Begin and end the automatic layout area inside the OnGUI function:

```
function OnGUI ()
{
    GUILayout.BeginArea (Rect (0,0,Screen.width,Screen.height));
    GUILayout.EndArea();
}
```

The area will be the width and height of the screen, and it will start at the screen origin at the top-left of the screen.

These two statements are like bookends or HTML tags. Any UI controls we build between these bookends will be created within the area we defined. Each new control will automatically stack vertically beneath the last. The controls will stretch to the width of the area, which in this case is the entire screen.

Have a go hero – don't take my word for it!

If you'd like to stray off the beaten path and build a few buttons between the area statements to see what happens, I won't hold you back! Use the code we learned earlier in the chapter to create a button or two at different positions. You could also try adjusting the width, height, and start values of the area to see how that affects your UI buttons' placement.

Build that grid

Between the area statements, we want to build the grid of card buttons. But, to keep the code from getting hard to understand, we could make a function call out to a separate piece of code, just to keep things looking clean and easy to read. Modify your OnGUI code:

```
function OnGUI () {
   GUILayout.BeginArea (Rect (0,0,Screen.width,Screen.height));
      BuildGrid();
   GUILayout.EndArea();
   print("building grid!");
}
```

That `building grid!` line is just so that you can be sure something's happening. I like to add statements like these so that I can see into the "mind" of my computer, and to make sure certain functions are getting executed. Remember that your `print` statements show up in the status bar at the bottom of the screen or in the console window if you have it open.

 Note that if we actually try to run the code now, we'll get an error. Unity has no idea what the `BuildGrid` function is, because we haven't written it yet!

Let's write that `BuildGrid` function. Add this code to the bottom of the script, outside and apart from the other chunks:

```
function BuildGrid()
{
   GUILayout.BeginVertical();
   for(var i:int=0; i<rows; i++)
   {
      GUILayout.BeginHorizontal();
      for(var j:int=0; j<cols; j++)
      {
         var card:Card = aGrid[i,j];
```

```
      if(GUILayout.Button(Resources.Load(card.img),
          GUILayout.Width(cardW)))
      {
        Debug.Log(card.img);
      }
    }
    GUILayout.EndHorizontal();
  }
  GUILayout.EndVertical();
}
```

What just happened – grokking the code

We start by wrapping the whole thing in vertical layout tags. Controls are stacked vertically by default within a layout area, but we're explicitly calling `BeginVertical` and `EndVertical` because of some fancy layout gymnastics that we're going to perform a few steps later.

Next, we build a nested loop. Just as before, we're looping through the columns and rows. We wrap the inner loop in a horizontal layout area with the `BeginHorizontal` and `EndHorizontal` calls. By doing this, each new card button we lay down will be stacked horizontally instead of vertically.

Finally, inside the inner loop, we're using an unfamiliar statement to create a button:

```
      if(GUILayout.Button(Resources.Load(card.img), GUILayout.Width(cardW)))
```

In that first parameter, we're passing `Resources.Load` to fill the button with a picture instead of a piece of text. We pass the name of the picture we want to the `Resources.Load` call. Because every card's `img` variable is set to `robot`, Unity pulls the picture labeled `robot` from the **Resources** folder in the **Assets** library and sticks it on the button.

The second parameter is a sort of an override. We don't want our card buttons stretching to fill the width of the layout area, so we pass the `cardW` (which is set to `100` pixels at the top of the script) to the `GUILayout.Width` method.

The net result is that we loop four times, and on each loop we lay down a row of four buttons, each with a picture of a robot.

Save the script and test your game. You should see a 4 x 4 grid of buttons, each with a yellow robot picture on it.

Now you're playing with power!

There's so much to learn about building Unity graphical user interfaces, and you've just taken the first important steps. So far, you know how to:

◆ Add button UI controls to the screen

◆ Tool up a custom GUI skin

◆ Create new scenes, add them to the Build List, and link them together using buttons

◆ Declare and define three different types of collections: a built-in array, a 2D Array and a Generic List

◆ Populate a 2D Array using a nested loop

◆ Lay out UI controls with both automatic and fixed positioning

As we delve deeper into our Robot Repair game, we'll learn more about automatic positioning so that we can center the game grid. We'll also figure out how to flip over cards, and add the crucial game logic to make everything function properly. Join us, won't you?

C# addendum

Converting the `TitleGUI` JavaScript to C# was pretty painless:

```csharp
using UnityEngine;
using System.Collections;

public class TitleGUICSharp : MonoBehaviour {
    private float buttonW = 100; // button width
    private float buttonH = 50;  // button height
    private float halfScreenW; // half of the Screen width
    private float halfButtonW; // half of the button width

    public GUISkin customSkin;
    private void Start()
    {
      halfScreenW = Screen.width/2;
      halfButtonW = buttonW/2;
    }
    private void OnGUI ()
    {
     GUI.skin = customSkin;
      if(GUI.Button(new Rect(halfScreenW-halfButtonW, 460,
        buttonW, buttonH), "Play Game"))
      {
          Application.LoadLevel("game");
      }
    }
}
```

Here are the changes:

We declared `buttonW` and `buttonH` as `floats` instead of `ints`, because the `Rect` structure later in the code accepts `float`, and we can't be bothered converting the `int` values to the `float` datatype. It's probably simpler and easier for them to begin their lives as floats anyway.

Earlier in our JavaScript code, we separated the declaration and definition of a few variables, but we didn't have to. We could have combined the declaration and definition in a single line, like so:

```
var halfScreenW:float = Screen.width/2;
```

We can't pull the same monkeyshines with C#. We're not allowed to simultaneously derive the value of Screen.width, perform a calculation on it, and store it as the value of halfScreenW. Just as we did with the JavaScript code, we've declared the variables at the top of the class, and define the variables (give them their values) in the Start function.

Note that in order for the customSkin variable to show up in Unity's **Inspector** panel, we need to use the public access modifier before declaring the variable. Try switching it to private, and observe that the variable disappears from the **Inspector** panel.

The only other change to this script, aside from the usual changes mentioned in the previous chapter, is that the Rect structure requires the new keyword in front of it in C#.

There are a few differences in the C# version of the GameScript script as well:

```
using UnityEngine;
using System.Collections;
using System.Collections.Generic;

public class GameScriptCSharp : MonoBehaviour {
    private int cols = 4; // the number of columns in the card grid
    private int rows = 4; // the number of rows in the card grid
    private int totalCards = 16;
    private int matchesNeededToWin;
    private int matchesMade = 0; // At the outset, the player has
        not made any matches
    private int cardW = 100; // Each card's width and height is 100
        pixels
    private List<Card> aCards; // We'll store all the cards we
        create in this array
    private Card[,] aGrid; // This 2d array will keep track of the
        shuffled, dealt cards
    private List<Card> aCardsFlipped; // This generic array list
        will store the two cards that the player flips over
    private bool playerCanClick; // We'll use this flag to prevent
        the player from clicking buttons when we don't want him to
    private bool playerHasWon = false; // Store whether or not the
        player has won. This should probably start out false :)

    // Use this for initialization
    private void Start () {
        matchesNeededToWin = totalCards / 2; // If there are 16 cards,
            the player needs to find 8 matches to clear the board
        playerCanClick = true; // We should let the player play, don't
            you think?
```

```
    // Initialize some empty Lists:
    aCards = new List<Card>(); // this Generic List is our deck of
        cards. It can only ever hold instances of the Card class.
    aGrid = new Card[rows,cols];  // The rows and cols variables
        help us define the dimensions of this 2D array
    aCardsFlipped = new List<Card>(); // This List will store
        the two cards the player flips over.

    // Loop through the total number of rows in our aGrid List:
    for(int i = 0; i<rows; i++)
    {
        // For each individual grid row, loop through the total
            number of columns in the grid:
        for(int j = 0; j<cols; j++)
        {
            aGrid[i,j] = new Card(); // stuff a new card instance into
                the 2D array
        }
    }

}
private void OnGUI()
{
    GUILayout.BeginArea (new Rect (0,0,Screen.width,
        Screen.height));
    BuildGrid();
    GUILayout.EndArea();
    print("building grid!");
}

private void BuildGrid()
{

    GUILayout.BeginVertical();
    for(int i = 0; i<rows; i++)
    {
```

```
        GUILayout.BeginHorizontal();
        for(int j = 0; j<cols; j++)
        {
          Card card = aGrid[i,j];

          if(GUILayout.Button(Resources.Load(card.img) as Texture,
            GUILayout.Width(cardW)))
          {
            Debug.Log(card.img);
          }
        }
        GUILayout.EndHorizontal();
      }
      GUILayout.EndVertical();
      print ("building grid!");
    }
  }
```

As with the **TitleGUI** script, we've moved the `matchesNeededToWin` declaration to the `Awake` function, because we need to know the value of `totalCards` to define it.

Here's a subtle difference. When we define the `aCardsFlipped` Generic List, note that JavaScript uses a dot, while C# does not:

```
aCardsFlipped = new List.<Card>(); // JavaScript
aCardsFlipped = new List<Card>(); // C#
```

The only other difference within this script is the `GUILayout.Button` call in the `BuildGrid` function:

```
if(GUILayout.Button(Resources.Load(card.img) as Texture,
  GUILayout.Width(cardW)))
```

The first parameter of `GUILayout.Button` should be `Texture`, but the `Resources.Load` method gives us an `Object`. Since we know that we're actually loading a valid texture (or pulling out a piece of chicken instead of a tennis shoe), we can explicitly tell Unity that this is, indeed, the `Texture` it requires.

We do that with the help of the `as` keyword. By telling Unity that this `Object` is, in fact, a valid `Texture`, we're said to be casting the `Object` to a `Texture` via `as`.

Finally, we've moved the `Card` class declaration into its very own separate script file:

```
using UnityEngine;
using System.Collections;

public class Card {

    public bool isFaceUp = false;
    public bool isMatched = false;
    public string img;

    public Card()
    {
        img = "robot";
    }
}
```

The sneaky bit here is that by default, C# classes in Unity inherit from a class called `MonoBehaviour`. When they do that, they can't actually have a constructor function. We can keep the constructor function (`Card()`) intact by simply removing the `Monobehaviour` bit from the class declaration so that this class stands alone. Everything else in the `Card` class is straightforward.

6
Game #2 – Robot Repair Part 2

As we've learned, building the game part of the game is only half the battle. A lot of your sweat goes into creating what's around the game—the buttons, menus, and prompts that lead the player in, around, and through your game. We're right in the middle of learning how to display buttons and other UI (user interface) controls on top of our Unity games. We'll take a break from the 3D environment, adding game logic to the UI controls to produce a fully functioning 2D game with the Unity GUI alone.

In this chapter, we'll:

- ◆ Discover some code to help us better position our UI controls on the screen
- ◆ Learn to control when the player can and can't interact with our game
- ◆ Unleash the terrifyingly awesome power of random numbers
- ◆ Hide and show UI controls
- ◆ Detect winning conditions
- ◆ Show a "Win" screen when the player finishes the game

From zero to game in one chapter

Let's make a quick list of the stuff we need to do to make this flip n' match memory game functional. Break all of the missing pieces into little bite-sized tasks. For smaller game projects, I like to put these steps in a list with checkboxes. Then, I can put a big 'X' in the box when I'm finished. There is no more satisfying thing I can do in any given workday than to put X's in boxes.

Here's what we need to do to get this game working:

- ☐ Center the grid on the screen.

- ☐ Put different images on the cards. (It would be great if the cards could be shuffled around every time you played!)

- ☐ Figure out how to break the robots and distribute their body parts on the cards properly.

- ☐ Make the cards flip over from back to front when you click them.

- ☐ Prevent the player from flipping over more than two cards in a turn.

- ☐ Compare two flipped-over cards to see if they match (note: if they match, we should remove the cards from the table. If they don't match, we should flip them back over).

- ☐ If all of the cards have been removed from the table, show a victory message and a **Play Again** button. The **Play Again** button should restart the game when you click on it.

Checkboxes are like ferocious dragons. Putting X's in boxes is like slaying those dragons. With each dragon you slay, you've become stronger and wiser, and you're getting closer to your goal. And sometimes, I like to pretend my desk chair is a pony.

> **Golly-GDD**
>
> The list we just created is a very simple example of a **GDD**, a **Game Design Document**. GDDs can be as simple as checklists, or as complicated as 1,000-page Word documents. I like to write my GDDs online in a wiki because it's easier to stay nimble and to change things. My whole team can commit new artwork, ideas, and comments to a living, breathing wiki GDD.
>
> **Putting a point on it**
>
> One interesting tip I've heard about writing GDDs is that you should end each task with a period. This gives the task more weight, as if you're saying, "It shall be so!" Periods, strangely, help to make GDD tasks seem more final, crucial, and concrete.

With this to-do list, and our description of gameplay from the previous chapter, we have our bare-bones GDD. Are you ready? Let's slay some dragons!

Finding your center

We've got our game grid set up, but it's crammed up to the top-left of the screen. That'll be the first thing we'll tackle. Advance warning: writing code isn't quite like writing a book. You rarely begin at the beginning and end at the ending. We're going to be bouncing around quite a bit from function to function. If it ever gets too hairy, don't worry: the complete script is listed at the end of this chapter, and you can always download the final working file from the Packt website.

Time for action – centering the game grid vertically

We'll use the `FlexibleSpace()` method of the `GUILayout` class to center the grid on the screen, first vertically and then horizontally.

1. Double-click on the **gameScript** script to open the code editor. Find the `BuildGrid()` function.

2. Insert two `GUILayout.FlexibleSpace()` calls inside the `GUILayout.BeginVertical()` and `GUILayout.EndVertical()` calls, like so:

    ```
    function BuildGrid()
    {
      GUILayout.BeginVertical();
      GUILayout.FlexibleSpace();
      for(i=0; i<rows; i++)
      {
        // the rest of the code is in here, but we've removed
           it for the sake of simplicity
      }
      GUILayout.FlexibleSpace();
      GUILayout.EndVertical();
    }
    ```

3. Save the script and test your game.

The game grid is now centered vertically on the screen. There's an equal amount of space above the grid as there is below it.

What just happened?

UI controls in an automatic layout like the one we're using want to fill all the space they're given, much like a goldfish will grow to fill the size of the tank it's in. The goldfish thing is actually a myth, but `FlexibleSpace()` is very, very real. Because we've given the grid the entire screen to fill by defining the size of our area rectangle with `Screen.width` and `Screen.height`, our UI controls want to spread out to fill all that space.

`FlexibleSpace` creates a kind of compactable spring that fills up any space that the UI controls aren't using. To get a better sense of what this invisible element does, try commenting the top `GUILayout.FlexibleSpace();` function call:

```
// GUILayout.FlexibleSpace();
```

Save the script and then test your game. There's no `FlexibleSpace` above the grid anymore, so the `FlexibleSpace` below the grid stretches out to fill as much of the area as possible. It automatically grabs any available space that's not filled by your UI controls.

Likewise, you can try commenting out only the bottom `FlexibleSpace()` function call and leave the top `FlexibleSpace` uncommented. Predictably, the top `FlexibleSpace` stretches its legs and pushes the grid to the bottom of the screen. Make sure both the `FlexibleSpace` lines are uncommented, and let's forge ahead.

Time for action – centering the game grid horizontally

By dropping two more `FlexibleSpace` function calls into your `BuildGrid()` function, you can horizontally center the grid on the screen.

1. Add a `GUILayout.FlexibleSpace();` function call between the `GUILayout.BeginHorizontal()` and `GUILayout.EndHorizontal()` calls:

```
function BuildGrid()
{
  GUILayout.BeginVertical();
  GUILayout.FlexibleSpace();
  for(i=0; i<rows; i++)
  {
    GUILayout.BeginHorizontal();
    GUILayout.FlexibleSpace();
    for(j=0; j<cols; j++)
    {
      // Again, the code here has been removed for the sake
        of brevity
    }
    GUILayout.FlexibleSpace();
    GUILayout.EndHorizontal();
  }
  GUILayout.FlexibleSpace();
  GUILayout.EndVertical();
}
```

2. Save the script and test your game. Hooray! The game grid is now centered on the screen, both horizontally and vertically.

What just happened – coding like a ninja

What we've done here is stuck two springy, compactible `FlexibleSpace` elements at either end of each of our horizontal grid rows. At this point, we have ten `FlexibleSpace` elements: one on the top, one on the bottom, and two on either side of our four grid rows.

As with any programming task, there are many different ways you could have approached this problem. You could wrap your four grid rows in a single horizontal area, and stick two `FlexibleSpace` elements inside that in order to have only four `FlexibleSpace` elements in total instead of ten. Or, you could do away with `FlexibleSpace` elements and automatic layouts altogether, and opt for a fixed layout. You could also put all of the buttons in an area (`GUILayout.BeginArea`) and center the area. Or, you could turn off your computer and go outside and play. It's up to you. This is just one solution available to you.

Any way you slice it, we've just knocked one item off our GDD task list:

☒   Center the grid on the screen

Take THAT, you fell beast! Giddy up, desk chair! Onward!

Down to the nitty griddy

Grids are a game development essential. As we saw in the previous chapter, a classic board game like *Battleship* is set up in a grid. So are about 50 other board games I can think of off the top of my head: *Connect Four, Guess Who, Stratego, chess, tic-tac-toe, Clue, checkers, chutes n' ladders, go, slider puzzles*, and so on—it's an absolutely huge list. Add to that the slew of digital games that use a grid layout: *MineSweeper, Tetris, Bejewelled, Puzzle League, Bomberman, Dr. Mario, Breakout*. And lest you think that only 2D games use grids, consider 3D turn-based strategy games—the action takes place on a grid! Grids are used in inventory screens, in image galleries, and on level select screens. A* (A-star), a popular method for moving characters around obstacles on the screen ("pathfinding"), can also use grids. In fact, your entire computer display is a grid of square pixels.

Mastering the grid is key to mastering game development. You'll use grids again and again, from the main mechanic to the interface to perhaps even the high score table at the end of the game. The 2D array method we learned in the last chapter is just one way of setting up a grid, but it's a great one to start with.

Do the random card shuffle

What fun is a flip n' match memory game if all the cards are face up, and they all have the same image on them? Answer: no fun. No fun at all. What we *want* is to deal out a bunch of different cards. And, as long as we're shooting for the moon here, why not deal out a *different* bunch of cards every time we play?

We're going to define a List to represent our entire deck of cards. Then, we'll randomly draw a card from that deck and put it on the table—just like we would in real life.

Time for action – preparing to build the deck

Let's set up a deck-building function called `BuildDeck`.

1. In the GameScript, create a new function called `BuildDeck`. Write this function outside of and apart from your other functions—make sure it's not trapped inside the curly brackets of one of your other functions.

   ```
   function BuildDeck()
   {
   }
   ```

2. Call the `BuildDeck` function in the `Start` function, just after you define the three card-related collections:

   ```
   function Start()
   {
     playerCanClick = true; // We should let the player play,
         don't you think?

     // Initialize some empty Collections:
     aCards = new List.<Card>(); // this Generic List is
        our deck of cards. It can only ever hold instances of
        the Card class.
     aGrid = new Card[rows,cols]; // The rows and cols
        variables help us define the dimensions of this 2D
        array
     aCardsFlipped = new List.<Card>(); // This List will
        store the two cards the player flips over.

     BuildDeck();

     // (the rest of this function has been omitted)
   }
   ```

The very first function that gets called in our script is the `Start` function. After we set our `playerCanClick` flag and create a few empty arrays, `BuildDeck()` is the very first thing the script will do. (If you've been reading the C# addenda, you'll know from the previous chapter the special `Awake` function is called even earlier than the `Start` function.)

Let's break some robots

The way our game works, we have four different robots—a yellow one, a blue one, a red one, and a green one. Each robot will be missing a body part. The player has to match each robot to its missing body part. That accounts for eight cards—four robots and four missing body parts. Because there are sixteen cards in our 4 x 4 grid, we need to use each robot twice—two yellow robots with two missing yellow body parts, two blue robots with two blue missing body parts, and so on: **2*8=16**.

Each robot has three body parts that we can knock off: its head, its arm, or its leg. We have to be careful when we build our deck that we don't repeat a robot and body part combination of the same color. For example, our two green robots can't both be missing a head. Our player won't know which head goes with which robot! It's also possible that the player might flip over two green heads, and wonder why they aren't considered a match. Let's do whatever we can to avoid that.

Time for action – building the deck

The strategy we'll use to build our deck is to create a list of possibilities, randomly choose one of those possibilities, and then remove that possibility as an option. Let's see how that works.

1. In the `BuildDeck` function, start off by declaring a few temporary variables:

    ```
    function BuildDeck()
    {

        var totalRobots:int = 4;  // we've got four robots to
          work with
        var card:Card; // this stores a reference to a card
    }
    ```

2. Next, build a loop to step through each of the four colored robot types:

    ```
    var card:Card; // this stores a reference to a card

    for(var i:int=0; i<totalRobots; i++)
    {
    }
    ```

That loop will run four times because `totalRobots` is set to 4. Next, create a Generic List of type `string` called `aRobotParts` that will house the names of the body parts we can knock off:

```
for(i=0; i<totalRobots; i++)
{
    var aRobotParts:List.<String> = new List.<String>();
    aRobotParts.Add("Head");
    aRobotParts.Add("Arm");
    aRobotParts.Add("Leg");
}
```

3. Now, we'll set up a nested loop to run twice. So, for all four robot types, we'll create two busted robots (in order to fill our 16-card quota):

```
for(var i:int=0; i<totalRobots; i++)
{
    var aRobotParts:List.<String> = new List.<String>();
    aRobotParts.Add("Head");
    aRobotParts.Add("Arm");
    aRobotParts.Add("Leg");
    for(var j:int=0; j<2; j++)
    {
    }
}
```

The meat of the `BuildDeck` code goes inside that inner loop:

```
for(var j:int=0; j<2; j++)
{
    var someNum:int = Random.Range(0, aRobotParts.Count);
    var theMissingPart:String = aRobotParts[someNum];

    aRobotParts.RemoveAt(someNum);

    card = new Card("robot" + (i+1) + "Missing" + theMissingPart);
    aCards.Add(card);

    card= new Card("robot" + (i+1) + theMissingPart);
    aCards.Add(card);
}
```

Here's how the BuildDeck function looks when you're finished:

```
function BuildDeck()
{
  var totalRobots:int = 4;   // we've got four robots to
    work with
  var card:Card; // this stores a reference to a card

  for(var i:int=0; i<totalRobots; i++)
  {
    var aRobotParts:List.<String> - new List.<String>();

    aRobotParts.Add("Head");
    aRobotParts.Add("Arm");
    aRobotParts.Add("Leg");

    for(var j:int=0; j<2; j++)
    {
      var someNum:int = Random.Range(0, aRobotParts.Count);
      var theMissingPart:String = aRobotParts[someNum];

      aRobotParts.RemoveAt(someNum);

      card = new Card("robot" + (i+1) + "Missing" +
        theMissingPart);
      aCards.Add(card);

      card= new Card("robot" + (i+1) + theMissingPart);
      aCards.Add(card);
    }
  }
}
```

What just happened – dissecting the bits

Let's step through that last chunk of code and figure out what it does:

```
var someNum:int = Random.Range(0, aRobotParts.Count);
```

First, we're declaring a variable called someNum (short for "some crazy old random number"), which will be an integer type. We're going to use this number to randomly refer to one of the body parts in the aRobotParts Generic List. So we use the Range() method of the Random class to pull that random number.

We supply the minimum and maximum ends of the range to pull from—in this case, the low end is 0 (because arrays are 0-based), and the high end is the length of the aRobotParts Generic List. The first time through the loop, aRobotParts.length is 3 ("Head", "Arm", and "Leg"). Our minimum and maximum values are 0 and 3. So, the first time through this loop, someNum will be a random number from 0-2.

> **Exclusive to the max**
>
> When using Random.Range with int data types, note that the minimum value is *inclusive*, while the maximum value is *exclusive*. That means that unless you supply the same number for your minimum and maximum values, Random.Range() will never pull your maximum value. In the previous example, you'll never get 3 from Random.Range(), even though we're supplying 3 as the maximum value.
>
> **Floats** work a little differently than **ints**. When randomizing with **floats**, the maximum value is inclusive.

Here, we use our random number to pull a body part out of the aRobotParts leneric list.

```
var theMissingPart:String = aRobotParts[someNum];
```

If someNum is 0, we get "Head". If someNum is 1, we get "Arm". If someNum is 2, we get "Leg". We store this result in a String variable called theMissingPart.

```
aRobotParts.RemoveAt(someNum);
```

The RemoveAt() method of the Array class rips an element out of the List at the specified index. We specify the someNum index we just used to grab a body part. This removes that body part from the List, so that it's no longer an option to the next robot. This is how we avoid ever having two green robots, each with a missing head—by the time we choose a missing body part for the second robot, "Head" has been removed from our list of options. Note that because it's declared and defined inside the loop, the aRobotParts array is "reborn" with each new robot type, so the first of each pair of robots gets its pick of a new batch of body parts. The second robot of each type always has one less option to choose from.

```
card = new Card("robot" + (i+1) + "Missing" + theMissingPart);
aCards.Add(card);
card= new Card("robot" + (i+1) + theMissingPart);
aCards.Add(card);
```

With these final lines, we create two new instances of the `Card` class, and add references to those cards to the `aCards` array using the Add method of the Generic List. The `aCards` Generic List is the deck of cards we'll use to deal out the game.

Each time we create a new card instance, we're passing a new argument between those round brackets—the name of the image we want displayed on the card. The first time through the nested loop, for the first (yellow) robot type, let's say we randomly choose to break its head.

This `String`:

```
"robot" + (i+1) + "Missing" + theMissingPart
```

resolves to:

```
"robot1MissingHead"
```

and

```
"robot" + (i+1) + theMissingPart
```

resolves to:

```
"robot1Head"
```

Take a quick look at the images in the `Resources` folder of the **Project** panel. `"robot1MissingHead"` and `"robot1Head"` just so happen to be the names of two of our images!

Time for action – modifying the img argument

Because we're passing a new argument to the `Card` class, we have to modify the `Card` class to accept it.

1. Change the `Card` class code from this:

```
class Card extends System.Object
{
  // (variables omitted for clarity)
  function Card()
  {
    img = "robot";
  }
}
```

to this:

```
class Card extends System.Object
{
    // (variables omitted for clarity)
    function Card(img:String)
    {
        this.img = img;
    }
}
```

2. Now, find the nested loop in the `Start` function where we added all our new cards to the `aGrid` array. Change it from this:

```
for(j=0; j<cols; j++)
{
    aGrid[i,j] = new Card();
}
```

to this:

```
for(j=0; j<cols; j++)
{
    var someNum:int = Random.Range(0,aCards.Count);
    aGrid[i,j] = aCards[someNum];
    aCards.RemoveAt(someNum);
}
```

What just happened?

This code should look familiar to you, because we're pulling a very similar trick as before. We have a deck of cards—the `aCards` List. After the `BuildDeck` function is finished, the `aCards` list is populated with all of the cards we need to deal out to the table.

We're grabbing a random number using `Random.Range()`, and we're supplying the length of the `aCards` array as the maximum value. This gives us a value that stays within the bounds of the total number of cards in `aCards`.

Then, we use that random number to pull a card out of the deck and stuff it in the `aGrid` 2D array (it gets *visually* dealt to the table later on, in the `BuildGrid()` function). Finally, we remove that card from the deck so that we don't accidentally deal it out in successive loops. This prevents us from dealing duplicate cards to the table.

Save the script and play your game! What you should see is an army of amputated androids. Awesome! Because the cards are dealt randomly and the deck itself is being built randomly, any pictures of the game that you see from here on may not match what you have on your screen.

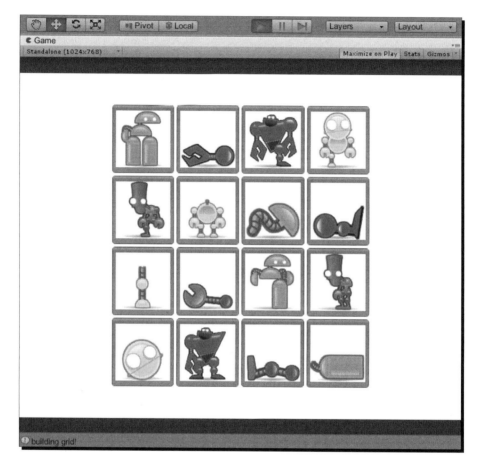

What exactly is "this"?

Did the `this.img` = `img;` line trip you up? Here's what's going on with that.

The `Card` class has an instance variable called `img`. We're also passing an argument to its constructor function with the exact same name, `img`. If we simply wrote `img` = `img;`, that means we'd be setting the value of the argument to the value of the argument. Hunh! That's not quite what we're after.

By specifying `this.img` = `img;`, we're saying that we want the `img` variable attached to this, the `Card` class, to have the same value as the *argument* called `img`.

It's a smidge confusing, I'll admit. So, why not just call the argument something different? You absolutely could! We did it this way because it's very common to see variables passed to the constructor function with the same name as the instance variables in the class. You may as well encounter it here with a full explanation, than come across it in the wild and let it gnaw your leg off.

Here's one more look at another, completely imaginary class that does the same kind of thing. Stare at it, absorb it, and be at peace with it:

```
class Dog extends System.Object
{
  // Declare some instance variables:
  var myName:String;
  var breed:String
  var age:int;

  function Dog(myName:String,breed:String,age:int)
  {
     this.myName = myName; // set the value of the instance variable
      "myName" to the value of the argument "myName"
     this.breed = breed; // set the value of the instance variable
      "breed" to the value of the argument "breed"
     this.age = age; // set the value of the instance variable "age"
      to the value of the argument "age"
  }
}
```

It might help your understanding to know that those arguments that are passed into the constructor function have a limited **scope**. They will disappear if we don't do something with them in the function. The instance variables declared at the top of the class have a broader **scope**—they exist outside of all the functions, and they persist no matter what happens inside the functions. We take the values of the ephemeral, soon-to-disappear arguments, and store them in the longer-term instance variables. We use the keyword `this` to tell the difference between the two.

Have a go hero – grokketh-thou Random.Range()?

As long as we're taking some time to let it all sink in, let's do another pass on this `Random.Range()` method. If `Random.Range()` is not clear to you yet, try building a test loop at the bottom of the `Start()` function and logging the results:

```
for(i=0; i<1000; i++)
{
    Debug.Log(Random.Range(0,10));
}
```

Test and run. Make sure that the **Console** window is open (**Window | Console**), and make sure that **Collapse** is unchecked—otherwise, you'll see only the last few log lines. You should also ensure there are no other `print()` or `Debug.Log()` statements cluttering the console. Use double-slashes `//` to comment those out for the time being.

The number Unity spits out should never equal ten (provided you're using ints and not floats). Play around with the minimum and maximum values until you're completely confident, then delete your test loop and check out the rest of this code.

Random reigns supreme

Being able to pull and effectively use random numbers is another game development essential. With random numbers, you can make sure every card deal is different, like you've just done with your **Robot Repair** game. You can make enemies behave unpredictably, making it seem as though they're acting intelligently (without having to bother with complicated Artificial Intelligence programming! See *Chapter 12, Game #5 –Kisses 'n' Hugs*, for more on this technique.) You can make spaceships attack from surprising angles. You can build an avatar system with a **Shuffle** button that randomly dresses up your player's character.

The best game developers use random numbers to make their games meatier, more visually appealing, and more fun! The *worst* game developers use random numbers in all the wrong ways. Imagine a game where, whenever you shot a gun, the bullet traveled in a completely random direction! Random numbers can dramatically help or hinder your gameplay. Use them wisely, and they're an incredibly effective weapon in your game design arsenal.

Second dragon down

We've got some card faces displaying in the game, and we randomized them. We just totally stabbed another one of our GDD dragons in the face (or cuddled another kitten, depending on the imagery you prefer). Well done!

- ☒ Put different images on the cards. (It would be great if the cards could be shuffled around every time you played!)

Time to totally flip

Let's move on to the next item in our list. **Robot Repair** lacks a certain amount of mystery at the moment. Let's add a bit of logic to make our cards two-sided, and to flip them over when the player clicks on them.

Time for action – making the cards two-sided

We'll write some logic so that the cards show one image or another depending on whether or not they've been flipped over.

1. Find this line in your `BuildGrid` function:

```
if(GUILayout.Button(Resources.Load(card.img),
    GUILayout.Width(cardW)))
```

2. Change `card.img` to `img` so that the line reads like this:

```
if(GUILayout.Button(Resources.Load(img),
    GUILayout.Width(cardW)))
```

3. Just above that line, find the `card` variable definition:

```
var card:Object = aGrid[i,j];
```

4. Insert this line just after it:

```
var img:String;
```

5. Finally, after that line, write this conditional statement:

```
if(card.isFaceUp)
{
   img = card.img;
} else {
   img = "wrench";
}
```

The whole function should look like this when you're finished:

```
function BuildGrid()
{

  GUILayout.BeginVertical();
  GUILayout.FlexibleSpace();
  for(var i:int=0; i<rows; i++)
  {
    GUILayout.BeginHorizontal();
    GUILayout.FlexibleSpace();
    for(var j:int=0; j<cols; j++)
    {
      var card:Card = aGrid[i,j];
      var img:String;
      if(card.isFaceUp)
      {
```

```
          img = card.img;
        } else {
          img = "wrench";
        }
        if(GUILayout.Button(Resources.Load(img),
          GUILayout.Width(cardW)))
        {
          Debug.Log(card.img);
        }
      }
    GUILayout.FlexibleSpace();
    GUILayout.EndHorizontal();
  }
  GUILayout.FlexibleSpace();
  GUILayout.EndVertical();
  //print ("building grid!");
}
```

So, instead of showing the card's image (`card.img`) when we draw each card button, we're showing the name of a card that we're storing in a new variable called `img`. Note that `img` and `card.img` are two different variables—`card.img` belongs to an instance of our `Card` class, while `img` is just a temporary variable that we're declaring inside our loop, with the line `var img:String;`.

Next, we have a conditional statement. If the `isFaceUp` Boolean flag on the card is `true`, we set the value of our temporary `img` variable to match the `card.img` name. But, if the card is not face up, we'll show a generic "wrench" picture. The wrench picture will be the standard reverse image for all of our cards. You can find it in the `Resources` folder of the **Project** panel, if you're the kind of person who likes to peek at presents before your birthday.

Time for action – building the card-flipping function

This card-flipping code looks pretty good, but there's no way to test it without adding some way of flagging that `isFaceUp` variable to `true`. Let's build a new function to do just that, and call it whenever a card button is clicked.

1. Create a new function called `FlipCardFaceUp`. As you did with the `BuildDeck` function earlier, write this function outside of and apart from your other functions— make sure it's not trapped inside the curly brackets of one of your other functions.

    ```
    function FlipCardFaceUp()
    {

    }
    ```

2. Call the `FlipCardFaceUp` function from inside the card creation code:

```
if(GUILayout.Button(Resources.Load(img), GUILayout.
  Width(cardW)))
{
    FlipCardFaceUp();
    Debug.Log(card.img);
}
```

3. We need to tell the `FlipCardFaceUp` function *which* card has been flipped. Modify the line to pass a reference to the clicked-on card as an argument:

```
FlipCardFaceUp(card);
```

4. Now, we need to accept that card as an argument in our function definition. Modify your `FlipCardFaceUp` definition:

```
function FlipCardFaceUp(card:Card){


}
```

5. Now that we're passing a reference to the clicked-on card to our `FlipCardFaceUp` function, and the function is receiving that reference as an argument, we can do as we please with the card:

```
function FlipCardFaceUp(card:Card)
{
    card.isFaceUp = true;
}
```

Mismatched arguments

The name of the variable that you pass as an argument to a function does not need to match the name of the argument you receive in that function. For example, we could pass a variable called `monkeyNubs` (`FlipCardFaceUp(monkeyNubs)`) and we could name the argument `butterFig` function (`FlipCardFaceUp(butterFig:Card)`). As long as the type of the thing getting passed and received is the same (in this case, an object of type `Card`), it'll work. We can't pass a `String` and receive an `int`, no matter what the variable is called on either end.

Reference versus value

Another picky thing about many programming languages, including UnityScript, is that some data types are passed to functions by **reference**, while some are passed by **value**. Data types like classes and arrays are passed by reference, which means that when we accept them as arguments in our functions and start fiddling around with them, we're making changes to the **actual** structure that was passed in. But when we pass something like an `int`, it gets passed by value. It's like we're getting a copy of it, not the original. Any changes we make to something passed by value does not affect the original variable.

Save the script and test your game. Because all of the cards default to `isFaceUp = false`, the grid is dealt "wrench side up". When you click on each of the cards, the `isFaceUp` Boolean for each clicked-on card is flagged to `true`. The next time the interface is redrawn `OnGUI` (which is fractions of seconds later), Unity sees that `isFaceUp=true` for the clicked-on cards, and loads `card.img` instead of "wrench".

What's that I smell? Why, it's the stench of a dying dragon (or a cuddled kitten). We figured out how to flip over the cards, so let's knock another item off our list:

☒ Make the cards flip over from back to front when you click them.

You'll notice, of course, that there's no way to flip the cards back over. Let's take care of that now.

Time for action – building the card-flipping function

The game will let the player flip over two cards. Then, it will pause for a brief moment and flip the cards back over. We'll worry about detecting matches for our grand finale in just a moment.

1. Add the following code to your `FlipCardFaceUp` function:

```
function FlipCardFaceUp(card:Card)
{
    card.isFaceUp = true;
    aCardsFlipped.Add(card);

    if(aCardsFlipped.Count == 2)
    {
        playerCanClick = false;

        yield WaitForSeconds(1);

        aCardsFlipped[0].isFaceUp = false;
        aCardsFlipped[1].isFaceUp = false;

        aCardsFlipped = new List.<Card>();

        playerCanClick = true;
    }
}
```

2. Then, make a small change to one line in the `BuildGrid` function:

```
if(GUILayout.Button(Resources.Load(img),
    GUILayout.Width(cardW)))
{
    if(playerCanClick)
    {
        FlipCardFaceUp(card);
    }
    Debug.Log(card.img);
}
```

3. Save and test. You should be able to flip over two cards before your incessant clicking falls on deaf ears. After a one-second pause, the cards flip back over.

What just happened – dissecting the flip

Let's take a look at what we've just done:

```
aCardsFlipped.Add(card);
```

In this line, we're adding the card to our `aCardsFlipped` generic list.

```
if(aCardsFlipped.Count == 2)
```

Next, our conditional checks to see if the player has flipped over two cards—in that case, the `Count` property should be 2. Remember that `aCardsFlipped` is from the `Generic List` class, not the `Array` class, and the two are different beasts. To check the length of an `Array`, we use `Length`. To check the length of `Generic List`, we use `Count`. The `Count` of our List goes up when we use the `Add()` method, which throws additional items into the list.

```
playerCanClick = false;
```

Our `playerCanClick` flag comes in handy here—by setting it to `false`, we prevent the fiendish player from flipping over more cards than he ought to.

```
yield WaitForSeconds(1);
```

This straightforward piece of code waits for one second before allowing the next lines of code to execute.

```
aCardsFlipped[0].isFaceUp = false;
aCardsFlipped[1].isFaceUp = false;
```

These lines flag the two flipped-over cards back to their unflipped states. The next time the `OnGUI` function runs, which will be very soon, the cards will be drawn wrench side up. The first flipped card is at index 0 of the `aCardsFlipped` list, and the second flipped card is at index 1.

```
aCardsFlipped = new List.<Card>();
```

By reinitializing the `aCardsFlipped` Generic List, we're emptying it out to hold two brand new flipped-over cards later on.

```
playerCanClick = true;
```

Now that it's safe to start flipping cards again, we'll flag the `playerCanClick` variable back to `true`.

```
if(playerCanClick)
{
    FlipCardFaceUp(card);
}
```

By adding this simple condition at the beginning of the `FlipCardFaceUp()` function call, we can control whether or not the player is allowed to flip over the card. If `playerCanClick` resolves to `false`, NO FLIPPY.

Pumpkin eater

If you hail from Cheaty-Pants land, you may have figured out that you can flip over the same card twice. This isn't technically cheating, but when you break the game, *you're only cheating yourself*. We also have to be careful because a click-happy player might accidentally double-click the first card, and then think that the game is broken when he can't flip over a second card. Let's wrap the `FlipCardFaceUp` in a conditional statement to prevent this from happening:

```
function FlipCardFaceUp(card:Card)
{
    card.isFaceUp = true;
    if(aCardsFlipped.IndexOf(card) < 0)
    {
        aCardsFlipped.Add(card);
        // (the rest of the code is omitted)
    }
}
```

What just happened?

This is where we finally get some mileage out of our `Generic List` class. `Generic List` has a method called `IndexOf` that searches itself for an element, and returns the index point of that element.

Take a look at this example (the log's "answers" are commented at the end of each line):

```
var aShoppingList: List.<String> = new List.<String>();
aShoppingList.Add("apples");
aShoppingList.Add("milk");
aShoppingList.Add("cheese");
aShoppingList.Add("chainsaw");
Debug.Log(aShoppingList.IndexOf("apples")); // 0
Debug.Log(aShoppingList.IndexOf("cheese")); // 2
Debug.Log(aShoppingList.IndexOf("bicarbonate of soda")); // -1
```

Since `"apples"` is the first element in the list, the method returns 0 when we test `IndexOf("apples")`. Since `"cheese"` is the third element, `IndexOf("cheese")` returns 2, and so on. Note that `List` returns -1 when the element can't be found.

So, for our purposes, we do a quick check of the `aCardsFlipped` List to make sure it doesn't already contain a reference to the card that was clicked. If the clicked card is already in `aCardsFlipped`, that means that the player clicked on the same card twice. If we do detect a double-flip, we simply don't execute the remainder of the card-flipping code. So there.

Even though its fixed-size feature makes the `Built-in Array` class faster, it doesn't have this handy `IndexOf()` method—we would have had to write our own. Thumbs up for less work!

Stabby McDragonpoker rides again

There's one more item off our checklist. Make an X, pat yourself on the back, and steel your will against the next challenge!

☒   Prevent the player from flipping over more than two cards in a turn

Game and match

The last piece of crucial functionality in our flip n' match game is to detect, and react to, a match. We currently have no way of knowing, through code, if two cards match, so we'll fix that first. Then, we'll detect the match and remove the cards from the table. After that, we just need to check for the endgame scenario (all matches found) before zipping it up and calling it a game.

Time for action – ID the cards

Let's revisit our card-creation code and give each card an ID number. We'll use that number to detect matches.

1. In the `BuildDeck` function, add this line:

```
function BuildDeck()
{
    var totalRobots:int = 4; // we've got four robots to
       work with
    var card:Object; // this stores a reference to a card
    var id:int = 0;
```

2. Look a little further down the code. Pass the `id` value to the `Card` class with each robot and missing body part card, and then increment the ID number:

```
card = new Card("robot" + (i+1) + "Missing" + theMissingPart,
    id);
```

```
aCards.Add(card);

card= new Card("robot" + (i+1) + theMissingPart, id);
aCards.Add(card);
id++;
```

3. Add id as a property of the Card class. Accept id as an argument in the Card class constructor function, and set the card's id instance variable to that value:

```
class Card extends System.Object
{
    var isFaceUp:boolean = false;
    var isMatched:boolean = false;
    var img:String;
    var id:int;

    function Card(img:String, id:int)
    {
        this.img = img;
        this.id = id;
    }
}
```

What just happened?

What you've done is given each matching set of cards its own ID number. A yellow robot with a missing head, and its missing head, will each have an ID of 0. The next two cards added to the deck might be a yellow robot with a missing arm, and its missing arm, which each get an ID of 1. With this logic in place, it should be much easier to tell if two cards match—we'll just compare their IDs!

Time for action – comparing the IDs

To compare the IDs, we need to make some changes to the FlipCardFaceUp function.

1. Note that we're folding two existing lines of code inside a new conditional statement:

```
function FlipCardFaceUp(card:Card)
{
    card.isFaceUp = true;

    if(aCardsFlipped.IndexOf(card) < 0)
    {
```

```
      aCardsFlipped.Add(card);

   if(aCardsFlipped.Count == 2)
   {
     playerCanClick = false;

     yield WaitForSeconds(1);

     if(aCardsFlipped[0].id == aCardsFlipped[1].id)
     {
         // Match!
         aCardsFlipped[0].isMatched = true;
         aCardsFlipped[1].isMatched = true;

     } else {
         aCardsFlipped[0].isFaceUp = false;
         aCardsFlipped[1].isFaceUp = false;
     }

     aCardsFlipped = new List.<Card>();

     playerCanClick = true;
   }
 }
}
```

Here, we check to see if the two flipped-over cards have the same ID value. If they do, we set each card's isMatched flag to true. If they don't match, we just flip the cards back over as before.

2. We should add a little bit of logic to our BuildGrid function to make sure the player can't flip over a card that's been matched:

```
function BuildGrid()
{
  // (some stuff was omitted here for clarity)
  var card:Object = aGrid[i][j];
  var img:String;
  if(card.isMatched)
  {
```

```
      img = "blank";
    } else {
      if(card.isFaceUp)
      {
        img = card.img;
      }
      else
      {
        img = "wrench";
      }
    }

    GUI.enabled = !card.isMatched;
    if(GUILayout.Button(Resources.Load(img), GUILayout.
      Width(cardW)))
    {
      if(playerCanClick)
      {
        FlipCardFaceUp(card);
        Debug.Log(card.img);
      }
    }
    GUI.enabled = true;
```

What just happened?

We wrapped our first piece of logic in a conditional check that says "if the card is matched, set its image to some blank white picture".

The next new lines are pretty interesting. We're setting GUI.enabled, which is a Boolean value, to whatever card.isMatched is NOT. The exclamation mark operator means "is not". So, if card.isMatched is true, then GUI.enabled is false. If card.isMatched is false, then GUI.enabled is true. GUI.enabled, as you probably guessed, enables or disables GUI control functionality.

When we're finished drawing our card button and setting its click behavior (which is ignored if GUI.enabled is false), we need to remember to re-enable the GUI—otherwise, none of our other cards will be clickable!

Save the script and repair some robots. Just like the second **Death Star**, your game is fully operational, baby!

On to the final boss

With that last step, we've slain or cuddled the penultimate dragon or kitten:

⊠ Compare two flipped-over cards to see if they match (note: if they match, we should remove the cards from the table. If they don't match, we should flip them back over).

The last checkbox awaits: detecting victory and showing the endgame message with a **Play Again** button. Onward, to victory!

Endgame

With the amount of emotional and temporal engagement you're expecting from your players with this game, it would be criminal to skimp on the endgame. Let's close the loop by showing the player a congratulatory message with an option to play again when we detect that all of the matches have been found.

Time for action – checking for victory

Our `matchesMade`, `matchesNeededToWin`, and `playerHasWon` variables have been standing at the ready this whole time. Let's finally make use of them.

1. Add these few lines to the `FlipCardFaceUp` function, where you're detecting a match:

```
if(aCardsFlipped[0].id == aCardsFlipped[1].id)
{
  // Match!
  aCardsFlipped[0].isMatched = true;
  aCardsFlipped[1].isMatched = true;

  matchesMade ++;

  if(matchesMade >= matchesNeededToWin)
  {
    playerHasWon = true;
  }
```

2. Add a new function call to the `OnGUI` function:

```
function OnGUI () {
    GUILayout.BeginArea (Rect (0,0,Screen.width,Screen.height));
    BuildGrid();
    if(playerHasWon) BuildWinPrompt();
    GUILayout.EndArea();
}
```

3. And, now, we'll use some `GUILayout` commands that we learned in the last chapter to display a "win" prompt to the player. Write this new function apart from the other functions, and make sure it's not wedged inside any other function's curlies:

```
function BuildWinPrompt()
{
    var winPromptW:int = 120;
```

```
    var winPromptH:int = 90;

    var halfScreenW:float = Screen.width/2;
    var halfScreenH:float = Screen.height/2;

    var halfPromptW:int = winPromptW/2;
    var halfPromptH:int = winPromptH/2;

    GUI.BeginGroup(Rect(halfScreenW-halfPromptW, halfScreenH-
      halfPromptH, winPromptW, winPromptH));
    GUI.Box (Rect (0,0,winPromptW,winPromptH), "A Winner is
      You!!");

    var buttonW:int = 80;
    var buttonH:int = 20;

    if(GUI.Button(Rect(halfPromptW-(buttonW/2),halfPromptH-
      (buttonH/2),buttonW,buttonH),"Play Again"))
    {
        Application.LoadLevel("Title");
    }
        GUI.EndGroup();
}
```

What just happened?

This method uses 90 % recycled knowledge. We store a few variables to help us remember where the middle of the screen is, store the half width and height of the prompt we're about to draw, and then draw and position it using a fixed layout (instead of an automatic layout, like our grid of cards).

The remaining unknown 10 % uses a wrapper called a **Group**, which helps us collect UI controls together.

```
    GUI.Box (Rect (0,0,winPromptW,winPromptH), "A Winner is You!!");
```

This draws a box at the origin point of the Group (which is centered on the screen). Feel free to change the box label, "**A Winner is You!**", to something equally sarcastic.

Inside that box, we draw a **Button** control with the label **Play Again**. When clicked, we link the player to the **Title Scene** where the game starts all over again and much fun is repeatedly had, until the player dies of old age and the Earth crashes into the sun.

Have a go hero – extra credit

As you now know how to create, label, and position buttons; create scenes, and link scenes to each other with buttons; and draw text and graphics to the screen, here are a few challenges for you that will give your already complete game even more bells and whistles:

♦ Create a **Credits** screen, and link to it from either the **Title Scene** or the **Play Again** prompt. Be sure to credit yourself for absolutely everything, with perhaps a token nod to Grandma. You've earned it!

- Create an **Instructions** screen. This is an excuse to throw some color into the game, and church up what is really just a simple flip n' match Memory game. Here's some copy for you to use and adapt:

  "Professor Wrecker had a wild night and smashed up the robotics lab again! Can you put the ruined robots back together while the Professor sleeps it off?"

  Hilarious *and* kid-friendly.

- Create some new elements near the edge of your grid—eight cards with silhouettes of the robots on them. As the player finds matches and the clickable cards are blanked out, swap the silhouettes for the repaired robots. This may give the player a stronger sense of a goal.

- Create a new set of graphics with four additional robots. Add them to your **Resources** folder, name them properly, and see if you can adjust the code so that all eight robots get dealt into the deck.

- Explore the other UI controls Unity has to offer. Try expanding those game instructions to a 30-page-long epic (NOT a good idea in real life, but we're just practising here). Hook those monstrous instructions up to a scroll bar. Add a checkbox for the player stating, "I have read and agreed to these instructions." Do not let your player play the game until he has scrolled to the bottom of the instructions. This is probably a terrible design decision, but we'll make some concessions for the sake of your education. Just be sure to hide your home address from the player so that you don't get any bricks through your window or flaming bags of poo on your doorstep.

Endgame

You've created a fully working flip n' match Memory game that'll be a sure-fire hit with Grandma, especially if she sees her shout-out in the credits. In this chapter, you:

- Used `FlexibleSpace` to center your automatic `GUILayout`
- Learned how to pull random numbers and bend them to your nefarious will
- Figured out how to disable the GUI, flip Boolean flags, pause code execution, and prevent the player from clicking on stuff he's not supposed to
- Built an entire functioning game using only the Unity GUI system
- Learned how to break a game's design into smaller functional steps that you can add to a to-do list

Remember that any 3D game will likely require a decent amount of 2D programming. User interfaces like shops, inventory screens, level select screens, and character creation tools usually display items in grid layouts with selectable buttons, changing pictures, control-limiting logic, and a lot of the same stuff we've covered off in this chapter. Consider these past two chapters training for all the amazing user interfaces you'll build for your games.

Astronauts don't train in space—they train in simulators. And, just like an astronaut in a NASA-constructed spinning thrill ride, this chapter may have left your head reeling! We covered a *lot* of ground here, but the good news is that the pages in this book aren't going anywhere. Meditate on them. Read them again and again. Take your time to let it all sink in before charging on to the next chapter.

Bring. It. On.

Are you ready to continue? Then it's time to slather that wonderful brain of yours with awesome sauce. With Unity UI mastery under your belt, you'll now learn how to build a one-off GUI component that you could end up using in every game you'll ever build. How's that for a cliffhanger ending? Turn that page!

Here is the completed GameScript for Robot Repair:

```
#pragma strict

import System.Collections.Generic;

var cols:int = 4; // the number of columns in the card grid
var rows:int = 4; // the number of rows in the card grid
var totalCards:int = 16;
var matchesNeededToWin:int = totalCards * 0.5; // If there are 16
    cards, the player needs to find 8 matches to clear the board
var matchesMade:int = 0; // At the outset, the player has not made
    any matches
var cardW:int = 100; // Each card's width and height is 100 pixels
var aCards:List.<Card>; // We'll store all the cards we create in
    this List
var aGrid:Card[,]; // This 2d array will keep track of the shuffled,
    dealt cards
var aCardsFlipped:List.<Card>; // This generic array list will
    store the two cards that the player flips over
var playerCanClick:boolean; // We'll use this flag to prevent the
    player from clicking buttons when we don't want him to
var playerHasWon:boolean = false; // Store whether or not the player
    has won. This should probably start out false :)
```

```
function Start () {
  playerCanClick = true; // We should let the player play, don't you
    think?

  // Initialize some empty Collections:
  aCards = new List.<Card>(); // this Generic List is our deck of
    cards. It can only ever hold instances of the Card class.
  aGrid = new Card[rows,cols]; // The rows and cols variables help
    us define the dimensions of this 2D array
  aCardsFlipped = new List.<Card>(); // This List will store the
    two cards the player flips over.

  BuildDeck();

  // Loop through the total number of rows in our aGrid List:
  for(var i:int = 0; i<rows; i++)
  {
    // For each individual grid row, loop through the total number
      of columns in the grid:
    for(var j:int = 0; j<cols; j++)
    {
      var someNum:int = Random.Range(0,aCards.Count);
      aGrid[i,j] = aCards[someNum];
      aCards.RemoveAt(someNum);


    }
  }


  /*
  // Uncomment this code to experiment with the Random.Range() method
  for(i=0; i<1000; i++)
  {
    Debug.Log(Random.Range(0,10));
  }
  */
}
```

```
function OnGUI()
{
  GUILayout.BeginArea (Rect (0,0,Screen.width,Screen.height));
  BuildGrid();
  if(playerHasWon) BuildWinPrompt();
  GUILayout.EndArea();
  //print("building grid!");
}

function BuildWinPrompt()
{
  var winPromptW:int = 120;
  var winPromptH:int = 90;

  var halfScreenW:float = Screen.width/2;
  var halfScreenH:float = Screen.height/2;

  var halfPromptW:int = winPromptW/2;
  var halfPromptH:int = winPromptH/2;

  GUI.BeginGroup(Rect(halfScreenW-halfPromptW, halfScreenH-
    halfPromptH, winPromptW, winPromptH));
  GUI.Box (Rect (0,0,winPromptW,winPromptH), "A Winner is You!!");

  var buttonW:int = 80;
  var buttonH:int = 20;

  if(GUI.Button(Rect(halfPromptW-(buttonW/2),halfPromptH-(buttonH/2),
    buttonW,buttonH),"Play Again"))
  {
    Application.LoadLevel("Title");
  }
  GUI.EndGroup();
}


function BuildGrid()
{

  GUILayout.BeginVertical();
  GUILayout.FlexibleSpace();
  for(var i:int=0; i<rows; i++)
  {
```

```
    GUILayout.BeginHorizontal();
    GUILayout.FlexibleSpace();
    for(var j:int=0; j<cols; j++)
    {
      var card:Card = aGrid[i,j];
      var img:String;
      if(card.isMatched)
      {
        img = "blank";
      } else {
        if(card.isFaceUp)
        {
          img = card.img;
        } else {
          img = "wrench";
        }
      }

      GUI.enabled = !card.isMatched;
      if(GUILayout.Button(Resources.Load(img),
        GUILayout. Width(cardW)))
      {
        if(playerCanClick)
        {
          FlipCardFaceUp(card);
          Debug.Log(card.img);
        }
      }
      GUI.enabled = true;
    }
    GUILayout.FlexibleSpace();
    GUILayout.EndHorizontal();
  }
  GUILayout.FlexibleSpace();
  GUILayout.EndVertical();
  //print ("building grid!");
}

function BuildDeck()
{
```

```
var totalRobots:int = 4;   // we've got four robots to work with
var card:Card; // this stores a reference to a card
var id:int = 0;

   for(var i:int=0; i<totalRobots; i++)
{
   var aRobotParts:List.<String> = new List.<String>();

   aRobotParts.Add("Head");
   aRobotParts.Add("Arm");
   aRobotParts.Add("Leg");

   for(var j:int=0; j<2; j++)
   {
      var someNum:int = Random.Range(0, aRobotParts.Count);
      var theMissingPart:String = aRobotParts[someNum];

      aRobotParts.RemoveAt(someNum);

      card = new Card("robot" + (i+1) + "Missing" + theMissingPart,
         id);
      aCards.Add(card);

      card= new Card("robot" + (i+1) + theMissingPart, id);
      aCards.Add(card);
      id++;
   }
  }
}


function FlipCardFaceUp(card:Card)
{
   card.isFaceUp = true;

   if(aCardsFlipped.IndexOf(card) < 0)
   {
   aCardsFlipped.Add(card);

   if(aCardsFlipped.Count == 2)
   {
      playerCanClick = false;

      yield WaitForSeconds(1);
```

```
      if(aCardsFlipped[0].id == aCardsFlipped[1].id)
      {
        // Match!
        aCardsFlipped[0].isMatched = true;
        aCardsFlipped[1].isMatched = true;

        matchesMade ++;

        if(matchesMade >= matchesNeededToWin)
        {
          playerHasWon = true;
        }

      } else {
        aCardsFlipped[0].isFaceUp = false;
        aCardsFlipped[1].isFaceUp = false;
      }

      aCardsFlipped = new List.<Card>();

      playerCanClick = true;
    }
  }
}



class Card extends System.Object
{
  var isFaceUp:boolean = false;
  var isMatched:boolean = false;
  var img:String;
  var id:int;

  function Card(img:String, id:int)
  {
    this.img = img;
    this.id = id;
  }
}
```

C# Addendum

Let's see what it takes to convert this script from Unity JavaScript to C#. The complete C# script is shown in the following code snippet:

```
using UnityEngine;
using System.Collections;
using System.Collections.Generic;

public class GameScriptCSharp : MonoBehaviour
{

    private int cols = 4; // the number of columns in the card grid
    private int rows = 4; // the number of rows in the card grid
    private int totalCards = 16;
    private int matchesNeededToWin;
    private int matchesMade = 0; // At the outset, the player has not
        made any matches
    private int cardW = 100; // Each card's width and height is 100
        pixels
    private int cardH = 100;
    private List<Card> aCards; // We'll store all the cards we create
        in this array
    private Card[,] aGrid; // This 2d array will keep track of the
        shuffled, dealt cards
    private List<Card> aCardsFlipped; // This generic array list
        will store the two cards that the player flips over
    private bool playerCanClick; // We'll use this flag to prevent
        the player from clicking buttons when we don't want him to
    private bool playerHasWon = false; // Store whether or not the
        player has won. This should probably start out false :)


    private void Start()
    {
        matchesNeededToWin = totalCards / 2; // If there are 16 cards,
            the player needs to find 8 matches to clear the board

        playerCanClick = true; // We should let the player play, don't
            you think?

        // Initialize some empty Collections:
        aCards = new List<Card>(); // this Generic List is our deck
            of cards. It can only ever hold instances of the Card class.
```

```
    aGrid = new Card[rows,cols]; // The rows and cols variables
      help us define the dimensions of this 2D array
    aCardsFlipped = new List<Card>(); // This List will store the
      two cards the player flips over.

    BuildDeck();

    // Loop through the total number of rows in our aGrid List:
    for(int i = 0; i<rows; i++)
    {
      // For each individual grid row, loop through the total
        number of columns in the grid:
      for(int j = 0; j<cols; j++)
      {
        int someNum = Random.Range(0,aCards.Count);
        aGrid[i,j] = aCards[someNum];
        aCards.RemoveAt(someNum);
      }
    }
}

private void OnGUI()
{
  GUILayout.BeginArea (new Rect (0,0,Screen.width,Screen.height));
  BuildGrid();
  if(playerHasWon) BuildWinPrompt();
  GUILayout.EndArea();
}

private void BuildWinPrompt()
{
  int winPromptW = 120;
  int winPromptH = 90;

  float halfScreenW = Screen.width/2;
  float halfScreenH = Screen.height/2;

  int halfPromptW = winPromptW/2;
  int halfPromptH = winPromptH/2;

  GUI.BeginGroup(new Rect(halfScreenW-halfPromptW, halfScreenH-
    halfPromptH, winPromptW, winPromptH));
```

```
    GUI.Box (new Rect (0,0,winPromptW,winPromptH), "A Winner
      is You!!");

    int buttonW = 80;
    int buttonH = 20;

    if(GUI.Button(new Rect(halfPromptW-(buttonW/2),
      halfPromptH-(buttonH/2),buttonW,buttonH),"Play Again"))
    {
      Application.LoadLevel("Title");
    }
    GUI.EndGroup();
}


private void BuildGrid()
{

  GUILayout.BeginVertical();
  GUILayout.FlexibleSpace();
  for(int i = 0; i<rows; i++)
  {
    GUILayout.BeginHorizontal();
    GUILayout.FlexibleSpace();
    for(int j = 0; j<cols; j++)
    {
        Card card = aGrid[i,j];
        string img;
        if(card.isMatched)
        {
          img = "blank";
        } else {

          if(card.isFaceUp)
          {
            img = card.img;
          } else {
            img = "wrench";
          }

        }

        GUI.enabled = !card.isMatched;
```

```
      if(GUILayout.Button((Texture2D)Resources.Load(img,
        typeof(Texture2D)), GUILayout.Width(cardW)))
      {
        print ("playerCanClick = " + playerCanClick);
        if(playerCanClick)
        {
          FlipCardFaceUp(card);
        }
      }
      GUI.enabled = true;
    }
    GUILayout.FlexibleSpace();
    GUILayout.EndHorizontal();
  }
  GUILayout.FlexibleSpace();
  GUILayout.EndVertical();
}

private void BuildDeck()
{
  int totalRobots = 4;  // we've got four robots to work with
  Card card; // this stores a reference to a card
  int id = 0;

  for(int i = 0; i<totalRobots; i++)
  {
    List<string> aRobotParts = new List<string>();

    aRobotParts.Add("Head");
    aRobotParts.Add("Arm");
    aRobotParts.Add("Leg");

    for(int j=0; j<2; j++)
    {
      int someNum = Random.Range(0, aRobotParts.Count);
      string theMissingPart = aRobotParts[someNum];

      aRobotParts.RemoveAt(someNum);

      card = new Card("robot" + (i+1) + "Missing" + theMissingPart,
        id);
      aCards.Add(card);
```

```
            card= new Card("robot" + (i+1) + theMissingPart, id);
            aCards.Add(card);
            id++;
        }
    }
}

private void FlipCardFaceUp(Card card)
{
    card.isFaceUp = true;

    if(aCardsFlipped.IndexOf(card) < 0)
    {
     aCardsFlipped.Add(card);

        if(aCardsFlipped.Count == 2)
        {
          playerCanClick = false;

          Invoke("CheckCards", 1);
        }
    }
}

private void CheckCards()
{
  if(aCardsFlipped[0].id == aCardsFlipped[1].id)
  {
    // Match!
    aCardsFlipped[0].isMatched = true;
    aCardsFlipped[1].isMatched = true;

    matchesMade ++;

    if(matchesMade >= matchesNeededToWin)
    {
      playerHasWon = true;
    }
```

```
  } else {
    aCardsFlipped[0].isFaceUp = false;
    aCardsFlipped[1].isFaceUp = false;
  }

  aCardsFlipped = new List<Card>();

  playerCanClick = true;
  }

}
```

Most of the conversion work here is standard. You have to change the way variables are declared by putting the type before the variable name, and deleting the colon. You should add the **private** access modifier to your functions and variables. You should add `void` to most functions, because they don't return a value. No problem! We've seen all this before.

The only significant change to the code is the way we're treating that `yield` command. In JavaScript, it's a trifle. In C#, using `yield` is a little more complex, and it involves splitting your code into a separate function and returning `IEnumerator` data types and all manner of things that curl the hair of a Beginner's Guide author.

To make things simple, we've replaced `yield` with the simple and elegant `Invoke` function. Here's how it works:

```
Invoke("CheckCards", 1);
```

This means that your code grinds to a halt for one second, after which it fires the `CheckCards` function. So we've moved the function's remaining code into a new function called `CheckCards`. When the player flips a second card, there's a 1 second pause, and then the `CheckCards` function runs.

The `Invoke` function is so simple and elegant; you could put it in a puffy dress and take it to prom.

7

Don't Be a Clock Blocker

We've taken a baby game like Memory and made it slightly cooler by changing the straight-up match mechanism and adding a twist: matching disembodied robot parts to their bodies. Robot Repair is a tiny bit more interesting and more challenging thanks to this simple modification.

There are lots of ways we could make the game even more difficult: we could quadruple the number of robots, crank the game up to a 20x20 card grid, or rig Unity up to some peripheral device that issues a low-grade electrical shock to the player's fiddly bits every time he doesn't find a match. NOW who's making a baby game?

These ideas could take a lot of time though, and the **Return-On-Investment** *(ROI) we see from these features may not be worth the effort. One cheap, effective way of amping up the game experience is to add a clock. Games have used clocks to make us nervous for time immemorial, and it's hard to find a video game in existence that doesn't include some sort of time pressure—from the increasing speed of falling Tetris pieces, to the countdown clock in every Super Mario Bros. level, to the hourglass timers packaged with many popular board games like Boggle, Taboo, and Scattergories.*

Apply pressure

What if the player only has *x* seconds to find all the matches in the Robot Repair game? Or what if, in our keep-up game, the player has to bounce the ball without dropping it until the timer runs out in order to advance to the next level? In this chapter, let's:

◆ Program a text-based countdown clock to add a little pressure to our games

◆ Modify the clock to make it graphical, with an ever-shrinking horizontal bar

◆ Layer in some new code and graphics to create a pie chart-style clock

| Text Clock | Bar Clock | Pie Clock |

That's three different countdown clocks, all running from the same initial code, all ready to be put to work in whatever Unity games you dream up. Roll up your sleeves—it's time to start coding!

Time for action – preparing the Clock Script

Open your Robot Repair game project and make sure you're in the **game Scene**. As we've done in earlier chapters, we'll create an empty **GameObject** and glue some code to it.

1. Navigate to **GameObject | Create Empty**.

2. Rename the empty GameObject `Clock`.

3. Create a new **JavaScript** and name it `ClockScript`.

4. Drag-and-drop the **ClockScript** onto the **Clock** GameObject.

No problem! We know the drill by now—we've got a **GameObject** ready to go with an empty script where we'll put all of our clock code.

Time for more action – preparing the clock text

In order to display the numbers, we need to add a **GUIText** component to the **Clock** GameObject, but there's one problem: **GUIText** defaults to white, which isn't so hot for a game with a white background. Let's make a quick adjustment to the game background color so that we can see what's going on. We can change it back later.

1. Select the **Main Camera** in the **Hierarchy** panel.

2. Find the **Camera** component in the **Inspector** panel.

3. Click on the color swatch labeled **Background**, and change it to something darker so that our piece of white **GUIText** will show up against it. I chose a "delightful" puce (R157 G99 B120).

4. Select the **Clock** GameObject from the **Hierarchy** panel. It's not a bad idea to look in the **Inspector** panel and confirm that **ClockScript** was added as a component in the preceding instruction.

5. With the **Clock** GameObject selected, navigate to **Component | Rendering | GUIText**. This is the **GUIText** component that we'll use to display the clock numbers on the screen.

6. In the **Inspector** panel, find the **GUIText** component and type `whatever` in the blank **Text** property.

7. In the **Inspector** panel, change the clock's **Position** to X: 0.8 Y: 0.9 Z: 0 to bring it into view. You should see the word **whatever** in white, floating near the top-right corner of the screen in the **Game** view.

8. Right, then! We have a **GameObject** with an empty script attached. That **GameObject** has a **GUIText** component to display the clock numbers. Our game background is certifiably hideous. Let's code us some clock.

Still time for action – changing the clock text color

Double-click on **ClockScript**. Your empty script, with the default the `Start()` and `Update()` functions and the `#pragma strict` line, should appear in the code editor. The very first thing we should consider is doing away with our puce background by changing the **GUIText** color to black instead of white. Let's get at it:

1. Replace the `Start` function with the built-in `Awake` function and change the **GUIText** color:

```
function Awake()
{
    guiText.color = Color.black;
}
function Update() {
}
```

2. Save the script and test your game to see your new black text.

As we've seen before, `Awake` is a built-in function just like `Start`, but it happens even earlier. `Awake` is the first function that gets called when our script runs.

If you feel comfy, you can change the game background color back to white by clicking on the **Main Camera** GameObject and finding the color swatch in the **Inspector** panel. The white **whatever** GUIText will disappear against the white background in the **Game** view because the color-changing code that we just wrote runs only when we test the game (try testing the game to confirm this). You can change the text color to black by default by clicking on the **Color** swatch in the **GUIText** component, but it's useful to prove that you can do the same thing through code.

If you're happy with the crummy-looking default font, you can move on to the **Prepare the clock code** section. But, if you want to put in a little extra elbow grease to *see* the text in a font of your choosing, follow these next steps.

Time for action rides again – creating Font Texture and Material

Ha! I knew you couldn't resist. In order to change the font of this **GUIText**, we need to import a font, hook it up to a **Material**, and apply that **Material** to the **GUIText**.

1. Find a font that you want to use for your game clock. I like the LOLCats standby *Impact*. If you're running Windows, your fonts are likely to be in the C:\Windows\Fonts directory. If you're a Mac user, you should look in the /Library/Fonts/ folder. Stick with a **.ttf (TrueType Font)** if you want to have the most success.

2. Drag the font into the **Project** panel in unity. The font will be added to your list of **Assets**. (Remember to create a Fonts folder to store it, if you want to keep your **Project** panel tidy).

3. Right-click (or alternate-click) on an empty area of the **Project** panel and navigate to **Create | Material**. You can also click on the **Create** button at the top of the panel.

4. Rename the new **Material** to something useful. Because I'm using the *Impact* font, and it's going to be black, I named mine BlackImpact (incidentally, "Black Impact" is also the name of my favorite exploitation film from the 1970s). Again, you can place the new Material in a folder that you create called Materials.

5. Click on the **Material** you just created in the **Project** Panel.

6. In the **Inspector** panel, click on the color swatch labeled **Main Color** and choose black (R0 G0 B0), then click on the little red **X** to close the color picker.

7. In the empty square area labeled **None (Texture 2D)**, click on the **Select** button, and choose your font from the list of textures (mine was labeled **impact - font texture**). If your font texture doesn't appear in the list, open the font in the **Project** panel, and drag-and-drop the font texture into the **None (Texture 2D)** area.

8. At the top of the **Inspector** panel, there's a drop-down labeled **Shader**. Select **GUI/ Text Shader** from the list.

9. Click on the **Clock** GameObject in the **Hierarchy** panel.

10. Find the **GUIText** component in the **Inspector** panel.

11. Click and drag your font—the one with the letter **A** icon—from the **Project** panel into the parameter labeled **Font** in the **GUIText** component. You can also click on the circular button next to the parameter labeled **None (Font)** and choose your font from the pop-up list.

12. Similarly, click-and-drag your **Material**—the one with the gray sphere icon—from the **Project** panel into the parameter labeled **Material** in the **GUIText** component. You can also click on the circle button (the parameter should say **None (Material)** initially) and choose your **Material** from the list.

Just as you always dreamed about since childhood, the **GUIText** changes to a solid black version of the fancy font you chose! Now, you can definitely get rid of that horrid puce background and switch back to white for the remainder of the project. If you made it this far and you're using a **Material** instead of the naked font option, or if you've changed the **Color** swatch to black in the **Inspector** Panel, it's also safe to delete the `guiText.material.color = Color.black;` line from the **ClockScript**.

Time for action – what's with the tiny font?

The Impact font, or any other font you choose, won't be very impactful at its default size. Let's change the import settings to biggify it.

1. Click on your imported font—the one with the letter **A** icon—in the **Project** panel.

2. In the **Inspector** panel, you'll see the **True Type Font Importer**. Change the **Font Size** to something respectable, like 32, and press the *Enter* key on your keyboard.

3. Click on the **Apply** button. Magically, your **GUIText** cranks up to 32 points (you'll only see this happen if you still have a piece of text like `"whatever"` entered into the **Text** parameter of the **GUIText** of the **Clock** GameObject component).

What just happened – was that seriously magic?

Of course, there's nothing magical about it. Here's what happened when you clicked on that **Apply** button.

When you import a font into Unity, an entire set of raster images is created for you by the True Type Font Importer. **Raster images** are the ones that look all pixelly and square when you zoom in on them. Fonts are inherently vector instead of raster, which means that they use math to describe their curves and angles. Vector images can be scaled up any size without going all Rubik's Cube on you.

But, Unity doesn't yet support vector fonts. For every font size that you want to support, you need to import a new version of the font and change its import settings to a different size. This means that you may have four copies of, say, the Impact font, at the four different sizes you require.

When you click on the **Apply** button, Unity creates its set of raster images based on the font that you're importing.

Time for action – preparing the clock code

Let's rough in a few empty functions and three variables that we'll need to make the clock work.

1. Open up the **ClockScript** by double-clicking on it. Update the code:

```
#pragma strict
var clockIsPaused : boolean = false;
var startTime : float; //(in seconds)
var timeRemaining : float; //(in seconds)
function Awake()
{
}

function Update() {
  if (!clockIsPaused)
  {
    // make sure the timer is not paused
    DoCountdown();
  }
}

function DoCountdown() {
}

function PauseClock()
{
    clockIsPaused = true;
}
```

```
function UnpauseClock()
{
    clockIsPaused = false;
}

function ShowTime()
{
}

function TimeIsUp()
{
}
```

What just happened – that's a whole lotta nothing

Here, we've created a list of functions that we'll probably need to get our clock working. The functions are mostly empty, but that's okay—roughing them in like this is a really valid and useful way to program. We have a DoCountdown() function that we call on every update, as long as our clockIsPaused flag is false. We have PauseClock() and UnpauseClock() functions—each of them needs only one simple line of code to change the clockIsPaused flag, so we've included that. In the ShowTime() function, we'll display the time in the **GUIText** component. Finally, we'll call the TimeIsUp() function when the clock reaches zero.

At the top of the script are three hopefully self-explanatory variables: a Boolean to hold the clock's paused state, a floating point number to hold the start time, and another to hold the remaining time.

Now that we have the skeleton of our clock code and we see the scope of work ahead of us, we can dive in and flesh it out.

Time for action – creating the countdown logic

Let's set the startTime variable, and build the logic to handle the counting-down functionality of our clock.

1. Set the startTime variable:

    ```
    function Awake() {
        startTime = Time.time + 5.0;
    }
    ```

> Five seconds to beat the game is a bit ridiculous. We're just keeping
> the time tight for testing. You can crank this variable up later.

2. Decrease the amount of time on the clock:

```
function DoCountdown()
{
    timeRemaining = startTime - Time.time;
}
```

3. If the clock hits zero, pause the clock and call the `TimeIsUp()` function:

```
timeRemaining = startTime - Time.time;
if (timeRemaining < 0)
{
    timeRemaining = 0;
    clockIsPaused = true;
    TimeIsUp();
}
```

4. Add some `Debug` statements so that you can see something happening:

```
function DoCountdown()
{
    // (other lines omitted for clarity)
    Debug.Log("time remaining = " + timeRemaining);
}

function TimeIsUp()
{
    Debug.Log("Time is up!");
}
```

5. Save the script and test your game.

You should see the `Debug` statements in the information bar at the bottom of the screen.
When the clock finishes ticking down through five seconds, you'll see the **Time is up!**
message... if you're a mutant with super-speed vision. The **Time is up!** message gets wiped
out by the next "time remaining" message, which continues to be called whether the clock
is at zero or not. If you want to see it with normal-people vision, open the Console window
(**Window | Console** in the menu) and watch for it in the list of printed statements.

If the **building grid!** print statement from the previous chapters is cluttering up your console window, it's safe to comment that line out with a double slash //.

```
Console
Clear | Collapse | Clear on Play | Error Pause                    ① 643  ⚠ 1  ⓘ 0
① time remaining = 0.1092467
  UnityEngine.Debug:Log(Object)
① time remaining = 0.0926795
  UnityEngine.Debug:Log(Object)
① time remaining = 0.07611322
  UnityEngine.Debug:Log(Object)
① time remaining = 0.05954647
  UnityEngine.Debug:Log(Object)
① time remaining = 0.04297972
  UnityEngine.Debug:Log(Object)
① time remaining = 0.02641344
  UnityEngine.Debug:Log(Object)
① time remaining = 0.009845734
  UnityEngine.Debug:Log(Object)
① Time is up!
  UnityEngine.Debug:Log(Object)
① time remaining = 0
  UnityEngine.Debug:Log(Object)
```

Time for action – displaying the time on-screen

We know from the Debug statements that the clock is working, so all we need to do is stick the timeRemaining value into our **GUIText** to see it on the screen. But, it won't look very clock-like unless we perform a tiny bit of math on that value to split it into minutes and seconds, so that five seconds displays as 0:05, or 119 seconds displays as 1:59.

1. Call the ShowTime() function from within the DoCountdown() function (you can delete or comment the Debug.Log() statement):

```
function DoCountdown()
{
    timeRemaining = startTime - Time.time;
    // (other lines omitted for clarity)
    ShowTime();
    //Debug.Log("time remaining = " + timeRemaining);
}
```

2. Create some variables to store the minutes and seconds values in the `ShowTime()` function, along with a variable to store the `string` (text) version of the time:

```
function ShowTime() {
    var minutes : int;
    var seconds : int;
    var timeStr : String;
}
```

3. Just below that, divide the `timeRemaining` by `60` to get the number of minutes that have elapsed:

```
var timeStr : String;
minutes = timeRemaining/60;
```

4. Store the remainder as the number of elapsed seconds:

```
minutes = timeRemaining/60;
seconds = timeRemaining % 60;
```

5. Set the text version of the time to the number of elapsed minutes, followed by a colon:

```
seconds = timeRemaining % 60;
timeStr = minutes.ToString() + ":";
```

6. Append (add) the text version of the elapsed seconds:

```
timeStr = minutes.ToString() + ":";
timeStr += seconds.ToString("D2");
```

7. Finally, push the `timeStr` value to the **GUIText** component:

```
timeStr += seconds.ToString("D2");
guiText.text = timeStr; //display the time to the GUI
```

8. To gaze at your clock longingly as it counts down every delectable second, crank up the `startTime` amount in the `Awake` function:

```
startTime = Time.time + 120.0;
```

9. Save and test.

Your beautiful new game clock whiles away the hours in your own chosen font at your own chosen size, formatted with a colon like any self-respecting game clock should be.

What just happened – what about that terrifying code?

There are a few kooky things going on in the code we just wrote. Let's home in on the new and weird stuff.

```
minutes = timeRemaining/60;
```

We set the value of the minutes variable by dividing `timeRemaining` by 60. If there were 120 seconds left, dividing by 60 means there are two minutes on the clock. If there were only 11 seconds left on the clock, dividing by 60 gives us 0.183 repeating.

The reason why we don't see 0.1833333 in the "minutes" portion of our clock is a sneaky data type trick: `timeRemaining` is a `float` (floating point number), so it can remember decimal places. Our `minutes` variable is an `int` (integer), which *can't* remember decimal places. So, when we feed 0.183333 into an `int` variable, it just snips off everything after the decimal. It can't remember that stuff, so why bother? The result is that `minutes` is set to 0, which is what we see on the clock.

I know that earlier, we said it's slightly less processor intensive to multiply than to divide. So why are we dividing by 60 to get our minutes count? Because the alternative is to multiply by 0.0166666666666666666666666666666667, which frightens me.

```
seconds = timeRemaining % 60;
```

This unnerving little percent-symbol beastie performs a *modulo* operation, which is like those exercises you did in grade three math class when you were just about to learn long division. A *modulo* operation is like a division, except it results in the remainder of your operation. Here are a few examples:

- 4 % 2 = 0, because 2 goes into 4 twice with no remainder

- 11 % 10 = 1, because 10 goes into 11 once with 1 as the remainder (10+1 = 11)

- 28 % 5 = 3, because 5 goes into 28 five times (5*5=25), with a remainder of 3 (25+3 = 28)

```
timeStr = minutes.ToString() + ":";
```

The `int.ToString()` method works exactly as advertised, converting an integer to a String. All data types have `ToString()` methods, though some are more helpful than others. At the end of this line, we're tacking on a colon (:) to visually separate the minutes from the seconds.

```
timeStr += seconds.ToString("D2");
```

The += operator, you'll remember, takes what we've already got and adds something new to it—in this case, it's seconds.ToString();. We're passing the special argument D2 to the ToString() method to round to the nearest two decimal places so that the clock looks like: 4:02 instead of 4:2.

Nifty!

Whatever is the problem?

If you still have **whatever** as your placeholder text, now's a good time to consider ditching it. It shows up on-screen for a split-second before the numbers appear. Yuck! Click on the **Clock** GameObject in the **Hierarchy** panel, and clear out the value marked **Text** in the **GUIText** component in the **Inspector** panel.

Picture it

Number clocks look alright, but graphical clocks really get me revved up and ready for some pressurized pants-wetting. Nothing denotes white-knuckled urgency like a bar that's slowly draining. We don't need to do much extra work to convert our number clock into a picture clock, so let's go for it!

Time for action – grabbing the picture clock graphics

As per our agreement, all the pretty pictures are pre-drawn for you. Download the Unity assets package for this chapter. When you're ready to import it, navigate to **Assets | Import Package | Custom Package...** and find the .unitypackage file. Open it up, and there she be! If only obtaining game graphics in a real production environment was this easy.

Let's get right to work by creating some code to make use of two of the graphics in the package—a blue clock background bar, and a shiny yellow foreground bar that will slowly shrink as time marches on.

1. Let's go back to the top of the **ClockScript** and create a variable to store the elapsed time as a percentage:

```
var clockIsPaused : boolean = false;
var startTime : float; //(in seconds)
var timeRemaining : float; //(in seconds)
var percent:float;
```

2. Create some variables to store the foreground (FG) and background (BG) textures, as well as the initial width of the yellow foreground bar:

```
var percent:float;
var clockBG:Texture2D;
var clockFG:Texture2D;
var clockFGMaxWidth:float; // the starting width of the
    foreground bar
```

3. Save the script and go back to Unity.

4. Click on the **Clock** GameObject in the **Hierarchy** panel.

5. Find the **ClockScript** component in the **Inspector** Panel.

6. The new `clockBG` and `clockFG` variables we just created are now listed there. Click-and-drag the `clockBG` texture from the **Project** panel to the `clockBG` slot, and then click-and-drag the `clockFG` texture into its slot.

What just happened – you can do that?

This is yet another example of Unity's drag-and-drop usefulness. We created the two `Texture2D` variables, and the variables appeared on the **Script** component in the **Inspector** panel. We dragged-and-dropped two textures into those slots, and now whenever we refer to `clockBG` and `clockFG` in code, we'll be talking about those two texture images. Handy, yes?

Time for action – Flex those GUI muscles

Let's take a trip down memory lane to the previous chapter, where we became `OnGUI` ninjas. We'll use the GUI techniques we already know to display the two bars, and shrink the foreground bar as time runs out.

1. In the `DoCountdown` function of the **ClockScript**, calculate the percentage of time elapsed by comparing the `startTime` and the `timeRemaining` values:

```
function DoCountdown()
{
  timeRemaining = startTime - Time.time;
  percent = timeRemaining/startTime * 100;
  if (timeRemaining < 0)
  {
```

```
            timeRemaining = 0;
            clockIsPaused = true;
            TimeIsUp();
        }
        ShowTime();
    }
```

2. Store the initial width of the `clockFG` graphic in a variable called `clockFGMaxWidth` in the `Awake` function:

```
function Awake()
{
    startTime = 120.0;
    clockFGMaxWidth = clockFG.width;
}
```

3. Create the built-in `OnGUI` function somewhere apart from the other functions in your script (make sure you don't create it inside the curly brackets of some other function!)

```
function OnGUI()
{
    var newBarWidth:float = (percent/100) * clockFGMaxWidth;
    // this is the width that the foreground bar should be
    var gap:int = 20; // a spacing variable to help us position
       the clock
}
```

4. Create a new group to contain the `clockBG` texture. We'll position the group so that the `clockBG` graphic appears 20 pixels down, and 20 away from the right edge of the screen:

```
function OnGUI()
{
    var newBarWidth:float = (percent/100) * clockFGMaxWidth;
    // this is the width that the foreground bar should be
    var gap:int = 20; // a spacing variable to help us position
       the clock
    GUI.BeginGroup (new Rect(Screen.width - clockBG.width - gap,
       gap, clockBG.width, clockBG.height));
    GUI.EndGroup ();
}
```

5. Use the `DrawTexture` method to draw the `clockBG` texture inside the group:

```
GUI.BeginGroup (new Rect (Screen.width - clockBG.width - gap,
  gap, clockBG.width, clockBG.height));
GUI.DrawTexture (Rect (0,0, clockBG.width, clockBG.height),
  clockBG);
GUI.EndGroup ();
```

6. Nest another group inside the first group to hold the `clockFG` texture. Notice that we're offsetting it by a few pixels (5,6) so that it appears inside the `clockBG` graphic:

```
GUI.BeginGroup (new Rect (Screen.width - clockBG.width - gap,
  gap, clockBG.width, clockBG.height));
GUI.DrawTexture (Rect (0,0, clockBG.width, clockBG.height),
  clockBG);
GUI.BeginGroup (new Rect (5, 6, newBarWidth, clockFG.height));
GUI.EndGroup ();
GUI.EndGroup ();
```

Here, I've indented the second group to make the code easier to read.

7. Now, draw the `clockFG` texture inside that nested group:

```
GUI.BeginGroup (new Rect (5, 6, newBarWidth, clockFG.height));
GUI.DrawTexture (Rect (0,0, clockFG.width, clockFG.height),
  clockFG);
GUI.EndGroup ();
```

Did you punch that in correctly? Here's what the entire function looks like all at once:

```
function OnGUI()
{
  var newBarWidth:float = (percent/100) * clockFGMaxWidth;
  // this is the width that the foreground bar should be
  var gap:int = 20; // a spacing variable to help us position
    the clock
  GUI.BeginGroup (new Rect (Screen.width - clockBG.width - gap,
    gap, clockBG.width, clockBG.height));
  GUI.DrawTexture (Rect (0,0, clockBG.width, clockBG.height),
    clockBG);
```

```
        GUI.BeginGroup (new Rect (5, 6, newBarWidth,
           clockFG.height));
        GUI.DrawTexture (Rect (0,0, clockFG.width,
           clockFG.height), clockFG);
        GUI.EndGroup ();
    GUI.EndGroup ();
}
```

Save the script and jump back into Unity. Let's turn off the old and busted number clock so that we can marvel at the new hotness—our graphical clock. Select the **Clock** GameObject in the **Hierarchy** panel. Locate the **GUIText** component in the **Inspector** panel, and uncheck its check box to turn off its rendering.

Now, test your game. Fantastic! Your new graphical clock drains ominously as time runs out. That'll really put the heat on, without compromising your player's doubtless lust for eye candy.

What just happened – how does it work?

The math behind this magic is simple ratio stuff that I, for one, conveniently forgot the moment I escaped the sixth grade and ran away to become a kid who enjoys watching the circus. We converted the time elapsed into a percentage of the total time on the clock. Then, we used that percentage to figure out how wide the `clockFG` graphic should be. Percentage of time elapsed is to 100, as the width of the `clockFG` graphic is to its original width. It's simple algebra from there.

The only math you need to know

I often say that this dead-simple ratio stuff is the only math you need to know as a game developer. I'm half-kidding, of course. Developers with a firm grasp of trigonometry can create billiard and pinball games, while Developers who know differential calculus can create a tank game where the enemy AI knows which way to aim its turret, taking trajectory, wind, and gravity into account (hey, kids! Stay in school).

But, when people ask sheepishly about programming and how difficult it is to learn, it's usually because they think you can only create games by using complex mathematical equations. We've hopefully debunked this myth by creating two simple games so far with equally simple math. These ratio calculations are used ALL THE TIME in gaming, from figuring out health bars, to player positions on a mini-map, to level progress meters. If you're arithmophobic like I am, and you relearn only one piece of math from your long-forgotten elementary school days, make it this one.

The incredible shrinking clock

We've seen in earlier chapters that the `GUI.BeginGroup()` and `GUI.EndGroup()` functions can wrap our fixed-position UI controls together so that we can move them around as a unit. In the preceding code, we made one group to hold the background bar, and another inside it to hold the foreground bar, offset slightly. The outer group is positioned near the right edge of the screen, using the gap value of 20 pixels to set it back from the screen edges.

When we draw the foreground clock bar, we draw it at its normal size, but the group that wraps it is drawn at the shrinking size, so it cuts the texture off. If you put a 500 x 500 pixel texture inside a 20 x 20 pixel group, you'll only see a 20 x 20 pixel portion of the larger image. We use this to our advantage to display an ever-decreasing section of our clock bar.

Keep your fork – there's pie!

The third type of clock we'll build is a pie chart-style clock. Here's what it will look like when it's counting down:

Pop quiz – how do we build it?

Before reading any further, stare at the picture of the pie clock and try to figure out how you would build it if you didn't have this book in front of you. As a new game developer, you'll spend a significant amount of time trying to mimic or emulate different effects you see in the games you enjoy. It's almost like watching a magic show and trying to figure out how they did it. So, how'd they do it?

(If you need a hint, take a look at the unused textures in the **Project** panel that you imported earlier in the chapter).

How they did it

The pie clock involves a little sleight of hand. Here are the pieces that make up the clock:

It's a bit like a sandwich. We start by drawing the blue background. Then, we layer on the two yellow half-moon pieces. To make the clock look pretty, we apply the lovely, shiny gloss picture in front of all these pieces.

We rotate the right half-moon piece halfway around the circle to make the slice of yellow time appear to grow smaller and smaller.

At the halfway point, we slap a half-moon section of the blue background on top of everything, on the right side of the clock. We're all done with the right half-circle, so we don't draw it.

Now, we rotate the left half-moon piece, and it disappears behind the blocker graphic, creating the illusion that the rest of the clock is depleting.

When time is up, we slap the red clock graphic in front of everything.

A little flourish of the wrist, a puff of smoke, and the audience doesn't suspect a thing!

Time for action – rigging up the textures

We know most of what we need to get started. There's just a little trick with rotating the textures that we have to learn. But, first, let's set up our clock with the variables we'll need to draw the textures to the screen.

1. Add variables for the new pie clock textures at the top of the **ClockScript**:

    ```
    var clockFGMaxWidth:float; // the starting width of the
        foreground bar
    var rightSide:Texture2D;
    var leftSide:Texture2D;
    var back:Texture2D;
    var blocker:Texture2D;
    var shiny:Texture2D;
    var finished:Texture2D;
    ```

2. In the **Hierarchy** panel, select the **Clock** GameObject.

3. Just as we did with the bar clock, drag-and-drop the pie clock textures from the **Project** panel into their respective slots in the **ClockScript** component in the **Inspector** panel. When you're finished, it should look like this:

Time for action – writing the pie chart script

With these `Texture2D` variables defined, and the images stored in those variables, we can control the images with our script. Let's lay down some code, and pick through the aftermath when we're finished:

1. Because of the switcheroo we have to pull off with the two yellow half-moon pieces, knowing when the clock has passed the halfway point is pretty important with this clock. Let's create an `isPastHalfway` variable inside our `OnGUI` function:

   ```
   function OnGUI ()
   {
       var isPastHalfway:boolean = percent < 50;
   ```

   (Confused? Remember that our `percent` variable means "percent remaining", not "percent elapsed". When percent is less than 50, we've passed the halfway mark).

2. Define a rectangle in which to draw the textures:

```
var isPastHalfway:boolean = percent < 50;
var clockRect:Rect = Rect(0, 0, 128, 128);
```

3. On the next line, draw the background blue texture and the foreground shiny texture:

```
var clockRect:Rect = Rect(0, 0, 128, 128);
GUI.DrawTexture(clockRect, back, ScaleMode.StretchToFill,
    true, 0);
GUI.DrawTexture(clockRect, shiny, ScaleMode.StretchToFill,
    true, 0);
```

4. Save the script and play the game. You should see your shiny blue clock glimmering at you in the top-left corner of the screen:

5. Next, we'll add a condition check and draw the red "finished" graphic over the top of everything when percent goes below zero (which means that time is up). Add that bit just above the "shiny" texture draw so that the shiny picture still layers on top of the red "finished" graphic:

```
GUI.DrawTexture(clockRect, back, ScaleMode.StretchToFill,
    true, 0);
if(percent < 0)
{
```

```
    GUI.DrawTexture(clockRect, finished, ScaleMode.StretchToFill,
        true, 0);
}
GUI.DrawTexture(clockRect, shiny, ScaleMode.StretchToFill,
    true,
    0);
```

6. Save the script and play the game again to confirm that it's working. When time runs out, your blue clock should turn red:

7. Let's set up a `rotation` variable at the top of the OnGUI function. We'll use the `percent` value to figure out how far along the 360 degree spectrum we should be rotating those yellow half-circle pieces. Note that once again, we're using the same ratio math that we used earlier with our bar clock:

```
var clockRect:Rect = Rect(0, 0,128,128);
var rot:float = (percent/100) * 360;
```

If you want to see it working, try adding a `Debug.Log()` or `print()` statement underneath to track the value of `rot`. The value should hit 360 when the clock times out.

8. We have to set two more variables before the fun begins—a `centerPoint` and a `startMatrix`. We'll go over both in a moment:

```
var rot:float = (percent/100) * 360;
var centerPoint:Vector2 = Vector2(64, 64);
var startMatrix:Matrix4x4  = GUI.matrix;
```

What just happened?

One important thing to know is that, unlike 3D **GameObjects** like the **Paddle** and **Ball** from our keep-up game, GUI textures can't be rotated. Even if you apply them to a **GameObject** and rotate the **GameObject**, the textures won't rotate (or will skew in a very strange way). We know we need to rotate those two half-circle pieces to make the pie clock count down, but because of this limitation, we'll have to find a creative workaround.

Here's the game plan: we're going to use a method of the GUIUtility class called RotateAroundPivot. The centerPoint value we created defines the point around which we'll rotate. RotateAroundPivot rotates the *entire GUI*. It's as if the GUI controls were stickers on a sheet of glass, and instead of rotating the stickers, we're rotating the sheet of glass.

So we're going to follow these steps to rotate those half-circles:

1. Draw the blue clock background.

2. Rotate the GUI using the rot (rotation) value we set.

3. Draw the yellow half-circle pieces in their rotated positions. This is like stamping pictures on a piece of paper with a stamp pad. The background has already been stamped. Then, we rotate the paper and stamp the half-circles on top of it.

4. Rotate the GUI back to its original position.

5. Draw or stamp the "finished" graphic (if the timer is finished) and the shiny image.

So, the background, the red "finished" image, and the shiny image all get drawn when the GUI is in its normal orientation, while the half-circle pieces get drawn when the GUI is rotated. Kinda neat, huh? That's what the startMatrix variable is all about. We're storing the matrix transformation of the GUI so that we can rotate it back to its "start" position later.

Time for action – commencing operation pie clock

Let's lay down some code to make those half-circle pieces rotate.

1. Set up a conditional statement so that we can draw different things before and after the halfway point:

```
GUI.DrawTexture(clockRect, back, ScaleMode.StretchToFill, true,
0);
if(isPastHalfway)
{
} else {
}
```

2. If we're not past halfway, rotate the GUI around the `centerPoint`. Draw the right side half-circle piece on top of the rotated GUI. Then, rotate the GUI back to its start position:

```
if(isPastHalfway)
{
} else {
  GUIUtility.RotateAroundPivot(-rot, centerPoint);
  GUI.DrawTexture(clockRect, rightSide,
    ScaleMode.StretchToFill, true, 0);
  GUI.matrix = startMatrix;
}
```

3. Save the script and test your game. You should see the right side half-circle piece rotating around the clock. But, we know it's not really rotating—the entire GUI is rotating, and we're stamping the image on the screen before resetting the rotation:

4. Draw the left half-circle once the GUI is back into position.

```
GUI.matrix = startMatrix;
GUI.DrawTexture(clockRect, leftSide, ScaleMode.StretchToFill,
  true, 0);
```

5. You can save and test at this point, too. The right half-circle disappears behind the left half-circle as it rotates, creating the illusion we're after:

6. It all comes crashing down after the halfway point, though. Let's fix that:

```
if(isPastHalfway)
{
    GUIUtility.RotateAroundPivot(-rot-180, centerPoint);
    GUI.DrawTexture(clockRect, leftSide, ScaleMode.StretchToFill,
        true, 0);
    GUI.matrix = startMatrix;
```

7. Save and test. Once we're past the halfway point, the left half-circle does its thing, but the illusion is ruined because we see it rotating into the right side of the clock:

We just need to draw that blue half-circle blocker graphic in front of it to complete the illusion:

```
GUI.matrix = startMatrix;
GUI.DrawTexture(clockRect, blocker, ScaleMode.StretchToFill,
    true, 0);
```

8. Save and test one last time. You should see your pie clock elapse exactly as described in the sales brochure.

What just happened – explaining away the loose ends

Hopefully, the code is straightforward. Notice that in this line:

```
GUIUtility.RotateAroundPivot(-rot, centerPoint);
```

We're sticking a minus sign on the `rot` value—that's like multiplying a number by negative one. If we don't do this, the half-circle will rotate in the opposite direction (try it yourself! Nix the minus sign and try out your game).

Similarly, in this line:

```
GUIUtility.RotateAroundPivot(-rot-180, centerPoint);
```

We're using the negative `rot` value, and we're subtracting 180 degrees. That's because the left half-circle is on the other side of the clock. Again, try getting rid of the `-180` and see what effect that has on your clock.

Another thing that you may want to try is changing the `centerPoint` value. Our pie clock graphics are 128x128 pixels, so the center point is at 64, 64. Mess around with that value and check out the funky stuff the clock starts doing.

```
GUI.matrix = startMatrix;
```

It's worth mentioning that this line locks the GUI back into position, based on the `startMatrix` value we stored.

```
GUI.DrawTexture(clockRect, leftSide, ScaleMode.StretchToFill,
   true,  0);
```

Did I catch you wondering what `ScaleMode.StretchToFill` was all about? There are three different settings you can apply here, all of which fill the supplied rectangle with the texture in a different way. Try looking them up in the Script Reference to read about what each one does.

Time for action – positioning and scaling the clock

The pie clock is pretty neat, but it's sadly stuck to the top-left corner of the screen. It would be great if we could make it any size we wanted, and if we could move it anywhere on the screen.

We're not far off from that goal. Follow these steps to get a dynamically positioned and scaled pie clock:

1. Create these variables at the top of the OnGUI function:

```
var pieClockX:int = 100;
var pieClockY:int = 50;

var pieClockW:int = 64; // clock width
var pieClockH:int = 64; // clock height

var pieClockHalfW:int = pieClockW * 0.5; // half the clock width
var pieClockHalfH:int = pieClockH * 0.5; // half the clock height
```

In this example, 100 and 50 are the X and Y values where I'd like the pie clock to appear on the screen. The clock builds out from its top-left corner. 64 and 64 are the width and height values I'd like to make the clock—that's exactly half the size of the original clock.

 Scaling the clock will result in some ugly image artifacting, so I don't really recommend it. In fact, plugging in non-uniform scale values like 57 x 64 will destroy the illusion completely! But, learning to make the clock's size dynamic is still a worthwhile coding exercise, so let's keep going.

2. Modify the clockRect declaration to make use of the new x, y, width, and height variables:

```
var clockRect:Rect = Rect(pieClockX, pieClockY, pieClockW,
    pieClockH);
```

3. Modify the centerPoint variable to make sure we're still hitting the dead-center of the clock:

```
var centerPoint:Vector2 = Vector2(pieClockX + pieClockHalfW,
    pieClockY + pieClockHalfH);
```

4. Save the script and test your game. You should see a pint-sized clock (with a few ugly pixels here and there) at x: 100 y: 50 on your screen.

Have a go hero – rock out with your clock out

There's lots more you could add to your clock to juice it up. Here are a few ideas:

- Add some logic to the `TimeIsUp()` method. You could pop up a new GUI window that says **Time is up!** with a **Try Again** button, or you could link to another **Scene** showing your player's character perishing in a blazing inferno... whatever you like!

- Create a **pause/unpause** button that starts and stops the timer. The `ClockScript` is already set up to do this—just toggle the `clockIsPaused` variable, create a variable to keep track of how many seconds elapse while the game is paused, and subtract that number from `timeRemaining`.

- In a few chapters, we'll talk about how to add sound to your games. Bring that knowledge back with you to this chapter to add some ticking and buzzer sound effects to your clock.

- Create a button that says **More Time!**. When you click on it, it should add more time to the clock. When you get this working, you can use this logic to add power-ups to your game that increase clock time.

- Use the skills that you've already acquired to tie this clock into any game that you create in Unity, including the keep-up and robot games you've built with this book.

Unfinished business

With this chapter, you've taken an important step in your journey as a game developer. Understanding how to build a game clock will serve you well in nearly all of the games you venture off to build. Games without some kind of clock or timer are uncommon, so adding this notch to your game developer tool belt is a real victory. Here are some skills you learned in this chapter:

- Creating a font material
- Displaying values on-screen with **GUIText**
- Converting numbers to strings
- Formatting string data to two decimal places
- Ratios: the only math you'll ever need (according to someone who doesn't know math!)
- Storing texture images in variables
- Scaling or snipping graphics based on script data
- Rotating, and then unrotating, the GUI
- Converting hardcoded script values to dynamic script values

With three chapters behind you on linking scenes with buttons, displaying title screens, adding clocks and on-screen counters, the keep-up game that we started so long ago is starting to seem a little weak. Let's return home like the mighty conquerors we are, and jazz it up with some of the new things we've learned. Then, we'll go even further, and start incorporating 3D models built in an actual 3D art package into our game **Scenes**.

C# Addendum

The **ClockScript** was fairly painless to convert to C#. These were the steps:

1. Copy/paste the JavaScript code into a new C# script (keeping the C# class definition and omitting the #pragma strict line)
2. Add the appropriate access modifier to the variable definitions (note: any variables that need to show up in the drag-n-drop Unity interface, like the ones that store the textures, need the `public` modifier. Use `private` for all other variables)
3. Change the syntax of all the variable definitions (declare the type before the variable name, and nix the colon)
4. Change the function declarations so that they start with the return type (`void` in all cases for this script) and an access modifier (`private` for all of these functions)
5. Add the `new` keyword when defining a `Rect` or a `Vector2` instance
6. Explicitly cast variables when you convert a float to an int. See this line for an example:

```
minutes = (int)(timeRemaining/60); // minutes is an int,
    while timeRemaining is a float
```

Remember that if you remove the Javascript component and attach a C# script instead, you'll have to re-drag-n-drop all of the textures into the variables, because Unity loses track of them entirely.

A fun exercise (depending on your definition of "fun") would be to create a new C# script, and to see if you can work through the errors one by one to completely convert this script yourself. Give it a try! The answer key is below, in case you get into trouble.

```
using UnityEngine;
using System.Collections;

public class ClockScriptCSharp : MonoBehaviour {


    private bool clockIsPaused = false;
```

```
private float startTime; //(in seconds)
private float timeRemaining; //(in seconds)
private float percent;
public Texture2D clockBG;
public Texture2D clockFG;
private float clockFGMaxWidth; // the starting width of the
  foreground bar
public Texture2D rightSide;
public Texture2D leftSide;
public Texture2D back;
public Texture2D blocker;
public Texture2D shiny;
public Texture2D finished;

private void Awake ()
{
  startTime = Time.time + 120.0f;
  clockFGMaxWidth = clockFG.width;
}

private void Update ()
{
  if (!clockIsPaused)
  {
    // make sure the timer is not paused
    DoCountdown();
  }
}

private void DoCountdown()
{
  timeRemaining = startTime - Time.time;
  percent = timeRemaining/startTime * 100;
  if (timeRemaining < 0)
  {
    timeRemaining = 0;
    clockIsPaused = true;
    TimeIsUp();
  }
  ShowTime();
  //Debug.Log("time remaining = " + timeRemaining);
}
```

```
private void PauseClock()
{
    clockIsPaused = true;
}

private void UnpauseClock()
{
    clockIsPaused = false;
}

private void ShowTime()
{
  int minutes;
  int seconds;
  string timeStr;
  minutes = (int)(timeRemaining/60);
  seconds = (int)(timeRemaining % 60);
  timeStr = minutes.ToString() + ":";
  timeStr += seconds.ToString("D2");
  guiText.text = timeStr; //display the time to the GUI
}

private void TimeIsUp()
{
  Debug.Log("Time is up!");
}

private void OnGUI()
{
  int pieClockX = 100;
  int pieClockY = 50;

  int pieClockW = 64; // clock width
  int pieClockH = 64; // clock height

  int pieClockHalfW = (int)(pieClockW * 0.5); // half the clock width
  int pieClockHalfH = (int)(pieClockH * 0.5); // half the clock
    height

  bool isPastHalfway = percent < 50;
  Rect clockRect = new Rect(pieClockX, pieClockY, pieClockW,
    pieClockH);
  float rot = (percent/100) * 360;
  Vector2 centerPoint = new Vector2(pieClockX + pieClockHalfW,
    pieClockY + pieClockHalfH);
```

```
Matrix4x4 startMatrix = GUI.matrix;

GUI.DrawTexture(clockRect, back, ScaleMode.StretchToFill,
  true, 0);

if(isPastHalfway)
{
  GUIUtility.RotateAroundPivot(-rot-180, centerPoint);
  GUI.DrawTexture(clockRect, leftSide, ScaleMode.StretchToFill,
    true, 0);
  GUI.matrix = startMatrix;
  GUI.DrawTexture(clockRect, blocker, ScaleMode.StretchToFill,
    true, 0);
} else {
  GUIUtility.RotateAroundPivot(-rot, centerPoint);
  GUI.DrawTexture(clockRect, rightSide, ScaleMode.StretchToFill,
    true, 0);
  GUI.matrix = startMatrix;
  GUI.DrawTexture(clockRect, leftSide, ScaleMode.StretchToFill,
    true, 0);
}


if(percent < 0)
{
  GUI.DrawTexture(clockRect, finished, ScaleMode.StretchToFill,
    true, 0);
}

GUI.DrawTexture(clockRect, shiny, ScaleMode.StretchToFill,
  true, 0);

float newBarWidth = (percent/100) * clockFGMaxWidth; // this is
  the width that the foreground bar should be
int gap = 20; // a spacing variable to help us position the clock
GUI.BeginGroup (new Rect(Screen.width - clockBG.width - gap, gap,
  clockBG.width, clockBG.height));
GUI.DrawTexture (new Rect (0,0, clockBG.width, clockBG.height),
  clockBG);
  GUI.BeginGroup (new Rect (5, 6, newBarWidth, clockFG.height));
    GUI.DrawTexture (new Rect (0,0, clockFG.width, clockFG.
      height), clockFG);
  GUI.EndGroup ();
GUI.EndGroup ();

  }
}
```

8
Hearty Har Har

Now that your veins are coursing with Unity GUI superpowers, the keep-up game that you built a few chapters ago is looking pretty feeble. Get used to it: as you grow your skills, you'll look at your earlier games and think, "Gee, I could have done that a different way and wound up with a much better product," or more likely, "MAN, that game is weak."

It's high time we revisit that keep-up game and add the stuff we said we will add to make it play properly. Open up your keep-up game Unity Project by going to **File** | **Open Project...**. *If you don't have the file any more, you can download it from the Packt website (*`http://www.packtpub.com/unity-4-x-game-development-by-example/book`*). When the project finishes loading, double-click on the Game Scene to see the ball and the paddle, just as we left them.*

In this chapter, we'll:

- ◆ Replace our boring primitives with real 3D models
- ◆ "Skin" the keep-up game to make it more awesome
- ◆ Add a keep-up counter to the screen to keep track of our score
- ◆ Detect when the player drops the ball, and then add a score recap and a **Play Again** button

Welcome to Snoozeville

Let's face it: the keep-up game is dull. You've got a ball and a paddle. We're going to add a score counter, but that's just not going to cut it. We need a fun theme to hold the player's interest, and to set our Unity game apart from the rest.

How's this? Let's call the game **Ticker Taker**. We'll replace the ball with a human heart, and the paddle with a pair of hands holding a teevee dinner tray. We'll string these bizarre elements together with a compelling story:

Mr. Feldman needs a heart transplant–stat–and there's no time to lose! Help Nurse Slipperfoot rush a still-beating human heart through the hospital hallways to the ER, while bouncing it on a dinner tray! Drop the heart, and it's lights out for Feldman!

With a simple story re-skin, we now have a time-limited life and death drama. Doesn't that sound more exciting than "bounce the ball on the paddle"? Which game would *you* rather play?

To pull this off, we need to import the assets package for this chapter. When the **Importing package** dialog pops up, leave everything selected and click the **Import** button.

Model behavior

Let's take a look at what we just added to the **Project** folder: two items with mysterious blue icons called **handsAndTray** and **heart**. These models were created in a free 3D software package called Blender and exported to the `.fbx` file format.

When things don't mesh

Remember that Unity doesn't actually ship with any 3D modeling tools. If you want your game to contain more than just primitives—spheres, boxes, cylinders, and so on—you'll need to get your hands on some 3D models. You can buy them, create them yourself, or cozy up with a 3D artist and bat your eyelashes at him.

Just as the 2D images for the Robot Repair game were created in a drawing package and then imported, these 3D models were built in Blender and brought into the project. All imported assets wind up in the **Assets** folder behind the scenes which, you'll recall, is not to be fiddled with outside of Unity. There is complex metadata keeping track of everything in that folder, and monkeying around with it could break your project. Check the *Appendix* of this book for different resources you can use to create or buy assets for your own games.

Time for action – exploring the models

Click on the little gray arrow next to the **handsAndTray** model. This model contains two separate meshes—a pair of hands, and a hospital dinner tray. There seem to be two instances of each, with two different icons next to them—a blue cube icon with a little white page and a black meshy/spiderwebby-looking icon.

Here's what's happening. The top-level **handsAndTray** parent is the `.fbx` file that Unity imported. Before you can use this file inside the program, Unity runs it through an import process to make sure that the models are the right size and orientation, along with a slew of other settings. The routine that preps the models for use in Unity is the **FBXImporter**. You can see it by clicking on the parent **handsAndTray** model in the **Project** panel.

There's a lot of fancy stuff going on with the **FBXImporter**. Thankfully, we don't have to touch much of it. Our biggest concern is that the models are facing the right way, and are the right size. Different models from different 3D software packages can import in funny ways, so this is like our check-in counter to make sure everything's okay before we admit the model into our *Hotel de Game*. At the very bottom of the **FBXImporter**, you can see what the model looks like.

Rank and file

Unity has superpowers. It's true. Even better, it's like one of those superheroes that can absorb other superheroes' powers. Unity doesn't have modeling or art tools itself, but, as we've seen, it can import meshes and images from the outside world. And if you have a supported 3D software package (like 3D Studio Max, Maya, or Blender) or 2D software package (like Photoshop) installed on your computer, Unity can import the native file format. That means your `.max`, `.ma`, `.blend`, and `.psd` files will be sitting right there in the **Assets** folder. If you double-click one of these assets, Unity is smart enough to launch the corresponding program for you. And if you make a change to the file and save it, the results are automatically updated right inside your project's **Assets** folder. No need to re-import the file!

You can also tell Unity which program you'd like to launch when you double-click a file with a format that can be read by many different programs, like `.fbx` or `.jpg`. Here's a list of native 3D file formats and software packages that Unity supported at the time of this writing:

- Maya `.mb` and `.ma`
- 3D Studio Max `.max`
- Cheetah 3D `.jas`
- Cinema 4D `.c4f`
- Blender `.blend`
- Carrara
- Lightwave
- XSI 5.x
- SketchUp Pro
- Wings 3D
- 3D Studio `.3ds`
- Wavefront `.obj`
- Drawing Interchange Files `.dxf`
- Autodesk FBX `.fbx`

The ability to handle native file formats for a number of major software applications is one of the coolest things about Unity. If you work a lot with Photoshop, you'll appreciate that you don't have to flatten your image and save it out to another format—just hide or show your various layers, and save the file. Unity automatically flattens the psd for you and updates the image.

Time for action – hands up!

Let's get the hands and tray into our **Scene**!

1. Navigate to **GameObject | Create Empty**. This is the **GameObject** that will contain the hands and tray models.

2. Rename the new **GameObject** HandsAndTray.

3. Click and drag the **HandsAndTray** model, which contains the **Tray_mesh** and **Hands_mesh** models, from the **Project** panel to the new **HandsAndTray** GameObject that you just created in the **Hierarchy** panel. You'll see the models appear indented beneath the **GameObject**, which will gain a gray arrow to indicate that it's now a parent.

4. Click on the top-level **HandsAndTray** Game Object in the **Hierarchy** panel, and change its Position/Rotation/Scale settings in the **Inspector** panel:

    Position   X: -0.18 Y: -0.4   Z: -0.2

    Rotation   X: 8   Y: 180   Z: 0

    Scale   X: 1   Y: 1   Z: 1

What just happened – size matters

When you change the Position and Rotation values, the **HandsAndTray GameObject** swings into view near our old **Paddle** GameObject, but the meshes are disappointingly tiny. Clearly, something went wrong during the FBX import process. We could scale the models' transforms up inside Unity, but strange things have been known to happen when you mess with a model's scale after it's been imported. Animations break, colliders stop colliding properly, the sun turns blood-red... it's a bad scene.

Time for action – changing the FBX import scale settings

Let's revisit the **FBXImporter** and crank up the scale to make our models the proper size with no breakage.

1. Click on the blue **HandsAndTray** model in the **Project** panel. The **FBXImporter** will appear in the **Inspector** panel.

2. Change the **Scale** factor near the top of the **FBXImporter** from **0.01** to **0.03**.

3. Click on the **Generate Colliders** checkbox. (We'll find out what this does very shortly.)

4. Click on the **Apply** button near the bottom of the **FBXImporter**. You may have to scroll down, depending on your screen size.

You should see the **handsAndTray** models scale up within the **Game** view to a reasonable size. That's better!

Auto-generating colliders

The checkbox that we ticked in the **FBXImporter** tells Unity to put a collider cage around our model once it's imported. You may remember that the spherical **Ball** GameObject and the cubic **Paddle** GameObject both got their own collider Components when we created them—a **Sphere Collider** for the **Ball**, and a **Cube Collider** for the **Paddle**.

Unity uses an additional copy of the mesh as the collision "cage" around the object. This is great if you have a strangely-shaped mesh, and you want things to collide with it naturally. The trouble is that your game will take a performance hit with a more complex collider (depending on the number of polygons in the collider). If you can get away with adding your own primitive (**Cube/Sphere/Capsule**) collider to your model to make things less complicated for the physics engine, you should. Our Ticker Taker game has very little complexity, so I think we can indulge ourselves with a fancier collider on our tray model. Maybe later, we'll take a long soak in the tub and paint our toenails?

Time for action – making the mesh colliders convex

Provided our mesh is made from fewer than 255 triangles, one thing that we can do to make our **Mesh Colliders** behave better is to mark them as "convex". (You can see how many triangles comprise a mesh by clicking the mesh and looking at the Preview section of the "Inspector" panel.) GameObjects that are in motion (like our **HandsAndTray** soon will be) tend to react better with other moving colliders if we make this small change.

1. In the **Hierarchy** panel, hold down the ALT key on your keyboard and click on the grey arrow next to the **HandsAndTray GameObject**. Instead of just expanding the top-level item, this expands the entire tree beneath the parent GameObject.

2. Select **Hands_Mesh**.

3. In the **Inspector** panel, under the **Mesh Collider Component**, check the box labeled **Convex**.

4. Do the same for **Tray_Mesh**.

5. As we did with the paddle before it, add a **Rigidbody** component to the **HandsAndTray** GameObject, and check the **Is Kinematic** box in the Inspector panel. As you'll remember, if a collider moves, it should have a **Rigidbody** to save us from unduly taxing the processor.

Now we're all set up to put some motion in the ocean. Let's turn our eyes toward making this imported mesh move around the same way our boring primitive paddle does.

Time for action – making the hands and tray follow the mouse

Any script that we create in Unity is reusable, and we can attach scripts to multiple GameObjects. Let's attach our **MouseFollow** script to the **HandsAndTray** GameObject.

1. Find the **MouseFollow** script in the **Project** panel (I put mine inside a "Scripts" folder), and drag it onto the **HandsAndTray** GameObject in the **Hierarchy** panel. (Make sure to drop it on the parent **HandsAndTray** GameObject, not the child **handsAndTray** model.)

2. Test your game by pressing the **Play** button.

The hands and tray should follow your mouse the very same way the paddle does. Because we generated a collider on the tray in the **FBXImporter** settings, the **Ball** should bounce on the tray just as it does with the **Paddle**.

The only trouble is that the hands and tray may be flipped backwards. That's because in the **MouseFollow** script, we're telling the paddle to constantly tilt towards y=0. Our HandsAndTray **GameObject** is rotated 180 degrees in the y axis. No worries—it's an easy fix.

Select the **HandsAndTray GameObject** and change its Y rotation to 0 (instead of 180). Then, open up the **GameObject** and select the **handsAndTray fbx** prefab instance inside. Change its Y rotation to 180. Now everything's aligned the way it should be.

What just happened – monkey see, monkey do

Because both the **Paddle** Game Object and the **HandsAndTray** Game Object have the same script attached, they both do exactly the same thing. Imagine a game where you have a number of enemies on-screen, all following the same **Script**:

1. Hunt the player.

2. Eat his face.

Reusable scripts make rampant face-eating possible, with just a single script.

Time for action – getting your heart on

Just as we did with the hands and tray models, we're going to create a new **Heart** GameObject and parent it to our imported heart model, with a few adjustments in the **FBXImporter**.

1. In the **Project** panel, click on the **heart** model.

2. Change the **Scale** factor of the **heart** model in the **Inspector** panel to 0.07.

3. Leave **Generate Colliders** unchecked.

4. Click on the **Apply** button.

5. Drag the heart model from the **Project** panel into the **Scene**.

6. In the **Inspector** panel, change the heart's position values to **X:0, Y:0, Z:0**.

7. In the **Hierarchy** panel, click on the gray arrow on the **heart** GameObject to reveal the **Heart_Mesh** inside.

8. Click to select the **Heart_Mesh**, and in the **Inspector** panel, change its **Transform** position to **X:0, Y:0, Z:0**.

   By setting everything to position 0, we ensure that the collider we're about to add will appear at roughly the same spot where the heart model is. Now instead of using a special **Mesh Collider**, let's add a more primitive **Capsule Collider**, and set up the heart so that it bounces.

9. Select the parent **heart** GameObject in the **Hierarchy** panel, and navigate to **Component | Physics | Rigidbody** to add a **Rigidbody** component to it. This includes the heart in the physics simulation. The heart's **Rigidbody** component appears in the **Inspector** Panel.

10. Navigate to **Component | Physics | Capsule Collider** to add a pill-shaped collider to the heart. A green cage-like **Collider** mesh appears around the heart in the **Scene** view.

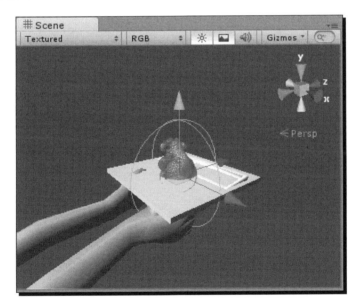

11. Change the settings on the **Capsule Collider** in the **Inspector** panel to:

> **Center**
>
> **X: -0.05   Y: 0.05   Z: 0**
>
> **Radius: 0.2**
>
> **Height: 0.6**

That should make the **Capsule Collider** fit snugly around the heart model.

12. Still in the **Capsule Collider** Component, click on the little circle button for the field labeled **Material**, and choose the custom **BouncyBall** PhysicMaterial (which we created in an earlier chapter). This is what will give the **heart** its bounce.

13. Finally, adjust the **heart** GameObject's **Transform** position in the **Inspector** panel to **X: 0.5 Y: 2 Z: -0.05**. This will place the **heart** right next to the **Ball**.

14. Save the **Scene** and test the game by clicking on the **Play** button. **Paddles**, trays, hearts, and balls should all be bouncing around. In fact, it's a smidge confusing. Let's take the old **Paddle** and **Ball** out of the equation and focus on the new stuff.

Time for action – ditching the Ball and Paddle

Click on the **Paddle** in the **Hierarchy** panel, and uncheck the checkbox next to its name in the **Inspector** panel to make it disappear. Do the same for the **Ball**. Retest the game. The **Ball** and **Paddle** are turned off; you should see only the **heart** bouncing on the tray.

What just happened – bypass the aorta

The reason we're using a **Capsule Collider** on the heart instead of a **Mesh Collider** is that the **heart** model is pretty weird and irregular. It could catch its aorta on the corner of the tray and go spinning unpredictably out of control. The **Capsule Collider** gives the **heart** a little more predictability, and it won't be glaringly obvious that the **heart** isn't colliding perfectly. (Of course, a capsule shape is a little wonkier than the **Sphere Collider** we were using earlier. This capsule is kind of a compromise.)

Time for action – material witness

Currently, the models we're using are about as exciting as clipping your toenails over the sink. All three models are a dull, default gray. Let's change that by creating some custom Materials, and applying them to the models.

Out with the old

If you had eaten your Wheaties this morning, you may have noticed that when we imported the models, their Materials were imported as well. The **Project** panel has a folder called **Materials** in it, which includes the three drab, boring Materials that we currently see on our models. Unity will import the materials that we create for our models depending on the 3D software package we used. Since these three models were not given Materials in Blender, they came in with default gray Materials. Now's a good time to select the **Materials** folder in the **Project** panel and press the *Delete* key (*command + Delete* if you're on a Mac) to get rid of it. After confirming this action, the models turn pinky-purple. Don't worry—we'll fix that.

1. Right-click/alternate-click any empty area in the **Project** panel (or click on the **Create** button at the top of the panel) and choose **Create | Material**. A **New Material** appears in the **Project** panel.

2. Rename the new material `Skin Material`.

3. Select the **Skin** Material and click on the color swatch (next to the eyedropper) in the **Inspector** panel.

4. Choose a skin color for Nurse Slipperfoot. I chose **R: 251 G: 230 B: 178** for a Caucasian nurse, but you feel free to make her whatever color you like.

5. Close the color window by clicking on the X icon in the top-right corner (top-left corner on a Mac).

6. Click and drag the **Skin** Material from the **Project** panel to the **Hands_Mesh** in the **Hierarchy** panel. You may have to click on the gray arrows to expand the parent/child tree beneath the **HandsAndTray** GameObject in order to see the **Hands_Mesh**.

In a twinkling, Nurse Slipperfoot's hands go from a hot fuschia to a rosy peach.

What just happened – understanding Materials

We've used Materials in a few other situations so far, for fonts and other goofy things, but applying Materials to models is the classic example. If meshes are like chicken wire, Materials are like the papier-mâché coating we lay over them to give them "skin". A **Material** is a collection of Shaders and textures that affect how light bounces off our models.

This diffuse, flat color is about as simple as a Material can get. If we wanted to go all-out, we could draw a more realistic image of Nurse Slipperfoot's skin, complete with freckles, beauty marks, and fingernails, in a program like Photoshop. Then we'd import the texture into Unity as an image file, and drag-and-drop it into that `Texture2D` slot that you see beneath the Material's color swatch. Suddenly, Nurse Slipperfoot's arms would look far more realistic. (It should be obvious, though, that realism isn't exactly what we're going for with this game.)

UV mapping

Any textures that we apply to our models this way may wind up disappointingly misaligned. There's a process in 3D texturing called UV mapping, which is where you adjust the position and orientation of your textures in relation to your models. Most textures that get wrapped around anything more complex than a primitive shape require some monkeying around with the models' UV settings, which happens in your 3D art package outside Unity.

You can use textures in combination with Shaders to pull off even more impressive effects. One popular Shader called a **Bump Map** (**Bumped Specular** or **Bumped Diffuse** in Unity) lets you paint the "high" and "low" areas that the light will hit. By creatively painting a flat 2D texture with light and dark tones, you can indicate which parts of the image you want to appear to be raised, and which ones should appear to recede. A bump map could give Nurse Slipperfoot's thumbs the illusion that there are modeled fingernails on their ends. The advantage is that you get this illusion without the cost of actually modeling these extra details—the Shader is doing all the work, and is tricking the light into seeing more complex geometry than we actually have. Remember that more polygons (mesh geometry) require more computer power to draw and move around the screen, so faking this complexity with a Shader is a great plan.

If you're so inclined, you can even program your own Shaders to pull off custom lighting and texturing effects on your models. That topic is way outside the scope of a beginner book, but if writing custom Shaders interests you, don't let me hold you back. Go forth and code! You can find some good resources for learning about more complex stuff like custom Shaders in the back of this book.

Have a go hero – adding materials to the other models

Now that you know how to create your own Materials, create two more Materials for your other models—one for the tray and one for the heart. I chose a bright red for the heart (R: 255 G: 0 B: 0), and made it revoltingly wet-looking and shiny by choosing **Specular** from the **Shader** dropdown. Then I cranked the "Shininess" slider up. If you had the inclination, you could draw a veiny texture in your favorite 2D program and import it into Unity, and then drag it onto the **Heart Material**. Gross!

When you're finished creating and adding new Materials to the tray and the heart, and dropping them into a new folder called "Materials", let's continue.

This just in – this game blows

Despite all the work we've done to add a fun theme, there's still a fundamental problem with our keep-up game. 2D is one thing, but because we're expecting the player to bounce the heart in three dimensions, the game is nigh impossible. I can only get a few bounces in before the heart goes flying off into Never-Neverland. But thanks to the miracle of cheating, we can actually fix this problem, and the player will feel much better about playing our game.

Time for action – multiple erections

We're going to erect four invisible walls around the play area to keep the heart reined in.

1. Navigate to **GameObject | Create Other | Cube**.

2. Rename the new **Cube** GameObject `Wall Back`.

3. Give the **Cube** these transform settings in the **Inspector** panel:

    Position   X: -0.15   Y: 1.4   Z: 1.6

    Rotation: X: 0   Y: 90   Z: 0

    Scale: X: 0.15   Y: 12   Z: 6

4. Uncheck the **Mesh Renderer** checkbox in the **Inspector** panel to make the back wall invisible to the player.

5. Repeat these steps to create three more Cubes called `Wall Front`, `Wall Left`, and `Wall Right`. The best way to do this is to duplicate the **Front Wall** three times. Just right-click/alternate-click the `Wall Front` GameObject and choose "Duplicate" from the context menu. These are the settings I used to place the other walls, but feel free to tweak them to suit your taste:

Wall Front

Position   X: -0.7   Y: 1.4   Z: -2.4

Rotation   X: 0   Y: 90   Z: 0

Scale   X: 0.15   Y: 12   Z: 6

Wall Left

Position   X: - 2   Y: 1.4   Z: 0.56

Rotation   X: 0   Y: 17.6   Z: 0

Scale   X: 0.15   Y: 12   Z: 6

Wall Right

Position   X: 1.6   Y: 1.4   Z: -0.06

Rotation   X: 0   Y: 348   Z: 0

Scale   X: 0.15   Y: 12   Z: 6

6. Remember to turn off the **Mesh Renderer** settings for each wall. You can turn them back on in case you need to fine-tune the positioning of each wall and you want to see the object in the **Scene** view.

7. I made a slight tweak to the **handsAndTray** transform, nudging the **X** rotation value to **16**.

It's like TRON up in here! Save the **Scene** and test the game. To the player, it seems as if the **heart** is bouncing off Nurse Slipperfoot's forehead, or the edges of the screen, but we know better. We've actually cheated in favor of the player, to help him have more fun and success with our game.

In defense of the Cube

If you've poked around Unity a little on your own, you may have wondered why we placed four cubes instead of four planes. For starters, planes are one-sided and they disappear when you look behind them, making it a little more difficult to position them into place. And because they're one-sided, we risk having the heart pass right through them if they're oriented the wrong way.

For the home stretch, we'll repeat a few of the steps we've already learned to display the number of hits the player achieves while playing, and to add a **Play Again** button when we detect that the heart has plummeted past the tray and into the abyss.

Time for action – creating a font texture

First, let's create a custom font texture to display some **GUIText** showing the player how many times he's bounced the heart.

1. Create a new **GUIText** object and call it **Bounce Count**. Follow the instructions in *Chapter 7, Don't Be a Clock Blocker* (in the *Creating Font Texture and Material* section) for creating a **GUIText** object and mapping a font material to it. This time, I chose a font called "Cajun Boogie" because it's ridiculous.

2. Change the font size in the Font Exporter. I chose 45 pt for the font I chose—your mileage may vary.

3. In the **Inspector** panel, set the **Bounce Count** transform position to **X: 0.9 Y: 0.9 Z: 0** to place it in the upper-right corner of the screen.

4. Choose **Anchor: Upper Right** and **Alignment: Right** from the **GUIText** component settings in the **Inspector** panel.

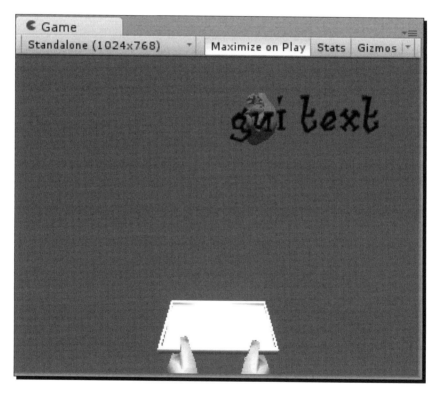

Now we have a fun on-screen **GUIText** GameObject to display the player's bounce score.

Time for action – create the HeartBounce script

We need to attach a new script to the **heart**. The script will respond to two important situations: when the **heart** hits the tray, and when the **heart** misses the tray completely and dive-bombs the Great Beyond. Let's create the script and add some simple code to it.

1. Right-click/alternate-click the **Project** panel (or use the **Create** button) and choose **Create | JavaScript**.

2. Rename the new script `HeartBounce`.

3. Double-click to open the script in the script editor.

4. Add the following code to the top of the script above the `Update` function:

```
function OnCollisionEnter(col : Collision) {
  if(col.gameObject.CompareTag("tray")) {
    Debug.Log("yes! hit tray!");
  }
}
```

What just happened – charting a collision course

There's some new code happening here. `OnCollisionEnter` is a built-in function that gets called when the GameObject's collider touches (or collides with) another GameObject's collider, as long as one of those colliders is attached to a GameObject with a non-kinematic **Rigidbody** Component (like our **heart**). We use the variable `col` (short for collision) to store the argument that gets passed in. That argument contains a reference to whatever it was we hit.

When Worlds Collide

There's a handy matrix in the Unity documentation describing how different colliders interact, and the messages they send when they collide. Give it a look:

`http://docs.unity3d.com/Documentation/Components/`
`class-MeshCollider.html`

One of the ways we can find out exactly what we hit is to ask for its `tag`. Here we're asking whether the Collision's **GameObject** is tagged **tray**. In order for this to work, we need to learn how to tag things.

Time for action – tagging the tray

Save and close the **HeartBounce** script—we'll come back to it in a jiffy. First, let's tag the **tray** GameObject so that we can determine if the **heart** has collided with it.

1. Click on the **HandsAndTray** GameObject in the **Hierarchy** panel.

2. In the **Inspector** panel, just beneath the GameObject's name, is a dropdown labeled **Tag**. Choose **Add Tag** from the bottom of this drop-down list. (By default, all Game Objects are marked "Untagged")

3. We're taken to the **Tag Manager**. Click on the gray arrow beside the word **Tags** at the top of the list.

4. There's an invisible text field next to the line labeled **Element 0**. This takes a leap of faith the first time you do it. Click on the blank area beneath the **1** on the **Size** line. Then type the word **tray**. Press the *Enter* key to make it stick. Notice that Unity adds a new blank tag for us, labeled **Element 1**.

⊙ Inspector	
⚙ TagManager	
▼ Tags	
Size	2
Element 0	tray
Element 1	
Builtin Layer 0	Default
Builtin Layer 1	TransparentFX
Builtin Layer 2	Ignore Raycast
Builtin Layer 3	
Builtin Layer 4	Water
Builtin Layer 5	
Builtin Layer 6	
Builtin Layer 7	
User Layer 8	
User Layer 9	
User Layer 10	
User Layer 11	
User Layer 12	
User Layer 13	

5. Click to select the **Tray_Mesh** in the **Hierarchy** panel (you may need to click on the gray arrows to expand the hierarchy beneath the **HandsAndTray** Game Object). When we chose "Add Tag," you may have thought that we were adding a tag called "tray" to the **HandsAndTray GameObject**. In fact, "Add Tag" actually means "add a tag to the list of tags we can choose from". The new tag isn't automatically added to any GameObject.

6. Now that we've *added* the **tray** tag, we can select it from the drop-down list. With the **Tray_Mesh** selected, choose **tray** from the **Tags** dropdown in the **Inspector** panel to tag the **Tray_Mesh**.

7. Tag the **Hands_Mesh** with the **tray** tag as well.

8. Click and drag the **HeartBounce** script to the **heart** GameObject to attach it.

Save the **Scene** and test your game. Keep an eye on the message bar at the bottom of the screen. When the heart hits the tray or hands models, you should see a message saying **yes! Hit tray!**

Time for action – tweaking the bounce

Now that we can detect when the heart is hitting the tray, there's no end to the fun we can have! While we're in the code, let's make a quick change to make the gameplay slightly better.

1. Double-click to open the **HeartBounce** script.

2. Type the following at the top of the script:

```
#pragma strict
var velocityWasStored = false;
var storedVelocity : Vector3;
function OnCollisionEnter(col : Collision) {
  if(col.gameObject.CompareTag("tray")) {
    Debug.Log("yes! hit tray!");
```

```
if (!velocityWasStored) {
  storedVelocity = rigidbody.velocity;
  velocityWasStored = true;
}
rigidbody.velocity.y = storedVelocity.y;
  }
}
```

Save the script and test the game. You may not notice a difference at first, but we've made a clear improvement to our mechanic.

What just happened – storing velocity

The trouble with Unity's physics simulation is that it's almost *too* good. Left to its own devices, our heart will bounce less and less until it eventually runs out of steam and comes to rest on the dinner tray. Realistically, this might actually be what a still-beating human heart would do, given the circumstances. I'm too squeamish to find out for sure.

But this isn't realism—this is video games, baby! This is the land of gigantic guns and anthropomorphic mushrooms! We want that heart to bounce forever, with no degradation over time when the heart bounces against the tray and the walls.

That's what our little script does. The first time the heart bounces, we store its velocity (distance over time) in a variable. Then we inject a little high-velocity serum into the heart every time it hits the tray, overriding the slowly degrading velocity that the heart suffers from hitting our invisible walls. We use the `velocityWasStored` flag to determine whether the heart has bounced yet.

Time for action – keeping track of the bounces

Let's introduce a few more variables to record how many times the player has bounced the heart.

1. Change the code to add these three variables at the top:

```
var hitCount:GUIText;
var numHits:int = 0;
var hasLost:boolean = false;
var velocityWasStored = false;
var storedVelocity : Vector3;
```

2. Save the script and return to Unity.

3. Select the **Heart** in the **Hierarchy** panel.

4. We've created a variable (bucket) to hold a GUIText object. Drag the **Bounce Count** GUIText GameObject from the **Hierarchy** panel into the **GUIText** slot of the heart in the **Inspector** panel (or choose it from the pop-up menu). Now, whenever we refer to hitCount in our script, we'll be talking about our **GUIText** GameObject.

5. Add the following code to the Update function:

```
function Update() {
  var str:String = "";

  if(!hasLost){
    str = numHits.ToString();
  } else {
    str = "Hits:" + numHits.ToString() + "\nYour best:" +
      bestScore;

    if(bestScore > lastBest) str += "\nNEW RECORD!";
  }

  hitCount.text = str;
}
```

What this script will do is check the hasLost flag on every Update, and change the hitCount **GUIText** to show either just the bounce count, or a big score recap at the end of the game that will look like this:

Hits: 32

Your Best: 12

NEW RECORD!

Note that we don't have any logic yet to flip the hasLost flag, nor do we have any code to increment the numHits variable. Let's add those two things next.

\n

This code creates a line break. Whenever you see it, you can think of it as if someone has hit the *Enter* key to space out some text. Be aware that it only works inside Strings.

Time for action – adding the lose condition

The easiest way to figure out if the player has lost is to check the `transform.position.y` value of the heart. If the heart has fallen through the floor, the player obviously isn't bouncing it on the tray any longer.

1. Add the logic for incrementing the player's score (number of hits/bounces before losing):

```
function OnCollisionEnter(col : Collision) {
  if(col.gameObject.CompareTag("tray")) {
    //Debug.Log("yes! hit tray!");
    if (!velocityWasStored) {
      storedVelocity = rigidbody.velocity;
       velocityWasStored = true;
    }
    if(rigidbody.velocity.y > 1) {
      numHits ++;
    }
   rigidbody.velocity.y = storedVelocity.y;
 }
```

2. Add the "lose the game" check to the `Update` function:

```
function Update() {
  var str:String = "";

  if(!hasLost){
     str = numHits.ToString();
  } else {
    str = "Hits:" +  numHits.ToString() + "\nYour best:" +
      bestScore;

    if(bestScore > lastBest) str += "\nNEW RECORD!";
  }
  hitCount.text = str;
  if(transform.position.y < -3){
    if(!hasLost) {
      hasLost = true;
      lastBest = bestScore;
      if(numHits > bestScore) {
        bestScore = numHits;
      }
    }
  }
}
```

3. Add these variables to the top of the script:

```
var hitCount:GUIText;
var numHits:int = 0;
var hasLost:boolean = false;
var bestScore:int = 0;
var lastBest:int = 0;
var velocityWasStored = false;
var storedVelocity : Vector3;
```

What just happened – understanding the code

We start by incrementing numHits whenever the heart hits the tray:

```
if(rigidbody.velocity.y > 1) {
   numHits ++;
}
```

By checking if the heart's velocity is greater than 1, we're making sure it's on the upward part of its bounce. We put this conditional check on the heart's velocity so that the player doesn't score any points if he catches the heart on the tray and it just starts rolling around. No bounce, no points.

```
if(transform.position.y < -3){
      if(!hasLost) {
         hasLost = true;
```

This is like saying "if the heart is through the floor (transform.position.y is less than negative 3), and the player hasn't lost yet, make the player lose".

Next, we record what the last high score was.

```
lastBest = bestScore;
```

If the number of hits the player pulled off in this round beats the player's best score, reset the best score to the player's number of hits.

```
if(numHits > bestScore) {
   bestScore = numHits;
}
```

Save the script and test the game. The on-screen score counter updates with every hit you get, and when you drop the heart, you get a recap of your last and best scores.

Time for action – adding the Play Again button

The very last thing we need to do is to add a button to the end of the game so that the player can play again. Let's revisit our good friend GUI from the last few chapters.

1. Add the OnGUI function to the **HeartBounce** script:

```
function OnGUI(){
  if(hasLost){
    var buttonW:int = 100; // button width
    var buttonH:int = 50; // button height

    var halfScreenW:float = Screen.width/2; // half of the
      Screen width
    var halfButtonW:float = buttonW/2; // Half of the
      button width

    if(GUI.Button(Rect(halfScreenW-halfButtonW,
      Screen.height*.8, buttonW, buttonH), "Play Again"))
    {
      numHits = 0;
      hasLost = false;
      velocityWasStored = false;
      transform.position = Vector3(0.5,2,-0.05);
      rigidbody.velocity = Vector3(0,0,0);
    }
  }
}
```

What just happened?

For GUI pros like us, this script is a piece of cake.

The whole function is wrapped in a "has the player lost the game?" conditional statement.

We start by storing some values for half of the Screen's width and height, and the width or height of the button.

```
var buttonW:int = 100; // button width
var buttonH:int = 50; // button height

var halfScreenW:float = Screen.width/2; // half of the Screen width
var halfButtonW:float = buttonW/2; // Half of the button width
```

Next, we draw the button to the screen, and reset some game variables if the button is clicked:

```
if(GUI.Button(Rect(halfScreenW-halfButtonW, Screen.height*.8,
    buttonW, buttonH),"Play Again")){
    numHits = 0;
    hasLost = false;
    velocityWasStored = false;
    transform.position = Vector3(0,2,0);
    rigidbody.velocity = Vector3(0,0,0);
}
```

It's important that we reset the heart's starting position and the velocity of its **Rigidbody** component. Try commenting either or both of these lines out and see what happens!

Save the script and try it out. Ticker Taker now uses 3D models and an on-screen score counter to elevate a standard, dull keep-up game to a madcap emergency ward adventure.

Ticker taken

Let's recap the mad skillz we picked up in this chapter. We:

- ◆ Added 3D models to our game

- ◆ Created some simple Materials

- ◆ Learned how to tag **GameObjects**

- ◆ Detected collisions between **GameObjects**

- ◆ Overrode the physics simulation with our own code

- ◆ Programmed an on-screen score counter and recap

We could still do a much better job of conveying the story and setting to the player in Ticker Taker, so let's put another pin in this game and return to it in a later chapter. In the next action-packed installment, we'll get a little more practice with **GameObject** collisions, and we'll learn all about **Prefabs**. Prefabs will change the way you use Unity! I can't wait.

C# Addendum

When converting this script to C#, there was only one small change to the **MouseFollow** script, which you can make quite easily.

There are no surprises whatsoever with the **HeartBounce** script. Here's how the script looks translated to C#:

```
using UnityEngine;
using System.Collections;

public class HeartBounceCSharp : MonoBehaviour {

  public GUIText hitCount;
  private int numHits = 0;
  private bool hasLost = false;
  private int bestScore = 0;
  private int lastBest = 0;
  private bool velocityWasStored = false;
  private Vector3 storedVelocity;

  private void OnCollisionEnter(Collision col)
  {
    if(col.gameObjectCompareTag("tray"))
      {
        Debug.Log("yes! hit tray!");
```

```
        if (!velocityWasStored)
        {
            storedVelocity = rigidbody.velocity;
            velocityWasStored = true;
        }

        if(rigidbody.velocity.y > 1)
        {
            numHits ++;
        }

        rigidbody.velocity = new Vector3(rigidbody.velocity.x,
        storedVelocity.y, rigidbody.velocity.z);
    }
}


void Update ()
{
  string str = "";

  if(!hasLost)
  {
    str = numHits.ToString();
  } else {
    str = "Hits:" + numHits.ToString() + "\nYour best:" + bestScore;

    if(bestScore > lastBest) str += "\nNEW RECORD!";
  }

  hitCount.text = str;

  if(transform.position.y < -3)
  {
    if(!hasLost)
    {
      hasLost = true;
      lastBest = bestScore;
      if(numHits > bestScore)
      {
        bestScore = numHits;
      }
    }
  }
}
```

```
void OnGUI()
{
  if(hasLost)
  {
    float buttonW = 100; // button width
    float buttonH = 50; // button height

    float halfScreenW = Screen.width/2; // half of the Screen width
    float halfButtonW = buttonW/2; // half of the button width

    if(GUI.Button(new Rect(halfScreenW-halfButtonW,
      Screen.height*.8f, buttonW, buttonH), "Play Again"))
    {
      numHits = 0;
      hasLost = false;
      velocityWasStored = false;
      transform.position = new Vector3(0.5f,2,-0.05f);
      rigidbody.velocity = new Vector3(0,0,0);
    }
  }
}
```

9

Game #3 – The Break-Up

We've been learning pieces of game development like Lego bricks. We've chugged along merrily on two tracks simultaneously: learning about what we need to build to have a complete game, and how we can use Unity to build those pieces.

The Break-Up will be a simple catch game. Catch is in a genre of what we now call mini-games—often, they are games within games. Catch, like keep-up, has a very simple mechanic. The player controls a thing, (like a paddle, a character, a bucket, or a trampoline), usually at the bottom of the screen, and other things fall or move towards the player-controlled thing from the top of the screen. In a catch game, the player has to connect his controllable thing with the falling things (people jumping out of buildings, cherries falling from a tree, and so on) to catch or collide with them. A common feature upgrade is to add bad things that the player must avoid.

That's how the unskinned mechanic works. Of course, you can skin it in a million different ways. One of the earliest catch games I ever played was called Kaboom! on the Atari 2600. The player controlled a group of buckets, and had to catch bombs dropped by the Mad Bomber villain at the top of the screen.

The skin I've cooked up for the Break-Up puts you in the role of a guy who's been kicked out of his apartment by his girlfriend. Your most prized possessions are your Beer Steins of the World collection and your cartoon bomb collection, and your ex-girlfriend is throwing both of them out of the window! The bombs, naturally, are lit. You have to catch the fragile beer steins and avoid the bombs.

That skin is clearly just a little west of nuts, but it shows how far you can go with the fictional wallpaper on a simple mechanic.

So what are we going to need? We should have some kind of backdrop to set the scene, some beer stein and bomb models, and a character. Ideally, that character should be animated. Oh, and we should probably learn how to blow stuff up too, because blowing stuff up is awesome. In this chapter, let's learn:

- ◆ How to set up animations from external models
- ◆ How to create particle effects like explosions and sparks
- ◆ How to use **Prefabs** to handle multiple copies of the same **GameObject**
- ◆ How to write one script to control multiple objects
- ◆ How to make things appear on-screen out of thin air

As before, the first thing you should do is start a new Unity project for this chapter, and call it TheBreakUp. Be sure to include the Particles.unityPackage file from the list. Once your project starts up, save the default **Scene** and call it Game. Next, download and import the assets package required for this chapter, and all of the goodies you need to build the game will show up in the **Project** panel, in their own **Materials** and **Models** folders.

Conversion perversion

As with the heart, hands, and tray models from our Ticker Taker project, these particular goodies were created in Blender, a free 3D modeling package. Then they were exported to the .fbx format, a common format among different 3D software packages. The drawback in converting your work to a common format is that certain things can be lost in translation—pieces of the geometry can be flipped inside out, textures can show up in the wrong place or not at all, and the model might not look the way you want it to. Remember that Unity can recognize a number of native 3D file formats. There are advantages and disadvantages to working with native file formats instead of common formats like .fbx, which you'll discover as you gain more experience with Unity.

Time for action – bombs away!

Let's cut right to the chase here: big round cartoon bombs are great. Real-life bombs aren't quite as much fun, so let's keep it cartoony. We'll set up our cartoon bomb model and add a special effect called a **Particle System** to make it look as though the fuse is lit.

1. In the **Project** panel, open the **Models** folder by clicking on the gray arrow to expand it.

2.   Drag the bomb model into the **Scene** view.

3.   In the **Inspector** panel, change the bomb's **Transform** Position values to **0**, **0**, **0** on the **X**, **Y**, and **Z** axes to place the bomb at the origin of your 3D world. You can also click on the gray gear icon and choose **Reset Position** from the dropdown.

4.   Hover your mouse over the **Scene** view and press the *F* key. This places focus on the bomb, which zooms into view.

5.   Navigate to **GameObject** | **Create Other** | **Particle System**.

6. In the **Inspector** panel, change the **X**, **Y**, **Z** position values of **Particle System** to 0, 3, 0. This places **Particle System** at the tip of the fuse.

7. In the **Hierarchy** panel, rename **Particle Effect** Sparks.

Particle systems give games their zest. They can be used to depict smoke, fire, water, sparks, magic, jetstreams, plasma, and a pile of other natural and unnatural phenomena. Essentially, they're a ton of tiny little flat images that turn to face the camera, in a common 3D technique called **billboarding**. Each little picture can be textured, just like the Material on a 3D model. The little pictures support transparency, so they don't have to look like squares. Particle systems have an emitter, which is where the particles come from. The built-in particle system that ships with Unity lets you control a dizzying array of additional parameters, such as the number, color, frequency, direction, and randomness of the particles.

In pursuit of shiny objects

Many game developers use particle effects as a cheap trick to reward their players. For many casual gamers, the best piece of feedback in a puzzle game is a satisfying sound effect paired with an explosion of particles. Games like Bejeweled and Peggle put particle systems to work with great results.

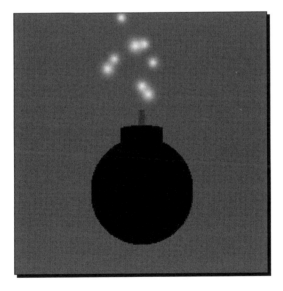

Right now, our particle effect looks like spooky forest fairy magic, floating around our bomb. We want something closer to the classic Warner Bros. Wile E. Coyote bomb, with sparks shooting out of the fuse. Let's explore the wide range of settings that Unity's particle systems offer.

Click on **Sparks** Particle System in the **Hierarchy** panel if it's not already selected.

Check out the **Inspector** panel. There are a metric ton of settings and dials for tweaking particle systems! We won't discuss them exhaustively because that's what software manuals are for. Suffice it to say, the best way to get what you want out of particle systems is to poke things until it looks right. Let's get poking!

Time for action – poke those particles

1. Adjust the dials on your **Particle System** to match these values:

   Top Section:

   - **Start Lifetime**: 0.1
   - **Start Speed**: 10
   - **Start Size**: 0.3

   Emission:

   - **Rate: 50**

   Shape:

   - **Shape: HemiSphere**

   Keep all other settings in these sections at their default.

Start Lifetime, the first value we tweaked, determines when the particles "die", or disappear from the player's view. Sparks shooting out of a hissing fuse don't last very long, so we've turned this value down quite a bit.

Start Speed is obviously-named. This value determines how fast the particles initially shoot out of our emitter.

Start Size controls how large the particle images are. Toning this value down makes the system look more *sparky*.

Under **Emission**, the **Rate** value controls the number of particles the emitter releases over time. Increasing this value gives us more particles, and a busier system.

Under **Shape**, selecting **HemiSphere** instead of the default **Cone** makes the particles shoot out more believably (or, if not more believably, more Looney Tunes-ably).

Move down to and check the **Color Over Lifetime** section. Here, we can make the particles animate through a range of colors. With something fast and frenetic like a bunch of sparks, we can choose a bunch of hot colors to give the particles a sparky kind of look. Click on the swatch next to the **Color** label. The **Gradient Editor** pops up.

In computer graphics parlance, a gradient is a spectrum of colors that moves from one color value to another, with 0 or more optional color values in between. The two little monopoly house-shaped markers at either end of the white bar define the start and end colors. Double-click each of them (or single-click and click on the resulting color swatch that appears), and set their colors to red on the right, and white on the left.

Next, single-click in the empty space between these markers to create additional markers. Create two new markers, and set their colors to orange and yellow, so that the gradient is a smooth blend from "cool" red on the right, to hot white on the left. If you place too many additional color markers, you can get rid of them simply by clicking and dragging them off the spectrum. You can click-and-drag to move these markers around to control how the colors on the spectrum blend.

Here are the color values I used, from left to right:

255 / 255 / 255 (white)

249 / 220 / 0 (yellow)

246 / 141 / 0 (orange)

255 / 0 / 0 (red)

Great! That's looking more sparky already! The particles move through the color spectrum as they travel through "life", before eventually expiring. It's ... *sniff* ... it's another touching example of the circle of life.

Time for action – creating a spark material

It's looking pretty good, but in order to really pull off this spark effect, we should add a material to the **Particle System**. This material will be applied to all of the little round fuzzy particles in our system.

1. Create a new material by either right-clicking/secondary-clicking in the **Project** panel and navigating to **Create | Material**, or by navigating to **Assets | Create | Material** in the menu.

2. Name the new **Material** Spark. The sphere icon helps us remember that this is a **Material**. Consider dragging this new material into the **Materials** folder to keep your project organized.

3.   In the **Inspector** panel, choose **Particles | Additive** as the **Shader** type.

4.   Click on the **Select** button in the square swatch labeled **Particle Texture** (it should say **None (Texture 2D)** inside the square), and choose the texture labeled **fire4** from the list. If you don't see it in the list, you may have forgotten to import the **Particles** assets package when you started your project. To rectify this, set your computer on fire, then go outside and enjoy the fresh air and sunshine. (Or if you're bound and determined to continue, import the **Particles** package under **Assets | Import Package | Particles**).

5.   In the **Hierarchy** panel, click again to select your **Sparks Particle System**.

6.   In the **Inspector** panel, uncheck **Cast Shadows** and **Receive Shadows** in the **Renderer** section. We're not exactly going for a realistic look here, so we can spare Unity the chore of rendering fancy shadow effects that no one will notice. (Note that real-time shadow casting is a Unity Pro feature. If you're not running Unity Pro, fuhgeddaboudit!)

7.   Still in the **Renderer** section in the **Inspector** panel, click on the circle next to the **Material** label, which by default contains the default-particle material.

8. In the resulting list, double-click to choose your newly created **Spark** Material.

There! Now it's looking even more sparky!

Have a go hero – time to ignite your creative spark

Do you like fiddling with buttons and knobs? Maybe your eyes lit up when you saw all the gory bits in Unity's **Particle System**? This is a great time to put the book down and fiddle to your heart's content (with Unity, that is). Maybe you can find some settings that make the sparks look even more sparky? You might try drawing your own texture that makes the sparks look sharper or pointier than the comparatively smooth and fluffy fire texture we're using. Or better yet, perhaps you could create another particle system and make a thin trail of gray smoke to flow up from your fuse? Check out the velocity settings, which give your particles direction, if you want to pull this off.

You can find a detailed explanation of every little **Particle System** setting in the Unity **User Guide** at this address:

```
http://docs.unity3d.com/Documentation/Manual/ParticleSystems.html
```

Time for action – prefabulous

Our game is going to contain not one bomb, but many. As with programming, doing something more than once in Unity completely stinks, so we're going to take a shortcut. We're going to create a built-in thing called a Prefab that will let us create a reusable bomb, much the same way we created a programmatic function that we could call multiple times in our script.

Follow these steps to create your first Prefab:

1. Right-click/secondary-click on the **Project** panel and navigate to **Create | Prefab**, or navigate to **Assets | Create | Prefab** in the menu. A gray box icon appears in your **Project** panel, labeled **New Prefab**. Because the box is gray, we know this Prefab is empty.

2. Rename the **Prefab** Bomb. Just like **Spark** Material, the icon helps us to keep track of what type of thing it is. For further clarity, consider adding the **Bomb Prefab** to a new folder, which you should call Prefabs.

3. In the **Hierarchy** panel, click-and-drag the **Sparks** Particle System to the **Bomb**
GameObject.

4. In the **Hierarchy** panel, click on the gray arrow next to the **bomb** model parent, and
you'll see the **Bomb** model and the **Sparks** Particle System nestled safely inside.
You've created a parent/child relationship between the two **GameObjects**. **Sparks**
will follow wherever **Bomb** leads.

5. In the **Hierarchy** panel, click-and-drag the parent **bomb** GameObject label, the one
that the **Bomb** model and the **Sparks** Particle System are nestled beneath, onto the
Bomb Prefab in the **Project** panel (remember, it has an empty gray cube icon next
to it). As a shortcut, you can also just drag-and-drop a **GameObject** into the **Project**
panel, and a Prefab will automatically be created for you.

When you pull the **bomb** GameObject into the empty **Prefab**, the gray **Prefab** icon lights
up blue. Filled Prefabs are blue, while empty Prefabs are gray. And 3D model icons look
suspiciously like filled Prefab icons, except that they have a little white page on their
blue boxes.

What just happened – what's a Prefab?

So what the heck is a Prefab, anyway? It's a container that holds stuff, and it's magically
reusable. Now that **Sparks** and **Bomb** are stowed safely inside a Prefab, we can populate
the **Scene** view with a whole pile of bombs. If you make any changes to the Prefab, all other
instances of the Prefab receive the same change. Let's see that in action:

1. Click on the **bomb** parent in the **Hierarchy** panel and press the *Delete* key on your keyboard (*Command + Delete* on a Mac) to get rid of it. It's okay. The **Bomb** model and **Sparks** are tucked inside our new **Prefab** down in the **Project** panel.

2. Click-and-drag the **Bomb** Prefab out from the **Project** panel into **Scene** lots of times. Populate your **Scene** with five or more **Bomb** Prefabs.

3. Move the bombs around **Scene**, so that they're not all stacked on top of each other.

4. In the **Project** panel, open up the **Bomb** Prefab by clicking on its gray arrow.

5. Click on the **Sparks** Particle System inside the **Bomb** Prefab.

6. In the **Inspector** panel, scroll down to the **Renderer** section.

7. Click on the **Particle Texture** swatch, where we originally chose the **fire4** texture, and choose a different texture from the list. Choose something silly, like the **soapbubble** texture.

8. All of the **Bomb** Prefabs in your **Scene** should update to display a **soapbubble** texture on their particle systems! Test your game to see this in action.

9. Be sure to change the texture back to **fire4** before continuing (unless you've got a weird sense of humor).

You've just proven that what happens to the master Prefab happens to all Prefabs. We'll come back to the bombs in a bit. For now, delete all of the **Bomb** Prefab instances from the **Hierarchy** panel to get back to an empty **Scene**.

Flashback

If you've ever used Flash, the concept of Prefabs may feel familiar. Prefabs behave very much like Flash Movieclips.

Time for action – lights, camera, and apartment

One of the models in the **Models** folder in the **Project** panel is called **brownstone**. This is the brownstone apartment building from which our hapless hero has been ejected. Let's set it up:

1. In the **Project** panel, click on the gray arrow to expand the **Models** folder.

2. Click-and-drag the **brownstone** model into **Scene**.

3. In the **Inspector** panel, set the apartment building's **Transform Position** to **X:0, Y:0, Z:0**.

4. Our camera is not exactly pointed the right way.

5. Let's adjust the camera's Transform to get a nice low-angle view of the brownstone building.

6. Click to select **Main Camera** in the **Hierarchy** panel.

7. In the **Inspector** panel, change its **Transform Position** to 35, 2.5, -38. (Note: that's negative thirty-eight).

8. Change its **Rotation** values to 333, 355, 0.4.

9. The brownstone should swing into view in your **Game** view.

10. Change the camera's field of view to 51, to hide the fact that the brownstone model is only two floors high. This place is rather dimly lit, so let's set up a light in our scene to simulate daytime.

11. Navigate to **GameObject | Create Other | Directional Light**. Put the light at the origin of your **Scene** (0,0,0) to make it easier to find.

12. In the **Inspector** panel, change the light's **Rotation** values to **X:45, Y:25, Z:0.**

Now the building is illuminated rather nicely.

Time for action – adding the character

The biggest missing piece at this point is the player character. Let's get him into the **Scene** view.

1. Create an empty Prefab and name it `Character`. (Drop it into the **Prefabs** folder if you'd like to keep your project organized.)

2. In the **Project** panel, click-and-drag the character model from the **Models** folder into the **Character** Prefab.

3. Click-and-drag an instance of the **Character** Prefab from the **Project** panel into the **Scene** view.

4. Use these settings to place the character:

Position: 24, 0, -16

Rotation: 0, 90, 0

These settings place the character at the foot of the brownstone. He looks like he's about to do some intensive aerobics with his arms out like that. This is called the "Christ pose" or the "T-pose", and it's the preferred position for a character model because it makes it easier to add a skeleton to the mesh, a process called **rigging**. A fully-rigged character is called a **character rig**. A skeleton is a virtual set of "bones" that distorts the mesh so that you can bend the limbs.

Time for action – registering the animations

The character model that we're using has been pre-animated in Blender. It has three animations: step, idle, and catch. Before we can play these animations using **Script**, we have to tell Unity the frame ranges the model uses.

1. In the **Project** panel, click on the character model inside the **Models** folder.

2. At the top of the **Inspector** panel, click on the **Animations** tab.

3. Click on the little plus icon at the right edge of the **Clips** box two times, to list a total of three animations.

4. Click on each animation in turn and, in the following section, name the animations `step`, `idle`, and `catch`.

5. Use these settings for the **Start**, **End**, and **Wrap Mode** parameters:

    ❑ **step 1-12, Loop**

    ❑ **idle 22-47, Loop**

    ❑ **catch 12-20, Once**

6. When you are finished, click on the **Apply** button.

Now that these animations have been named and identified, we can call them up with code.

Time for action – scripting the character

Let's do exactly that! We'll create a new **Script**, and use what we already know about following the mouse, to snap the player character to our mouse movement. Then we'll tell the character which animation cycle to use when he's moving around.

1. Create a new **JavaScript**. Rename it `Character`. If you're keeping your project tidy, consider creating a new folder called `Scripts` and dropping your new script into it.

2. Open the script and type in this code beneath the `#pragma` strict line:

```
var lastX:float; // this will store the last position of
   the character
var isMoving:boolean = false; //flags whether or not the
   player is in motion
function Start()
{
    animation.Stop();  // this stops Unity from playing the
       character's default animation.
}

function Update()
{
    transform.position.x = (Input.mousePosition.x)/20;
}
```

So far, all this should look very familiar. We're using the same type of commands we used with the keep-up game to make the **GameObject** follow the mouse around, but this time the player is locked to the x axis, so he'll only be able to move from side-to-side.

Now, we'll add a chunk of logic in the `Update` function to determine whether or not the player is moving.

 Note that the value `20` we've used here is a "magic number", which is programming parlance for a bad practice where the utility of a number is not explained. Your mileage with this number will vary based on your screen width. Adjust this evil magic number to taste like paprika in your favorite stew recipe.

3. Add the following code to your `Update` function:

```
function Update()
{
    var halfW:float = Screen.width / 2;
    transform.position.x = (Input.mousePosition.x)/20;
```

```
if(lastX != transform.position.x)
{
  // x values between this Update cycle and the last one
  // aren't the same! That means the player is moving the
  // mouse.
  if(!isMoving)
  {
    // the player was standing still.
    // Let's flag him to "isMoving"
    isMoving = true;
    animation.CrossFade("step");
  } else {
  // The player's x position is the same this Update cycle
  // as it was the last! The player has stopped moving the
  // mouse.
  if(isMoving)
  {
    // The player has stopped moving, so let's update the
        flag
    isMoving = false;
    animation.CrossFade("idle");
  }
}
}
lastX = transform.position.x;
}
```

4. Save the script. Now attach the script to your **Character** Prefab in the **Project** panel. I find it tricky to master the click-and-drag process when it comes to Prefabs. Unity always thinks I'm trying to drag my script above or below the **Prefab**. For a sure-fire way to stick that script to your character, click on the **Character** Prefab in the **Project** panel. Then, in the menu, navigate to **Component | Scripts | Character**. You should see the **Character** script get added as a component in the **Inspector** panel.

5. Play your game to try it out. When you move the mouse, the character loops through his "step" animation. When you stop moving the mouse, he transitions back to his "idle" animation, looking for more stuff to catch.

 Note: If your character doesn't animate and you get an error reading, **The animation state idle could not be played because it couldn't be found!**, you need to attach the animation clips to the Prefab's animation class.

1. Click on the **Character** Prefab in the **Project** window.

2. In the **Inspector** window, change the **Animations Size** to 3.

3. Attach each of the three animation clips we added to the model earlier.

What just happened – stepping through the "step" code

The comments should help clarify this code. This crucial line:

```
if(lastX != transform.position.x)
```

means "if the last x position of the character does not equal the character's current x position...", We base the rest of the logic on that check.

If he was moving and he just stopped, flag him as "not moving" and crossfade to the "idle" animation. If he was not moving and he just started moving since the last Update cycle, flag him as "moving" and crossfade to the "step" animation.

Time for action – open the pod bay door, Hal

I don't know about you, but I'm about ready to drop some bombs on this chump. We could do what we've done before and add a **Rigidbody Collider** Component to the bomb, as we did with the ball/heart in the keep-up game, and let Unity's physics take care of the rest. But in this case, we might like a little more control over the velocity of the bombs. So let's add Rigidbody and Collider Components to the bomb, but exclude it from Unity's gravity calculations.

1. In the **Project** panel, click on the **Bomb** Prefab.

2. Navigate to **Component | Physics | Rigidbody**. You should see the new **Rigidbody Component** appear in the **Inspector** panel.

3. In the **Inspector** panel, uncheck the **Use Gravity** checkbox. This will exempt the bomb from Unity's gravitational pull. PROTIP: I kind of wish I had this checkbox on my own body. That would be fun.

4. Navigate to **Component | Physics | Sphere Collider**. We don't need any fancy poly-perfect **Mesh Collider** in this case because the bomb is basically a sphere anyway.

5. In the **Inspector** panel, enter a value of 2 for the **radius** of **Sphere Collider**. That should fit the bomb snugly. You can confirm this by placing a **Bomb** Prefab in your **Scene** and checking it out, or you can take my word for it.

You'll remember from the keep-up game that the **Rigidbody** and **Sphere** Collider/Capsule Collider Components work together to make code respond when **GameObjects** touch each other.

Time for action – collision-enable the character

Now that the bomb is all rigged up, we'll be able to determine through code when it hits the player character. However, the player character is missing its Collider Component too! Let's fix that.

1. Click to select the **Character** Prefab in the **Hierarchy** panel.

2. Navigate to **Component | Physics | Box Collider** in the menu.

3. In the **Inspector** panel, update the **Size** and **Center** settings for your new **Box Collider** with these values:

    ❑   **Center**: -1, 8, 1

    ❑   **Size**: 5, 16, 10

Just like we did with the bomb, we'll forego using a computationally complex **Mesh Collider** in favor of a rough-hewn primitive. We've made a big, ugly green box around the character. This will make less work for Unity, and for our game's purposes, anything fancier would be overkill.

Add a **Rigidbody** component to the character, and mark it **Is Kinematic**, as we've done before. Remember the rule: if it has a collider and it moves around, it needs a Rigidbody (or else we'll make Unity do more work than it needs to).

Time for action – apocalypse now?

Enough prattle. It's bomb time!

1. Create a new **JavaScript** and name it Bomb. Drop it in the **Scripts** folder if you're keeping things tidy.

2. Open up the script and type the following code:

```
function Update()
{
    transform.position.y -= 50 * Time.deltaTime;
    if(transform.position.y < 0)
    {
        transform.position.y = 50;
        transform.position.x = Random.Range(0,60);
        transform.position.z = -16;
    }
}
```

We've seen these keywords before, so there should be no surprises here. On every update cycle, move the bomb down in the y axis by 50 units per second:

```
transform.position.y -= 50 * Time.deltaTime;
```

If the bomb has fallen through the floor:

```
if(transform.position.y < 0) {
```

pop the bomb back up to the top of the apartment building:

```
transform.position.y = 50;
```

and use Random.Range to make it appear in a different spot along the top of the building. This will create the illusion that there are multiple bombs falling from the sky.

Save this script. Just as we did with the **Character** Prefab, click on the **Bomb** Prefab in the **Project** panel, and navigate to **Component | Scripts | Bomb**, to add the new script to the bomb.

Drag the **Bomb** Prefab into your **Scene**, and give it the following **Transform Position: X:-9, Y:36, Z: -16**. Now playtest your game.

Zut alors! There are sparky, lit bombs falling from the top of that apartment building! For added amusement, try catching one on your character's face. We haven't done any collision handling yet, so our ousted friend gets a grill full of bomb.

Time for action – go boom

I must say, there's a distinct missing element to our bomb-centric game to this point. What could it be, what could it be? Ah, yes. ASSPLOSIONS. When they hit the ground OR the player, those bombs need to blow up real good. Sounds like a particle system would do just the trick.

1. Make sure you're no longer testing the game.

2. Navigate to **GameObject | Create Other | Particle System**. Rename it `Explosion` (or `Assplosion` if you want to be awesome about it).

3. Create a new **Prefab** and name it `Explosion`. Drop it into your **Prefabs** folder to keep the project organized.

4. From the **Hierarchy** panel, click-and-drag the **Explosion** Particle System into the **Explosion** Prefab container.

5. Re-select the **Explosion** GameObject in the **Hierarchy** panel. Point your mouse at the **Scene** view, and press the *F* key to bring the new Particle System into focus.

6. In the **Inspector** panel, adjust the **Explosion** settings thusly:

- **Duration**: `0.1`
- **Looping**: Unchecked
- **Start Lifetime**: `0.15`
- **Start Speed**: `60`
- **Start Size**: `5`

Emission

- **Rate**: `1000`

Shape

- **Shape: Sphere**
- **Random Direction**: Checked

7. By unchecking the **Looping** checkbox, we're creating a Particle System that will fire once, and expire—a crucial characteristic of an explosion. The one drawback is that you'll no longer get constant visual feedback. With the game stopped, click on the **Simulate** button on the **Particle Effect** tool in the **Scene** view to view your Particle System's playback.

8. As before, check the **Color over Lifetime** circle. Click on the color swatch, and modify the gradient to move from white on the left, through yellow and orange, to red on the right, just as we did with the **Spark** system.

9. In the **Renderer** section, uncheck **Cast Shadows** and **Receive Shadows**. (These matter only for Unity Pro users.) Drag the **Spark** material that we used for our bomb fuse into the **Material** slot.

✓ Renderer		
Render Mode	Billboard	▼
Normal Direction	1	
Material	Spark	⊙
Sort Mode	None	▼
Sorting Fudge	0	
Cast Shadows	☐	
Receive Shadows	☐	
Max Particle Size	0.5	

10. You'll see from the **Scene** view that this explosion is a little too dramatic, flowering violently in a fiery bloom. Yes, it will do nicely.

11. Change the **Transform Position** and **Rotation** values of **Explosion** to **X:0 Y:0 Z:0**.

Time for action – kill kill murder die

An explosion like this can't be allowed to roam the streets, wreaking its flaming spite on unsuspecting civilians. It must be stopped. And you, being a video game programmer, are the only person who can stop it.

Write a quick script to determine when the last particle in the explosion has run its course, and then destroy the explosion. It's the only way.

1. Create a new JavaScript called `DestroyParticleSystem`, and attach it as a component to **Explosion**.

2. Modify the script thusly:

```
function LateUpdate ()
{
  if (!particleSystem.IsAlive())
  {
```

```
    Destroy (this.gameObject);
    }
  }
}
```

The built-in `LateUpdate` function fires after all `Update` function calls have finished.

3. At the moment, if you click to view the **Explosion** Prefab in the **Project** panel, you may notice—to your horror—that all of the recent changes you made to your **Explosion** Particle System have not "stuck" in the Prefab. To commit all of the **Hierarchy** panel's **Explosion** changes to the Prefab mothership, click on the **Apply** button at the top of the **Inspector** panel.

Time for action – the point of impact

We're finished tweaking the explosion, so you should delete the instance of the **Explosion** Prefab from the **Scene** view. The original stays safe and sound in the **Prefab** container in your **Project** panel. Naturally, we want this explosion to appear whenever we detect that the bomb has hit the ground. We've already put the logic in place to detect a ground hit—remember that we're moving the bomb back up into the sky as soon as it drops below ground level. So it should be a reasonable hop, skip, and jump towards making that explosion happen. And luckily, it is!

1. Open up your **Bomb** Script and add the following variable at the very top:

```
var prefab:GameObject;
```

2. Then, just after the code where we detect a ground hit, add this line:

```
if(transform.position.y < 0)
{
  Instantiate(prefab, transform.position,
    Quaternion.identity);
```

We created a variable called `prefab` at the top of the script to store some sort of **GameObject**. Note that small-p "prefab" is not a Unity keyword—we're calling it that because calling it "monkeybutt" would make the code even more confusing.

The `Instantiate` command does exactly what you suspect it does. We need to pass it a reference to a **GameObject** (in our case, we've got one stored in the `prefab` variable), along with arguments to determine the position and the rotation of the thing. Then Unity goes looking for the **GameObject** we specified, and places it in the game at the position/rotation we specify.

What do we pass for the position value? The bomb's own position, before we move the bomb to the top of the apartment building. And what do we pass in for its rotation? SCARY MATH! BLAH!!

Once again, I'm not even going to pretend that I understand Quaternion mathematics. What I do know is that `Quaternion.identity` means "no rotation"—the object is aligned perfectly with the world or parent axes.

Time for action – hook up the explosion

"But wait," you say. How do we actually tell the Script what we want to instantiate? Ah, there's the magic of Unity yet again. Save the **Bomb** Script, and follow these next steps:

1. In the **Project** panel, select the **Bomb** Prefab.

2. In the **Inspector** panel, find the **Bomb** (Script) Component. Notice that the variable we called `prefab` is listed there. (If you actually did call your variable "monkeybutt", you'll see that instead.)

3. Click-and-drag the **Explosion** Prefab from the **Project** panel into the **Prefab** variable slot in the **Inspector** panel. You should see a little red green and blue icon appear in the slot, with the label **Explosion** Prefab. I've got a good feeling about this!

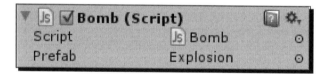

Test out your game. The bomb falls from the top of the building, "hits" the ground, and calls in the **Explosion** Prefab before popping back up to the top of the building at some random X position. The **Explosion**, because of its **DestroyParticleSystem** Script, does its thing and then disappears from the scene. It's a beautiful thing.

Summary

So! Do we have a game yet? Not quite. Catching a bomb with your face sounds like a great party trick, but our game is obviously missing a few things to make it playable. We still need to handle the collision of the bomb against the player, and we need to get those beer steins in there. They're apparently worth breaking up with your girlfriend, so they sound pretty important.

In the next chapter, we'll do all these things and more. Buckle your seatbelt and turn that page!

C# addendum

Here are the C# translations you so richly deserve. Among the very few changes here is the fact that you can't individually change the x/y/z transform.position values in C# as you can in JavaScript—you have to change all three values at the same time by creating a new instance of the Vector3 class.

BombCSharp

```
using UnityEngine;
using System.Collections;
```

```
public class BombCSharp : MonoBehaviour {

  public GameObject prefab;

  void Update ()
  {
    transform.position = new Vector3(transform.position.x,
      transform.position.y - 50 * Time.deltaTime,
      transform.position.z);
    if(transform.position.y < 0)
    {
      Instantiate(prefab, transform.position,
        Quaternion.identity);
      transform.position = new Vector3(Random.Range(0,60), 50,
        -16);
    }
  }
}
```

DestroyParticleSystemCSharp

```
using UnityEngine;
using System.Collections;

public class DestroyParticleSystemCSharp : MonoBehaviour
{

  void LateUpdate ()
  {
    if (!particleSystem.IsAlive())
    {
      Destroy (this.gameObject);
    }
  }
}
```

CharacterCSharp

```
using UnityEngine;
using System.Collections;

public class CharacterCSharp : MonoBehaviour {

  private float lastX; // this will store the last position of
    the character
```

```
private bool isMoving = false; //flags whether or not the player
  is in motion

void Start()
{
  animation.Stop();  // this stops Unity from playing the
    character's default animation.
}

void Update()
{

  transform.position = new Vector3((Input.mousePosition.x)/20,
    transform.position.y, transform.position.z);

  if(lastX != transform.position.x)
  {
    // x values between this Update cycle and the last one
    // aren't the same! That means the player is moving the mouse.
    if(!isMoving)
    {
      // the player was standing still.
      // Let's flag him to "isMoving"
      isMoving = true;
      animation.CrossFade("step");
    }
  } else {
    // The player's x position is the same this Update cycle
    // as it was the last! The player has stopped moving the mouse.
    if(isMoving)
    {
      // The player has stopped moving, so let's update the flag
      isMoving = false;
      animation.CrossFade("idle");
    }
  }
  lastX = transform.position.x;

}

}
```

Game #3 – The Break-Up Part 2

When last we left our put-upon protagonist, he had been kicked out of his apartment by his girlfriend, who began throwing lit bombs at him from the fourth floor. Luckily, our hero is bizarrely invulnerable to bombs, and what's more, he can defy the laws of physics by balancing those bombs on his nose. Clearly, we've got some work ahead of us if we want this game to make any sense.

As we continue to round out The Break-Up, we'll add the beer steins and their smash animations. We'll write a collision detection script to make the character react when he catches things. We'll learn how to save time by using one script for two different objects. Then we'll add some sound effects to the game, and we'll figure out how to throw a random number to play different sounds for the same action. Let's get gaming.

Time for action – amass some glass

If the whole point of the game is to catch mugs from the character's precious Beer Steins of the World collection, then adding the steins should be our next step.

1. Create a new **Prefab**. Remember, you can either right-click/alternate-click in the **Project** panel and choose **Create | Prefab**, or you can create one through the menu by clicking on **Assets | Create | Prefab**.

2. Name the new **Prefab** Stein. Drop it into your Prefabs folder.

3. Locate the **Stein** model in the `Models` folder of the **Project** panel.

4. Click-and-drag the **Stein** model into the empty **Stein Prefab** container. As we saw before, the icon should light up blue to indicate that the **Prefab** has something in it.

Time for action – create a particle system

We've learned these steps before—no surprises here. Now let's review how to create a **Particle System** so that we can get a shattering glass effect for when our steins hit the pavement:

1. Go to **GameObject | Create Other | Particle System** in the menu.

2. Rename the new **Particle System** as `Glass Smash`.

3. Hover the cursor over the **Scene** view and press the *F* key to focus the camera on your **Particle System**. You may have to orbit the camera if the apartment building gets in the way (hold down the *Alt* key and click/drag to do this).

4. In the **Inspector** panel, use the following settings (keep all other settings at their default):

   - **Duration**: 0.25
   - **Looping**: Unchecked
   - **Start Lifetime**: 0.2
   - **Start Speed**: 100
   - **Start Size**: 0.75
   - **Gravity Multiplier**: 50

   In the **Emission** section:

   - **Rate**: 100

In the **Shape** section:

- ❏ **Shape**: **HemiSphere**
- ❏ **Radius**: **3**
- ❏ **Emit from Shell**: Checked

5. Finally, uncheck **Cast Shadows** and **Receive Shadows** in the **Renderer** section.

What just happened – getting smashed

After punching in these settings, you should see a reasonable approximation of a shatter. We get this splash effect by applying a gravitational force with the **Gravity Multiplier** setting. The particles are then pulled back to Earth the moment they escape the emitter. (You won't see this effect if you're in the top isometric view. Rotate your **Scene** into a **Perspective** view to see what's happening.) Try increasing and decreasing this setting to see what sort of effect it has on the **Particle System**.

Time for action – make it edgier!

The particles look a bit like snowflakes at the moment. We want something more like sharp glass fragments, so let's set up a new **Material** with a sharper-edged texture on it to make this effect look more convincing:

1. In the **Project** panel, right-click or alternate-click on an empty area and choose **Create | Material**.

2. Name the **Material** Glass.

3. In the **Inspector** panel, choose **Particles/Additive** in the **Shader** dropdown.

4. Click on the **Select** button in the texture swatch, and choose `glassShard.png` from the list. (This image is in the `assetsPackage` file of `Chapter 10`. Import the package if you haven't already.)

5. Select the **Glass Smash Particle System** from the **Hierarchy** panel.

6. In the **Inspector** Panel, scroll down to the **Particle Renderer** component.

7. In the **Materials** section, choose the **Glass** material from the pop-up menu.

What just happened – I fall to pieces

Once we swap in these harder-edged textures, the effect is much improved! Now our **Glass Smash Particle System** looks a little more like an explosion of glass chunks than a violent headshot to *Frosty the Snowman*.

Time for action – contain the explosion

Let's place this **Glass Smash Particle System** into a **Prefab** so that it's ready to use with our falling beer steins:

1. In the **Project** panel, right-click or alternate-click and choose **Create | Prefab**.

2. Rename the new **Prefab** as Glass Smash.

3. Click-and-drag the **Glass Smash Particle System** from the **Hierarchy** panel into the empty **Glass Smash Prefab**. The icon lights up blue. That's how you know it's working.

4. With the **Particle System** tucked safely away into the **Prefab**, delete the **Glass Smash Particle System** from the **Scene** (select it in the **Hierarchy** panel, and press the *Delete* key on your keyboard, or *Command + Delete* if you're using a Mac).

Clean up

I've kept my **Project** panel neat and tidy by putting all of my Prefabs into a folder. I've done the same thing with my scripts, my materials, my models, and my dirty sweat socks. Because there's not a lot going on in this project, it may seem like wasted effort. Still, organizing assets into folders is a good habit to get into. It can save your sanity on larger projects.

```
▼ 📁 Prefabs
  ▶ 🔩 Bomb
  ▶ 🔩 Character
    🔩 Explosion
    🔩 Glass Smash
  ▶ 🔩 Stein
```

What just happened – duped?

We've almost duplicated the same process we followed to get the bomb working. Have you noticed? With both the bomb and the stein, we put an imported model into a **Prefab**, and we created a particle system and put it in its own **Prefab**. Then we created a script to move the bomb down the screen. We attached that script to the bomb. Then we dragged the bomb's explosion particle system into the prefab variable of its **Script** component.

This is all starting to sound familiar—too familiar. In fact, remember when we said earlier that programmers are always finding ways to do less work? We saw that if you type the same line of code twice, you may not be writing your code to be as maintenance-friendly as possible. The same holds true for this bomb/beer mug situation. If the bomb and the beer mug both need to do the exact same thing, why don't we make life easier for ourselves and use the same script for both?

Time for action – let's get lazy

There's no need to create an entirely separate script for the stein. Follow these steps to get more bang for your buck out of a single script:

1. Find the script you called **Bomb Script** in the **Project** panel, and rename it **FallingObject**. Because we'll be using the script more generically, we should give it a more generic name.

     Renaming a Script in the Editor is fine for UnityScript, but you'll cause problems if you rename a C# Script in this way, without also changing the Class declaration at the top of the Script in MonoDevelop.

2. In the **Project** panel, select the **Stein Prefab** (not the **Stein Model**).

3. Choose **Component | Scripts | FallingObject** in the menu to attach the script to the **Prefab**.

4. In the **Inspector** panel, you should see that the **FallingObject** has been added as a **Script** component to the **Stein Prefab**.

5. As we did earlier with the **Bomb Prefab**, find the **Glass Smash Prefab** in the **Project** panel. Click-and-drag it into the stein's `prefab` variable. By doing this, you're telling the **Script** which thing you want to add to the screen when the stein falls on the ground. In the bomb's case, it's the explosion. In the stein's case, it's the glass smash.

6. Add a **Capsule Collider** component to the beer stein.

7. Click to select the **Cylinder** child inside the Stein (click on the grey arrow to expand the child list to see it). Change the Cylinder's X/Y/Z Position values to 0.

8. Jump back up to the parent **Stein** node. Change the parameters of its capsule collider:

> **Radius: 2**
>
> **Height: 5.5**

9. Add a **Rigidbody** component to the beer stein.

10. Uncheck **Use Gravity** in the `Rigidbody` component settings. Recall that we're handling the beer stein's movement programmatically in the **FallingObject** script.

Two birds, one stone; or rather, two objects, one script. To test out the beer stein, drag the **Beer Stein Prefab** into your **Scene**. Add the **DestroyParticleSystem Script** as a component of the **Glass Smash** prefab to ensure the smash gets destroyed when it finishes playing. Hit the **Play** button to try it all out.

What just happened – FallingObject: The PuppetMaster

Just like the bomb, the beer stein plummets from a random X position at the top of the screen and explodes in a shower of particles when it hits the "ground". The bomb explodes and the glass smashes, but both are controlled by an identical script. Unfortunately, they both come to a gentle stop on top of the character's face when they collide, but that's what we'll take a look at next.

Very variable?

You may already be sending up warning flags about this madcap plan to use one script for two different objects. What if we wanted the bomb to travel at a different speed than the beer stein? And don't we want two completely different reactions depending on whether the player collides with the bomb or the stein?

We'll answer the collision question a little later in the chapter, and we'll tackle the variable speed question now. But before we do, fire up your gray matter. How would you solve this problem? How would you make the objects move at two different speeds, with two different collision reactions, and still use the same script?

Terminal velocity is a myth – bombs fall faster

Ignoring the laws of physics for a second, let's look at how to make the two objects fall at different speeds using the same script. One solution is to declare a variable called `speed` at the top of the **FallingObject** script.

```
var speed:int;
```

Change the following line:

```
transform.position.y -= 50 * Time.deltaTime;
```

to:

```
transform.position.y -= speed * Time.deltaTime;
```

Then for each object—the bomb and stein Prefabs—input a different number for the speed value in the **Inspector** panel. Try 30 for the stein and 50 for the bomb. Two objects, one script, and two different speeds. Awesome? Confirmed: awesome.

Know when to double down

At some point, objects become different enough that sharing a script is no longer saving you time and effort, it's causing you grief. As a game developer, you need to decide what sort of structure best suits your game-creating goal. Programmers have all kinds of tricks to save themselves work and to logically structure their code. The object-oriented programming pillar called inheritance (which we've looked at briefly) is another way to get two objects to share code, while ensuring that they function as two different things.

Wait till Sunday to take your code to church

When it comes down to just getting your game finished and playable, don't ever feel foolish about making mistakes and writing your game the wrong way. A great rule, especially when you're starting out, is to get the game working first, and then go back to make the code elegant. Totally a fact—tuning up your code and making it as organized and pretty as possible is called refactoring. When you're just starting out, worry more about functional code than elegant code.

What just happened – when game objects collide?

Bombs plummet from the top floor of the apartment building and explode around our character, as his beloved beer steins shatter on the pavement with every step he takes. These are the origins of a competent catch game! Now, let's worry about what happens when the player catches a stein or comes in contact with a bomb.

There are a few different ways we can go about this. We can write the collision detection code into the **FallingObject Script**, but that might get complicated. We're using the same script for both objects, and the objects need to do different things when they hit the player. It makes more sense to me to put the collision detection on the player character. We'll check to see when he gets hit by something, and then based on what hits him, he'll react in different ways.

Time for action – tag the objects

As we saw before with our bouncing heart, we can tag objects in the **Scene**, and then refer to objects in code using their tag names. Let's tag the bomb and the stein so that the player character can tell what hit him.

1. Select the **Bomb Prefab** in the **Project** panel. (You can actually select anything in this step. We're not actually applying a tag—just creating one. But we need to select something so that we see the tag interface show up in the **Inspector** panel. You can also reach it by navigating to **Edit | Project Settings | Tags** in the **Unity** menu.)

2. At the top of the **Inspector** panel, press and hold on the drop-down labeled **Tag**, and select **Add Tag…**.

3. Click on the gray arrow to expand the **Tags** list near the top of the **TagManager**.

4. Click in the blank area beside the **Element 0** label, and type the tag name bomb. Then punch in a tag called stein.

5. Select the **Bomb Prefab** again in the **Project** panel. (This is when it counts.)

6. In the **Inspector** panel, choose your new **bomb** tag from the drop-down list labeled **Tag**.

7. Follow the same process to tag the **Stein Prefab**.

With the bomb and stein properly tagged, we can write our collision detection code.

Time for action – write the collision detection code

Pop open the **Character Script** and let's get bizzay.

1. Type up the following function within the script. Be sure to follow the rules we've learned about where to properly write a new function (that is, "outside" of your other functions):

```
function OnCollisionEnter(col : Collision)
{

    if(col.gameObject.CompareTag("bomb"))
    {
      // I got hit by a bomb!
    } else if (col.gameObject.CompareTag("stein"))

    {
       animation.CrossFade("catch"); // Ima catch that stein!
    }
    col.gameObject.transform.position.y = 50;
    col.gameObject.transform.position.z = -16;
    col.gameObject.transform.position.x = Random.Range(0,60);
}
```

Once again, our prior knowledge of useful game code serves us well. This line should already look familiar:

```
function OnCollisionEnter(col : Collision) {
```

We're declaring a function—in this case, a special built-in Unity function called OnCollisionEnter—and accepting a variable called col as an argument. The value of col is a collision that Unity's physics calculations detect whenever rigid bodies smack into each other.

```
    if(col.gameObject.CompareTag("bomb"))
```

col.gameObject refers to whatever thing hits the GameObject to which this script is attached (the **Character**). gameObject.CompareTag, naturally, checks the argument against whatever tag that GameObject has stuck to it. We stuck **bomb** and **stein** tags on the **Bomb Prefab** and **Stein Prefab**, so that's what we should get when they hit. We use a branching conditional (if) statement to react to either the bomb or the stein.

```
    animation.CrossFade("catch"); // Ima catch that stein!
```

If the player gets hit by a beer stein, we'll play the `"catch"` animation stored in the
Character model.

```
col.gameObject.transform.position.y = 50;
col.gameObject.transform.position.z = -16;
col.gameObject.transform.position.x = Random.Range(0,60);
```

No matter what hits the player, we're going to throw the colliding object back up to the top
of the screen at some random **X** position and let it fall back down. This becomes problematic
if we end up having other stuff hit the player that doesn't need to respawn at the top of the
building, but let's get this script working simply for the time being.

But wait! Ees problem, señor. Save the script and try the game out. Then see if you can
spot the problem.

Time for action – animation interrupts

The trouble is that we're telling the character to play his `"catch"` animation when
he collides with a stein, but it's not happening. We see, at best, the first frame of that
animation, and then it's interrupted by either the `"idle"` or `"step"` animation:

1. Luckily, we can add a condition to the script to prevent these glory-hog animations
   from playing if we're trying to catch a beer stein. Dip back into your **CharacterScript**
   and make these changes:

   ```
   if(lastX != transform.position.x) {
     if(!isMoving) {
       isMoving = true;
       if(!animation.IsPlaying("catch")){
         animation.CrossFade("step");
       }
     }
   } else {
     if(isMoving) {
       isMoving = false;
       if(!animation.IsPlaying("catch")) {
         animation.CrossFade("idle");
       }
     }
   }
   ```

By wrapping the `animation.Play` calls in these `animation.isPlaying` conditionals, we can ensure that the character isn't busy playing his catch animation when we determine it's time to step or idle. Remember that!

2. Save the script and try it out. Your player character should start catching those steins like a champ!

What just happened – the impenetrable stare

The magical properties of our character's iron-clad bomb-catching face continue to amaze—now, the bombs hit the character straight in the schnozz and wondrously disappear! I don't know how many cartoons you watch, but the last time I saw someone get hit in the face with a bomb, there was a satisfying explosion, along with (possibly) a snickering mouse nearby.

How convenient. We just happen to have a reusable **Prefab** that contains a satisfying bomb explosion. Wouldn't it be great if we could trigger that explosion to happen right on top of the character's face? (The character might disagree with us, but I say let's go for it!)

Time for action – add facial explosions

Just as we did when our falling object hit the ground, we'll use the `Instantiate` command to make a copy of a **Prefab** appear in the game world. This time around, when we determine that the player has been hit in the face by a bomb, we'll instantiate the **Explosion Prefab** on top of his head.

1. Add the following line to the top of the code:

```
var lastX:float;
var isMoving:boolean = false;
var explosion:GameObject;
```

2. Later on, in the conditional statement that determines when the player is hit by a bomb, add the `Instantiate` command:

```
if(col.gameObject.CompareTag("bomb"))
{
  // I got hit by a bomb!
  Instantiate(explosion, col.gameObject.transform.position,
    Quaternion.identity);
    } else if (col.gameObject..CompareTag("stein")) {
```

3. Save the **Script**.

4. In the **Project** panel, select the **Character Prefab**.

5. In the **Inspector** panel, locate the **Explosion** variable in the **Script** component.

6. Click-and-drag the **Explosion Prefab** into the **Explosion** variable slot.

What just happened – raindrops keep 'sploding on my head

We already know how the Instantiate command works, so we won't dissect it again. Suffice it to say, when the bomb drops on the player's head, it appears to explode. The explosion removes itself when it's finished, because it has the **DestroyParticleSystem** script attached. Of course, we know what's really going on: we're just moving the bomb to the top of the building and setting it to some random position along the X-axis so that the player thinks it's a new bomb. Meanwhile, we're instantiating a new copy of the **Explosion Prefab** at the exact spot where the bomb was when it collided with the player. Sneaky!

Time for action – make some noise

So far, the games we've made have been completely silent. I count this as a terrible tragedy; audio in a game can account for *half* of the player's emotional experience. In the case of games like **Rock Band**, there would be no game without audio (hilarious little plastic instruments notwithstanding). Audio is so important to games that even crummy little low-rent sounds effects (like the ones we're about to add to this game!) can increase the game's awesomeness by a factor of WOW... to the power of GEE GOLLY—something like that. It's all very scientific.

Let's rig up our **Bomb** and **Stein Prefabs** so that they can emit sounds.

1. In the **Project** panel, click on the **Bomb Prefab**.

2. In the menu, navigate to **Component | Audio | Audio Source** to add the **Audio Source** component.

3. Repeat those steps to add an **Audio Source** component to your **Stein Prefab**.

Now hear this

You may have noticed that Unity also offers an **Audio Listener** component. What's the deal? Well, in the case of a 3D game, you don't necessarily want the player to hear everything that's going on all the time. You want him to hear audio fading in and out as he moves closer to or farther from the source (the **Audio Source**, to be specific). By default, an **Audio Listener** component is attached to the **Main Camera** in any **Scene**. In something like a first-person perspective game, the **Audio Listener** will only pick up sounds from Audio Source-enabled game objects if it's within range. If we tweak the settings just right, the player won't hear a noisy washing machine GameObject from the other side of the level. Each scene can only have one **Audio Listener** at a time.

Unity also offers a **Unity Reverb Zone** component. This is a spherical gizmo that lets you define an area where the sound is "pure" and unaffected, with a candy-coated craziness shell around it that lets you define echoes and other potentially oddball effects.

With the **Bomb** and **Stein Prefabs** so enabled, we can add a few lines to the **FallingObject** to make them play sounds when they hit the ground.

Time for action – add sounds to FallingObject

Let's drop a couple of lines into the **FallingObject** script to fire off a few sounds:

1. Open the **FallingObject** script.

2. Declare a `clip1` variable at the top of the script:

```
var prefab:GameObject;
var speed:int;
var clip1:AudioClip;
```

3. Just after we determine that the falling object has hit the ground, play the `clip1` sound:

```
if(transform.position.y < 0)
{
    audio.PlayOneShot(clip1);
```

By now, you've probably guessed that there's one more step involved. The script really has no idea what `clip1` actually is—it's just a variable placeholder. Let's add some actual sound files to the **Bomb** and **Stein** Prefabs to get this party started:

1. In the **Project** panel, click to open the SFX folder. Yay—sounds!!

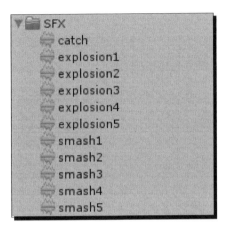

2. Again in the **Project** panel, click to select the **Bomb Prefab**.

3. In the **Inspector** panel, locate the `clip1` variable in the **FallingObject** component.

4. Click-and-drag the sound effect labeled **explosion1** into the `clip1` variable slot.

5. Repeat the previous steps for the **Stein Prefab**, but this time, choose the **smash1** sound effect.

Test your game. Whenever the bomb hits the dirt, there's a satisfying (if retro) sound effect to accompany it. Likewise, there's an 8-bit approximation of glass smashing whenever the beer stein shatters.

Silent 'Splosion

Even in 8 lo-fi bits, these sound effects don't have nearly the impact we need them to. Why are they so quiet? The answer is in the **Import Settings**, where both sound effects have been marked as **3D Sound**.

Since Unity thinks these are 3D sounds, the sounds will be quieter the further away the camera is from the audio sources attached to our objects. You can test this by moving the camera in closer to where the objects land.

To let Unity know we want these sounds to play at a consistent volume regardless of their proximity to the camera, we have to uncheck **3D Sound** in the **Import Settings**, and then click on **Apply** to make sure the change was registered. Do this for all of the sounds in the SFX folder.

After you make this change, test your game again. The sounds will be noticeably louder.

What's the catch?

Using the same method that you used earlier, you should be able to figure out how to add that "catch" sound effect to the player character when he catches a beer stein. Likewise, you want to enable the **explosion1** sound effect if the player gets hit by a bomb. If you can't figure it out on your own, take a deep breath, and then go nag someone else to figure it out for you. That's called **delegating**, and it's a perfectly legit way to develop a game.

Perfect for smashing

Unity has all kinds of complex sound controls for playing music and other effects. The `audio.PlayOneShot` command is perfect for collision sound effects. If you'd like to learn more about adding sounds and music to your game, look up **AudioSource** class, **AudioListener** class, and **AudioClip** class in the Unity Script Reference.

Lo-fi, high fun

The sound effects that we're using for our game were created with a freeware sound effects generator called **BFXR**. The sounds are all free to use and adorable, hearkening back to a time when dragons looked like ducks and heroes had big white 4-pixel squares for heads. Download a copy of BFXR to generate your own temporary (or even final) game audio. Look for a download link for BFXR and scads of other helpful resources in the *Appendix* at the back of this book.

Have a go hero – sound off

If you're not a big fan of the retro sounds, it's possible that you may have missed out on the cavalcade of cheese we now know as the 1980s. Feel free to create and import your own sound effects for the game. There are a few different ways you can go about this:

- Get busy with a microphone and record your own effects. This is the only way you can truly be happy with the results and get exactly what's in your head into the game. The industry term for sound effect scores is called "foley". You could use the method acting approach and actually smash glass and detonate high-powered explosives next to your computer (not recommended), or you could say "boom!" and "smash!" into the microphone. It's a style thing.

- There are a number of companies that sell royalty-free sound effects for film, television, and movies. I'll give you two warnings about using these—the first is that royalty-free sound effects collections can be very expensive on a hobbyist's budget. The second is that once you get enough experience with these popular collections under your belt, movies and teevee shows will be forever ruined for you. You'll hear these same sound effects everywhere! It's tough to stay immersed in a tense film when all you're thinking is "Hey, that's track #58 from disc 2 of the Explosive Ballistics Collection."

- There are less expensive royalty-free sound effects websites online, but I've found that a good number of them contain pirated sound effects from pricy collections that are passed off as legit effects. *Caveat emptor*, which is Latin for "You probably won't get sued, but do the right thing anyway."

Time for action – mix it up a bit

One of my personal beefs about sound design in games is when the sound effects are too samey. In our game, hearing the same two sound effects over and over again is wearying. One of the things I like to do is to create a bunch of slightly different sound effects for the same event, and when the time comes to play a sound, I just choose one of them at random. This can really vary the soundscape of the game and keep your player from overdosing on the same sound effects.

You probably noticed that the SFX folder contained five versions of the **smash** and **explosion** sound effects. Let's learn how to set them up to play randomly:

1. Open the **FallingObject** script.
2. Delete the line where you define the `clip1` variable, and replace it with an array declaration:

    ```
    var prefab:GameObject;
    var speed:int;
    var audioClips : AudioClip[];
    ```

3. Modify the line where you play the sound:

    ```
    audio.PlayOneShot(audioClips[Random.Range(0,audioClips.length)]
    );
    ```

    Let's take a closer look at this new code:

    ```
    var audioClips : AudioClip[];
    ```

This is a special built-in array; it is statically typed, which means we're telling Unity what kind of thing it's going to contain. In this case, it's going to be a list of **AudioClip** types. A normal array (`var myArray = new Array()`) won't show up in the **Inspector** panel, but a built-in array will.

```
audio.PlayOneShot(audioClips[Random.Range(0,audioClips.length)]);
```

What we're doing here is picking a random number from 0 to the built-in array's length. We're using the resulting number as the index of the `audioClip` in the array that we want to play.

The last step is to click-and-drag the **explosion** and **smash** sound effects into the new built-in array in the **Inspector** panel:

1. Select the **Bomb Prefab** in the **Project** panel.
2. In the **Inspector** panel, locate the **FallingObject** component.
3. Click on the gray arrow to expand the **Audio Clips** array.

4. Enter a value of 5 in the **Size** label. The list expands even further to accommodate five empty slots for **Audio Clips** objects.

5. Click-and-drag the five explosion sound effects into the various indices of the array.

6. Repeat these steps for the **Stein Prefab** using the **smash** sound effects.

▼ Js ☑ **Falling Object (Script)**		🖺 ⚙▾
Script	Js FallingObject	⊙
Prefab	Glass Smash	⊙
Speed	30	
▼ Audio Clips		
Size	5	
Element 0	smash1	⊙
Element 1	smash2	⊙
Element 2	smash3	⊙
Element 3	smash4	⊙
Element 4	smash5	⊙

7. Run the game.

Now the falling objects make different-ish noises when they hit the ground. Variety is the spice of life. Paprika is also reasonably delicious.

Have a go hero – filling in the gaps

Consider this the jumping-off point for your catch game. With the basics roughed in, there are a number of finer elements missing from the experience:

♦ Title screen with **Play** button

♦ Instructions page

♦ Credits screen

♦ End game

♦ **Play Again** button

♦ On-screen scoring (counting the number of steins the player has collected)

Sounds for when the player gets hit by something bad

We already know how to do a lot of this stuff. We've built a **Title** screen with a **Play** button for Robot Repair, and it's the same process to build in the other screens, like Credits and Instructions. We've created an on-screen counter for Ticker Taker. We've built a timer for use in our games as well.

If you imagine all of these elements as ingredients in a cake, you should know how to bake a pretty scrumptious dessert by now. There are a few different decisions you can make about how the game plays:

Score points

Let the player catch beer steins. Count up each one he catches. End the game when he gets hit by a bomb. Show the player his last and best scores, and add a message when he beats his best score, exactly as we did with Ticker Taker.

Survive

Add the timer from *Chapter 8, Hearty Har Har*, to the screen. The player has to keep collecting beer steins until the timer runs out. He's allowed to miss only three beer steins—if he drops his third stein, or gets hit by a bomb, the game ends. This is different from the last scenario because there's a definite win scenario, whereas the other method kept the player playing until he inevitably lost. This win scenario doesn't lend itself as well to adding a high score board, and it doesn't have as much replay value. But certain players (myself included) just can't get excited about games they can't win.

Quota

Clocks are a great and frequently used gameplay tool, but sometimes they just give players the jitters. Another way you can determine player's success is by defining a quota: "You must catch x beer steins to finish the game."

Levels

One possibility that a "win" scenario opens up is a multilevel structure for your game. If the player makes it through the first level, you increase the number of bombs (or the falling speed of the objects). Maybe a bus periodically drives through the screen, and the player has to jump down a manhole to avoid it? Maybe the mugs get smaller and harder to catch, or the bombs get larger and harder to avoid? If you are using a timer for a survival mode, increase the length of time the player has to spend to survive. If you're using a quota system, increase the number of steins the player has to catch to finish the level.

In this way, you combine the best of both worlds—the game has finite successes because the player can finish and feel accomplished. But the player is also guaranteed to lose, because the quota keeps getting larger and more impossible to fill. You could even loop it right back around and put a level cap on the game; after finishing level 10, the player wins once and for all. Perhaps his high score is the lowest time it took him to complete all ten levels?

Health points

You could create some *The Legend of Zelda*-style heart graphics and display them at the top-right of the screen. Every time the player gets hit by a bomb, remove a heart. If the player loses all his health, the game ends. This feature works with both the "score points" and "survive" ideas, and helps to give the player much more of a fighting chance. The player is usually more willing to play your game if he perceives that the rules are "fair" and if he can own any mistakes he makes. He should never feel like the game "made him die". Keep in mind that "fair" can sometimes mean "unfairly advantageous to the player"—as long as the computer doesn't "cheat", it's fair in the player's eyes.

Catch unlit bombs

You could create another **bomb Prefab** that doesn't have the sparking fuse, and ask that the player catch both beer steins AND unlit bombs. The objects would probably need to fall more slowly (or you'd need to pull the camera back to reveal a larger play area), and you may need to increase the size of the fuse sparks to help the player differentiate a lit bomb from an unlit one. Better yet, to make it even more "fair", you could put a bright red texture on the lit bombs.

Vary the landscape

Doesn't this guy have anything in his apartment other than cartoon bombs and Oktoberfest souvenirs? In order to make the game more visually interesting, you could import a few new models and chuck *those* out the window. Tighty whities, action figures, and naughty magazines might make nice additions to the fiction.

Summary

The savings don't stop there! We've already been able to take a scant knowledge of programming and a few simple Unity concepts and turn them into three capable beginner games, with a lot of potential. In the next chapter, we'll actually milk even more mileage out of our blossoming game development skills by applying a graphics re-skin to The Break-Up to turn it into a completely different game! Join us, won't you?

C# Addendum

This was another very straightforward port to C#. The only thing that could potentially trip you up is realizing that in C# version of the **FallingObject** script, the built-in array's `Length` property starts with a capital L, while Unity JavaScript uses a lowercase l.

Here's the code:

FallingObjectCSharp.cs

```csharp
using UnityEngine;
using System.Collections;

public class FallingObjectCSharp : MonoBehaviour {

  public GameObject prefab;
  public int speed;
  public AudioClip[] audioClips;

  void Update ()
  {
    transform.position = new Vector3(transform.position.x,
      transform.position.y - speed * Time.deltaTime,
      transform.position.z);
    if(transform.position.y < 0)
    {
      audio.PlayOneShot(audioClips[Random.Range(0,
        audioClips.Length)]);
      Instantiate(prefab, transform.position, Quaternion.identity);
      transform.position = new Vector3(Random.Range(0,60), 50, -16);
    }
  }
}
```

CharacterCSharp.cs

```csharp
using UnityEngine;
using System.Collections;

public class CharacterCSharp : MonoBehaviour {

  private float lastX; // this will store the last position of
    the character
  private bool isMoving = false; //flags whether or not the player is
    in motion
  public GameObject explosion;

  void Start()
  {
```

```
    animation.Stop();  // this stops Unity from playing the
      character's default animation.
}


void Update()
{

  transform.position = new Vector3((Input.mousePosition.x)/20,
    transform.position.y, transform.position.z);

  if(lastX != transform.position.x)
  {
    // x values between this Update cycle and the last one
    // aren't the same! That means the player is moving the mouse
    if(!isMoving)
    {
      // the player was standing still.
      // Let's flag him to "isMoving"
      isMoving = true;
      if(!animation.IsPlaying("catch")){
        animation.CrossFade("step");
      }
    }
  } else {
    // The player's x position is the same this Update cycle
    // as it was the last! The player has stopped moving the mouse
    if(isMoving)
    {
      // The player has stopped moving, so let's update the flag
      isMoving = false;
      if(!animation.IsPlaying("catch")){
        animation.CrossFade("idle");
      }
    }
  }
  lastX = transform.position.x;

}


void OnCollisionEnter(Collision col)
{
```

```
        if(col.gameObject.CompareTag("bomb"))
        {
          // I got hit by a bomb!
          Instantiate(explosion, col.gameObject.transform.position,
            Quaternion.identity);
        } else if (col.gameObject.CompareTag("stein")) {
          animation.CrossFade("catch"); // Ima catch that stein!
        }
        col.gameObject.transform.position = new
          Vector3(Random.Range(0,60), 50, -16);
      }
    }
```

11

Game #4 – Shoot the Moon

Way back in Chapter 2, Let's Start with the Sky, we talked about the difference between a game's mechanics and its skin. We've used Unity to create some very simple games with funny, strange, or interesting skins. In this chapter, we'll investigate the enormous difference a new skin can make to our games.

*We're going to re-skin **The Break-Up** from the last few chapters as a completely different game: a sci-fi space shooter (think **Galaga**, **Space Invaders**, **Centipede**, and so on). We're going to leverage the work we've already done on The Break-Up to create a game with a very different feel, but the guts will be the same. In the industry, we call this getting more products for less effort, and it's a very good plan. When you break it down, there's not much difference between a catch game and a space shooter. In both games, you're moving your character back and forth across the screen. In a catch game, you're trying to collide with valuable objects, while in a space shooter, you're trying to avoid dangerous objects—namely, enemy ships. Luckily, our catch game includes both colliding with and avoiding objects, so we're all set. The only other real difference is that a space shooter, by definition, requires shooting. You may be surprised to see how easy it is to include a new shooting feature based on techniques you've already learned!*

Here is a preview of the game we'll build in this chapter:

Time for action – duplicate your game project

Unity does not provide us with a **Save as** option to duplicate a project. You have to do it through your computer's operating system.

1. Close Unity.

2. Navigate to the folder where you saved your finished game, The Break-Up, from the previous two chapters.

3. Copy the folder.

4. Paste the folder wherever you'd like your new Shoot the Moon game to live.

5. Rename the copied folder `Shoot the Moon` (or `ShootTheMoon` if you're picky about spaces).

Unity copies over our whole `Assets` folder and everything in it, so you should have an exact duplicate of The Break-Up, with a different project name. Let's open the new project:

1. Open up Unity, and then go to **File | Open Project…**.

> **Protip**
>
> If you hold down the *Alt* key on your keyboard after double-clicking on the file to open Unity, the Project picker prompt will appear, enabling you to choose a project without opening the most recent one.

2. Navigate to your new `Shoot the Moon` project folder and open it.

3. Your project may open on a blank scene. Find the **Game** Scene in the **Project** panel and double-click on it. You should see the brownstone apartment building, the bomb, the stein, and all the other game goodies as you left them at the end of the last chapter.

4. Import the new assets package for this chapter, which includes two spaceship models and their materials, a new sound effect, and a new background texture. Tuck all of the new stuff into appropriate folders to keep everything organized.

Time for action – space the shooter up a bit

I've never known a space shooter to take place in front of an apartment building, so let's get rid of our old backdrop. Then we'll pull a fun trick with multiple cameras to add a space backdrop to our game.

1. Click on the brownstone apartment building GameObject and delete it from the **Scene**.

2. Go to **GameObject | Create Other | Camera** to add a second camera to the scene.

3. Rename the camera `SpaceCam`.

4. In the **Project** panel, select the **starfield** texture.

5. Go to **GameObject | Create Other | GUI Texture**.

Suddenly, the starfield image appears in the **Game** view as shown in the following screenshot:

Suddenly, the starfield image appears in the Game view, but it completely takes over, blocking everything in the Scene! Let's fix this.

1. In the **Hierarchy** panel, click on the **starfield** GUITexture that you just created.

2. In the **Inspector** panel, we'll create a new layer. Click on the **Layer** dropdown and select **Add Layer...**.

3. Look down the list, past all the built-in layers. The next available slot is going to be **User Layer 8**. Click on the empty field beside that label and type `starfield`. Press the *Enter* key when you're finished to commit the layer name.

4. In the **Hierarchy** panel, click to select **starfield** GUITexture.

5. In the **Inspector** panel, click on the **Layer** dropdown and choose the new **starfield** layer you just created.

With the **starfield** GUITexture placed in a layer, we'll modify the **SpaceCam** camera so that it only ever "sees" that **GUITexture**.

1. In the **Hierarchy** panel, click to select **SpaceCam**.

2. In the **Inspector** panel, remove the **Flare Layer** and **Audio Listener** components (right-click/secondary-click on the names of the Components and choose **Remove Component**, or pick this option by clicking on the small black gear icon to the right of the **Component** label, next to the blue book icon). We can have only one **Audio Listener** in the Scene, so let's leave that job up to the **Main Camera** by getting rid of this extraneous listener. Likewise, we don't need this secondary camera to render any lens flare effects, which is why we're nixing the **Flare Layer**.

3. Find the **Clear Flags** drop-down at the top of the **Camera** component. It defaults to **Skybox**. Instead, set it to **Solid Color**.

4. Change the **Depth** to **-1**.

5. In the **Culling Mask** dropdown, choose **Nothing**. This deselects all other options in the list, and the little Camera Preview window in the Scene view is cleared.

6. Again in the **Culling Mask** dropdown, select the **starfield** layer.

We've now told our **SpaceCam** component to only render (draw, look at) stuff that's on the **starfield** layer. Currently, the only thing on the **starfield** layer is our **starfield** GUITexture. We changed the **SpaceCam** depth to a low number, because we want whatever it sees to appear behind everything our **Main Camera** sees. Let's make a few changes to the **Main Camera** to blend the two cameras' views.

1. In the **Hierarchy** panel, select **Main Camera**.

2. In the **Inspector** panel, set its **Clear Flags** to **Depth only**.

3. In the **Culling Mask** dropdown, click to uncheck the **starfield** layer. When you do this, you're deselecting the **starfield** layer so that the **Main Camera** sees everything else. The value of **Culling Mask** changes to **Mixed**, and the character model pops into view.

4. Ensure that the **Depth** value of the **Main Camera** is set to **1**.

   Because the **Main Camera's** depth is 1 and the **SpaceCam's** depth is -1, the **Main Camera's** imagery gets layered in front of the **SpaceCam's** picture.. You should now see the jilted lover character from The Break-Up floating in the vacuum of space. As if the poor guy wasn't having a bad enough day already!

Resizing a GUI Texture

If you're running a very high resolution on your monitor, the 1024 x 768 pixel **starfield** image may not be large enough to cover your screen's real estate. You can always select the GUITexture in the **Hierarchy** panel, and adjust its Width and Height properties under the **Pixel Inset** heading. Keep in mind, though, that scaling up a bitmap image will lead to an increasingly poorer-quality picture. The very best thing, as we've learned in other chapters, is to choose your target resolution and to build all of your texture assets to work with that resolution.

Clear Flags

The **Clear Flags** setting we just used determines what a camera renders in all the empty space that isn't *stuff* (models, particle effects, and so on). The default is to render the skybox, which is an inverted cube to which you can map, among other things, a sky texture, to provide the illusion that the open world continues on for miles in any direction (which it does not).

The **Clear Flags** dropdown lets us fill that empty space with a skybox, a solid color, or depth only. With Depth Only, the camera just draws the stuff in its **Culling Mask** list. Any empty areas are gaping holes that get filled with whatever the camera at a lower depth is showing. The final **Clear Flags** option is **Don't Clear**, which Unity doesn't recommend because of the resulting "smear-looking effect".

Time for action – enter the hero

Because the hero from our last game does a lot of the same stuff we want our spaceship to do, we really only have to replace the dude with the ship for fast, fun results.

1. In the **Project** panel, find the **Hero Ship** model and drag it into the **Scene**.

2. In the **Hierarchy** panel, click on the gray arrow to expand the **Character** Prefab.

3. Delete the child object called **Armature**.

4. Click on **Continue** if Unity warns you about losing the connection to the **Prefab**. Aaand... poof! No more dude.

5. In the **Hierarchy** panel, drag the **heroShip** model into the recently gutted **Character** prefab. (Do this all within the **Hierarchy** panel—not in the **Project** panel.)

6. In the **Inspector** panel, punch in all of the default transform values (or choose **Reset Position** by clicking on the little black gear icon) for the **heroShip**. Then tweak the rotation:

> **Position**: **X**:0, **Y**:0, **Z**:0
>
> **Rotation**: **X**:0, **Y**:-180, **Z**:-180
>
> **Scale**: **X**:1, **Y**:1, **Z**:1

7. In the **Hierarchy** panel, click to select the parent, the **Character** prefab.

8. In the **Inspector** panel, position the **Character Prefab** thusly:

> **Position**: **X**:25, **Y**:5, **Z**:0

9. Set all **Rotation** values to 0 and all **Scale** values to 1. The **HeroShip** model swings into view near the bottom of the **Game** view. I changed the **Field of View** setting of Main Camera to 60 to pull it back out a smidge.

The **HeroShip** GameObject becomes a child of the **Character** Prefab, instead of the human model and armature bones. This means that it keeps all of the components we tacked onto our character—the **Box Collider**, the **Script**, the **Audio Source**, and so on. This is way faster than recreating this **Prefab** from the ground up!

Save the project and play the game. Some wacky things may be going on with the bomb and stein, but notice that the spaceship controls beautifully.

Time for action – it's a hit!

Now we'll do a little fiddling to bring the **Character** Prefab in line with its new, smaller spaceship model. You remember when we added that gigantic green box collider to the human character? Well it's still there, and it's not going to cut it for this game. We fix!

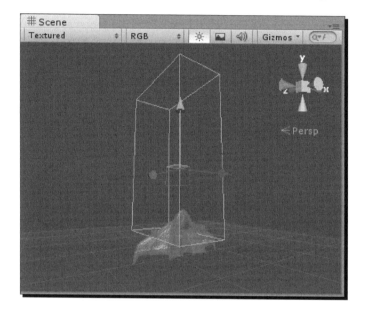

1. In the **Hierarchy** panel, click to select the **Character** Prefab.

2. Point your mouse cursor over the **Scene** view, and press the *F* key on your keyboard to focus in on the ship.

3. In the **Inspector** panel, find the **Box Collider** component.

4. In the menu, go to **Component | Physics | Mesh Collider**. A prompt asks us whether we want to **Replace** or **Add** the new collider. Click on **Replace** to knock out the oversized collider and replace it with the new one.

5. In the **Project** panel, find the **heroShipCollisionCage** model.

6. Click on the gray arrow to expand the list of goodies inside **heroShipCollisionCage**. One of these goodies should be a mesh called **CollisionCage** (remember that a mesh has a black grid pattern icon beside its name).

7. In the **Hierarchy** panel, click again to select the **Character Prefab**.

8. Click and drag the **CollisionCage** mesh into the **Inspector** panel, in the **Mesh** field of the **Mesh Collider** component.

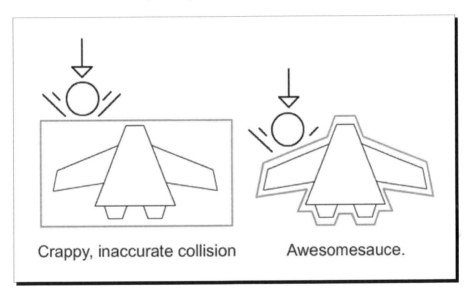

9. At the top of the **Inspector** panel, click on the **Apply** button to commit all of these changes to the **Prefab**.

Instead of a coarse, bulky box collider around our ship, we've used a special, separate model to determine its collision contours. Now, objects won't hit the empty space above the wings, on either side of the nose cone, as they would if we kept using a box collider.

Custom colliders

You may have guessed that we could have used the **HeroShip's** own mesh in its **Mesh Collider**. The trouble with that plan is that the **HeroShip** mesh is too complex. If you're making a game where you're trying to squeeze every last ounce of performance out of Unity, you might consider modeling a separate, simpler mesh to use as the **Mesh Collider** for your spaceship—one that roughly approximates the ship's shape, but with less detail, which is what we've done here. Unity can chew through its calculations faster if you use optimized mesh colliders. If you want Unity to turn your **Mesh Collider** into a convex **Mesh Collider**, like we did with the hands and tray models in **Ticker Taker**, the mesh has to have fewer than 256 triangles. You'll recall that convex mesh colliders give us better results when testing collisions between moving objects. An unoptimized mesh, like a poorly constructed wall, can actually let other colliders pass right through it, which is called "tunneling". Be sure to optimize your collider meshes to prevent tunneling. Thin, flimsy colliders are good candidates for unwanted tunneling.

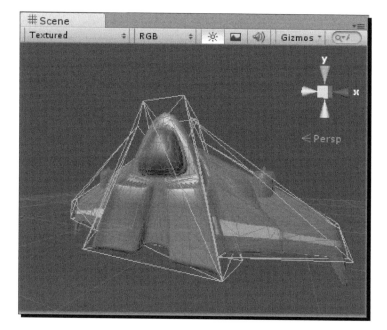

Time for action – bring on the bad guys

Unlike **The Break-Up**, where we had good items and bad items, we'll have only bad items in our space shooter **Shoot the Moon**. Those bad items will be evil enemy spaceships that are hell-bent on destroying the universe, or whatever. Let's nix the beer steins, and leverage the work we've already done on our **Bomb** Prefab to swap them out for our enemy spacecraft.

1. In the **Hierarchy** panel, click on the **Stein** Prefab and delete it. So much for space beer. You can get rid of the stein model and the stein **GameObject** while you're at it.

2. Drag the **EnemyShip** model from the **Project** panel into the **Scene**.

3. In the **Hierarchy** panel, click on the gray arrow to expand the contents of **Bomb**.

4. Delete the **Bomb** child. Click on **Continue** at the **Losing Prefab** prompt.

5. Delete the **Sparks** child in the same way.

6. Drag the **EnemyShip** GameObject into the **Bomb** GameObject (all within the **Hierarchy** panel). As before, the **EnemyShip** becomes a child of the **Bomb** GameObject.

7. Ensure that the transform of **EnemyShip** is set to default (the **Reset** option under the gear icon will handle this quickly):

> **Position: X**:0, **Y**:0, **Z**:0
>
> **Rotation: X**:0, **Y**:0, **Z**:0
>
> **Scale: X**:1, **Y**:1, **Z**:1

8. In the **Hierarchy** panel, click on the **Bomb** GameObject. In the **Inspector** panel, position it like so:

> **Position: X**:25, **Y**:71, **Z**:0

9. In the **Inspector** panel, within the **Rigidbody** component, check the **Freeze Rotation** boxes for **X**, **Y**, and **Z** under the **Constraints** fly-out. This will prevent the enemy ship from spinning all over the place after a collision.

10. Click on the **Apply** button at the top of the **Inspector** panel to commit these changes to the **Prefab**.

11. Try out the game.

Positions are still nutty, but check it out—we've got a "good" spaceship that we can move across the screen, and a "bad" spaceship that uses the old **FallingObject** Script to slither down the screen.

Time for action – do some housekeeping

We're most of the way to a brand new game, and we barely broke a sweat! Let's take a moment to rename a few things before we make some script adjustments.

1. Rename the **Bomb** and **Character** Prefabs EnemyShip and HeroShip, respectively. You should make this change in both the **Hierarchy** and **Project** panels.

2. In the **Project** panel, rename the **Character** Script to HeroShip.

3. Likewise, rename the **FallingObject** Script to EnemyShip.

 If you've been working through the book using the C# examples, you should also rename the class inside the script when you rename the script file.

4. In the **Hierarchy** panel, click to select the **EnemyShip** Prefab (formerly the **Bomb** Prefab).

5. Hover your mouse cursor over the **Scene** view and press the *F* key to focus in on the **EnemyShip**. You may notice that the **Sphere Collider** is too large. Let's fix that.

6. In the **Inspector** panel, change the **radius** of the **Sphere Collider** to 1.7.

7. Click on the **Apply** button to apply these changes to the source **Prefab** when you're finished. It's safe to delete the Bomb and Stein models from the **Project** panel if you like.

▼ ☑ Sphere Collider		
Is Trigger	☐	
Material	None (Physic Mate	⊙
Center		
X 0	Y 0	Z 0
Radius	1.7	

Time for action – fixing the fall

In The Break-Up, our falling objects were larger, and they fell through a smaller vertical range. Now that there's no ground to hit and the sky's the limit, we should tweak a few lines of code in our **EnemyShip** Script (formerly the **FallingObject** Script). Double-click on the **EnemyShip** Script and roll up your sleeves:

Change:

```
if(transform.position.y < 0)
```

to:

```
if(transform.position.y < -4)
```

This allows the enemy ship to reposition itself when it moves off the bottom edge of the screen, instead of when it hits the non-existent ground plane at $y:0$.

Change:

```
transform.position.y = 50;
```

to:

```
transform.position.y = 71;
```

When the **EnemyShip** is repositioned, cranking up its y value will start it just above the top edge of the screen.

Change:

```
transform.position.x = Random.Range(0, 60);
```

to:

```
transform.position.x = Random.Range(-11, 68);
```

This gives the **EnemyShip** a corrected horizontal range at which to spawn—somewhere between -11 and 68 along the X-axis. You can either delete or comment out these two lines (remember, to turn a line into a comment, you just add a double slash // to the beginning of the line):

```
// audio.PlayOneShot(audioClips[Random.Range(0,audioClips.length)]);
// Instantiate(prefab, transform.position, Quaternion.identity);
```

We're commenting out/deleting these lines because we don't really want the **EnemyShip** to explode and make a noise when it moves off the bottom of the screen. In space, no one can hear you get all blowed up.

Change the value in this line:

```
transform.position.z = 0;
```

Just below the position.z line, add this line:

```
transform.position.z = 0;
rigidbody.velocity = Vector3.zero;
```

Here's how the complete Update function should look:

```
function Update(){
    transform.position.y -= speed * Time.deltaTime;
    if(transform.position.y < -4) {
      //audio.PlayOneShot(audioClips[Random.Range(
          0,audioClips.length)]);
        //Instantiate(prefab, transform.position,
            Quaternion.identity);
        transform.position.y = 71;
        transform.position.x = Random.Range(-11,68);
        transform.position.z = 0;
        rigidbody.velocity = Vector3.zero;
    }
}
```

What's with that rigidbody.velocity reset? Well, when GameObjects smack into each other, it's possible for them to get knocked out of orbit, or for the physics engine to apply a velocity to the GameObject's **rigidbody**. We'll just use those two lines to flatten everything to zero when the ship starts a new descent down the screen.

The **EnemyShip** looks like a pretty cool buzzsaw thing. In a single line, we can throw a rotation on there that'll make the ship spin and look all scary-cool.

Add this line within the Update function:

```
function Update () {
    transform.position.y -= speed * Time.deltaTime;
    transform.Rotate(0,0,Time.deltaTime * -500); // buzzsaw!!
```

You'll remember from earlier chapters that multiplying by `Time.deltaTime` sets things to the tempo of time, rather than updates. This way, an enemy ship takes two seconds to travel across the screen, regardless of how fast or slow the player's computer is. It's hardly fair to give players with slow computers a twitch advantage.

Save the **EnemyShip** Script and play your game. The angry-looking enemy ship bent on universal annihilation or some such now makes a complete trip from the top to the bottom of the screen. It respawns properly at the top, at some random X position. And it spins just like a sharp, pointy bad guy should.

Time for action – tweak the hero

There are a few changes we should make to the **HeroShip** Script (formerly the **Character** Script) to suit our new game. Let's do it:

1. Open the **HeroShip** Script.

2. Delete the `else if` condition handling the steins. Get rid of everything in this snippet in bold:

```
if(col.gameObject.tag == "bomb")
{
    audio.PlayOneShot(explosionSound);
    Instantiate(explosion, col.gameObject.transform.position,
        Quaternion.identity);
} else if (col.gameObject.tag == "stein") {
    animation.Play("catch"); // Ima catch that stein!
}
```

Shoot the Moon doesn't have beer steins, so we can safely kill this chunk.

3. Delete all of the code controlling the character model animation. Get rid of this whole section in bold:

```
if(lastX != transform.position.x) {
    // x values between this Update cycle and the last one
    // aren't the same! That means the player is moving the
    // mouse.
    if(!isMoving) {
        // the player was standing still.
        // Let's flag him to "isMoving"
        isMoving = true;
        if(!animation.IsPlaying("catch")){
        animation.Play("step");
        }
    }
}
```

```
    } else {
        // The player's x position is the same this Update cycle
        // as it was the last! The player has stopped moving the
        // mouse.
        if(isMoving) {
            // The player has stopped moving, so let's update the
                flag.
            isMoving = false;
            if(!animation.IsPlaying("catch")){
            animation.Play("idle");
            }
        }
    }
}
lastX = transform.position.x;
```

4. Delete the `isMoving` variable from the top of the script:

```
var isMoving:boolean = false; // flags whether or not the
    player is in motion
```

5. Delete the `lastX` variable definition from the top of the script:

```
var lastX:float; // this will store the last position of the
    character
```

6. Delete the entire `Start` function:

```
function Start() {
    animation.Stop();  // this stops Unity from playing the
        character's default animation.
}
```

The hero ship doesn't have any default animation, so this code is unnecessary.

Here's how the complete, freshly preened script should look:

```
var explosion:GameObject;

function Update() {
    transform.position.x = (Input.mousePosition.x)/20;
}

function OnCollisionEnter(col : Collision) {
    if(col.gameObject.tag == "bomb")
    {
```

```
    // I got hit by a bomb!
    Instantiate(explosion, col.gameObject.transform.position,
      Quaternion.identity);
  }
  col.gameObject.transform.position.y = 50;
  col.gameObject.transform.position.x = Random.Range(-11,68);
  col.gameObject.transform.z = -16;
}
```

Our human character in The Break-Up had animation cycles that we tapped into, but the **HeroShip** model doesn't. Unity will keep throwing complaints that it can't find these animations unless we tidy up the code as described above.

What just happened – hooray for lazy!

Take a look at these three lines in our **HeroShip** Script:

```
col.gameObject.transform.position.y = 50;
col.gameObject.transform.position.x = Random.Range(-11,68);
col.gameObject.transform.z = -16;
```

Those are the lines we used to reposition the falling object when it hit the player. We have similar lines in our **EnemyShip** Script that we just updated with new values. Should we do the same thing here? What if the values have to change again later? Then we'll have to update the code in two different scripts. And that, in professional parlance, is irritating.

It makes sense to fold this code into some kind of `ResetPosition` function that both scripts can call, yes? Then we'll only ever have to update the values in one place. BUT can you really call a function on one script from a completely different script? Yes, Virginia, there is a Santa Claus.

Time for action – give up the func

Let's get that function set up in the **EnemyShip** Script first. Double-click to open the **EnemyShip** Script, and get typing.

1. Write this new function outside of and apart from the other functions in the script:

```
function ResetPosition(){
  transform.position.y = 71;
  transform.position.x = Random.Range(-11, 68);
  transform.position.z = 0;
  rigidbody.velocity = Vector3.zero;
}
```

These are the very same repositioning lines we already have. You can even just type the shell of the function, and copy/paste those lines right in there. Either way, you need to go back and eradicate those lines from the `Update` function and replace them with a `ResetPosition()` function call.

2. Erase these bolded lines:

```
if(transform.position.y < -4) {
  transform.position.z = 0;
  transform.position.y = 71;
  transform.position.x = Random.Range(-11, 68);
  rigidbody.velocity = Vector3.zero;
}
```

And replace them with the `ResetPosition()` function call:

```
if(transform.position.y < -4) {
  ResetPosition();
}
```

When the interpreter hits that `ResetPosition()` function call, it'll jump into the `ResetPosition` function and run those repositioning lines.

Save the **EnemyShip** Script. Next, hop over to the **HeroShip** Script to make some changes.

3. Get rid of those old repositioning lines from the **HeroShip** Script. Delete the lines in bold:

```
function OnCollisionEnter(col : Collision) {
    // (a few lines omitted here for clarity)
    col.gameObject.transform.position.y = 50;
    col.gameObject.transform.position.z = -16;
    col.gameObject.transform.position.x = Random.Range(-11,68);
```

4. Replace those lines with these ones:

```
function OnCollisionEnter(col : Collision) {
    // (a few lines omitted here for brevity)
    if(col.gameObject.GetComponent(EnemyShip))
    {
        col.gameObject.GetComponent(EnemyShip).ResetPosition();
    }
}
```

Here's how the whole `OnCollisionEnter` function should look:

```
function OnCollisionEnter(col : Collision) {
  if(col.gameObject.tag == "bomb")
  {
  // I got hit by a bomb!
    Instantiate(explosion, col.gameObject.transform.position,
    Quaternion.identity);
  }

  if(col.gameObject.GetComponent(EnemyShip))
  {
      col.gameObject.GetComponent(EnemyShip).ResetPosition();
  }
}
```

Let's break those new lines down.

```
if(col.gameObject.GetComponent(EnemyShip)){
```

The value of `col` is something of type `Collision`. The `Collision` class has a variable called `gameObject`, which refers to the GameObject involved in the collision. The `Game Object` class has a function called `GetComponent`. You can pass the name of the script you want to access as an argument.

In this case, we're referring to the **EnemyShip** Script attached to whatever hit the **HeroShip**. By wrapping it in an `if` statement, we're effectively saying "if whatever just hit the **HeroShip** has a component called **EnemyShip** attached to it..."

```
col.gameObject.GetComponent(EnemyShip).ResetPosition();
```

... then call the `ResetPosition()` function on that script.

Our conditional check confirms that such a script even exists on the colliding object, by returning (answering) `true` or `false`. (Recall that conditional `if` statements always have to boil down to one of these two boolean states: `true` or `false`.)

Later, if a hypothetical **FallingStar** GameObject hits the ship, and it doesn't have a script called **EnemyShip** attached to it, we would get an error when trying to refer to the **EnemyShip** script. The conditional statement protects us from getting that error. We check to see if that script exists on the colliding object before we go calling any functions on it.

The end result of all this is that when the **EnemyShip** hits the bottom of the screen, it calls the `ResetPosition()` function and pops back up to the top. When the **EnemyShip** (or any **GameObject** with the **EnemyShip** Script component attached) hits the **HeroShip**, the **HeroShip** Script calls the **EnemyShip** Script's `ResetPosition()` function, and the **EnemyShip** pops back to the top of the screen.

Save the script and give your game a try! The enemy ship resets its position in both of these cases. Success!

Optimization

Here's one example of how we could optimize our code to make it more efficient. The `GetComponent` function is an "expensive" operation, which means that it takes longer for the computer to execute than other built-in functions. You'll notice that we're calling the function here twice. We could store the results of the `GetComponent` function in a variable. Then we'd have to call that function only once. Look here:

```
var other = col.gameObject.GetComponent(EnemyShip);
if (other) {
    other.ResetPosition();
}
```

As with refactoring (making the code pretty), we should focus on getting our code to work first. Then we can go back to make it faster and cleaner.

Time for action – itchy trigger finger

This is a whole lot of nerd-talk and not enough shooting. Let's build a bullet so that we can take these alien bad boys down.

1. In the menu, navigate to **GameObject | Create Other | Sphere**. Rename the resulting Sphere `bullet`.

2. In the **Hierarchy** panel, click to select your newly minted bullet.

3. In the **Inspector** panel, reset the bullet's **Transform** values, and then punch in `0.5` for all three **Scale** values:

   Position: X:`0`**, Y:**`0`**, Z:**`0`

   Rotation: X:`0`**, Y:**`0`**, Z:**`0`

   Scale: X:`0.5`**, Y:**`0.5`**, Z:**`0.5`

4. Hover over the **Scene** view and press the *F* key to focus it within the **Scene**.

Time for action – futurize the bullet

A dull, gray bullet just won't cut it in a sci-fi game. Let's make a neon-green **Material** and apply it to the bullet, because in the distant future, bullets are obviously neon-green. I have this crazy hunch.

1. In the **Project** panel, create a new **Material**. Rename the new **Material** `Bullet`.

2. Click to select the new **Bullet** Material.

3. In the **Inspector** panel, click on the Material's color swatch and choose neon space-bullet green. I chose these values:

    R: 9

    G: 255

    B: 0

4. In the **Hierarchy** panel, select the **Bullet** GameObject.

5. In the **Inspector** panel, find the **Mesh Renderer** component.

6. Apply the **Bullet** Material to the **Bullet**. You can either do this by choosing the **Bullet** Material in the Element 0 popup of the **Materials** section, or by clicking and dragging the **Bullet** Material into the slot. (You may have to click on the gray arrow to open the Material list first.) You can also drag the Material onto the GameObject in either the **Hierarchy** or the **Scene** view.

7. Uncheck **Cast Shadows** and **Receive Shadows** in the **Mesh Renderer** component.

Time for action – building Halo

OK, don't get too excited. We're not actually going to build **Halo**... we're going to build a halo to make our bullet look all glowy and awesome.

1. Ensure that the **Bullet** GameObject is still selected.

2. In the menu, go to **Component | Effects | Halo**. This adds a cool halo effect to the bullet.

3. In the **Inspector** panel, click on the color swatch for the **Halo** Component. Enter the same neon-green color values as before:

    R: 9

    G: 255

    B: 0

4. Change the halo's **Size** value to 0.5.

Now let's get the bullet ready to move around in the physics engine.

5. Make sure the **Bullet** GameObject is still selected.

6. In the menu, go to **Component | Physics | Rigidbody**.

7. In the **Inspector** panel, uncheck **Use gravity**.

8. At the top of the **Inspector** panel, click on **Add Tag...** in the **Tag** dropdown.

9. Create a new tag called `bullet`. (If you want to keep your file tidy, you can delete the old **bomb** and **stein** tags left over from the previous project, and shrink the list size down to 2.)

10. Click again to select the **bullet** GameObject.

11. In the **Inspector** panel, choose the new **bullet** tag from the **Tag** dropdown to apply it to the **bullet** GameObject.

We'll create a very simple Script and hook it up to the bullet.

12. In the **Project** panel, create a new **JavaScript**.

13. Rename the new Script **Bullet**.

14. Give the **Bullet** Script this `Start` function:

```
function Start() {
    rigidbody.velocity.y = 100;
}
```

This gives the bullet some oomph to get it moving along the Y-axis.

15. Add the following lines to the `Update` function:

```
function Update () {
  if(transform.position.y > 62) {
    Destroy(gameObject);
  }
}
```

16. In the **Hierarchy** panel, click to select the **Bullet** GameObject.

17. Attach the Script to the bullet by either clicking and dragging the Script on top of the **Bullet** GameObject or navigating to **Component | Scripts | Bullet** from the menu.

Finally, we'll create a new Prefab to house the **Bullet** GameObject.

18. In the **Project** panel, create a new Prefab and call it `Bullet`. (Remember to keep your project organized by dropping your assets into their respective folders.)

19. Drag the **Bullet** GameObject from the **Hierarchy** panel into the empty **Bullet** Prefab container. The gray icon lights up blue to indicate that the **Prefab** is full.

20. Select and delete the **Bullet** GameObject from the **Hierarchy** panel. It's safe inside the **Prefab** now.

Put your toys away

If you've been keeping all of your assets organized into folders to this point, things should be humming along nicely. If not, you may be facing a growing mess of similarly named assets and disused pieces from the previous project. Take some time to go through the **Project** panel and clean the house. We don't need the bomb, brownstone, stein, or character models any more, and their **Materials** can get chucked as well. A clean project is a happy project.

Time for action – fire!

In order to have something for the ship to fire, we have to create a variable at the top of the script called `bullet`, and then click-and-drag the **Bullet** Prefab into the variable slot in the **Inspector** panel. Otherwise, the script will have no idea what we're talking about when we try to instantiate something called `bullet`.

Follow these steps:

1. Add the variable declaration at the top of the **HeroShip** Script:

   ```
   var bullet:GameObject;
   ```

2. Save the script.

3. In the **Hierarchy** panel, select the **HeroShip** Prefab.

4. In the **Inspector** panel, find the **HeroShip** Script component.

5. Hook up the **Bullet** Prefab to the `bullet` variable.

Let's add a few lines of code to the **HeroShip** Script to make the bullet fire when you click on the mouse button, because shooting is cool.

```
function Update ()
{
    transform.position.x = (Input.mousePosition.x )/20;
    if(Input.GetMouseButtonDown(0)){
      Instantiate(bullet, transform.position + new Vector3(-3,2,0),
      Quaternion.identity);
      Instantiate(bullet, transform.position + new Vector3(3,2,0),
      Quaternion.identity);
      }
}
```

Let's review:

```
if(Input.GetMouseButtonDown(0)){
```

This line returns `true` if the left (or primary) mouse button (which has an ID of 0) has been pushed down within this `Update` cycle.

```
Instantiate(bullet, transform.position+new Vector3(-3,2,0),
    Quaternion.identity);
Instantiate(bullet, transform.position+new Vector3(3,2,0),
    Quaternion.identity);
```

We've used the `Instantiate` command before—this time, we're creating two new **Bullet** Prefab instances in the same position as the **HeroShip**, with the same rotation. In the same statement, we're moving the bullets two units along the Y-axis, which places them at the wings of our hero ship. The left bullet gets nudged `-3` units along the X-axis, while the right bullet is nudged `3` units the other direction, which places the bullets right around the ship's wing-mounted cannons. The bullets start moving up the screen because of `rigidbody.velocity` we applied in the bullet script's `Start` function.

Now test your game. When you click on the left mouse button, two new instances of the **Bullet** Prefab are added to the **Scene**. A force is applied to their **Rigidbody** components that will eventually send them careening up to the top of the screen. Then they're positioned at the wing cannons of the **HeroShip**. The script attached to each bullet detects when the bullet has passed the top edge of the play area, and destroys the **Bullet** Prefab instance and everything in it.

Put more simply: CLICK MOUSE. MAKE SHOOT.

Time for action – code do-si-do

Because the needs of our game have changed, we might reconsider how and where our code is written. In The Break-Up, it made sense for the player character to detect all collisions. But in Shoot the Moon, all the significant collisions actually happen on the enemy ship. The enemy ship has to know when it hits the hero ship, and it needs to know when it hits a bullet. So we can actually localize all of the collision code on the enemy ship. This makes a lot of sense, so let's make that change by transplanting some code:

1. In the **HeroShip** Script, delete the `OnCollisionEnter` function.

2. Delete the `explosion` variable declaration from the top of the script.

3. Save the **HeroShip** Script.

    As we did with the `ResetPosition()` function, let's build a reusable `Explode()` function, and fold the explosion-related code into it.

4. In the **EnemyShip** Script, create an `Explode()` function outside and apart from the other functions:

```
function Explode()
{
audio.PlayOneShot(audioClips[Random.Range(0,audioClips.length)]);
 Instantiate(prefab, transform.position, Quaternion.identity);
}
```

5. Give the **EnemyShip** an `OnCollisionEnter` function, and call the `Explode` and `ResetPosition` functions. The enemy ship will explode regardless of what it hits:

```
function OnCollisionEnter(col : Collision) {
    Explode();
    ResetPosition();
}
```

6. Next, we'll set up a conditional statement in the `OnCollisionEnter` function to determine whether the enemy ship has hit a bullet, or the hero ship:

```
function OnCollisionEnter(col : Collision) {
    Explode();
    ResetPosition();
    if(col.gameObject.tag == "bullet") {
      Destroy(col.gameObject);
    } else if (col.gameObject.tag == "heroShip") {
      // This enemy ship hit the player!
    }
}
```

7. At the very top of the **EnemyShip** Script, rename the `prefab` variable `explosion`:

```
var explosion:GameObject;
```

8. Change the `Explode()` function to call the new variable:

```
Instantiate(explosion, transform.position,
    Quaternion.identity);
```

9. Save the script.

10. Since we changed the name of our `prefab` variable to `explosion`, we should duck out to the **Inspector** panel and make sure that the **Explosion** Prefab is still set as the proper value. Changing variable names like this can sometimes cause Unity to lose track of things. Drag and drop the **Explosion** Prefab into the `explosion` variable's slot to bring Unity back up to its speed.

What just happened – eat lead

Try out the game. When the enemy ship hits either a bullet or the hero ship, it runs the `Explode()` function and repositions itself at the top of the screen. Specifically, if it hits a bullet, the bullet gets destroyed. If it hits the hero ship, it looks like it's behaving properly. But if you try putting a `print` command inside the conditional that says `//This enemy ship hit the player!`, you'll realize that the code isn't getting executed.

This is because we haven't tagged the **HeroShip**. Without that tag, our **EnemyShip** Script has no idea that it hit the hero ship. It just knows that it's hit *something*, so it shows an explosion and bounces back up to the top of the screen. You may notice a small but unwanted side effect of our code. Because we're instantiating the explosion using the enemy ship's `transform.position`, the explosion appears exactly where the enemy ship used to be. This makes sense when a bullet hits the enemy ship, but it doesn't quite make sense when the enemy ship hits the hero. It makes it seem as though the hero ship is impenetrable—that anything that crashes into it will burst into flames. It's actually the HERO ship's position that we need for that explosion.

Thankfully, this is a quick fix using the maaaagic of aaarguments.

Time for action – the maaagic of aaaarguments

To make the explosion happen on the thing that hits the enemy ship, rather than on the enemy ship itself, we'll pass the position of the colliding GameObject to the `Explode()` function.

1. Open the **EnemyShip** Script, and make these changes:

2. In the `OnCollisionEnter` function, pass the `transform.position` of the colliding object's GameObject to the `Explode()` function:

   ```
   Explode(col.gameObject.transform.position);
   ```

3. Now make sure that the `Explode()` function accepts this argument:

   ```
   function Explode(pos:Vector3){
   ```

4. And finally, position the instantiated explosion to the `pos` variable that receives the argument value:

   ```
   function Explode(pos:Vector3){
     audio.PlayOneShot(audioClips[Random.Range(0,
       audioClips.length)]);
     Instantiate(explosion, pos, Quaternion.identity);
   }
   ```

5. Save the script and try it out. The explosions go off at the site of the collision, and it makes a lot more visual sense.

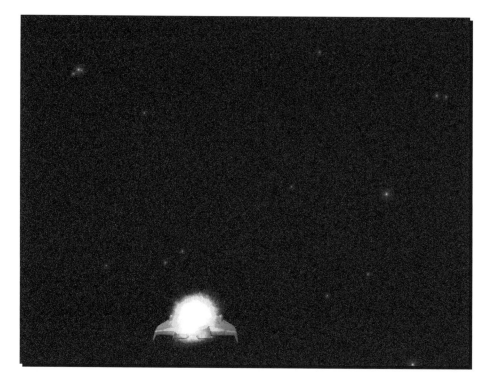

Time for action – add the most important part of any space shooter

We're almost ready to close the book on the main functionality of our space shooter game. We can fire bullets and explodify enemy ships. Although it may well defy the laws of physics, a satisfying fiery explosion occurs in the oxygen-free vacuum of space. But there's just something... missing, yes?

Numerous studies have been conducted to determine the most scientifically accurate sound for a neon-green irradiated bullet being fired through space, and the results have settled unanimously on the onomatopoeic "pew". Luckily, we have just such a sound effect in our `Assets` folder, so let's get it going.

1. At the top of the **HeroShip** Script, declare a variable to hold the "pew" sound effect:

```
var pew:AudioClip;
```

2. In the left-mouse button firing section of the code, play the "pew" sound effect:

```
if(Input.GetMouseButtonDown(0)){
    audio.PlayOneShot(pew);
```

3. Save and close the script.

4. Find the "pew" sound effect in the **Project** panel.

5. In the **Hierarchy** panel, click to select the **HeroShip**.

6. Click and drag the "pew" sound effect into the **HeroShip** Script component in the **Inspector** panel, in the slot labeled "pew".

7. Click on **Apply** to apply the changes to the source **Prefab**.

   Now when you fire, the spaceship goes "pew". And lo, all became right with the world!

Last year's model

We've taken a game about a guy who gets kicked out of his apartment and turned it into a game about destroying an onslaught of alien spacecraft. That's the difference a theme makes. The underlying bones of both games are quite similar, and it wasn't an enormous effort to make these changes. It's the rough equivalent of throwing a new coat of paint and some seat warmers on last year's model and selling it as a brand new car.

And I say "why not"? The beautiful thing about game development is that you don't have to reinvent the wheel every time. You should absolutely build things with a mind towards reusing them in future projects. The momentum you build up will make you an unstoppable game dev machine.

Have a go hero – filling in the empty space

This game, like The Break-Up, has a number of missing elements that I'll let you fill in, based on what you've learned in previous chapters. But in addition to the title screen, instructions, credits, win/lose conditions, and player health that we discussed earlier, here are a few ideas to strive for if you decide to develop **Shoot the Moon** further:

◆ Build a couple of neat-looking jet trail particle systems and hook them up to the exhaust pipes sticking out the back of your hero ship.

◆ Make the ship angle as it moves left and right. You might try repurposing some of your paddle code from the code of *Chapter 8, Hearty Har Har*, to do this.

◆ Add some power-ups that appear randomly in the void of space. If the player collides with them, you can give him awesome skillz... maybe he becomes invincible for a short period of time? Or you could crank up the number of bullets that he can fire, for a triple-shot effect. That's a very easy change to make based on the code you've already written.

◆ Duplicate and reupholster an enemy ship to paint it purple or something. Give that type of ship some hit points so that it doesn't explode until it's been hit by *three* bullets.

◆ Mess around with the enemy ship's movement script. Using mathemagic, can you make the ships travel diagonally, or even in spirals or waves? Can you do it without math?

◆ Make it so that when you hold down the mouse button, you charge up a super shot, and when you let go, some crazy-huge bullet blasts out of your ship's nose cone.

◆ Make the enemy ships fire back!

◆ After the player has shot down x enemy ships, introduce the big boss: THE MOON. Give the moon a big pile of hit points and some missiles. Then, and only then, will the title of the game make sense... which I'm sure has been keeping you up at night.

Summary

We've learned something today: the value of friendship, the importance of kayak safety, and the dangers of eating mysterious red berries you find in the forest. But most of all, we've learned how to:

◆ Set up a 2-camera system to composite two different views together

◆ Change existing Prefabs to use different models

◆ Apply a mesh collider

◆ Use the Halo component

◆ Fire bullets

◆ Completely re-skin a game in a single chapter

C# Addendum

The code in this chapter represents another straightforward C# port. Here it is:

HeroShipCSharp.cs

```csharp
using UnityEngine;
using System.Collections;

public class HeroShipCSharp : MonoBehaviour {

    public GameObject bullet;
    public AudioClip pew;

    private void Update()
    {
        transform.position = new Vector3(Input.mousePosition.x/20,
          transform.position.y, transform.position.z);
        if(Input.GetMouseButtonDown(0))
        {
            audio.PlayOneShot(pew);
            Instantiate(bullet, transform.position +
              new Vector3(-3,2,0), Quaternion.identity);
            Instantiate(bullet, transform.position +
              new Vector3(3,2,0), Quaternion.identity);
        }
    }
}
```

EnemyShipCSharp.cs

```
using UnityEngine;
using System.Collections;

public class EnemyShipCSharp : MonoBehaviour {

    public GameObject explosion;
    public int speed;
    public AudioClip[] audioClips;

    private void Update ()
    {
        transform.position = new Vector3(transform.position.x,
          transform.position.y - speed * Time.deltaTime,
          transform.position.z);
        transform.Rotate(new Vector3(0,0,Time.deltaTime * -500));
        // buzzsaw!!
        if(transform.position.y < -4)
        {
            ResetPosition();
        }
    }

    private void ResetPosition()
    {
        transform.position = new Vector3
          (Random.Range(-11, 68), 71, 0);
        rigidbody.velocity = Vector3.zero;
    }

    private void Explode(Vector3 pos)
    {
        audio.PlayOneShot(audioClips[Random.Range(
          0,audioClips.Length)]);
        Instantiate(explosion, pos, Quaternion.identity);
    }
```

```
    private void OnCollisionEnter(Collision col)
    {
        Explode(col.gameObject.transform.position);
        ResetPosition();
        if(col.gameObject.tag == "bullet") {
            Destroy(col.gameObject);
        } else if (col.gameObject.tag == "heroShip") {
            // This enemy ship hit the player!
        }

    }

}
```

12

Game #5 – Kisses 'n' Hugs

Cast your memory back to the earliest chapters in this book. You were younger then, and you probably still had all your hair. We were talking about the amount of effort involved in creating games for a single player versus multiple players, on one computer or many, turn-based or real-time.

*The games we've created to this point have been single-player, with the player playing against him or herself. The computer presented the player with obstacles or challenges—cards to flip, bombs to avoid—but there really wasn't much decision-making or "thinking" happening on the part of the computer. What if we wanted our player to square off against an artificially intelligent computer opponent? That would be **way** beyond the scope of a beginners book, wouldn't it? As it turns out, maybe not!*

Computers that think

Artificial Intelligence (AI) is the name computer scientists have given to their attempts at simulating human-like thought, and sometimes learning, in one or more computers. AI has a long history with games, with one of the most famous examples being the 1997 match between chess world champion Garry Kasparov and IBM's Deep Blue chess-playing computer. Deep Blue defeated Kasparov, while many of us re-watched Terminator 2: Judgment Day and trembled.

AI programming is a very complex and ever-evolving discipline. It's what makes first person shooter enemies shoot at you from behind cover. It's the engine behind the parsers in text adventure games. It's the driving force behind every non-human video game opponent you've ever faced. In this chapter, you'll create a simple 2-player Tic Tac Toe (Noughts and Crosses, X's and O's) game suitable for a pair of humans. In the following chapter, you'll program an artificially intelligent computer opponent to square off against a human player.

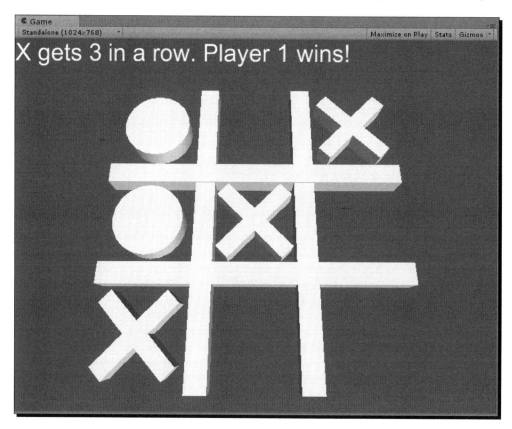

Unity has everything we need to build a solid Tic Tac Toe game, without having to import 3D models. We can build the whole game with primitives—cubes, cylinders, and so on. Let's get to work.

Time for action – haul in the hallway

Launch Unity, and follow these standard steps to set up the project:

1. Create a brand-spanking-new Unity project.

2. Navigate to **File | Save Scene As**, and call the Scene "**Game**".

3. Add a directional light to the Scene.

Fantastic! We're nearly there.

Time for action – hash it out

We'll stretch some cube primitives to create the hashtable grid that houses the game.

1. Change to a top, isometric view in your Scene.

2. Navigate to **GameObject | Create Other | Cube** to create a cube primitive on the screen.

3. Scale the cube up to z:15, and set **Position** to 0,0,0.

4. Duplicate the cube with *Ctrl/command* + *D*, and move it 5 units to the right along the X-axis.

5. Select both cubes by clicking on them while holding *Ctrl* or *command*. Duplicate them as in the previous step.

6. Press the *E* key to call up the **Rotate** gizmo. Click the tool handle above the Scene view until it reads **Center** (not **Pivot**). Rotate the pair of duplicated cubes to y:90. You can fine-tune the rotation by typing a value of 90 into the Rotation:Y field in the **Inspector** panel after you begin the rotation.

7. Create an empty GameObject by navigating to **GameObject | Create Empty**, and rename it Grid. Reset its position to the origin.

8. In the **Hierarchy** panel, click and drag the four elongated cubes into the Grid GameObject to make them its children.

9. Position the Grid GameObject at 0,0,-25.

10. Set the camera to **Position** 2.5,15,-30 and its **Rotation** to 72,0,0. This brings our grid nicely into view.

One Script to rule them all

We're going to create a single script to do most of the heavy lifting in our Tic Tac Toe game. Let's set it up.

1. Create an empty GameObject, and rename it `GameLogic`.

2. Create a new JavaScript and rename it `GameLogic`.

3. Drag the `GameLogic` script onto the `GameLogic` GameObject to add it as a **Component**.

The `GameLogic` script will be the central control for the game.

Time for action – it's hip to be square

The way that players interact with a Tic Tac Toe is to place an X or an O piece in the empty spaces on the grid. If we create an invisible, clickable GameObject to sit in those spaces and respond to clicks, we'll have nailed down most of the game's interactivity. Follow these steps to create that clickable square:

1. Create a cube. Position it at `-2.8,1,-19.7` with a scale of `4.2,1,4.2`. This puts the square in the top-left cell of the grid, sized appropriately.

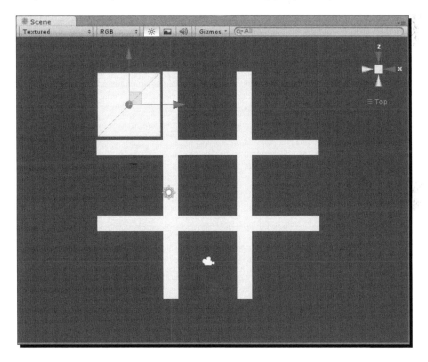

2. Rename it `Square`.

3. Create a new Javascript and rename it `Square`.

4. Drag the `Square` script onto the `Square` GameObject.

5. Add this to the `GameLogic` script:

```
function ClickSquare(x:int, y:int)
{
   print("Square " + x + "," + y + " was clicked");
}
```

6. Double-click to open the `Square` script and punch in this code:

```
#pragma strict
var x:int;
var y:int;

var gameLogic:GameObject;

function Start ()
{
   gameLogic = GameObject.Find("GameLogic");
}

function OnMouseDown()
{
   gameLogic.GetComponent(GameLogic).ClickSquare(x, y);
}
```

What just happened – find and click

Let's have a gander at that code.

```
gameLogic = GameObject.Find("GameLogic");
```

In the `Start` function of the `Square` script, we use the `GameObject.Find()` method to get a reference to the `GameLogic` "mothership" GameObject. Unity searches through the Hierarchy, looking for an element with a matching name. Since this is an "expensive" (read: slow) operation, we only do it once at the beginning of the game, instead of, say, repeatedly in the `Update` function, or every time the player clicks on the square.

function onMouseDown () The `OnMouseDown` function is called when the primary mouse button (most often the left mouse button, unless the player has an unusual system configuration) is pressed and the mouse cursor intersects this GameObject's Collider.

Test the game. When you click on the square, the message is sent to the `GameLogic` script, and we see a printout of the `Square's x and y coordinates`:

> **Square 0,0 was clicked**

Try changing the x and y values of `Square` in the **Inspector** panel, then run the game and click on the `Square` to see the results. Change the x and y values to 9,9 when you're finished testing.

Why 9,9? The reason will become clear after a few more steps.

Squaring the Square

Now that we have one working `Square`, let's create eight more to fill in the remaining gaps. But before we do that, we should encapsulate the `Square` in a **Prefab**, so that any duplicates will share the changes we make.

1. Create a Prefab and rename it `Square`.

2. Drag the `Square` GameObject from the **Hirearchy** panel inside the `Square` Prefab in the Project panel. The Prefab lights up that familiar shade of blue.

3. In the **Scene** view, duplicate the first square until you have a total of 9 squares in the grid gaps. An easy way to do this is to duplicate the top-left square twice, and drag the copies to the top-middle and top-right spaces to complete the first row. Then select all 3 squares and duplicate them. Move the three duplicates down to the middle row. Duplicate again, and move the last three squares to the bottom row.

4. Click on each square and, in the **Inspector** panel, its x and y values appropriately. When the value is bold, that means it's overriding the Prefab's default value of 9,9 that we set earlier. Make sure that the top-left square in the **Scene** view is also the top-left square in the camera view, by moving it around a little. If your Scene view is disoriented, rotate the view until you're seeing things correctly.

The x and y values for the squares should be set like so:

Notice that when you change the default x and y values of 9,9, the values are bold, indicating that this instance of the Prefab has overridden the default values.

Test the game and confirm that all the values work by clicking on each square in turn and watching the message.

Time for action – now you see it...

Because the squares are visible, our Tic Tac Toe game looks more like an oversized novelty calculator. We can fix that, so let's follow the listed steps:

1. Select the top left `Square`.

2. In the **Inspector** panel, uncheck the **Mesh Renderer**. The square disappears.

3. While you're at it, check the **Is Trigger** box in the `Box Collider` component. We'll see why that's important shortly.

4. Click on the **Apply** button at the top of the **Inspector** panel. All of the squares that are derived from the `Square` Prefab disappear from sight, as shown in the following screenshot:

Family values

The explanation for why we used 9,9 as the initial x / y values for the Square is a little bit twisty, but here goes:

If we hadn't first set that initial x and y values of Square to 9,9 (say, for example, if the initial values of Square were 0,0), then any Square that had an x value of 0 or a y value of 0 would not be overridden. You wouldn't have seen the value turn bold in the **Inspector** panel. Non-overridden values are not "protected"—they're at risk of being modified whenever a change from another instance is applied to the Prefab.

Imagine yourself making the above changes to the bottom-right Square, which has its x and y values set to 2,2. Once you click on **Apply**, x:2 y:2 become the default values for all squares whose values were *not* overridden. That means that any Square matching the initial default values of x:0 or y:0 would have those values replaced with x:2 or y:2. The top-middle square, with its overridden value of X:1 and its default value of Y:0, would see its unprotected Y value replaced with 2.

This is the reason that we set the default x and y values of the Prefab to 9,9 (any value greater than 2,2 would also work). Because those values are not shared by any of the squares, we overrode the X and Y values for each of the squares, and protected them from being inadvertently changed. In this way, none of the squares' values were overwritten when we clicked on **Apply**.

Time for action – X marks the spot

Just as we created the Tic Tac Toe grid from cube primitives, we can create the X player piece in a similar way.

1. Create a Cube, and position it at 0,0,0.
2. Change the Cube's scale to 0.8,1,4.5.
3. Rotate it -45 degrees in the y-axis.
4. Duplicate it.

5. Change the duplicate Cube's y rotation to 45. You should have an X shape, as shown in the following screenshot:

6. Create an empty **GameObject**.

7. Rename it as X.

8. Position it at 0,0,0.

9. Drag both cubes inside it in the **Hierarchy** panel make them children of the X GameObject.

10. Add a **Rigidbody** component to the X **GameObject**.

11. Create a **Prefab** and rename it X.

12. Drag the X GameObject from the **Hierarchy** panel into the X **Prefab** in the **Project** panel.

13. Delete the X **GameObject** from the **Hierarchy** panel.

Time for action – boy O boy

Unity doesn't have a Tube primitive that we can use to create the O player piece, but we can use the Cylinder primitive to create an "un-holey" approximation.

1. Create a Cylinder.

2. Rename it as O.

3. Scale it to 3.5,0.5,3.5.

4. Add a Box Collider to the Cylinder (by navigating to **Component | Physics | Box Collider**). Unity asks if you want to replace the existing Capsule Collider with a Box Collider. Yes you do!

5. Add a Rigidbody Component.

6. Position the O at 0,0,0.

7. Create a **Prefab** and name it O.

8. Drag the O **GameObject** inside the O **Prefab**.

9. Delete the O GameObject from the **Hierarchy** panel.

Time for action – bottoming out

When the player clicks on the invisible `Square` GameObjects, the X and O pieces are going to fall gently into place. The rigidbodies attached to each piece will include them in the physics engine, and gravity will take over. However, the pieces will fall straight into oblivion unless we build a "floor" beneath the grid to stop them.

Let's create a floor to keep the falling pieces contained

1. Create a `Plane`.
2. Rename it as `floor`.
3. Scale it up so that it is larger than the Grid GameObject.

4. Switch to a Right view in the Scene view and position the Floor so that it sits just beneath the `Grid` GameObject.

5. In the **Inspector** panel, turn off the **Mesh Renderer** option for `floor`.

As with the Squares, the floor disappears when its **Mesh Renderer** option is disabled, but its Collider stays active, which is all we care about.

Here comes the drop

With this groundwork literally laid, we're ready to add some code so that the X and O pieces fall into the Grid when the Squares are clicked.

Declare the following variables at the top of the GameLogic script, beneath the `#pragma strict` line:

- var XPiece:GameObject;
- var OPiece:GameObject;

Click on the GameLogic GameObject. Drag the X and O pieces into the Inspector in those variable slots.

Add this line to the `ClickSquare` function:

```
print("Square " + x + "," + y + " was clicked");
Instantiate(XPiece, new Vector3(-2.8,1,-19.7), Quaternion.identity);
```

This line creates a new instance of the XPiece Prefab at a hard-coded position on the screen.

What just happened – to collide or not to collide?

Test the game and click on any of the invisible Squares. The X settles nicely into the top-left slot on the grid, as shown in the following screenshot. (If this doesn't happen, it's possible that you forgot to set the X or its Cube children's positions to 0,0,0 while you were creating the piece).

The X does not collide with the `Box Collider` of the Square because the `Box Collider` component is marked as "**Is Trigger**". Try unchecking that option on the Prefab to see the difference that option makes. `Is Trigger` enables a GameObject's Collider component to respond to things like mouse clicks and collision events in code, but it is removed from the physics simulation and doesn't hinder the movement of the pieces that collide with it.

The X piece does collide reliably with the invisible floor. However, you can click to place many X's, and they start erupting like popcorn and falling over the edge of the invisible floor, making our Tic Tac Toe game look more like a game of Perfection™ (as played by wombats).

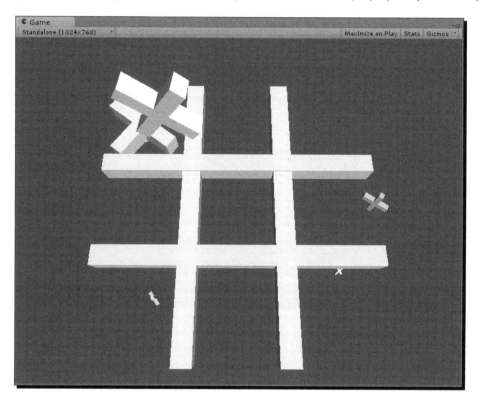

Time for action – +9 accuracy

Let's change the code a little so that we can put the X at the same place as the square that was clicked.

Change this line in the `Square` script:

```
gameLogic.GetComponent(GameLogic).ClickSquare(gameObject);
```

Modify the following `ClickSquare` function in the GameLogic script:

```
function ClickSquare(square:GameObject)
{
  Instantiate(XPiece,  square.transform.position,
    Quaternion.identity);
}
```

Delete the print statement we had in there earlier.

Instead of passing the x and y values of `Square` to the `ClickSquare` function, we're passing a reference to the entire `Square` GameObject itself, with the reference name lowercase-s `square`. (Remember that Unity JavaScript is case-sensitive, so `Square` is not the same animal as `square`).

Test the game, and click on the Squares. Now the X's are all falling in their proper places as you click on the different Squares, as shown in the following screenshot:

Time for action – solve for X

The problem remains that if you click too many times, you still get too many X's.
Let's fix that.

In the Square script, add the following code:

```
var x:int;
var y:int;
var isUsed:boolean;

function OnMouseDown()
{
  if(!isUsed)
  {
    gameLogic.GetComponent(GameLogic).ClickSquare(gameObject);
    isUsed = true;
  }

}
```

What just happened – lockdown

Now you can't place an X in a square more than once, because the isUsed boolean
locks it. isUsed is false by default, and it gets set to true as soon as you click on a square.
When you click the square again, the code checks the isUsed boolean, finds that it's true,
and skips over the line inside the conditional statement.

Time for action – it takes two to Tic Tac Toe

A one-playerTic Tac Toe game sounds like a recipe for a bad time. Let's get the O's in there
to liven things up.

Add this line to the GameLogic script:

```
var XPiece:GameObject;
var OPiece:GameObject;
var currentPlayer:int = 1;
```

And later:

```
function ClickSquare(square:GameObject)
{
  var piece:GameObject;
```

```
if(currentPlayer == 1)
{
  piece = XPiece;
} else {
  piece = OPiece;
}

Instantiate(piece, square.transform.position, Quaternion.identity);

currentPlayer ++;
if(currentPlayer > 2) currentPlayer = 1;
}
```

Try it out. Now when you click, the game alternates between X's and O's.

What just happened – alternating between players

Let's take a closer look at that code.

```
var currentPlayer:int = 1;
```

We begin the game with `currentPlayer` set to 1.

```
var piece:GameObject;
if(currentPlayer == 1)
{
  piece = XPiece;
} else {
  piece = OPiece;
}
```

This chunk of code defines a variable called `piece`. If `currentPlayer` is 1, it gets set to `XPiece` (which is defined at the top of the script, and currently contains a reference to our X Prefab). If `currentPlayer` is 2, we store a reference to the `OPiece` value, which in turn refers to our O Prefab.

```
Instantiate(piece, square.transform.position, Quaternion.identity);
```

Instead of explicitly instantiating `XPiece` or `OPiece`, we instantiate whichever piece is stored in the `piece` variable.

```
currentPlayer ++;
if(currentPlayer > 2) currentPlayer = 1;
```

After a piece is played, we increment the `currentPlayer` variable, so that 1 becomes 2, and 2 becomes 3. In the next line, if we reach 3, then we bust the value back down to 1. In this way, with each move, `currentPlayer` toggles between 1 and 2.

Time for action – designer to player. Come in, player.

Most people over the age of zero know how to play Tic Tac Toe, but just to be safe, let's rig up a down-and-dirty onscreen prompt to let the players know whose turn it is.

1. Create a new GUI Text.
2. Position it at 0,1,0 with a font size of 36.

3. Rename it as `Prompt`.

4. Store a reference to it in the `GameLogic` script:

```
var XPiece:GameObject;
var OPiece:GameObject;
var currentPlayer:int = 1;
var prompt:GUIText;
```

5. Save the script.

6. Select the `GameLogic` GameObject.

7. Drag the `Prompt` GUIText GameObject into the `prompt` variable of `GameLogic` in the **Inspector** panel.

8. Back in the GameLogic script, create a function, as follows, to show the players whose /turn it is:

```
function ShowPlayerPrompt()
{
  if(currentPlayer == 1)
  {
    prompt.text = "Player 1, place an X.";
  } else {
    prompt.text = "Player 2, place an O.";
  }
}
```

9. Call this function at the beginning of the game, and again after a move is made.

```
function Start ()
{
  ShowPlayerPrompt();
}
```

and later:

```
function ClickSquare(square:GameObject)
{
  // (prior code omitted for brevity)
  ShowPlayerPrompt();
}
```

10. Test the game.

What just happened – prompt service

Hopefully, the new code is easy to parse. The ShowPlayerPrompt does a condition check on the currentPlayer variable. If it's player 1's turn, the GUIText text is set to say "**Player 1, place an X**." Otherwise, the prompt says "**Player 2, place an O**."

```
ShowPlayerPrompt();
```

The new function gets called from two different places: right at the beginning of the game in the built-in Start function, and on an ongoing basis after a piece has been played.

Slowly building to a climax

What we very nearly have now is a functional Tic Tac Toe game for two players. Why waste money on a paper and pencil, when you can spend hundreds or thousands of dollars on a computer to play Tic Tac Toe?

Two human players can see for themselves whenever X or O gets 3-in-a-row and wins the game, but ideally, the game will be able to check for a win through code. We don't quite have the right elements in place to detect a win state, but we're going to spend the rest of the chapter getting there.

Have a go hero – think it through

Ask yourself: what does the code need to know in order to determine when a player has won? How would you go about figuring that out? Put the book down for a moment and puzzle through this question, because it's exactly the type of problem you'll face when you begin building your own games.

I strongly urge you not to keep reading at this point. This isn't like one of those kids' shows where the little Mexican girl says "flap your arms like a chicken, everybody!", and you just sit on your couch eating snacks like a slug. *Actually* sit down and work out what it might take to determine a win condition in this game. When you've given it an honest shot (whether you think your solution is successful or not), come back to the book and work through the solution I devised, which is one of many possible solutions.

Read after thinking

One of the crucial pieces of information we're missing is which player's piece is inside each square. Thanks to the `isUsed` boolean, we know when a square has a piece in it, but we have no idea which piece it is. Keeping better track of which piece occupies which square is the first step to detecting a win condition.

`isUsed` isn't a very information-packed variable. By replacing it with an `int`, we can use it to store more valuable data.

In the Square script, replace this:

```
var isUsed:boolean;
```

with this:

```
var player:int;
```

In the logic check, change this:

```
if(!isUsed)
```

to this:

```
if(player == 0)
```

and remove this line from the OnMouseDown function:

```
isUsed = true;
```

Altogether, the Square script should look like this:

```
#pragma strict
var x:int;
var y:int;
var player:int;

var gameLogic:GameObject;

function Start ()
{
  gameLogic = GameObject.Find("GameLogic");
}

function OnMouseDown()
{
  if(player == 0)
  {
    gameLogic.GetComponent(GameLogic).ClickSquare(gameObject);
  }
}
```

What just happened – building a more complex lock

Read that code over one more time. Being an int, the player variable defaults to 0. So an unused Square has a player value of 0. If a Square's player value is 0, we know it's safe to place a piece there. But how does the value get changed to 1 or 2?

In the game logic script, add this just after the `Instantiate` line:

```
Instantiate(piece, square.transform.position, Quaternion.identity);
square.GetComponent.<Square>().player = currentPlayer;
```

We've used the familiar `GetComponent` command to get a reference to the `Square` script attached to the `Square` GameObject that the player clicked on (a reference to which is passed into this function with the variable name lower-case s `square`). This line sets the player variable on the clicked square to the value of the `currentPlayer` variable, which toggles between `1` and `2`.

If it's player 1's turn, the clicked `square`'s player variable is set to `1`. If it's player 2's turn the clicked `square`'s player variable is set to `2`. A value of `0` indicates that the square is empty.

Test out the game again. There should be no outward change, but behind the scenes, there's a whole lot more knowledge flying around.

On deaf ears

Now that all the Squares know which piece is inside them, we can theoretically poll any square and ask its status. The trouble is that the `GameLogic` script is only set up to be *reactive*. The `ClickSquare` function responds to the player's action of clicking on a square. We need to *actively* ask a square what's up.

Currently, there's no real way for us to do that, since we haven't created any references to our squares. As we did with the Robot Repair game, it would be really handy to create a two-dimensional array, so that we can refer to Squares by their coordinate addresses. So let's!

Time for action – pretty maids all in a row

We're going to create a 2D array referencing our squares in an interesting way. Follow along.

1. Create a standard one-dimensional array to hold the squares by adding this declaration to the `GameLogic` script:

```
var XPiece:GameObject;
var OPiece:GameObject;
var currentPlayer:int = 1;
var prompt:GUIText;
var aSquares:GameObject[];
```

2. Select the `GameLogic` GameObject. Set the Size of the `aSquares` array to `9` in the **Inspector** panel.

3. One by one, making sure you get all 9 unique squares with no repeats, click and drag the 9 `Square` GameObjects from the **Hierarchy** panel into the array slots in the **Inspector** panel. Another way to accomplish this in a single shot is to leave the array size at `0`, and then select the `GameLogic` GameObject and lock the Inspector (click the little lock icon at the top right of the panel). With the `GameLogic` Inspector locked, you can select all the Squares and drag them en masse onto the array in the **Inspector** panel.

4. We're part of the way there. The `aSquares` array gives us references in code to the Squares, but it would be difficult to access the squares by their coordinate values with this flat, 1-dimensional array.

5. Off the top of the game, we can pick through the list of Squares and place them in a second two-dimensional array, based on their X and Y values.

6. Modify the `GameLogic` scrip:

```
var aSquares:GameObject[];
var aGrid:GameObject[,];
function Start ()
{
  currentPlayer = 1;
  ShowPlayerPrompt();

  aGrid = new GameObject[3,3];

  var theSquare:GameObject;
  var theScript:Square;

  for(var i:int =0; i < aSquares.Length; i++)
  {
    theSquare = aSquares[i];
    theScript = theSquare.GetComponent.<Square>();
    aGrid[theScript.x,theScript.y] = theSquare;
  }
}
```

What just happened – order!

The new code parcels the Squares into an easily-accessible 2D array, much like the one we used in Robot Repair to store our `Card` instances.

```
var aGrid:GameObject[,];
```

This following line of code defines a 2D array:

```
aGrid = new GameObject[3,3];
```

This line in the `Start` function defines that 2D array as having 3 elements, each of which contain 3 elements. The net result is, essentially, a matrix of columns and rows.

```
var theSquare:GameObject;
var theScript:Square;
```

We declare these two variables above the for loop instead of inside the for loop, so that Unity doesn't have to recreate them on every iteration. This will really only matter with a very performance-intensive loop (which this isn't) and Unity's compiler takes care of any inefficiencies from declaring the variables inside the loop anyway, but it helps to know these tips in case you need them down the road in other languages. Declaring the variables outside the loop in Unity can be argued as a stylistic decision.

theSquare will hold a reference to the Square GameObject that we pull out of the aSquares array, while theScript is a reference to the Square script attached to that Square GameObject.

```
for(var i:int =0; i < aSquares.Length; i++)
{
    theSquare = aSquares[i];
    theScript = theSquare.GetComponent.<Square>();
    aGrid[theScript.x,theScript.y] = theSquare;
}
```

This for loop has us iterating through all 9 elements of the aSquares array, which contains references to each Square in the grid. For each Square, we store a reference to its attached Square script. Then we insert a reference to the Square into the 2D array, using the x and y values found in the Square script attached to it.

Regardless of the order in which the Squares appear in the aSquares array, we wind up with a 2D array with all the squares sorted by their x and y values for easy reference:

```
aGrid[x,y]
```

> There actually is a formula for treating a 1-dimensional array like a 2-dimensional array:
>
> *x + width * y*
>
> Picture a Tic Tac Toe grid laid out like this:
> ```
> A B C
> D E F
> G H I
> ```
> The 1D array would look like this:
> ```
> [A, B, C, D, E, F, G, H, I]
> ```
> The coordinate address of square H is x:1 y:2. The width of the grid is 3 cells. So the equation becomes:
>
> *1 + 3 * 2*
>
> The result is 7. If we count along the 1D array, starting at the 0th element with A, the seventh element is H. It works!

Winner is coming

We now have all the information we need to check the Squares, to determine which piece they contain, and to call the match if we find 3-in-a-row. In the `GameLogic` script, scaffold the mighty hard-fought `CheckForWin` function:

```
function CheckForWin(square:GameObject):boolean
{

}
```

Did you notice something different about this function declaration? It's got a big, ugly `boolean` stuck to the side of its face. (Gee—it should really get that looked at).

This function declares a return type. We've already called numerous functions that have a return value, but this is the first time we've set one up in our own custom code. All it means is that somewhere along the way, this function will spit out a boolean value. In fact, it *must* spit out a boolean value, or else we'll get script error.

To spit out a value, we'll use the `return` keyword. This `CheckForWin` function must, at some point, return either `true` or `false`, or a statement that resolves to true or false, such as `(2+2)==4` (true!) or `beeStings=="awesome"` (false!).

The function is ready. Please fasten your seatbelt, because coding it is going to be turbulent.

Codesplosion

In earlier chapters, I've said that it's more important to get your code working than to make it elegant. However in some situations, like the one you're about to experience, the code is so preposterously inelegant that it cries out to be refactored on the spot.

Just like in math class where they make you add numbers up a million times before teaching multiplication, let's start by doing this the long way. Don't bother writing any of this code down. Just follow along, and look for ways in which it can be cleaned up.

We can look for 3-in-a-row as follows:

```
// Check the first row:
if(aGrid[0,0].GetComponent.<Square>().player == currentPlayer &&
   aGrid[1,0].GetComponent.<Square>().player == currentPlayer &&
   aGrid[2,0].GetComponent.<Square>().player == currentPlayer) return
   true;
```

```
// Check the second row:
if(aGrid[0,1].GetComponent.<Square>().player == currentPlayer &&
   aGrid[1,1].GetComponent.<Square>().player == currentPlayer &&
   aGrid[2,1].GetComponent.<Square>().player == currentPlayer) return
   true;
```

... and so on. That will give us 8 gigantic statements: 3 for the rows, 3 for the columns, and 2 for the diagonals.

> In this example, we're returning a value of true in two places. That's okay. As soon as the interpreter hits the first return statement, it auto-ejects out of the function and skips the rest of the code like a pilot with his mech on fire.

Need-to-know basis

By writing the line in this long-winded way, we're checking all of the possible win scenarios by searching the whole grid, when we should really only be concerned about the square where the current player just finished placing a piece.

Given any square's x and y values, we can just check the squares in the same row and column, instead of checking every single win scenario. Here's what a line of code looks like if we only check the square's row:

```
if(aGrid[0, square.GetComponent.<Square>().y].GetComponent.<Square>().
   player == currentPlayer && aGrid[1,
   square.GetComponent.<Square>().y].GetComponent.<Square>().player ==
   currentPlayer && aGrid[2,
   square.GetComponent.<Square>().y].GetComponent.<Square>().player ==
   currentPlayer) return true;
```

Need-to-know basis

It's an improvement, but that line is still monstrous! Notice the repeated element square.GetComponent.<Square>().y. Why say it three separate times, when we can say it once and store it in a variable?

We'll probably need to know `square.GetComponent.<Square>().x` as well to check the columns. So let's just store the first part, `square.GetComponent.<Square>()`, in a variable as follows:

```
function CheckForWin(square:GameObject):boolean
{
   var theScript:Square = square.GetComponent.<Square>();
```

So now the code for checking the square's column becomes:

```
if(aGrid[0,theScript.y].GetComponent.<Square>().player ==
   currentPlayer && aGrid[1, theScript.y].GetComponent.
   <Square>().player == currentPlayer && aGrid[2,
   theScript.y].GetComponent.<Square>().player == currentPlayer)
   return true;
```

Clean-up on aisle code

It's more succinct than it was, but this code is still a nightmare to read and update. Let's try to refactor it a little more.

There's a lot of `GetComponent.<Square>().player` happening throughout the line. What if we made one function that would do that job, just to shorten up our code and make it a little more readable?

By setting up a function that accepts x and y as arguments, and spits out the value of a square's player variable, we'll have a handy and reusable piece of code for all kinds of situations. You should start writing the code into your project again.

```
function GetPlayer(x:int, y:int):int
{
   return aGrid[x,y].GetComponent.<Square>().player;
}
```

What just happened – vending machine

Just like our vending machine analogy from an earlier chapter, the `GetPlayer` function accepts two integers called x and y as inputs (these are like quarters and nickels). It uses these values to look up a Square in the grid and, using the `return` keyword, the function spits out an `int` referring to the value of the square's player variable (this is like a bag of corn chips).

This function allows us to easily poll any Square by its grid coordinates to find out which piece has been played on it.

Shave and a haircut

Thanks to the `GetPlayer` function, we can shorten up our monstro code quite nicely. Add the following lines to the `CheckForWin` function:

```
var theScript:Square = square.GetComponent.<Square>();
//Check the squares in the same column:
if(GetPlayer(theScript.x,0) == currentPlayer &&
  GetPlayer(theScript.x,1) == currentPlayer &&
  GetPlayer(theScript.x,2) == currentPlayer) return true;
// Check the squares in the same row:
if(GetPlayer(0,theScript.y) == currentPlayer &&
  GetPlayer(1,theScript.y) == currentPlayer &&
  GetPlayer(2,theScript.y) == currentPlayer) return true;
```

That reduces our column and row checks to two somewhat long, but still much more manageable lines.

Finally, we'll hard-code the values in two more statements to check the diagonals, because checking the diagonals in some pithy, clever loop is a more trouble than it's worth:

```
function CheckForWin(square:GameObject):boolean
{
    var theScript:Square = square.GetComponent.<Square>();

    //Check the squares in the same column:
    if(GetPlayer(theScript.x,0) == currentPlayer &&
      GetPlayer(theScript.x,1) == currentPlayer &&
      GetPlayer(theScript.x,2) == currentPlayer) return true;
    // Check the squares in the same row:
    if(GetPlayer(0,theScript.y) == currentPlayer &&
      GetPlayer(1,theScript.y) == currentPlayer &&
      GetPlayer(2,theScript.y) == currentPlayer) return true;
    // Check the diagonals:
    if(GetPlayer(0,0) == currentPlayer && GetPlayer(1,1) ==
      currentPlayer && GetPlayer(2,2) == currentPlayer) return true;
    if(GetPlayer(2,0) == currentPlayer && GetPlayer(1,1) ==
      currentPlayer && GetPlayer(0,2) == currentPlayer) return true;
    return false; // If we get this far without finding a win, return
    false to signify "no win".
    }
```

What just happened – hunting for a win

The `CheckForWin` function accepts `square` as its only argument. That `square` happens to the be Square the current player just clicked on to place a piece. Hand-in-hand with the `GetPlayer` function, `CheckForWin` first searches for the three Squares in the same column as the Square that was just clicked on.

If all of the pieces in those Squares are the same, that makes three-in-a-row. The `return` keyword spits the good news back to whichever part of the code called this function.

Failing that, the function checks the three Squares in the same row as the Square that was just clicked on. If it finds three-in-a-row, it returns a value of `true` and the rest of the code is similarly skipped.

We repeat the same process to check the two diagonals, regardless of whether the recently-clicked Square was on a diagonal, because to do otherwise is a pain in the butt and requires extraneous code.

If no wins are found on the diagonals, the function returns a value of `false`.

Time for action – check for a win

The `CheckForWin` function is ready to start cranking out the hits! Add a win check to the `ClickSquare` function:

```
square.GetComponent.<Square>().player = currentPlayer;
if(CheckForWin(square)) print("player " + currentPlayer + "
  wins!!!");
```

Smashed into a single succinct line, this code runs the `CheckForWin` function, passing it a reference to the Square that was just clicked. If that function call resolves to `true` (because `CheckForWin` returns true), then Unity should print a statement saying that the current player has won.

Here is the long form version of that same code:

```
if(CheckForWin(square) == true)
{
  print("player " + currentPlayer + " wins!!!");
}
```

Test the game. Try letting either X or O win the game. It works, and the message is displayed to the bottom of the Unity interface, and to the **Console** window:

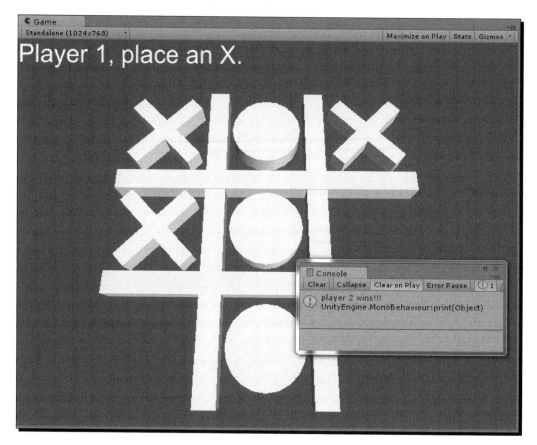

Sore loser

You've no doubt noticed that when one player wins, the game obliviously prompts the next player to make a move.

We need to create a boolean flag that we can flip when a player wins, and show the players a different message when the game is over.

Add this following boolean to the `GameLogic` script:

```
var aGrid:GameObject[,];
var gameIsOver:boolean;
```

Expand the `CheckForWin()` conditional statement:

```
if(CheckForWin(square))
{
  gameIsOver = true;
  ShowWinnerPrompt();
  return;
}
```

We can use the `return` statement like that, too. A naked `return` statement just bails us out of running the rest of the code in a function, without even returning a value. If the game is truly over, there's no need to bother with the rest of the function. Let's just get the heck out of here.

Time for action – notify the winner

Let's create that `ShowWinnerPrompt` function we just called:

```
function ShowWinnerPrompt()
{
  if(currentPlayer == 1)
  {
    prompt.text = "X gets 3 in a row. Player 1 wins!";
  } else {
    prompt.text = "O gets 3 in a row. Player 2 wins!";
  }
}
```

Hopefully, this code is straightforward, but since I'm contractually obligated to explain it, I will offer that this conditional statement evaluates the `currentPlayer` value, and shows one message or another depending on the result.

Test the game, and play until one player wins.

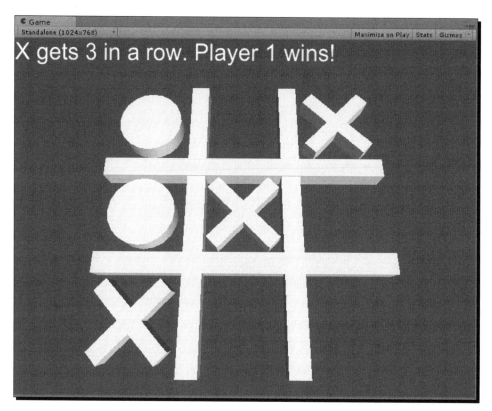

Time for action – you win. Now what?

We get the right message, but the game doesn't do anything after that. Let's build in a bit of a pause, and then reload the Game Scene after a win occurs.

At the bottom of the `ShowWinnerPrompt` function, add these two lines:

```
yield WaitForSeconds(3);
Application.LoadLevel(0);
```

We pause for 3 seconds so the players can read the "win" message and grasp the full weight of the situation, and then we automatically reload the level for a new game.

The remaining problem with the game is that if we arrive at a stalemate where neither player wins and there are no more moves to make, the game doesn't know it, and prompts the next player to place a piece anyway. The game should somehow be able to figure out when the game is a draw, and react to that situation.

Have a go hero – draw, pardner

Just as you did earlier in the chapter, take a moment to flap your arms like a chicken. Then think about how you would determine that the game is a draw. Compare your solution(s) with the one you're about to implement.

Nice moves

It seems simple enough to create an `int` variable to keep track of the number of moves that have been made, which we'll increment every time a player places a piece. If we're up to the ninth move with no winner, that means all of the squares have been filled and we've reached a stalemate.

At the top of the script, declare a `moves` variable:

```
var gameIsOver:boolean;
var moves:int;
```

Just above the `Instantiate` command in the `ClickSquare` function, increment `moves`:

```
moves ++;
Instantiate(piece, square.transform.position, Quaternion.identity);
```

Tack on an `else` to the `CheckForWin` condition check that ends the game if we've reached 9 moves with no winner:

```
if(CheckForWin(square))
{
  gameIsOver = true;
  ShowWinnerPrompt();
  return;
} else if(moves >= 9) {
  gameIsOver = true;
  ShowStalematePrompt();
  return;
}
```

Why are we checking if `moves` is equal to or greater than 9? Isn't that impossible? Yes it is, but I've adopted the habit of being abundantly confident in my condition checks to cover possible *and* impossible scenarios. It's that extra layer of security that makes programmers so cuddly.

Since we call it, we need to make sure the `ShowStalematePrompt` function exists. Drop this into the `GameLogic` script:

```
function ShowStalematePrompt()
{
  prompt.text = "Stalemate!  Neither player wins.";

  yield WaitForSeconds(3);
  Application.LoadLevel(0);
}
```

Time for action – the final bug

The last bug in the game is that in the pause between someone winning and the game reloading, players can still click on spaces to place their pieces. Let's add a quick condition check to the top of the `ClickSpace` function. If the game is won, prevent the rest of the code from executing:

```
function ClickSquare(square:GameObject)
{
    if(gameIsOver) return;
```

Push the red return button! Eject! Eject!

All done but for the shouting

We have succeeded in creating a fully functional local multiplayer turn-based strategy game for a couple of flesh-and-blood players, entirely out of things we found around the house (and Primitives we found in Unity's GameObject menu). We could stop right there, but you were promised AI programming, and AI programming you shall have.

Before we charge into the next chapter, let's take a look back on some of the concepts covered in the warm-up.

You have learned how to:

◆ Build a working game in Unity with no imported assets

◆ Prevent GameObjects from colliding using the **Is Trigger** checkbox

◆ Refactor code for improved readability and maintenance

◆ Create a custom function that returns a value

◆ Use the `return` keyword to spit out a value from within a function

◆ Return no value in order to escape the rest of a function

Don't go away! The fun continues one page from now. If you want to have a few games of digital Tic Tac Toe before moving on, indulge yourself!

C# addendum

The full C# code translation for the Tic Tac Toe game awaits you at the end of the next chapter! Standing in for it in this chapter is a Japanese ASCII emoticon of an adorable Himalayan kitty. Feast your eyes!

○人○

D'awwwww.

13

AI Programming and World Domination

In the previous chapter, we left off with a working 2-player Tic Tac Toe game. We could easily hang up our hats and call it a day. The sad truth is that for many, playing video games is a solitary activity, and we, as game programmers, need to devise computer-controlled "friends" to challenge our human players. As game budgets and networking capabilities improve, games are increasingly returning to their social, multiplayer roots. Despite this, there will always be a call for "smart" computer opponents in case—God forbid—the Internet goes down.

Artificial Intelligence is so-called because it's an attempt at making a computer seem like it's thinking, when in reality, it's just robotically following instructions like it always has. Through careful design, we can create the illusion that the computer is strategizing, and even making mistakes, just like a human being would. By the end of this chapter, you will have written your own AI routine to "teach" the computer to mercilessly dominate your Tic Tac Toe game.

Take it away, computer

Currently, the Tic Tac Toe game has one function, `ClickSquare`, that enables human players to play their pieces. The computer player doesn't actually have to click anything, and since the AI routine is going to contain special, computer player-specific instructions, it makes sense to build a special function to govern the computer's turn-taking.

Time for action – add computer control

Let's build a function so that the computer can take a turn. Add a `ComputerTakeATurn` function to the `GameLogic` script:

```
function ComputerTakeATurn()
{
}
```

When do we want the computer to take a turn? After player 1, the human, has taken a turn, and the `currentPlayer` variable updates to 2.

Therefore in the `ClickSquare` function, after we show the player prompt, let's let the computer take a turn:

```
ShowPlayerPrompt();
    ComputerTakeATurn();
```

Herpa derp derp

Just to get this up and running, we'll make the artificial intelligence as dumb as possible. The computer will scan the grid for empty Squares, choose one at random, and place an O there.

We'll accomplish this by looping through our 1-dimensional array of Square references, adding any empty Squares to a separate list, and then choosing a Square at random from that list.

Add this code to the `ComputerTakeATurn` function:

```
function ComputerTakeATurn()
{
  var square:GameObject;
  var aEmptySquares:List.<GameObject> = new List.<GameObject>();

  for(var i:int = 0; i < aSquares.Length; i++)
  {
    square = aSquares[i];
    if(square.GetComponent.<Square>().player == 0)
      aEmptySquares.Add(square);
  }
  square = aEmptySquares[Random.Range(0,aEmptySquares.Count)];
}
```

Add this line to the top of the script:

```
#pragma strict
import System.Collections.Generic;
```

What just happened – making a list, checking it twice

Let's break this code down.

```
var square:GameObject;
```

This variable will store a reference to a square that we pull from the array. As before, we declare this variable outside the upcoming for loop.

```
var aEmptySquares:List.<GameObject> = new List.<GameObject>();
```

We're going to get a lot of use out of the Generic Array collection type in this chapter. Here, we declare an `aEmptySquares` array to store all of the Square GameObjects that do not have a player piece in them. (The `import` statement we added to the top of the script makes it possible for us to use Generic Arrays).

```
for(var i:int = 0; i < aSquares.Length; i++)
```

We use a for loop to pick through the squares in the 1-dimensional `aSquares` array.

```
square = aSquares[i];
```

Inside the loop, we store a reference to the square in the ith position of the array.

```
if(square.GetComponent.<Square>().player == 0)
    aEmptySquares.Add(square);
```

If the square has a player value of 0, that means it's empty, so we add it to our list of empty squares.

```
square = aEmptySquares[Random.Range(0,aEmptySquares.Count)];
```

Outside the loop, after we've picked through all of the squares, we randomly choose one of the empty squares from the list.

Unpacking the code

If you saw a similar line of code in the previous chapter and were a little mystified by it, here is a clearer, longer-form breakdown of what's happening (do not add this code to your script):

```
var someRandomIndex:int = Random.Range(0,aEmptySquares.Count);
```

Choose a random number between 0 and the length of the `aEmptySquares` array minus one. For example, if the `aEmptySquares` array has 5 squares in it, we'll get a number between 0 and 4.

```
square = aEmptySquares[someRandomIndex];
```

Retrieve a square from the `aEmptySquares` array at the index point we randomly chose. For example, if the randomly chosen number between 0 and 5 was 2, then retrieve the element at index 2 of the `aEmptySquares` array.

The line we actually used in our script is just those two lines above, condensed into a single line:

```
square = aEmptySquares[Random.Range(0,aEmptySquares.Count)];
```

Why go through all this trouble to compose a list of empty squares, and then randomly choose one from the list? Why don't we just stop at the first empty square we find, and play the computer's piece there?

This is the first lesson in artificial intelligence: *randomness creates the illusion of thought.*

Let's say the Squares are listed in the array in order, and the first square in the array is the top-left square. If we always stop our search at the first empty square we find, then the computer will always play its piece in the top-left square (unless player 1 takes that square, and then the computer will always play its piece in the next square in the array).

If you were playing Tic Tac Toe against someone who always, always placed his or her piece in the same squares, and in always in the same order, would you consider that player intelligent? No! You would probably start looking around for a helmet and gloves to prevent your opponent from hurting himself.

By having the computer choose a random square, we can improve the illusion that the computer is "thinking". But as you'll soon see, that illusion breaks down pretty quickly.

Time for action – code consolidation

We've chosen the square that the computer player will take. What are the next steps? Well, we need to increment the `moves` variable. We need to instantiate a piece **Prefab**. We need to update the Square with the player who claimed it. We need to check for a win or a stalemate, and update the player number.

By golly, all these steps are identical to the steps we already take when the human player places a piece! We should encapsulate those steps in a function that both the human and computer player can call.

Take all of the lines that are bolded below in the `ClickSquare` function, and move them into a new function called `PlacePiece()`:

```
function ClickSquare(square:GameObject)
{
    if(gameIsOver) return;
```

```
var piece:GameObject;
if(currentPlayer == 1)
{
  piece = XPiece;
} else {
  piece = OPiece;
}

moves ++;

Instantiate(piece, square.transform.position, Quaternion.identity);
  square.GetComponent.<Square>().player = currentPlayer;

if(CheckForWin(square))
{
  gameIsOver = true;
  ShowWinnerPrompt();
  return;
} else if(moves >= 9) {
  gameIsOver = true;
  ShowStalematePrompt();
  return;
}



currentPlayer ++;
if(currentPlayer > 2) currentPlayer = 1;

ShowPlayerPrompt();

ComputerTakeATurn();
}
```

In place of the lines highlighted above, call the PlacePiece() function. The new ClickSquare function should look like the following:

```
function ClickSquare(square:GameObject)
{
  if(gameIsOver) return;

  PlacePiece();

  ComputerTakeATurn();
}
```

The `PlacePiece` function should look like the following:

```
function PlacePiece()
{
  var piece:GameObject;
  if(currentPlayer == 1)
  {
    piece = XPiece;
  } else {
    piece = OPiece;
  }
  moves ++;
  Instantiate(piece, square.transform.position, Quaternion.identity);
  square.GetComponent.<Square>().player = currentPlayer;
  if(CheckForWin(square))
  {
    gameIsOver = true;
    ShowWinnerPrompt();
    return;
  } else if(moves >= 9) {
    gameIsOver = true;
    ShowStalematePrompt();
    return;
  }
  currentPlayer ++;
  if(currentPlayer > 2) currentPlayer = 1;
  ShowPlayerPrompt();
}
```

At the top of the `PlacePiece` function, we have a conditional check to determine whether we should place an X or an O depending on the `currentPlayer` variable. Now that we're discretely calling this function, we can actually pass in the piece we want placed, and omit the conditional check.

Change the `PlacePiece()` function call in the `ClickSquare` function, so that you're explicitly passing a reference to the **XPiece** Prefab:

```
PlacePiece(XPiece);
```

In the `PlacePiece` function, accept `piece` as a parameter:

```
function PlacePiece(piece:GameObject)
```

Delete the whole `currentPlayer`-checking conditional from the `PlacePiece` function, bolded below:

```
var piece:GameObject;
if(currentPlayer == 1)
{
  piece = XPiece;
} else {
  piece = OPiece;
}
```

The `Instantiate` command still refers to a `GameObject` called `piece`, which is now coming from the parameter, instead of being defined in the conditional statement. Here's how the `PlacePiece` function should look when you're finished:

```
function PlacePiece(piece:GameObject)
{
  moves ++;
  Instantiate(piece, square.transform.position, Quaternion.identity);
  square.GetComponent.<Square>().player = currentPlayer;

  if(CheckForWin(square))
  {
    gameIsOver = true;
    ShowWinnerPrompt();
    return;
  } else if(moves >= 9) {
    ShowStalematePrompt();
    return;
  }
  currentPlayer ++;
  if(currentPlayer > 2) currentPlayer = 1;
  ShowPlayerPrompt();
}
```

In moving this code into the `PlacePiece` function, we may not have noticed that the `PlacePiece` code now has no idea what `square` is, since it's no longer defined inside the function. Let's also pass that in when we call `PlacePiece`. Modify the function signature:

```
function PlacePiece(piece:GameObject, square:GameObject)
```

From the `ClickSquare` function, pass in the clicked `square` when you call `PlacePiece`:

```
PlacePiece(XPiece, square);
```

Down in the `ComputerTakeATurn` function, call the `PlacePiece` function and pass it the computer player-specific piece and square references:

```
square = aEmptySquares[Random.Range(0,aEmptySquares.Count)];
PlacePiece(OPiece, square);
```

Let's test the game and look for bugs.

Tic Tac Toe at the speed of light

Whoa... okay. The computer player plays a piece, but it does so instantly after the human clicks to place a piece. This is what happens when you play a game against a superior intellect!

To dull the game down to human-comprehensible speed, let's build in a brief pause before the computer makes a move just before the function call in the `ClickSquare` function.

```
yield WaitForSeconds(2);
ComputerTakeATurn();
```

Try the game again. There is now a nice 2-second pause before the computer makes a move, providing the illusion that the computer is "thinking" (when really, it's just randomly throwing darts at the wall). This Artificial Intelligence stuff is looking more and more like a magic trick, isn't it?

Sore loser

You may notice, however, that the computer cheats. If the human gets three Xs in a row, the computer will place an O even after the game is won. That's because our code is telling the computer to do this. We always call `ComputerTakeATurn` after the human's move, with no conditions.

Let's wrap our `ComputerTakeATurn` call in a conditional statement to check whether the game is won:

```
if(!gameIsOver)
{
   yield WaitForSeconds(2);
   ComputerTakeATurn();
}
```

That should prevent the computer from getting in a cheater-pants cheap shot after the game has ended.

Click-spamming for fun and profit

The human player can also cheat, and place an X during the pause while the computer is "thinking". Try "click-spamming" the grid to place more Xs than you ought to. If you're very quick, you can fill the grid with Xs before the computer places a single O.

By adding a conditional check to the `ClickSquare` function, we can make sure the human can only place a piece when it's his or her turn:

```
function ClickSquare(square:GameObject)
{
   if(gameIsOver || currentPlayer == 2) return;
```

The double-pipe means "OR". If either of the statements separated by || in the conditional check resolve to true, then the code within the conditional is executed.

So if the human clicks to place a piece, if either the game is over or it's the computer's turn, we use the return statement to eject out of the function and prevent the rest of the code from executing.

Test the game again. Now, neither player can cheat.

Artificial stupidity

Once again, we can end the project here. We now have a 2-player turn-based strategy game with a computer opponent. The human player can win and, with a little luck (and some rotten playing on the human's part), the computer player can win.

Try playing a few rounds of the worst Tic Tac Toe of your life. The computer player can win, but it's almost a challenge to play so badly that you lose to your artificially "intelligent" opponent.

Randomly choosing an empty Square isn't going to cut it. We need to make the computer opponent smarter. To do that, we have to sit down and study Tic Tac Toe until we understand what makes it ... ahem ... *tick*. We need to be experts at how to play, and win, Tic Tac Toe. The computer scientists who programmed Big Blue to defeat Kasparov had to go through the same process with a considerably more complicated game, studying the intricacies of chess so they could teach a computer how to strategize.

Have a go hero – solve Tic Tac Toe

Tic Tac Toe is what ludologists (people who study games) call a "solved game". A solved game is one where you can reliably predict the outcome of a match from any point, as long as both players play "perfectly", or optimally, without making any strategic errors. The process of solving a game can involve mapping out all of the game's possible states in a flowchart-like "game tree", and from that chart, deriving a set of steps to follow that will produce the best possible outcome for either player.

The game tree for Tic Tac Toe terminates in 138 different end states, as long as you don't include symmetries or board rotations. If you're feeling plucky, why not grab a pencil and a piece of paper and map out the game tree for Tic Tac Toe? Here's a nudge to get you started.

At first glance, it seems like player 1 has nine different options for placing an X—after all, there are nine empty squares in the grid. Consider, though, that an X placed in the top left-hand corner is identical to an X placed in the bottom right-hand corner, if you rotate the board. It's the same story with the sides.

In reality, at the beginning of a Tic Tac Toe game, there are only three unique moves a player can make: a corner, a side, or the center.

Consequently, the top of our game tree looks like this:

Pursue the first branch of the diagram where X takes a corner. O can respond with five possible moves: an adjacent side, an opposite side, an adjacent corner, an opposite corner, or the center.

The Tic Tac Toe game tree begins to look more like a maniacal football coach's playbook.

From those five options, you can keep branching out until you find the inevitable conclusion for each one. Then go back, and doodle the possibilities for the remaining unexplored paths.

If drawing this game tree scratches a ludological (or obsessive-compulsive) itch for you, keep going until you find all the 138 terminal board positions. Finishing the game tree is not crucial to completing this chapter, but it will give you a good feel for the lengths to which some computer scientists will go to find the answers to burning questions, like "how do you win at Tic Tac Toe?".

Time for action – winning is everything

To determine the best course of action for the computer opponent, we need to create a prioritized list of rules for the computer to follow when deciding how to place a piece, which changes depending on the situation on the board. Let's pretend we are the computer, and we see this situation:

It wouldn't make sense to place an O anywhere but in X's way—otherwise, the computer loses. So we have our first rule:

◆   Block opponent from winning

Now let's look at this situation:

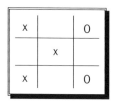

Sure, X is about to win, but O also has an opportunity to win. Which is more important: for O to keep X from winning, or for O to win? Clearly, it's more important for O to claim victory and win the game. So we have our second rule:

◆   Win

We just said that it's *more important* for O to claim victory than to block X, so we've also established a preferred order for these two rules:

◆   Win
◆   Block

Notice that our two statements are already written in pseudocode. `Win()` and `Block()` could just as easily be written as function calls. If we keep this up, we can just convert our plain English statements into Unity JavaScript and, theoretically, our code will work in-game.

It's a trap!

What are the most powerful ways in which to play this game? Tic Tac Toe neophytes suppose that the most powerful square on the grid is the middle. After all, doesn't the most high-profile washed-up celebrity get the center square on Hollywood Squares?

However, as any discerning Tic Tac Toe player knows, playing the corners is perhaps a wiser move, because it facilitates a trap, where scoring 3-in-a-row is possible in two different places. Blocking one path simply allows the player to win with the second path.

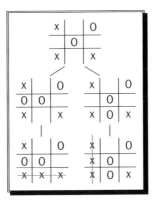

So in this situation, blocking is not an option. The only viable options are to win, if possible, or to have prevented the opponent from creating a trap to begin with. So that gives us one more rule for our AI player:

◆   Prevent a trap

And really, if it's possible to set a trap for the opponent, we want our artificially intelligent computer player to try to do that. So we have:

◆   Prevent a trap
◆   Create a trap

Where do these two things fit in our existing prioritized list of rules?

◆   Win
◆   Block

Since a player's victory is more important than an opponent's victory, setting one's own trap is of higher priority than blocking the opponent's trap. Our prioritized list of rules then becomes:

◆   Win
◆   Block
◆   Prevent a trap
◆   Create a trap

The leftovers

From there, the computer player can either take the center, a corner, or a side. Which of these three positions is the most powerful, and therefore of the highest priority?

If you had mapped out all of the possible board positions in a game tree, you would already know the answer. Or, you could save a boatload of time by just reading the Tic Tac Toe article on Wikipedia. At the time of this writing, it was an excellent primer on the thinking that goes into determining the best strategy for this game, and others of its kind. Since Wikipedia is editable by anyone, it's possible that by the time you read the article, it will be full of cat pictures. Let's hope not.

We'll stand on the shoulders of giants and crib the rest of our notes from Wikipedia. According to the article, taking a corner position provides more opportunities for your opponent to make a mistake, but this only matters if 1. it's the first move and 2. your opponent actually makes a mistake. Otherwise, the preferred order of play is center, corner, side.

Since we're not planning on allowing our computer player to make a mistake (yet), our prioritized list then becomes:

◆ Win
◆ Block
◆ Prevent a trap
◆ Create a trap
◆ Play the center
◆ Play a corner
◆ Play a side

To put this in more pseudocode terms, we might say:

◆ Try to win

◆ If you can't win, try to block

◆ If you can't block, try to set a trap

◆ If you can't set a trap, try to prevent the opponent from setting a trap

◆ If there's no trap to prevent, play the center

◆ If the center is taken, play a corner

◆ If there's no free corner, play a side

Doesn't it matter *which* corner or side we play? Possibly. We won't know unless we map out that gigantic game tree and strap on our taped-up specs for some right nerdy analysis, or just try this code and see if it works. I vote for the latter.

Time for action – pseu pseu pseudocode

To translate our prioritized peudocode strategy list into actual code, I propose that we turn each attempt at playing a piece into its own function. If we find a valid move, the function will return the square where the computer should play a piece. If there's no valid move, the function will return `null`, which is the computer code equivalent of "does not exist/totally isn't a thing".

In the `ComputerTakeATurn` function, let's get rid of (or comment out) the code that randomly chooses a square, which is bolded in the following code:

```
function ComputerTakeATurn()
{
  var square:GameObject;

  var aEmptySquares:List.<GameObject> = new List.<GameObject>();

  for(var i:int = 0; i < aSquares.Length; i++)
  {
    square = aSquares[i];
    if(square.GetComponent.<Square>().player == 0)
      aEmptySquares.Add(square);
  }
  square = aEmptySquares[Random.Range(0,aEmptySquares.Count)];

  PlacePiece(OPiece, square);
}
```

We'll replace it with our pseudocode-turned-real-code list of attempted moves:

```
var square:GameObject;
square = Win();
if(square == null) square = Block();
if(square == null) square = CreateTrap();
if(square == null) square = PreventTrap();
if(square == null) square = GetCentre();
if(square == null) square = GetEmptyCorner();
if(square == null) square = GetEmptySide();
if(square == null) square = GetRandomEmptySquare();
PlacePiece(OPiece, square);
```

What just happened – stepping through the strategy

Each of the items in our prioritized strategy list is represented by a (currently non-existent) function. Each function will attempt to find a valid square for the computer player to place its piece, by returning a reference to a square `GameObject`.

```
square = Win();
```

By writing this, we're setting the value of the `square` variable to whatever gets spit out of the `Win` function vending machine. If the `Win` function finds a winning square, the returned item will be a square `GameObject`. If the `Win` function fails to find a winning square, it will return a value of null.

```
if(square == null) square = Block();
```

In the next lines, we check to see if the value of square is null. If it is, then we'll try the next strategic move, and the next, in decreasing order of preference, until the computer just plays a random empty square, which is the weakest move it can make.

Time for action – begin at the end

There's no shame in starting simple. Let's start writing these functions from the bottom up, until we reach the most complex ones at the top.

The `GetRandomEmptySquare()` function does what our stupidest possible computer player does: finds any empty square and marks it with no thought to strategy. We can just reuse code we've already written:

```
function GetRandomEmptySquare():GameObject
{
  var square:GameObject
  var aEmptySquares:List.<GameObject> = new List.<GameObject>();

  for(var i:int = 0; i < aSquares.Length; i++)
  {
    square = aSquares[i];
    if(square.GetComponent.<Square>().player == 0)
      aEmptySquares.Add(square);
  }
  square = aEmptySquares[Random.Range(0,aEmptySquares.Count)];
  return square;
}
```

This will be our fall-through code. If all else fails and none of the other functions manage to return a square, we can count on this line to just grab an empty space in the grid.

The GetEmptySide function needs to look at all four of the side squares, and return an empty one (if one exists). We could just return the first one we find, but as we saw earlier, that might break the illusion that the computer is "thinking" intelligently. A better approach is to make a list of all the empty sides, and choose one at random, just as we did with the empty squares in the unintelligent version of our computer player.

We know we'll need a list. We'll add any empty side we find to that list. Then, if the list has at least one empty side in it, we'll return a random side from the list. Otherwise, we'll return null.

In pseudocode, it looks like this:

The GetEmptySide function returns a GameObject.

1. Create an empty list.

2. If the top side is empty, add it to the list.

3. If the left side is empty, add it to the list.

4. If the right side is empty, add it to the list.

5. If the bottom side is empty, add it to the list.

6. If the list has at least one thing in it, choose a thing at random and return it.

7. Otherwise, return null.

In UnityScript, it looks like this:

```
function GetEmptySide():GameObject
{
  var aEmptySides:List.<GameObject> =
    new List.<GameObject>();
  if(GetPlayer(1,0) == 0) aEmptySides.Add(aGrid[1,0]);
  if(GetPlayer(0,1) == 0) aEmptySides.Add(aGrid[0,1]);
  if(GetPlayer(2,1) == 0) aEmptySides.Add(aGrid[2,1]);
  if(GetPlayer(1,2) == 0) aEmptySides.Add(aGrid[1,2]);
  if(aEmptySides.Count > 0) return
    aEmptySides[Random.Range(0,aEmptySides.Count)];
  return null;
}
```

It's a nearly identical process to return an empty corner. Add this function to your code:

```
function GetEmptyCorner():GameObject
{
  var aEmptyCorners:List.<GameObject> = new List.<GameObject>();

  if(GetPlayer(0,0) == 0) aEmptyCorners.Add(aGrid[0,0]);
  if(GetPlayer(2,0) == 0) aEmptyCorners.Add(aGrid[2,0]);
  if(GetPlayer(0,2) == 0) aEmptyCorners.Add(aGrid[0,2]);
  if(GetPlayer(2,2) == 0) aEmptyCorners.Add(aGrid[2,2]);

  if(aEmptyCorners.Count > 0) return aEmptyCorners
    [Random.Range(0,aEmptyCorners.Count)];

  return null;
}
```

It's an even simpler task to get the status of the center square and return it if it's empty. Tack on this function to your code:

```
function GetCentre():GameObject
{
  if( GetPlayer(1,1) == 0 ) return aGrid[1,1];
  return null;
}
```

Keep in mind throughout these three functions that a `return` statement prevents all other code in the function from executing. In the `GetCentre` function, for example, if the code finds an empty square in the center, it returns the square and bounces back out of the function, so that the `return null` line is never executed.

Time for action – the final four

That leaves us with four more functions to write: `Win()`, `Block()`, `CreateTrap()`, and `PreventTrap()`. Note that for the remainder of the chapter, we'll be using the word "row" to refer both to a horizontal line, and to three squares in a line regardless of their orientation, as in "in-a-row".

A very interesting thing happens if we carefully work out what needs to happen in each of these functions. Take the `Win` and `Block` functions first.

*To determine whether we can **win**, we need to look at three spaces in a row. If two of the spaces in a row contain our piece, and the third is empty, we can win the game.*

*To determine whether we can **block**, we need to look at three spaces in a row. If two of the spaces contain the opponent's piece, and the third is empty, we can block.*

Code one, get one free

I don't know about you, but I'm seeing double. The pseudocode to determine a chance to win and a chance to block looks exactly the same. That means we can probably combine the `Win` and `Block` checks into one efficient function. Let's give it a shot.

Start by combining the two `ComputerTakeATurn` lines from this:

```
square = Win();
if(square == null) square = Block();
if(square == null) square = CreateTrap();
if(square == null) square = PreventTrap();
```

Into this:

```
square = WinOrBlock();
if(square == null) square = CreateTrap();
if(square == null) square = PreventTrap();
```

I'll confess that it took quite a bit of trial and error to write a working `WinOrBlock()` function. As with any code, there may be better ways to accomplish the same goal, but this is the solution I painstakingly arrived at. I will step through the conclusions I reached in building this function. As you read, picture the mountains of crumpled-up paper and torn-out hair that led to this amazing breakthrough in computer programming.

Have a go hero - stump the author

Before you hear my solution, puzzle through it yourself and see if you can devise a good way to determine whether the computer can win or block. Full disclosure: the solution we're going to build actually uses two functions!

The actual intelligence behind artificial intelligence

The function needs to check all eight opportunities to score: 3 columns, 3 rows, and 2 diagonals. The big "aha" moment came when I realized that I couldn't just eject out of the function with a return statement the moment I discovered a chance to block, because (according to our handy prioritized strategy list), winning is of higher priority than blocking. By immediately returning the first opportunity to block I came across, I might be leaving an unsearched opportunity to win on the table.

It became clear that I would need to store a list of opportunities to block, and a list of opportunities to win. Once I search through all eight scoring scenarios, the function should return a random opportunity to win from the list (if any exist). If not, the function should return a random opportunity to block from the second list (if any existed). If there are no opportunities to block or win, the function should return null.

For example, in the preceding image, the search will find one opportunity to win (by playing the square on the right side), and one opportunity to block (by playing the square on the left side). Those options will each go into a different list. Since winning is a higher priority than blocking, the code will pull a random item out of the list of opportunities to win (there's only one in the list), and the rest of the function will be skipped over.

In the preceding situation, the search will only find one opportunity to block in the left side square. The code will check the list of opportunities to win, and since that list is empty, it will choose a random square from the list of opportunities to block (there's only one on the list).

In this example, there are no opportunities to win or block, so the two lists will be empty after the search is conducted. Since that's the case, the function will return `null`.

The second important breakthrough was parceling out the actual search steps into a separate function, and accepting three individual squares as inputs. It's tough to write a concise loop to pick through the rows, columns, and particularly diagonals in a Tic Tac Toe game, so defining a function that takes three discrete squares as inputs seems like a great way to keep the code simple and concise.

Time for action – score!

Because the solution requires two functions that each need to access the lists of win and block opportunities, those lists need to be defined at the top of the code as member variables that any function can access:

```
var aGrid:GameObject[,];
var gameIsOver:boolean;
var moves:int;
var aBlockOpportunities:List.<GameObject>;
var aWinOpportunities:List.<GameObject>;
```

This is the combined `WinOrBlock` function:

```
function WinOrBlock():GameObject
{
  aBlockOpportunities = new List.<GameObject>();
  aWinOpportunities = new List.<GameObject>();
  // Empty out these lists before we start searching.
  // Check the rows for 2 in a row:
  CheckFor2InARow([Vector2(0,0), Vector2(1,0), Vector2(2,0)]);
```

```
    CheckFor2InARow([Vector2(0,1), Vector2(1,1), Vector2(2,1)]);
    CheckFor2InARow([Vector2(0,2), Vector2(1,2), Vector2(2,2)]);
    // Check the columns for 2 in a row:
    CheckFor2InARow([Vector2(0,0), Vector2(0,1), Vector2(0,2)]);
    CheckFor2InARow([Vector2(1,0), Vector2(1,1), Vector2(1,2)]);
    CheckFor2InARow([Vector2(2,0), Vector2(2,1), Vector2(2,2)]);
    // Check the diagonals for 2 in a row:
    CheckFor2InARow([Vector2(0,0), Vector2(1,1), Vector2(2,2)]);
    CheckFor2InARow([Vector2(0,2), Vector2(1,1), Vector2(2,0)]);
    // If there are any opportunities to win, return one at random:
    if(aWinOpportunities.Count > 0) return
       aWinOpportunities[Random.Range(0, aWinOpportunities.Count)];
    // If there are any opportunities to block, return one at random:
    if(aBlockOpportunities.Count > 0) return
       aBlockOpportunities[Random.Range(0, aBlockOpportunities.Count)];
    // There are no opportunities to win or block, so return null:
    return null;
}
```

Each `CheckFor2InARow` call updates the `aWinOpportunities` and `aBlockOpportunities` lists if the function finds two X's or O's in a row. Finally, here is the `CheckFor2InARow` companion function:

```
function CheckFor2InARow(coords:Vector2[])
{
  var p1InThisRow:int = 0; // the number of X's in this row
  var p2InThisRow:int = 0; // the number of O's in this row
  var player:int;
  var square:GameObject = null;
  var coord:Vector2;
  // Step through each of the 3 Square coordinates
    that were passed in:
  for (var i:int = 0; i<3; i++)
  {
    coord = coords[i];
    player = GetPlayer(coord.x,coord.y);
    // Find the piece in this Square
    if(player == 1)
    {
      p1InThisRow ++; // Tally up an X
    } else if(player == 2) {
      p2InThisRow ++; // Tally up an O
    } else {
```

```
        square = aGrid[coord.x,coord.y];
        // This Square is empty. Store it for later.
    }
  }

  if(square != null)
  {
    // We found an empty Square in this row.
    if(p2InThisRow == 2)
    {
      // There are two O's in a row with an empty Square.
      aWinOpportunities.Add(square);
      // Add a win opportunity to the list.
    } else if (p1InThisRow == 2) {
      // There are two X's in a row with an empty Square.
      aBlockOpportunities.Add(square);
      // Add a block opportunity to the list.
    }
  }
}
```

What just happened – the search is on

The `WinOrBlock` function kicks off by emptying out the `aBlockOpportunities` and `aWinOpportunities` arrays.

```
aBlockOpportunities = new List.<GameObject>();
aWinOpportunities = new List.<GameObject>();
// Empty out these lists before we start searching.
```

By doing this, we ensure that any results leftover from earlier searches are swept out, and we start fresh.

The next eight lines are nearly identical. They all pass a different set of three squares to the `CheckFor2InARow` function.

```
CheckFor2InARow([Vector2(1,0), Vector2(1,1), Vector2(1,2)]);
```

This call, for example, passes in the three squares in the column that runs straight down the middle of the grid.

```
if(aWinOpportunities.Count > 0) return aWinOpportunities
  [Random.Range(0, aWinOpportunities.Count)];
```

This line, like the one that follows it, determines whether there's at least one element in the aWinOpportunities array. If there is, it grabs one at random and returns it.

Let's take a closer look at the CheckFor2InARow function.

```
var p1InThisRow:int = 0; // the number of X's in this row
var p2InThisRow:int = 0; // the number of O's in this row
var player:int;
var square:GameObject = null;
var coord:Vector2;
```

These variable declarations at the top are all used inside the loop, as we've seen before.

```
for (var i:int = 0; i<3; i++)
```

We loop through the three coordinates that were passed in through the coords array in the function definition.

```
coord = coords[i];
```

First, we pull out a pair of coordinates at the ith index and store it in the coord variable.

```
player = GetPlayer(coord.x, coord.y);
// Find the piece in this Square
```

Next, we use our prebuilt GetPlayer function to return the value of the player variable on the square at the specified coordinates.

```
if(player == 1)
{
   p1InThisRow ++; // Tally up an X
```

If the square's player value is set to 1, we increment the value of the p1InThisRow variable.

```
} else if(player == 2) {
   p2InThisRow ++; // Tally up an O
```

Otherwise, if the square's player value is 2, we increment the p2InThisRow variable.

```
} else {
   square = aGrid[coord.x, coord.y]; // This Square is empty.
      Store it for later.
}
```

If the player value is neither 1 nor 2, then the square is empty. Store a reference to it in the square variable for safekeeping.

```
if(square != null)
```

If we really did find an empty square somewhere in that row, it's possible that there's a win or block opportunity here.

```
if(p2InThisRow == 2)
```

More specifically, if there was an empty square and there were two Os in the row, this is a win opportunity.

```
aWinOpportunities.Add(square);
```

We want to add this square to the list of win opportunities.

```
} else if (p1InThisRow == 2) {
```

Likewise, if there was an empty square and there are two Xs in the row.

```
aBlockOpportunities.Add(square);
```

we'll keep track of this square as a block possibility.

Shut your trap

We're closing in on a completed AI routine. The last check we have to make is to set a trap if an opportunity exists, or to prevent a trap if the opponent has that chance. If you're getting antsy, you can test the game now by using double slashes to comment out these two lines of code:

```
// if(square == null) square = CreateTrap();
// if(square == null) square = PreventTrap();
```

You'll figure out pretty quickly how important trap-blocking intelligence is. Just place an X in a corner.

The artificial intelligence steps through its logic as follows:

- ◆ Try to win or block (fail)
- ◆ If you can't block, try to set a trap (this step is commented out)
- ◆ If you can't set a trap, try to prevent the opponent from setting a trap (this step is commented out)
- ◆ If there's no trap to prevent, play the center (done!)

The computer plays the center. Then you play the opposite corner.

The computer steps through its logic again, from the top:

- Try to win or block (fail)
- If you can't block, try to set a trap (this step is commented out)
- If you can't set a trap, try to prevent the opponent from setting a trap (this step is commented out)
- If there's no trap to prevent, play the center (fail)
- If the center is taken, play a corner (done!)

This leaves you to take that third corner, and to set an unwinnable trap for the computer. In this way, you can reliably win against the computer every single time.

Detecting the tri-corner trap

As John Rambo once said, "to win Tic Tac Toe, you gotta *become* Tic Tac Toe". Before we can prevent or set a trap, we need to understand what constitutes a trap.

There are four possible trap scenarios in Tic Tac Toe:

Because our artificial intelligence does what it does, the only possible trap scenario we can manage against the computer is the **Tri-Corner**. Try it yourself. You won't be able to set up **Interior-L**, **Exterior-L**, or **Staggered Row** traps, because of the steps the computer already takes. That's good news! That means that the Tri-Corner trap is the only one we have to worry about.

Just as we did with the `Win()` and `Block()` functions, let's look at what it will take to detect a Tri-Corner trap for both the player and the opponent:

♦ To create a trap, count up the number of corners I control. If I control two corners and a third corner is available, take it.

♦ To prevent a trap, count up the number of corners the opponent controls. If the opponent controls two corners, take a side to force him to defend (thus preventing him from grabbing that third corner).

As before, it looks like there's considerable overlap between these two functions. We can probably combine them into a single function like we did with the `Win` and `Block` functions.

Time for action – to catch a competitor

Combine these two separate function calls:

```
square = Win();
if(square == null) square = Block();
if(square == null) square = CreateTrap();
if(square == null) square = PreventTrap();
```

into this unified call:

```
square = Win();
if(square == null) square = Block();
if(square == null) square = PreventOrCreateTrap();
```

The `PreventOrCreateTrap` function is very straightforward:

```
function PreventOrCreateTrap():GameObject
{
  var aP1Corners:List.<GameObject> = new List.<GameObject>();
    // Create an empty list to store X-controlled corners
  var aP2Corners:List.<GameObject> = new List.<GameObject>();
    // Create an empty list to store O-controlled corners
  var aOpenCorners:List.<GameObject> = new List.<GameObject>();
    // Create an empty list to store unoccupied corners

  var aCorners:GameObject[] = [aGrid[0,0],aGrid[2,0],aGrid[0,2],
    aGrid[2,2]];
    // Create an array to store the corner coordinates

  var player:int;
  var square:GameObject;

  // Loop through the corner coordinates:
  var i:int;
  for(i = 0; i < 4; i++)
  {
    square = aCorners[i];
    player = square.GetComponent.<Square>().player;
      // Find the piece that's in this corner
    if(player == 1)
    {
      aP1Corners.Add(square);
        // If it's an X, add it to the X-controlled corners lists
    } else if (player == 2) {
      aP2Corners.Add(square);
        // If it's an O, add it to the X-controlled corners lists
    } else {
      aOpenCorners.Add(square);
        // If it's empty, add it to the empty corners list
    }
  }
```

```
// Set a trap!
// If O has two corners and there's at least one empty corner,
// randomly return an empty corner from the empty corners list:
if( aP2Corners.Count == 2 && aOpenCorners.Count > 0)
    return aOpenCorners[Random.Range(0,aOpenCorners.Count)];

// Prevent a trap!
// If X has two corners, take a side to force him to defend:
if(aP1Corners.Count == 2) return GetEmptySide();

// If there's no trap to set or prevent, return null:
return null;
}
```

What just happened – I'm running out of trap puns

Let's zero in on what's happening in that code.

```
var aP1Corners:List.<GameObject> = new List.<GameObject>();
    // Create an empty list to store X-controlled corners
var aP2Corners:List.<GameObject> = new List.<GameObject>();
    // Create an empty list to store O-controlled corners
var aOpenCorners:List.<GameObject> = new List.<GameObject>();
    // Create an empty list to store unoccupied corners
```

We kick off the `PreventOrCreateTrap` function by creating three empty Generic Lists to store references to the corner squares player 1 has claimed, references to the corner squares player 2 has claimed, and the list of corner squares neither player has claimed.

```
var aCorners:GameObject[] =
    [aGrid[0,0],aGrid[2,0],aGrid[0,2],aGrid[2,2]];
    // Create an array to store the corner coordinates
```

Then, we define a Generic List of the corner squares, pulling them from the `aGrid` array by their coordinates. We can loop through this List later (and, in fact, we do!).

```
var player:int;
var square:GameObject;
```

These two variables are needed in the loop:

```
var i:int;
for(i = 0; i < 4; i++)
```

This is a standard iterative loop setup that we've used numerous times before. The `i` iterator variable is declared outside the loop, allowing us to reuse the iterator in other loops throughout this function, if need be. (In this situation, `i` is only used in one iterative loop.)

```
square = aCorners[i];
```

Grab a reference to the ith square in the `aCorners` List, and assign it to the lowercase-s variable `square`.

```
player = square.GetComponent.<Square>().player;
  // Find the piece that's in this corner
```

Store a reference to the **Square's** player value (which will be `0`, `1`, or `2`).

```
if(player == 1)
{
  aP1Corners.Add(square);
    // If it's an X, add it to the X-controlled corners lists
} else if (player == 2) {
  aP2Corners.Add(square);
    // If it's an O, add it to the X-controlled corners lists
} else {
  aOpenCorners.Add(square);
    // If it's empty, add it to the empty corners list
}
```

If player 1 controls this **Square**, add the **Square** to the `aP1Corners` List. If player 2 controls it, add the **Square** to the `aP2Corners` List. If neither player controls the **Square**, add its reference to the `aOpenCorners` List.

```
if( aP2Corners.Count == 2 && aOpenCorners.Count > 0)
   return aOpenCorners[Random.Range(0,aOpenCorners.Count)];
```

If player 2 (the computer player) has claimed two corners and there's at least one empty corner in the `aOpenCorners` List, this **Square** represents a chance for the computer to set a Tri-Corner trap! Spit out a randomly-chosen empty corner from the `aOpenCorners` List.

```
if(aP1Corners.Count == 2) return GetEmptySide();
```

If player 1, the human player, has claimed two corners, the computer can't allow him to claim a third corner and set a trap. Playing an O in one of the side **Squares** will force the human into a defensive position, so pull a random empty side **Square** using the existing `GetEmptySide` function and return it.

Perfection Horrible, horrible perfection.

With your computer player's "brain" completely programmed, test your game.

Egad! We've created the Deep Blue of Tic Tac Toe-playing computers! The computer plays so well that every single game ends in either a win for the computer, or a draw. There's no possible way to win. We've created a monster! It won't be long before Skynet starts sending Terminators back in time. What have we wrought??

Time for action – programming fallibility

As we've discovered in the other games we've built, if the human player ain't happy, ain't nobody happy. We need to tweak the code so that our hideously perfect computer intellect makes mistakes every so often. But how do you program fallibility, an excruciatingly human trait, into the cold, unerring calculations of an unfeeling computer?

Well, you just throw some dice around.

By grabbing a random number as a success condition at each step of the computer's "thinking", we can simulate an error in judgment where the computer makes a "mistake".

Set the `square` variable to null off the top of the `ComputerTakeATurn` function, and then add in a few dice throws:

```
function ComputerTakeATurn()
{
  var square:GameObject = null;
  if(Random.value > 0.5f) square = WinOrBlock();
  if(square == null && Random.value > 0.5f) square =
    PreventOrCreateTrap();
  if(square == null && Random.value > 0.5f) square = GetCentre();
  if(square == null && Random.value > 0.5f) square = GetEmptyCorner();
  if(square == null && Random.value >0.5f) square = GetEmptySide();
  if(square == null) square = GetRandomEmptySquare();
  PlacePiece(OPiece, square);
}
```

What just happened – roll for initiative

At each step of the computer's "thought" process, we're pulling a random number. If there's no valid move from the previous step and the computer passes a Dungeons and Dragons-style "roll for initiative", the computer is allowed to complete the next (and most desirable) check for a move.

If the computer fails the random number roll, the logic falls through to the next prioritized strategic move, where the computer player must again survive a random number check. The result is that by failing a "die roll" (when the random number is, randomly, less than 0.5f, about half the time), the computer makes a mistake and misses an important strategic step.

When you play the game, you'll see that it's now much more possible to defeat the computer player, because we've used random numbers to simulate errors in judgment (or, to put it in more human terms, "brain farts").

Failing a dice roll on the `WinOrBlock()` function makes the computer seem *especially* stupid. When given the chance, who *wouldn't* spot a chance to win the game or block the opponent? You might consider removing the conditional statement before the `WinOrBlock()` function call to prevent your human player from catching on that you're deliberately dumbing down your AI.

Turning it up to "Smart"

Interestingly, this 0.5f float value handily represents the computer's level of intellect. If we crank that number up, it becomes less likely that the computer will fail a random number check, and the computer becomes "smarter" by messing up less often. By tuning the number down, the computer becomes more prone to error. Simply put, we can create a dumber computer with the turn of a dial, by replacing all those instances of 0.5f with a variable called `difficulty`, and setting that variable off the top of the game.

Having a master knob to mess around with the computer's artificial intellect is very useful, because it enables us to create different difficulty levels. We can allow the player to choose easy, medium, or hard, or a number from 1 to 10 at the beginning of the game, and tweak the float value behind the scenes to react accordingly. We can even adjust the variable up or down depending on how often the human player is winning or losing!

Code encore

In case your own intellect was dialed down to 0.2f and you goofed somewhere along the way, here's the complete GameLogic code for the Tic Tac Toe game all in one shot:

```
#pragma strict

import System.Collections.Generic;

var XPiece:GameObject;
var OPiece:GameObject;
var currentPlayer:int = 1;
var prompt:GUIText;
var aSquares:GameObject[];
var aGrid:GameObject[,];
var gameIsOver:boolean;
var moves:int;
var aBlockOpportunities:List.<GameObject>;
var aWinOpportunities:List.<GameObject>;


function Start ()
{
  ShowPlayerPrompt();

  aGrid = new GameObject[3,3];

  var theSquare:GameObject;
  var theScript:Square;
```

```
  for(var i:int =0; i < aSquares.Length; i++)
  {
    theSquare = aSquares[i];
    theScript = theSquare.GetComponent.<Square>();
    aGrid[theScript.x,theScript.y] = theSquare;
  }

}


function ClickSquare(square:GameObject)
{
  if(gameIsOver) return;

  PlacePiece(XPiece,square);

  if(!gameIsOver)
  {
    yield WaitForSeconds(2);
    ComputerTakeATurn();
  }

}


function PlacePiece(piece:GameObject,square:GameObject)
{

  moves ++;
  Instantiate(piece, square.transform.position, Quaternion.identity);
  square.GetComponent.<Square>().player = currentPlayer;
  if(CheckForWin(square))
  {
    gameIsOver = true;
    ShowWinnerPrompt();
    return;
  } else if(moves >= 9) {
    gameIsOver = true;
    ShowStalematePrompt();
    return;
  }
```

```
    currentPlayer ++;
    if(currentPlayer > 2) currentPlayer = 1;

    ShowPlayerPrompt();
}

function ComputerTakeATurn()
{

    var square:GameObject = null;

    if(Random.value > 0.5f) square = WinOrBlock();
    if(square == null && Random.value > 0.5f)
      square = PreventOrCreateTrap();
    if(square == null && Random.value > 0.5f) square = GetCentre();
    if(square == null && Random.value > 0.5f)
      square = GetEmptyCorner();
    if(square == null && Random.value > 0.5f) square = GetEmptySide();


    PlacePiece(OPiece, square);
}

function GetRandomEmptySquare():GameObject
{
  var square:GameObject
  var aEmptySquares:List.<GameObject> = new List.<GameObject>();

  for(var i:int = 0; i < aSquares.Length; i++)
  {
    square = aSquares[i];
    if(square.GetComponent.<Square>().player == 0)
      aEmptySquares.Add(square);
  }
  square = aEmptySquares[Random.Range(0,aEmptySquares.Count)];
  return square;
}

function WinOrBlock():GameObject
{
  aBlockOpportunities = new List.<GameObject>();
  aWinOpportunities = new List.<GameObject>();
    // Empty out these lists before we start searching.
```

```
// Check the rows for 2 in a row:
CheckFor2InARow([Vector2(0,0), Vector2(1,0), Vector2(2,0)]);
CheckFor2InARow([Vector2(0,1), Vector2(1,1), Vector2(2,1)]);
CheckFor2InARow([Vector2(0,2), Vector2(1,2), Vector2(2,2)]);

// Check the columns for 2 in a row:
CheckFor2InARow([Vector2(0,0), Vector2(0,1), Vector2(0,2)]);
CheckFor2InARow([Vector2(1,0), Vector2(1,1), Vector2(1,2)]);
CheckFor2InARow([Vector2(2,0), Vector2(2,1), Vector2(2,2)]);

// Check the diagonals for 2 in a row:
CheckFor2InARow([Vector2(0,0), Vector2(1,1), Vector2(2,2)]);
CheckFor2InARow([Vector2(0,2), Vector2(1,1), Vector2(2,0)]);

// If there are any opportunities to win, return one at random:
if(aWinOpportunities.Count > 0)
    return aWinOpportunities[Random.Range(0,
      aWinOpportunities.Count)];

// If there are any opportunities to block, return one at random:
if(aBlockOpportunities.Count > 0)
    return aBlockOpportunities[Random.Range(0,
      aBlockOpportunities.Count)];

// There are no opportunities to win or block, so return null:
return null;
}

function PreventOrCreateTrap():GameObject
{
  var aP1Corners:List.<GameObject> = new List.<GameObject>();
    // Create an empty list to store X-controlled corners
  var aP2Corners:List.<GameObject> = new List.<GameObject>();
    // Create an empty list to store O-controlled corners
  var aOpenCorners:List.<GameObject> = new List.<GameObject>();
    // Create an empty list to store unoccupied corners

  var aCorners:GameObject[] =
    [aGrid[0,0],aGrid[2,0],aGrid[0,2],aGrid[2,2]];
      // Create an array to store the corner coordinates

  var player:int;
  var square:GameObject;

  // Loop through the corner coordinates:
  var i:int;
```

```
for(i = 0; i < 4; i++)
{
  square = aCorners[i];
  player = square.GetComponent.<Square>().player;
    // Find the piece that's in this corner
  if(player == 1)
  {
    aP1Corners.Add(square);
      // If it's an X, add it to the X-controlled corners lists
  } else if (player == 2) {
    aP2Corners.Add(square);
      // If it's an O, add it to the X-controlled corners lists
  } else {
    aOpenCorners.Add(square);
      // If it's empty, add it to the empty corners list
  }
}


// Set a trap!
// If O has two corners and there's at least one empty corner,
//randomly return an empty corner from the empty corners list:
if( aP2Corners.Count == 2 && aOpenCorners.Count > 0)
  return aOpenCorners[Random.Range(0,aOpenCorners.Count)];

// Prevent a trap!
// If X has two corners, take a side to force him to defend:
if(aP1Corners.Count == 2) return GetEmptySide();

// If there's no trap to set or prevent, return null:
return null;
}



function CheckFor2InARow(coords:Vector2[])
{
  var p1InThisRow:int = 0; // the number of X's in this row
  var p2InThisRow:int = 0; // the number of O's in this row
  var player:int;
  var square:GameObject = null;
  var coord:Vector2;
  // Step through each of the 3 Square coordinates
  // that were passed in:
```

```
for (var i:int = 0; i<3; i++)
{
  coord = coords[i];
  player = GetPlayer(coord.x,coord.y);
    // Find the piece in this Square
  if(player == 1)
  {
    p1InThisRow ++; // Tally up an X
  } else if(player == 2) {
    p2InThisRow ++; // Tally up an O
  } else {
    square = aGrid[coord.x,coord.y]; // This Square is empty.
      //Store  it for later.
  }
}

if(square != null)
{
  // We found an empty Square in this row.
  if(p2InThisRow == 2)
  {
    // There are two O's in a row with an empty Square.
    aWinOpportunities.Add(square);
    // Add a win opportunity to the list.
  } else if (p1InThisRow == 2) {
    // There are two X's in a row with an empty Square.
    aBlockOpportunities.Add(square);
    // Add a block opportunity to the list.
  }
}
}


function GetEmptySide():GameObject
{
  var aEmptySides:List.<GameObject> = new List.<GameObject>();
  if(GetPlayer(1,0) == 0) aEmptySides.Add(aGrid[1,0]);
  if(GetPlayer(0,1) == 0) aEmptySides.Add(aGrid[0,1]);
  if(GetPlayer(2,1) == 0) aEmptySides.Add(aGrid[2,1]);
  if(GetPlayer(1,2) == 0) aEmptySides.Add(aGrid[1,2]);
  if(aEmptySides.Count > 0)
    return aEmptySides[Random.Range(0,aEmptySides.Count)];
  return null;
}
```

```
function GetEmptyCorner():GameObject
{
  var aEmptyCorners:List.<GameObject> = new List.<GameObject>();

  if(GetPlayer(0,0) == 0) aEmptyCorners.Add(aGrid[0,0]);
  if(GetPlayer(2,0) == 0) aEmptyCorners.Add(aGrid[2,0]);
  if(GetPlayer(0,2) == 0) aEmptyCorners.Add(aGrid[0,2]);
  if(GetPlayer(2,2) == 0) aEmptyCorners.Add(aGrid[2,2]);

  if(aEmptyCorners.Count > 0)
    return aEmptyCorners[Random.Range(0,aEmptyCorners.Count)];

  return null;
}

function GetCentre():GameObject
{
  if( GetPlayer(1,1) == 0 ) return aGrid[1,1];
  return null;
}




function ShowPlayerPrompt()
{
  if(currentPlayer == 1)
  {
    prompt.text = "Player 1, place an X.";
  } else {
    prompt.text = "Player 2, place an O.";
  }
}

function ShowWinnerPrompt()
{
  if(currentPlayer == 1)
  {
    prompt.text = "X gets 3 in a row. Player 1 wins!";
  } else {
    prompt.text = "O gets 3 in a row. Player 2 wins!";
  }

  yield WaitForSeconds(3);
  Application.LoadLevel(0);

}
```

```
function ShowStalematePrompt()
{
  prompt.text = "Stalemate!  Neither player wins.";

  yield WaitForSeconds(3);
  Application.LoadLevel(0);
}




function CheckForWin(square:GameObject):boolean
{
  var theScript:Square = square.GetComponent.<Square>();

  //Check the squares in the same column:
  if(GetPlayer(theScript.x,0) == currentPlayer &&
    GetPlayer(theScript.x,1) == currentPlayer &&
      GetPlayer(theScript.x,2) == currentPlayer) return true;

  // Check the squares in the same row:
  if(GetPlayer(0,theScript.y) == currentPlayer &&
    GetPlayer(1,theScript.y) == currentPlayer &&
    GetPlayer(2,theScript.y) == currentPlayer) return true;

  // Check the diagonals:
  if(GetPlayer(0,0) == currentPlayer &&
    GetPlayer(1,1) == currentPlayer &&
    GetPlayer(2,2) == currentPlayer) return true;
  if(GetPlayer(2,0) == currentPlayer &&
    GetPlayer(1,1) == currentPlayer &&
    GetPlayer(0,2) == currentPlayer) return true;

  return false; // If we get this far without finding a win,
    return false to signify "no win".


}


function GetPlayer(x:int, y:int):int
{
  return aGrid[x,y].GetComponent.<Square>().player;
}
```

Summary

If you're the kind of reader who's in it for the pictures, you may have found this chapter challenging. An important skill of a computer programmer is to describe nonvisual things, like thought, in concrete steps that a computer can easily digest. But first you, as a human, have to properly digest them!

By using the example of a fairly simple game like Tic Tac Toe, you've walked half a block in the shoes of the computer scientists who programmed a computer to defeat the world's best chess player at his, and humankind's, own game.

In this chapter, you:

- Learned to break a strategy game down into its core elements
- Explored game trees, and how they can be used to map out all of the branching positions possible in a strategy game
- Prioritized a list of strategic options to create a preferred plan of attack.
- Used the | | (or) operator to build more sophisticated conditional statements
- Discovered how to create the illusion of thought by adding pauses in the computer's actions, and by choosing randomly from a list of preferred moves
- Taught a computer to simulate mistakes by testing against a random number

More hospitality

The last chapter is nigh! In our final hurrah, we'll leverage our dual-camera technique from **Shoot the Moon** to add environmental ambience to the **Ticker Taker** game. Then we'll explore the animation tools, and learn how to publish our games so that anyone can play them.

C# addendum

As promised, the complete translated C# code for the Tic Tac Toe game follows. There were a few tricky spots in the code that required a bit of tap dancing:

When a function returns a value, the value type needs to be declared in the function signature before the function name. So this function declaration in Unity Javascript:

```
function CheckForWin(square:GameObject):boolean
```

is translated like this in C#:

```
private bool CheckForWin(GameObject square)
```

In an earlier chapter, we dodged the requirements of the `waitForSeconds` method and used a different function entirely. Now that we've had more experience with return statements, we can discuss what's required.

In C#, this line:

```
yield WaitForSeconds(3);
```

becomes:

```
yield return new WaitForSeconds(3);
```

The `WaitForSeconds` method returns a result of type `IEnumerator`. Therefore, any C# function that uses `WaitForSeconds` must return `IEnumerator`. The `ShowStalematePrompt` declaration, for example, which uses the `WaitForSeconds` method, translates from this:

```
function ShowStalematePrompt()
```

to this:

```
private IEnumerator ShowStalematePrompt()
```

Remember that any variable that you want to access in the Inspector panel needs the `public` access modifier. The `x` and `y` variables in the C# `SquareCSharp` script are a good example:

```
public int x;
public int y;
```

Because the `SquareCSharp` script accesses the `ClickSquare` method in the `GameLogicCSharp` script, the `ClickSquare` method also has to be set to `public`:

```
public IEnumerator ClickSquare(GameObject square)
```

Note that the `ClickSquare` method also uses `WaitForSeconds`, so it needs to return a value of type `IEnumerator`. This poses a problem, because this line:

```
if(gameIsOver) return;
```

Since the function is expecting us to `return` a value of type `IEnumerator`, we can't use a naked `return` keyword, because it doesn't return anything. We can get around the issue by replacing `return` with this:

```
yield break;
```

Here, then, are the two Tic Tac Toe scripts completely translated into C#:

SquareCSharp.cs

```
using UnityEngine;
using System.Collections;

public class SquareCSharp : MonoBehaviour {

  public int x;
  public int y;
  public int player = 0;
  private GameObject gameLogic;


  private void Start ()
  {
    gameLogic = GameObject.Find("GameLogic");
  }

  private void OnMouseDown()
  {
    print ("player = " + player);
    if(player == 0)
    {
      print ("let's do this");
      gameLogic.GetComponent<GameLogicCSharp>().
        ClickSquare(gameObject);
    }
  }
}
```

GameLogicCSharp.cs

```
using UnityEngine;
using System.Collections;
using System.Collections.Generic;

public class GameLogicCSharp : MonoBehaviour
{

  public GameObject XPiece;
  public GameObject OPiece;
  private int currentPlayer = 1;
  public GUIText prompt;
  public GameObject[] aSquares;
```

```
private GameObject[,] aGrid;
private bool gameIsOver;
private int moves;

private List<GameObject> aBlockOpportunities;
private List<GameObject> aWinOpportunities;

private void Start()
{
  ShowPlayerPrompt();

  aGrid = new GameObject[3,3];

  GameObject theSquare;
  SquareCSharp theScript;

  for(int i = 0; i < aSquares.Length; i++)
  {
    theSquare = aSquares[i];
    theScript = theSquare.GetComponent<SquareCSharp>();
    aGrid[theScript.x,theScript.y] = theSquare;
  }

}


public IEnumerator ClickSquare(GameObject square)
{
  print ("click square!");
  if(gameIsOver || currentPlayer == 2) yield break;

  PlacePiece(XPiece, square);

  print ("keep going");

  if(!gameIsOver)
  {
    yield return new WaitForSeconds(0.5f);
    ComputerTakeATurn();
  }
}
```

```
private void ComputerTakeATurn()
{
  GameObject square = null;

  if(Random.value > 0.5f) square = WinOrBlock();
  if(square == null && Random.value > 0.5f)
    square = PreventOrCreateTrap();
  if(square == null && Random.value > 0.5f) square = GetCentre();
  if(square == null && Random.value > 0.5f)
    square = GetEmptyCorner();
  if(square == null) square = GetEmptySide();

  PlacePiece(OPiece, square);

}

private GameObject GetEmptySide()
{
  List<GameObject> aEmptySides = new List<GameObject>();

  if(GetPlayer(1,0) == 0) aEmptySides.Add(aGrid[1,0]);
  if(GetPlayer(0,1) == 0) aEmptySides.Add(aGrid[0,1]);
  if(GetPlayer(2,1) == 0) aEmptySides.Add(aGrid[2,1]);
  if(GetPlayer(1,2) == 0) aEmptySides.Add(aGrid[1,2]);

  if(aEmptySides.Count > 0) return
    aEmptySides[Random.Range(0,aEmptySides.Count)];

  return null;
}

private GameObject GetEmptyCorner()
{
  List<GameObject> aEmptyCorners = new List<GameObject>();

  if(GetPlayer(0,0) == 0) aEmptyCorners.Add(aGrid[0,0]);
  if(GetPlayer(2,0) == 0) aEmptyCorners.Add(aGrid[2,0]);
  if(GetPlayer(0,2) == 0) aEmptyCorners.Add(aGrid[0,2]);
  if(GetPlayer(2,2) == 0) aEmptyCorners.Add(aGrid[2,2]);

  if(aEmptyCorners.Count > 0) return
    aEmptyCorners[Random.Range(0,aEmptyCorners.Count)];

  return null;
}
```

```
private GameObject GetCentre()
{
  if( GetPlayer(1,1) == 0 ) return aGrid[1,1];
  return null;
}
private GameObject WinOrBlock()
{
  aBlockOpportunities = new List<GameObject>();
  aWinOpportunities = new List<GameObject>();
    // Empty out these lists before we start searching.

  // Check the rows for 2 in a row:
  CheckFor2InARow(new Vector2[] {new Vector2(0,0),
    new Vector2(1,0), new Vector2(2,0)});
  CheckFor2InARow(new Vector2[] {new Vector2(0,1),
    new Vector2(1,1), new Vector2(2,1)});
  CheckFor2InARow(new Vector2[] {new Vector2(0,2),
    new Vector2(1,2), new Vector2(2,2)});

  // Check the columns for 2 in a row:
  CheckFor2InARow(new Vector2[] {new Vector2(0,0),
    new Vector2(0,1), new Vector2(0,2)});
  CheckFor2InARow(new Vector2[] {new Vector2(1,0),
    new Vector2(1,1), new Vector2(1,2)});
  CheckFor2InARow(new Vector2[] {new Vector2(2,0),
    new Vector2(2,1), new Vector2(2,2)});

  // Check the diagonals for 2 in a row:
  CheckFor2InARow(new Vector2[] {new Vector2(0,0),
    new Vector2(1,1), new Vector2(2,2)});
  CheckFor2InARow(new Vector2[] {new Vector2(0,2),
    new Vector2(1,1), new Vector2(2,0)});

  // If there are any opportunities to win, return one at random:
  if(aWinOpportunities.Count > 0) return
    aWinOpportunities[Random.Range(0, aWinOpportunities.Count)];

  // If there are any opportunities to block, return one at random:
  if(aBlockOpportunities.Count > 0) return
    aBlockOpportunities[Random.Range(0,
    aBlockOpportunities.Count)];

  // There are no opportunities to win or block, so return null:
  return null;
}
```

```
    private void CheckFor2InARow(Vector2[] coords)
{

   int p1InThisRow = 0; // the number of X's in this row
   int p2InThisRow = 0; // the number of O's in this row
   int player;
   GameObject square = null;
   Vector2 coord;

   // Step through each of the 3 Square coordinates that
      were passed in:
   for (int i = 0; i<3; i++)
   {
     coord = coords[i];
     player = GetPlayer((int)coord.x, (int)coord.y);
       // Find the piece in this Square
     if(player == 1)
     {
       p1InThisRow ++; // Tally up an X
     } else if(player == 2) {
       p2InThisRow ++; // Tally up an O
     } else {
       square = aGrid[(int)coord.x, (int)coord.y];
         // This Square is empty. Store it for later.
     }
   }

   if(square != null)
   {
     // We found an empty Square in this row.
     if(p2InThisRow == 2)
     {
       // There are two O's in a row with an empty Square.
       aWinOpportunities.Add(square);
       // Add a win opportunity to the list.
     } else if (p1InThisRow == 2) {
       // There are two X's in a row with an empty Square.
       aBlockOpportunities.Add(square);
       // Add a block opportunity to the list.
     }
```

```
    }
}


private GameObject PreventOrCreateTrap()
{
  List<GameObject> aP1Corners = new List<GameObject>();
    // Create an empty list to store X-controlled corners
  List<GameObject> aP2Corners = new List<GameObject>();
    // Create an empty list to store O-controlled corners
  List<GameObject> aOpenCorners = new List<GameObject>();
    // Create an empty list to store unoccupied corners

  GameObject[] aCorners = new GameObject[]
    {aGrid[0,0],aGrid[2,0],aGrid[0,2],aGrid[2,2]};
      // Create an array to store the corner coordinates


  int player;
  GameObject square;

  // Loop through the corner coordinates:
  int i;
  for(i = 0; i < 4; i++)
  {
    square = aCorners[i];
    player = square.GetComponent<SquareCSharp>().player;
      // Find the piece that's in this corner
    if(player == 1)
    {
      aP1Corners.Add(square);
        // If it's an X, add it to the X-controlled corners lists
    } else if (player == 2) {
      aP2Corners.Add(square);
        // If it's an O, add it to the X-controlled corners lists
    } else {
      aOpenCorners.Add(square);
        // If it's empty, add it to the empty corners list
    }
  }

  // Set a trap!
  // If O has two corners and there's at least one empty corner,
    randomly return an empty corner from the empty corners list:
```

```
    if( aP2Corners.Count == 2 && aOpenCorners.Count > 0)
      return aOpenCorners[Random.Range(0,aOpenCorners.Count)];

    // Prevent a trap!
    // If X has two corners, take a side to force him to defend:
    if(aP1Corners.Count == 2) return GetEmptySide();

    // If there's no trap to set or prevent, return null:
    return null;

  }


  private void PlacePiece(GameObject piece, GameObject square)
  {
    moves ++;

    Instantiate(piece, square.transform.position,
      Quaternion.identity);
    square.GetComponent<SquareCSharp>().player = currentPlayer;

    if(CheckForWin(square))
    {
      gameIsOver = true;
      ShowWinnerPrompt();
      return;
    } else if(moves >= 9) {
      gameIsOver = true;
      ShowStalematePrompt();
      return;
    }

    currentPlayer ++;
    if(currentPlayer > 2) currentPlayer = 1;

    ShowPlayerPrompt();
  }
```

```
private void ShowPlayerPrompt()
{
  if(currentPlayer == 1)
  {
    prompt.text = "Player 1, place an X.";
  } else {
    prompt.text = "Player 2, place an O.";
  }

}

private IEnumerator ShowWinnerPrompt()
{
  if(currentPlayer == 1)
  {
    prompt.text = "X gets 3 in a row. Player 1 wins!";
  } else {
    prompt.text = "O gets 3 in a row. Player 2 wins!";
  }

  yield return new WaitForSeconds(3);
  Application.LoadLevel(0);
}

private IEnumerator ShowStalematePrompt()
{
  prompt.text = "Stalemate!  Neither player wins.";

  yield return new WaitForSeconds(3);
  Application.LoadLevel(0);
}

private bool CheckForWin(GameObject square)
{
  SquareCSharp theScript = square.GetComponent<SquareCSharp>();

  //Check the squares in the same column:
  if(GetPlayer(theScript.x,0) == currentPlayer &&
    GetPlayer(theScript.x,1) == currentPlayer &&
    GetPlayer(theScript.x,2) == currentPlayer) return true;
```

```
    // Check the squares in the same row:
    if(GetPlayer(0,theScript.y) == currentPlayer &&
      GetPlayer(1,theScript.y) == currentPlayer &&
      GetPlayer(2,theScript.y) == currentPlayer) return true;

    // Check the diagonals:
    if(GetPlayer(0,0) == currentPlayer &&
      GetPlayer(1,1) == currentPlayer &&
      GetPlayer(2,2) == currentPlayer) return true;
    if(GetPlayer(2,0) == currentPlayer &&
      GetPlayer(1,1) == currentPlayer &&
      GetPlayer(0,2) == currentPlayer) return true;

    return false; // If we get this far without finding a win,
      return false to signify "no win".

  }

  private int GetPlayer(int x, int y)
  {
    return aGrid[x,y].GetComponent<SquareCSharp>().player;
  }
}
```

14
Action!

When last we left Ticker Taker, our slightly demented hospital-themed keep-up game, we had two hands bouncing a heart on a dinner tray. The game's mechanics were pretty functional, but we hadn't fully delivered on the skin. If Ticker Taker is about a nurse rushing a heart to the transplant ward, then where is the hospital?

In this final chapter, we'll:

◆ Use the dual-camera technique from *Shoot the Moon* to render a fully-3D environment

◆ Set up a movable lighting rig for our **Scene**

◆ Dive into Unity's animation tools to animate GameObjects

◆ Publish a Unity game so that we can unleash our masterpiece on an unsuspecting public

Open heart surgery

To get started, open the last version of the Ticker Taker game. You can also copy the game files to another folder, as we did with *The Break-Up* and *Shoot the Moon*.

Once the project is open, find the **Game Scene** in the **Project** panel and double-click to open it (if it doesn't open by default). You should see the **Scene** just as we left it: heart, hands, and tray.

I took the time to organize the different assets into folders to tidy up the project. Neatness saves sanity.

Once that's all in order, download and import the assets package for this chapter. Now we're ready to dig in.

Time for action – haul in the hallway

The assets package contains a hallway model. Created in the free 3D software package Blender, it's essentially a square donut with the normals flipped so that it appears inside out.

 What's a normal? Usually, only one side of a 3D object's faces is "painted" (which is why you can zoom into the inside of a 3D object and it seems to disappear). Normals determine which side of each individual mesh polygon is painted.

We're going to set up one camera to bounce up and down, as if the character is running, and send it flying through the hallway. Then we'll set that view as the background for our **Main Camera**, which is aimed at the heart-and-tray action. By using **Depth** as our **Clear Flags** setting on the foreground camera, the background camera will show through the empty space to make it appear as though the player is running through the hallway.

1. Find the hallway model in the **Project** panel. It's the one with the blue cubic "model" icon next to it—not to be confused with the model *texture*, which uses a little image thumbnail as its icon.(I placed my models in the folder called `Models`, and dropped my textures into a `Textures` folder to keep them sorted.)

2. Drag the hallway model into the **Scene**.

3. Adjust the hallway's **Transform** properties in the **Inspector** panel:

   Position: X:0, Y:2, Z:-25

   Rotation: X:0, Y:0, Z:180

   These settings place the hallway behind the **Main Camera** in our **Scene** so that it's out of the way while we work with it. In the **Hierarchy** panel, select the hallway GameObject and press *F* to frame the selected object.

4. In the **Inspector** panel, add a new layer called `hallway`, as we did when we created the **starfield** layer in our *Shoot the Moon* project. Be sure that you're adding a new Layer, not a new Tag.

5. In the **Hierarchy** panel, select **hallway**. Choose the new `hallway` layer in the **Layer** dropdown. Unity will pop up a dialog asking you whether you want to put the child objects of **hallway** in the `hallway` layer as well. Answer with **Yes, change children**.

Time for action – meet me at camera two

In order to pull off this foreground/background effect, we'll need two cameras. Let's create the second camera and set it up to look at the **hallway**.

1. In the menu, navigate to **GameObject | Create Other | Camera**.

2. Rename the new camera `hallwayCam`.

3. Change the **Transform** settings of `hallwayCam` to:

   Position: X:`6.5`, **Y:**`1.2`, **Z:** `-31.5`

   Set the **Scene** view to **Top**, and you'll see that the `hallwayCam` is now positioned at one corner of the **hallway** model.

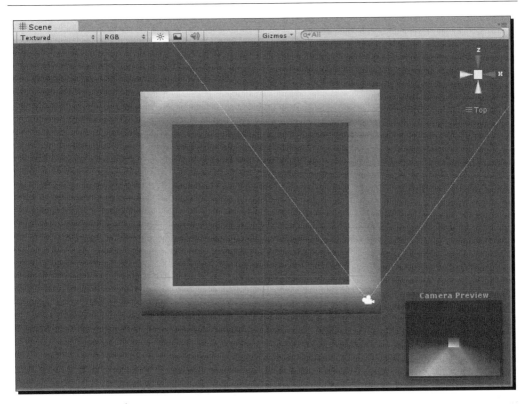

4. Select the `hallwayCam` in the **Hierarchy** panel.

5. In the **Inspector** panel, adjust the following settings:

   ▫ **Clear Flags: Solid Color**

   ▫ **Culling Mask: nothing** (This deselects everything in the culling mask list.)

   ▫ **Culling Mask: hallway** (This selects only the `hallway` layer, which contains our **hallway** model.)

   ▫ **Depth: -1**

   ▫ **Flare Layer**: unchecked/removed

   ▫ **Audio Listener**: unchecked

No surprises here—these are the very same settings we used for the background camera in *Shoot the Moon*.

Time for action – adjust Main Camera

As before, we'll nudge a few settings on the **Main Camera** in order to composite the two views together.

1. In the **Hierarchy** panel, select **Main Camera**.

2. In the **Inspector** panel, adjust the following settings:

   ❑ **Clear Flags: Depth only**

   ❑ **Culling Mask**—uncheck hallway (it now says **Mixed...**)

   ❑ **Depth: 1**

The two cameras' views are now layered together in the **Game** view. That's a good start!

Time for action – deck the halls

This bland gray hallway model looks less like a hospital and more like the white light patients see when they shuffle off their mortal coil. Luckily, there's a quick fix: the **Project** panel contains a texture that we'll apply to the model to make it look more—you know—*hospitable*.

1. In the **Hierarchy** panel, click on the gray arrow next to the hallway to expand its list of children.

2. The hallway contains one child, also called `Hallway`, which contains the **Mesh Renderer** and **Mesh Filter** components. Select the `Hallway` child.

3. Find the `hallway` texture in the **Project** panel, and click-and-drag it into the texture swatch in the **Inspector** panel, under the hallway's Material.

Wonderfully, the **hallway** texture wraps itself around the hallway model. In a twinkling, we're inside a hospital!

Time for action – turn on the lights

This hospital texture is great and all, but our level looks like something straight out of a survival horror game. Every hospital that I've ever visited has been bright and shiny. Let's add some lights to the level to perk it up some.

1. Click on the green Y-axis cone in the axis gizmo at the top-right of the **Scene** view. This swings us around to a Top view, looking down on our **Scene**.

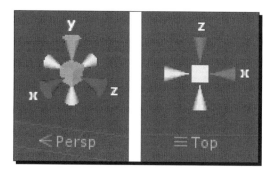

2. Pan and zoom the **Scene** view to center the hallway model.

3. In the menu, navigate to **GameObject | Create Other | Point Light**.

4. Create a new Prefab and call it `hallwayLight`.

5. In the **Hierarchy** panel, click to select **Point Light**, and reset its **Transform** in the **Inspector** panel.

6. Drag **Point Light** into the `hallwayLight` **Prefab**.

7. Delete **Point Light** from the **Hierarchy** panel.

8. Drag an instance of the `hallwayLight` **Prefab** from the **Project** panel into your **Scene**. Position it at the top-right corner of the hallway—around `x:` `6.3` `y:1` `z:-19.7`.

> Note: We could have kept the **Point Light** in the **Scene**, as it's connected to the `hallwayLight` **Prefab**, but I think it's easier to work with the project when **Prefab** instances are named consistently.

9. Create an empty **GameObject** and call it `LightingRig`. This GameObject will hold all of our lights, so we can keep them organized. Move the lighting rig to `x:0 y:0 z:-25`.

10. In the **Hierarchy** panel, click-and-drag the `hallwayLight` instance onto the `LightingRig` **GameObject**. This makes the light a child of the rig, and we see that familiar gray arrow appear indicating a parent/child relationship.

11. Select and then duplicate the `hallwayLight` instance by pressing *Ctrl + D* (*command + D* on a Mac). Notice that the second light is also a child of the `LightingRig` **GameObject**.

12. Move the duplicated light to the top-middle of the `hallway` model.

13. Duplicate a third light, and move it to the top-left corner of the level.

14. Hold down the *Shift* key on your keyboard and click on the other two lights, until all three lights are selected at once. (It may be easier to shift-select the three lights in the **Hierarchy** panel instead of the **Scene** view.)

15. Duplicate the trio of lights, and move them down across the middle of the level. You may need to zoom out slightly to see the transformed gizmo handles.

16. Duplicate the set of three lights again, and move them down to the bottom of the level. You should now have an array of nine lights.

17. Click on a blank area in the **Scene** view to deselect all the lights.

18. Click to select the light in the middle of the level and delete it. Now there's a light in each corner, and a light in the middle of each hallway section.

Unity 3D supports "expensive" pixel lighting, and less "expensive" vertex lighting. Pixel lighting is more taxing on the player's computer, but it's more believable and it can pull off fancier tricks like cookies (think of the "bat symbol" from the Batman comics) and normal-mapping, which creates the illusion of detail on a flat polygon. In trying to preserve performance, Unity only lets us have two active pixel lights and drops the other lights down to vertex quality, which interpolates (makes a calculated guess) at the light levels on a triangle by calculating light levels at its vertices. The result is a really rough guess that can make your scene look like junk.

In order for our lighting rig to light the hallway well, we need to tell Unity that it can use all of our lights as pixel lights. This is sort of a lazy solution, but we can get away with it because our geometry is so simple. In more complex games, you may need to employ real ingenuity to present your scene in the best possible "light" with minimal performance trade-off.

Follow these steps to increase the number of pixel lights that Unity will allow:

1. In the menu, navigate to **Edit | Project Settings | Quality**. Unity allows us to create different quality profiles, and to apply those profiles to different scenarios: playing a game standalone, using the web player, deploying to mobile, and viewing a game in the editor. Note that all of these scenarios default to using the **Good** profile.

2. With the **Good** profile selected, punch in 8 to increase the number of pixel lights Unity will allow.

Once you make this change, you should see the light levels in your scene punch up. Now Unity is rendering proper lighting effects for every pixel on the screen based on all eight lights, rather than calculating only two lights and fudging the others.

The light! It bliiiiiiinds! Luckily, these eight lights are all instances of the same **Prefab**, so by adjusting one of them, we'll affect the rest.

19. Click to select the `hallwayLight` **Prefab** in the **Project** panel.

20. In the **Inspector** panel, change the intensity to `0.5` and the range to `20`.

That should mute all the lights to the point where they look like they belong in a hospital, and not like a hospital built on the surface of the sun.

When you rotate your **Scene** view, you should see all eight lights nestled within the `hallway` model. If they ended up far above or below the level, just move the `LightingRig` **GameObject** around to move all eight lights as a single unit.

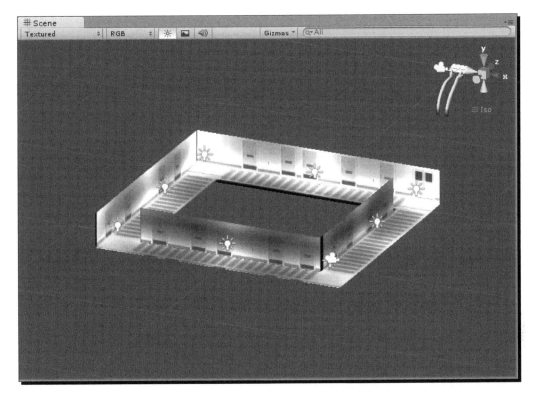

Time for action – set up the camera rig

We want to depict the player running through these hallways. There are at least two ways we can handle the animation of `HallwayCam`. We can use a **Script** to control the camera motion, or we can use Unity's built-in animation tools to record some camera motion that we'll play back during gameplay. We've already done a bunch of scripting, so let's see what the Unity IDE can do to help us pull off our running-through-the-hallway effect without writing any code.

We're going to build a camera rig, where the camera is a child of a GameObject that bounces up and down, and that GameObject is a child of another GameObject that runs through the hallways.

Order of operations

Because of the way Unity's built-in animations work, it's super important to set up your objects' parent-child relationships *before* you animate. The values we set in our animation clips become relative to an object's parent. In short, that means "bad news" if you animate first before setting up your rig. Existing animations can swing wildly out of position. Because redoing work is for chumps, let's get it right the first time.

1. Create an empty GameObject and name it bouncer.

2. Set its **Transform** using these values:

   ❏ **Position: X: 6.5, Y:1.2, Z:-31.5**

   These are the same values as for the hallwayCam.

3. Duplicate the bouncer GameObject and call it runner.

4. In the **Hierarchy** panel, make the hallwayCam a child of bouncer by clicking and dragging hallwayCam onto bouncer.

5. Make bouncer a child of runner by clicking and dragging bouncer onto runner.

```
≔ Hierarchy
 Create ▼  Q▾All
   Ball
   Bounce Count
   Directional light
 ▼ hallway
     Hallway
 ▶ HandsAndTray
 ▶ heart
 ▼ LightingRig
     hallwayLight
     hallwayLight
     hallwayLight
     hallwayLight
     hallwayLight
     hallwayLight
     hallwayLight
     hallwayLight
   Main Camera
   Paddle
 ▼ runner
   ▼ bouncer
       hallwayCam
   Wall Back
   Wall Front
   Wall Left
   Wall Right
```

Time for action – animate the bouncer

We'll use the Unity Animation tool to create an animation clip for our bouncer GameObject.

1. In the **Hierarchy** panel, click to select the bouncer GameObject.

2. In the menu, navigate to **Window | Animation** to bring up the **Animation** window. If you so choose, you can dock it within the interface like the **Hierarchy** and **Project** panels. I prefer not to because I like having a lot of space for this window. I resize the window so that it covers most of the right half of my screen. You can drag the middle line that splits the **Animation** window (dividing the dark and light parts of the window) to give more or less real estate to the key view (dark side).

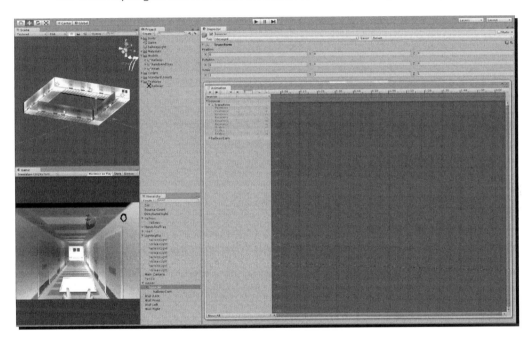

3. Press the round reddish-pink **Record** button near the top-left of the window.

4. Unity asks you to name your new **Animation** clip. Save it as animBounce.

What just happened – red and raging

When you save your Animation clip, two things happen: the clip becomes a tangible, reusable asset in your **Project** panel, and the Record, Play, Pause, and Step buttons all light up red to notify you that you're in animation mode.

Why make such a big, noticeable deal out of it? Because whenever you move your recorded **GameObject** around, Unity is going to remember its position, rotation, and scale in a keyframe. **Keyframe** is a term borrowed from classical animation. Animation software packages store the position, rotation, and scale values of objects in keyframes, and use **interpolation** to figure out how to animate an object between those keys. In classical animation, this is called **in-betweening**.

If you create a keyframe for a GameObject on frame 1 and another on frame 10 where the GameObject has moved across the screen, Unity will interpolate between those two keyframes, filling in the blanks to make the GameObject move from one side of the screen to the other.

Time for action – I like to move it move it

In the case of our `bouncer` GameObject, we'll set up three keyframes: one for the up position, one for the down position, and a third to bring it back to the top of the bounce.

1. Click on the red X cone in the **Scene** view's axis gizmo to view the level from the side.

2. In the **Animation** view, enter an initial value of -0.5 for the Position.y value of bouncer. A little diamond-shaped keyframe symbol appears on frame 1 at the top of the **Animation** view. This means that Unity is remembering the position, rotation, or scale of the GameObject on that frame. The colored diamond next to any given value means that Unity is storing a value on this frame for that specific parameter.

3. Click-and-drag the vertical red line (not the keyframe diamond) to frame 10, or enter the number 10 into the frame field at the top of the **Animation** window (next to the playback controls). It's very important not to mistake frame 10 with the 10:00 second mark!

4. On frame 10, punch in a Position.y value of -0.1. A second keyframe is created for us on frame 10, storing the new values.

5. Go to frame 20.

6. Enter the initial Position.y value of -0.5 to bring the bouncer back to the top of its bounce. A third diamond keyframe icon appears.

7. At the bottom of the **Animation** view, click the drop down labeled **Default** and choose **Loop** instead.

8. The animation arc between keyframes for the bouncer's y position spans into infinity to indicate that the animation loops. (You may have to pan and zoom around the **Animation** view to see this using the same controls that you use to pan and zoom around your 3D **Scene**.)

9. Click on the **Record** button to stop recording.

10. Test the game.

Now, Nurse Slipperfoot bounces the heart on the tray while running on the spot! That's great for her personal calisthenics routine, but not so hot for her poor transplant patient.

Note: If it doesn't work, check to make sure that the `animBounce` animation Component is attached to the `bouncer` GameObject.

Have a go hero – bounce your brains out

You can click-and-drag animations onto any GameObject you like. Try removing the `animBounce` animation from the `bounce` GameObject and applying it to `hallway`.

When you test your game, you should see the hallway snap to the X and Z position defined in our `animBounce` animation keyframes. The entire `hallway` model bounces up and down just like our `bounce` GameObject did. You can apply the same animation to the heart or the tray. Just as you can apply one script to many different GameObjects, a single animation can go a long way.

Time for action – animate the runner

Let's get that RN RuNning!

1. Click on the green Y-axis cone to switch into Top view. Pan and zoom so that the hallway fills the **Scene** view, like it did when we were building our lighting rig.

2. In the **Hierarchy** panel, select the `runner` GameObject.

3. In the **Animation** window, click on the **Record** button.

4. Name the new animation `animRun`. A new, reusable animation appears in the **Project** panel.

5. Punch in the following values on frame 0:

   Position.x: 6.5

   Position.y: 1.2

   Position.z: -31.5

If those values are already punched in when you create the animation, click on one of them and press the *Enter* key to make sure Unity registers a diamond-shaped keyframe to remember those settings.

6. Click on the little gray dash symbol to the right of the `Rotation.x` value. You'll find a small drop-down menu. Choose **Add Curves** from that list. We're adding curves to the rotation values because we'll need to modify them later.

![Animation panel showing runner Transform values and a drop-down menu with Add Curves, Delete Curves, Add Key, Delete Key]

7. Go to frame 120.

8. Move `runner` up along the Z-axis to the top-right corner of the building, or type in `-19.4` for its `Position.z` value.

 You'll have to press the *Enter* key on all three x, y and z values to make them "stick" on this keyframe if you decide to key in the values by hand. Watch to ensure that the little colored ovals are turning into little colored diamonds.

9. Go to frame 240.

10. Move `runner` along the X-axis to the top-left corner of the level, or key in `-6.5` for `Position.x`.

11. Move to frame 360.

12. Move `runner` down in the Z-axis to `-31.5` to the bottom-left corner of the hallway.

13. Go to frame 480.

14. Move runner along the X-axis back to the bottom-right corner where it started.

> **Position.x: 6.5**
>
> **Position.y: 1.2**
>
> **Position.z: -31.5**

15. Set this **Animation** clip to **Loop**, just like the bounce.

16. Uncheck the pink round "Animate" button to stop recording, and then test your game!

What just happened – holy hospital rampage, Batman!

At this point, it looks like Nurse Slipperfoot herself may be in serious need of medical attention. True, we haven't rotated her to look down the hallways, but even so, she flies through the emergency ward like a banshee, busting through walls and generally freaking me out.

That's because like other 3D programs, Unity gives us Bezier control over our keyframe values. A **Bezier** is a line that you can bend with little handles, which can either work separately or in tandem to create smooth motion. This enables us to ease animations in and out so that they look less robotic (or not, depending on our needs).

Time for action – how to "handle" Nurse Slipperfoot

You can mess around with each node's Bezier handles by clicking on the dots in the **Animation** window, selecting a handle style from the right-click menu, and pulling the little gray handles around, provided the keyframes are set to Flat, Broken, or Free Smooth. To correct this animation simply, we're going to apply a boring straight line between all of the key points.

1. In the **Animation** window, press *Ctrl/command + A* to select all of the nodes in the animation.

2. Right-click/alternate-click on any one of the nodes.

3. Navigate to **Both Tangents | Linear** to flatten the curves between the nodes.

4. Test your game.

That's better! Nurse Slipperfoot's still not facing the right direction as she runs, but at least she's no longer in need of an exorcism.

> Note: If Nurse Slipperfoot is still phasing through walls, you may need to revisit your keyframes and make sure she's positioned correctly at each corner of the hallway on frames 0 (bottom-right), 120 (top-right), 240 (top-left), 360 (bottom-left), and 480 (bottom-right). If she's not ending up where you think she should be, you may have forgotten to punch *Enter* to confirm all three position axes—x, y and z—on all of the frames we just modified.

Time for action – you spin me right round

Let's correct that little issue of the nurse careening sideways and backwards through the hallway by adding rotation values for the `runner` GameObject, to make her face the proper direction.

1. In the **Animation** window, go to frame 100. This is 20 frames before our second keyframe.

2. Click on the little button with the white diamond and plus symbol—the "add keyframe" button—to tell Unity to remember the runner's position/rotation/scale on this frame.

3. Go to frame 120.

4. Enter a `Rotation.y` value of `-90` to face the camera down the next hallway.

5. Move the runner down the second hallway just a bit, maybe to `Position.x 6.0`, to make the motion slightly less robotic.

6. Go to frame 220 and add a new keyframe.

7. On frame 240, rotate the `runner` to `Rotation.y:-180` to aim it down the third hallway.

8. Keep repeating these steps through the rest of the animation. Set a keyframe 20 frames before the existing one, and then move to the corner keyframe and set the Y rotation. Use `-270` and `-360` for the next two Y rotation values.

9. Select all of the keyframes and set their curves to linear.

10. Stop recording the animation, and test your game.

The runner tears down the hallways, turning the corners and facing the proper direction. Having a hospital background cranks up the credibility and polish of this game so much! It's like a doctor-prescribed injection of awesomeness.

> **Anticipating the turns**
>
> Are you wondering why we dropped a keyframe 20 frames before turning the corner? If we had simply rotated the runner at each corner, Unity would have tweened towards that new rotation the entire time the nurse was running down the hallway. We want the rotation to stay constant almost to the end of the hallway, so we set a keyframe as a sort of break point to tell Unity "okay, you can start tweening the rotation right here".

Have a go hero – give Robo-Nurse a soul

With straight Bezier curves connecting our nodes, our `runner` animation tends to look a little artificial or robotic. Now that you've seen the right-click menu to adjust the smoothness of those Beziers, why not spend some time fiddling with the handles to see if you can eke out a more natural motion through the hallway? But first, a warning: adjusting Bezier handles for 3D animation can be very time-consuming! If you get bogged down, or lose heart, just select the nodes and slap "Linear" on them to be done with it. That's the equivalent of blowing up a building and walking away in slow motion like a badass while a giant fireball ignites the sky. Aww yeah.

Have a go hero – use your new-found powers for good

Just as we did with our other games, let's whip up a quick list of modifications and improvements we could make to Ticker Taker to make it a complete game.

- Title Screen, Instructions, Credits—these all go without saying.
- Sound Effects—you know how to hook these in, so why dontcha? Ticker Taker cries out for a big wet *squish* whenever the heart hits the tray. You could also add the frantic clippity-clop sounds of Nurse Slipperfoot's Doc Martens slapping the linoleum as she makes her mad dash down the hallway.
- Returning to the debate of creating an endless, player-always-loses game versus one the player can finish, what if you built a GUI element that depicted a 2D nurse icon running from point A to point B, like the progress meters you see in racing games? All the player has to do is keep the heart aloft until the nurse icon reaches the end of the progress bar to win.
- To add a bit of difficulty, you could add a little ECG heart monitor to the corner of the screen that beeps every time the player bounces the heart with enough force. Add a timer so that if x seconds elapse without the player bouncing the heart hard enough, the heart stops beating and the player loses the game. This will ensure that the player doesn't simply let the heart roll around gently on the tray until the nurse reaches the transplant ward.
- The player's going to catch on pretty quickly that Nurse Slipperfoot is running in a circle! How about building two connected hallways, and making her run a figure-8 course for added visual variety?
- The hallway is pretty flat and bland at the moment. Perhaps you could add spice to the environment by placing gurneys, IV stands, and even other patients in the level.

Time for action – deploy your game

You may be wondering why the section on deploying your game has been squeezed into a tiny section at the very end of the book. That's because Unity makes it so darned simple to package up your game, that we don't need any more space. Here's how to do it:

1. In the menu, navigate to **File | Build Settings...**.

2. We need to add the **Scenes** to this list that we want bundled into our **game** file. The first **Scene** we add to the list will be the first one Unity displays to our player, so that's where our preloader or title screen should normally go.

    Because we have only one **Scene** in this game so far, click on the **Add Current** button to pop it into the list. In games with multiple **Scenes**, you can simply click-and-drag those **Scenes** into the list to add them to the build. Be sure to choose **Web Player** as your deployment preference if you'd like a file that can be played in a browser.

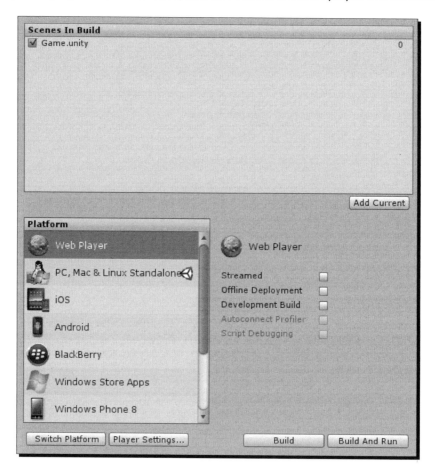

3. Click on the **Build And Run** button.

4. Unity asks where you want to save the `.unity3d` game file. Choose a folder and click on the **Save** button.

5. In the background, Unity cranks out a `.unity3d` file and an `.html` file to house it. Then Unity throws us to our default web browser and opens the HTML file. And there's our game, running beautifully within the browser.

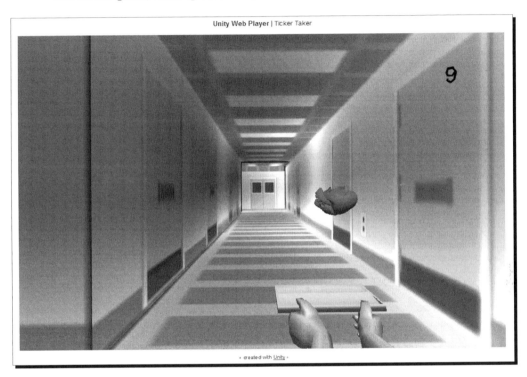

6. To publish the game live to the world, just upload the `.unity3d` file and the `.html` file to your web host, or pop it onto one of the Unity game portals we looked at off the top of the book. Unity support grows on a daily basis, so there are bound to be many more places hosting Unity games by the time you read this paragraph.

Note that you can also deploy your game as a standalone version to run on the Mac, PC and Linux platforms. And if you spring for additional Unity licenses and development kits, you can deploy your content to a growing list of platforms, including popular consoles, phones and tablets.

Time to grow

The theme in all of this is "growth". Since its release, Unity has made a huge splash in the game development world by offering a suite of tools that blew the lid off of 3D browser-based gaming, while making it easier for people without serious C-based programming knowledge to develop for once-unfathomable devices.

It's a complete cliché, but practice really is the one thin line separating you from developing those big projects you put up in jars on the shelf at the beginning of the book. Start building a game with what you know. With each project, set a new attainable challenge for yourself. This book has taught you how to set lights in a flat-looking hallway environment. But you've heard this term "lightmap" when reading about 3D games and models. What's that all about? Well, why not build a new game using the skills you've already developed, and commit to incorporating one lightmapped object in it? When you finish the game, you'll have added one extra tool to your tool belt, and you'll have a new, finished game for your portfolio.

How do you make a skybox so that the corner seams are invisible? How do you make your player take damage when he steps in lava? What's normal mapping? How do you program an enemy to follow and shoot at the player? How do you create your own models, textures, and animations? How do you put a different hat, gun, or pair of pants on a character model? How do you detect when one GameObject is near another, without colliding?

With each new thing you want your game to do, you'll come up with a question. Too many questions could discourage you and sink your ship before it even gets out to sea. Pick one thing and lock onto it with your laser scope. Do whatever it takes to discover the answer to your question, the solution to your problem, and build that solution into your game. Problem solved. Dragon slain. Checkbox checked. You will slay many dragons/cuddle many kittens in your journey as a game developer, but there's no need to take on the entire dragon/kitten army all at once. Take it one step at a time.

Be sure to check out the resources listed at the end of the book for places to turn to when you're stuck. You can also use that section to source new information when you're ready to add new tools to your tool belt.

Beyond the book

If you're starting from scratch and you made it this far, I hope you've found Unity to be well within your ability to develop your own 3D and 2D games. If you're sidling over from another development tool like Flash, GameMaker Pro, or Unreal Engine, I hope this book has provided you a sampling of the slick pipeline and process that Unity makes possible. A book like this can only ever scratch the surface of such an enormously powerful tool as Unity; if you've enjoyed what you've done with Unity so far, a fantastically supportive community and a deliciously deep development tool await you beyond the back cover of this book.

Appendix

As promised, here is a collection of resources that you can use as a launching point to your life as a game developer. Remember to start small, and to claim small victories as you learn.

Online resources

Here's a list of websites where you can tap into the Unity development community to find answers and to ask questions. Please remember to be courteous and respectful of more experienced developers' time. As with any online forum, be sure to search existing content for an answer before you ask a question.

Unity Manual: When you're new to a technology and you ask naive or poorly researched questions, you may hear "RTFM" a lot, which stands for "would you please be so kind as to review the product manual?" Well, here's the link to the product manual, which covers both beginner and advanced topics, including examples on writing your own custom Shaders:

```
http://unity3d.com/support/documentation/Manual/index.html
```

Google: A search engine should be the first place you look for answers. If the solution is plainly available with a simple query, you'll quickly exhaust the goodwill of the real-life people you petition for help online:

```
http://lmgtfy.com/
```

Unity Answers: This Unity sub-domain bills itself as "The best place to ask and answer questions about development with Unity", and it's not lying. Many of your Google searches will lead you here:

```
http://answers.unity3d.com/
```

Internet Relay Chat (IRC): This is an old-school chat system. You can download an IRC client to reach one of its many servers. IRC users split themselves into channels by topic. The very best channel available for Unity discussion is *#unity3d* on the server group `irc.freenode.net`. Wikipedia hosts this list of IRC client programs:

```
http://en.wikipedia.org/wiki/Comparison_of_Internet_Relay_Chat_
clients
```

Unity 3D Tutorials: The creators of Unity host a growing number of tutorials on the program's official site:

```
http://unity3d.com/learn/tutorials/modules
```

YouTube: The Internet's most popular video sharing site has tons of Unity 3D tutorials. Just search "Unity 3D" to get started:

```
http://www.youtube.com
```

Twitter: The best place to get up-to-the-minute news and information about practically everything is on Twitter. Follow as many Unity developers as you can find, and keep a watch on the `#unity3D` hash tag to become the smartest kid on your block. Twitter: it's not just about what your friends are having for lunch:

```
http://www.twitter.com
```

Unify Community Wiki: This is an excellent Unity resource where developers can help each other out. I've linked specifically to an excellent page outlining the differences and uses of various Collections (Arrays, Lists, Hashtables, among others), which was very helpful to me.

```
http://wiki.unity3d.com/index.php?title=Which_Kind_Of_Array_Or_
Collection_Should_I_Use?
```

Offline resources

Local User Groups: Lots of Unity developers are banding together to form user groups, which usually meet monthly. If your town doesn't already have a user group, why don't you start one?

Unite: This annual Unity 3D conference is the premiere Unity event. It's the best place to go to meet the planet's top Unity developers and to hear exciting announcements about the future of the product. See you there!

```
http://unity3d.com/unite/
```

Free development tools

There are a number of great development tools that integrate well with Unity 3D, like 3D Studio Max and Maya. However, many of these programs can cost thousands of dollars (like 3D Studio Max and Maya). Here are some links to free tools that may help you to develop your games:

Graphics

Blender: A 3D modeling and animation program with its own built-in game engine. Blender has a steep, often infuriating learning curve, but if you buy a book you'll be fine:

```
http://www.blender.org/download/
```

GIMP: A 2D photo manipulation program, somewhat like Photoshop:

```
http://www.gimp.org/downloads/
```

Paint.NET: Another 2D photo manipulation program, with perhaps a simpler interface than GIMP:

```
http://www.getpaint.net/
```

Sound

BFXR: For lo-fi sound effects creation. The sounds in this book were created with SFXR, its precursor:

```
http://www.bfxr.net
```

Audacity: For audio editing and processing:

```
http://audacity.sourceforge.net/
```

The Unity Asset Store

There were once many different companies that offered packages of Unity-ready materials and models that you could license for use in your games. Unity consolidated them under one roof in their online Unity Asset Store. To access the store, open Unity 3D and navigate to **Window | Asset Store**. Here are a few stand-out innovations that have seen a lot of use in the Unity community:

2DToolkit: Prior to the release of Unity 4.3, creating 2D games in Unity was tough, but not impossible. Packages like 2DToolkit provided sprite sheet and texture packing systems to ease 2D development.

NGUI: Another very popular package is NGUI, which does a great deal of GUI heavy lifting for you, using a more user-friendly system than Unity's built-in immediate mode GUI.

playMaker: This snap-together system provides LEGO-like behavior blocks that you can link together; no programming required.

Asset packs: There is a vast number of asset packages with everything from modeled airplanes to medieval dungeons that you can use to prototype your games. I strongly urge you to use whatever help you can to get your game finished. Paying $30 to save yourself months of work isn't cheating—it's just using your head. If it comes down to a choice between paying a few bucks and never finishing your game, it's time to break open your piggy bank.

The cats over at Unity Technologies aren't stupid. If they see a certain tool performing very well on the Unity Asset Store, it's a safe bet that they're planning to add it to a future release of Unity. That's why tools like NGUI and 2DToolkit see less use as their popularity peaks: Unity recreates or even hires the creators of these systems to improve their core product!

Game portals

We kicked off the book by looking at some Unity games. Here are some of the portals and distribution services specializing in Unity 3D games:

```
http://www.wooglie.com/
```

```
http://blurst.com/
```

```
http://www.kongregate.com/unity-games
```

Index

About Packt Publishing

Packt, pronounced 'packed', published its first book "Mastering phpMyAdmin for Effective MySQL Management" in April 2004 and subsequently continued to specialize in publishing highly focused books on specific technologies and solutions.

Our books and publications share the experiences of your fellow IT professionals in adapting and customizing today's systems, applications, and frameworks. Our solution-based books give you the knowledge and power to customize the software and technologies you're using to get the job done. Packt books are more specific and less general than the IT books you have seen in the past. Our unique business model allows us to bring you more focused information, giving you more of what you need to know, and less of what you don't.

Packt is a modern, yet unique publishing company, which focuses on producing quality, cutting-edge books for communities of developers, administrators, and newbies alike. For more information, please visit our website: www.PacktPub.com.

Writing for Packt

We welcome all inquiries from people who are interested in authoring. Book proposals should be sent to author@packtpub.com. If your book idea is still at an early stage and you would like to discuss it first before writing a formal book proposal, contact us; one of our commissioning editors will get in touch with you.

We're not just looking for published authors; if you have strong technical skills but no writing experience, our experienced editors can help you develop a writing career, or simply get some additional reward for your expertise.

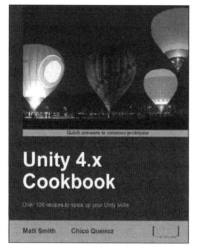
Unity 4.x Cookbook

ISBN: 978-1-84969-042-3   Paperback: 386 pages

Over 100 recipes to spice up your Unity skills

1. A wide range of topics are covered, ranging in complexity, offering something for every Unity 4 game developer

2. Every recipe provides step-by-step instructions, followed by an explanation of how it all works, and alternative approaches or refinements

3. Book developed with the latest version of Unity (4.x)

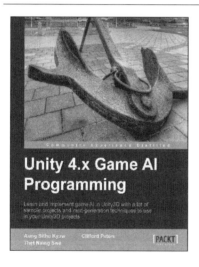

Unity 4.x Game AI Programming

ISBN: 978-1-84969-340-0   Paperback: 232 pages

Learn and implement game AI in Unity3D with a lot of sample projects and next-generation techniques to use in your Unity3D projects

1. A practical guide with step-by-step instructions and example projects to learn Unity3D scripting

2. Learn pathfinding using A* algorithms as well as Unity3D pro features and navigation graphs

3. Implement finite state machines (FSMs), path following, and steering algorithms

Please check **www.PacktPub.com** for information on our titles

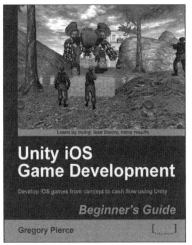
Unity iOS Game Development
Beginner's Guide

ISBN: 978-1-84969-040-9   Paperback: 314 pages

Develop iOS games from concept to cash flow using Unity

1. Dive straight into game development with no previous Unity or iOS experience

2. Work through the entire lifecycle of developing games for iOS

3. Add multiplayer, input controls, debugging, in app and micro payments to your game

4. Implement the different business models that will enable you to make money on iOS games

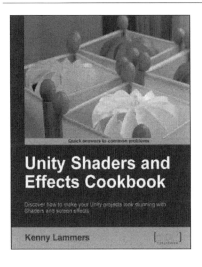

Unity Shaders and Effects Cookbook

ISBN: 978-1-84969-508-4   Paperback: 268 pages

Discover how to make your Unity projects look stunning with Shaders and screen effects

1. Learn the secrets of creating AAA quality Shaders without having to write long algorithms

2. Add realism to your game with stunning Screen Effects

3. Understand the structure of Surface Shaders through easy to understand step-by-step examples

Please check **www.PacktPub.com** for information on our titles

Made in the USA
San Bernardino, CA
13 June 2014